International Political Economy Series

W9-CBG-781

General Editor: **Timothy M. Shaw**, Professor of Political Science and International Development Studies, Dalhousie University, Halifax, Nova Scotia

Titles include:

Leslie Elliott Armijo (*editor*)
FINANCIAL GLOBALIZATION AND DEMOCRACY IN EMERGING MARKETS

Robert Boardman
THE POLITICAL ECONOMY OF NATURE
Environmental Debates and the Social Sciences

Gordon Crawford
FOREIGN AID AND POLITICAL REFORM
A Comparative Analysis of Democracy Assistance and Political Conditionality

Matt Davies
INTERNATIONAL POLITICAL ECONOMY AND MASS COMMUNICATION
IN CHILE
National Intellectuals and Transnational Hegemony

Martin Doornbos
INSTITUTIONALIZING DEVELOPMENT POLICIES AND RESOURCE
STRATEGIES IN EASTERN AFRICA AND INDIA
Developing Winners and Losers

Fred P. Gale
THE TROPICAL TIMBER TRADE REGIME

Keith M. Henderson and O. P. Dwivedi (*editors*)
BUREAUCRACY AND THE ALTERNATIVES IN WORLD PERSPECTIVES

Angela W. Little
LABOURING TO LEARN
Towards a Political Economy of Plantations, People and Education
in Sri Lanka

John Loxley (*editor*)
INTERDEPENDENCE, DISEQUILIBRIUM AND GROWTH
Reflections on the Political Economy of North–South Relations at the
Turn of the Century

Don D. Marshall
CARIBBEAN POLITICAL ECONOMY AT THE CROSSROADS
NAFTA and Regional Developmentalism

Susan M. McMillan
FOREIGN DIRECT INVESTMENT IN THREE REGIONS OF THE SOUTH AT
THE END OF THE TWENTIETH CENTURY

James H. Mittelman and Mustapha Pasha (*editors*)
OUT FROM UNDERDEVELOPMENT
Prospects for the Third World (Second Edition)

Lars Rudebeck, Olle Törnquist and Virgilio Rojas (*editors*)
DEMOCRATIZATION IN THE THIRD WORLD
Concrete Cases in Comparative and Theoretical Perspective

Howard Stein (*editor*)
ASIAN INDUSTRIALIZATION AND AFRICA
Studies in Policy Alternatives to Structural Adjustment

International Political Economy Series
Series Standing Order ISBN 0–333–71708–2 hardcover
Series Standing Order ISBN 0–333–71110–6 paperback
(*outside North America only*)

You can receive future titles in this series as they are published by placing a standing order.
Please contact your bookseller or, in case of difficulty, write to us at the address below with
your name and address, the title of the series and one of the ISBNs quoted above.

Customer Services Department, Macmillan Distribution Ltd, Houndmills, Basingstoke,
Hampshire RG21 6XS, England

Financial Globalization and Democracy in Emerging Markets

Edited by

Leslie Elliott Armijo
Visiting Scholar
Reed College
Portland
Oregon

Foreword by

Thomas J. Biersteker
Henry Luce Professor of Political Science
Brown University
Providence

palgrave

Selection, editorial matter, Introduction and Chapters 1 and 14
© Leslie Elliot Armijo 1999, 2001
Foreword © Thomas J. Biersteker 1999, 2001
Chapters 2–13 © Macmillan Press Ltd (now Palgrave) 1999, 2001

All rights reserved. No reproduction, copy or transmission of
this publication may be made without written permission.

No paragraph of this publication may be reproduced, copied or
transmitted save with written permission or in accordance with
the provisions of the Copyright, Designs and Patents Act 1988,
or under the terms of any licence permitting limited copying
issued by the Copyright Licensing Agency, 90 Tottenham Court
Road, London W1P 0LP.

Any person who does any unauthorised act in relation to this
publication may be liable to criminal prosecution and civil
claims for damages.

The authors have asserted their rights to be identified
as the authors of this work in accordance with the
Copyright, Designs and Patents Act 1988.

First published in hardcover 1999

First published in paperback 2001 by
PALGRAVE
Houndmills, Basingstoke, Hampshire RG21 6XS and
175 Fifth Avenue, New York, N. Y. 10010
Companies and representatives throughout the world

PALGRAVE is the new global academic imprint of
St. Martin's Press LLC Scholarly and Reference Division and
Palgrave Publishers Ltd (formerly Macmillan Press Ltd).

ISBN 0–333–73090–9 hardback (*outside North America*)
ISBN 0–312–22014–6 hardback (*in North America*)
ISBN 0–333–93067–3 paperback (*worldwide*)

This book is printed on paper suitable for recycling and
made from fully managed and sustained forest sources.

A catalogue record for this book is available
from the British Library.

The Library of Congress has cataloged the hardcover edition as follows:
Financial globalization and democracy in emerging markets / edited by
Leslie Elliott Armijo ; foreword by Thomas J. Biersteker.
    p. cm. — (International political economy series)
    Papers presented at a conference organized by the Watson Institute
for International Studies in Brown University in November 1995.
    Includes bibliographical references and index.
    ISBN 0–312–22014–6 (cloth)
    1. Investments, Foreign—Developing countries. 2. Capital
movements—Developing countries. 3. Financial crises—Developing
countries. I. Armijo, Leslie Elliott. II. Series.
HG5993.F557 1999
332.67'3—dc21
                              98–40013
                                CIP

10 9 8 7 6 5 4 3 2 1
10 09 08 07 06 05 04 03 02 01

Printed in Great Britain by Antony Rowe Ltd, Chippenham, Wiltshire

Contents

List of Tables

List of Figures

Notes on the Contributors

Leslie Elliott Armijo is Visiting Scholar at Reed College, Portland, Oregon.

Thomas J. Biersteker is Henry Luce Professor of Political Science and Director of the Watson Institute of International Studies at Brown University, Providence.

Carlos Elizondo Mayer-Serra is Professor, and currently Director, of the Centro de Investigaciones y Docéncia Económica (CIDE), Mexico City.

John Echeverri-Gent is Associate Professor of Government and International Affairs at the University of Virginia, Charlottesville.

William C. Gruben is Director of the Center for Latin American Economics at the Federal Reserve Bank of Dallas.

Mary Ann Haley teaches at Fairfield University, Connecticut.

Jonathan Haughton is Assistant Professor of Economics at Suffolk University, Boston, and Faculty Associate of the Harvard Institute for International Development.

Peter R. Kingstone is Associate Professor of Political Science at the University of Connecticut, Storrs.

Stefano Manzocchi is Assistant Professor of Economics at the University of Ancona, Italy.

Walter Molano is Head of Research BCP Securities, LLC.

Tony Porter is Assistant Professor of Political Science at McMaster University, Ontario.

Randall W. Stone is Assistant Professor of Political Science at the University of Rochester, New York.

Danny Unger Assistant Professor of Political Science at Northern Illinois University.

Jeffrey A. Winters is Associate Professor of Political Science at Northwestern University, Chicago.

Foreword

Thomas J. Biersteker

Financial globalization and its consequences have moved to the center of the global stage. Mexico's 1994 financial crisis had ripple effects in markets around the world, but the Asian financial crisis of 1997 has had even more far-reaching consequences. The interdependence of global financial markets has become increasingly apparent, as markets in the United States react to daily developments in the markets of Asia and Europe. International financial news that was previously relegated to the back pages of the business sections of major newspapers is today's front-page news. Financially troubled South Korea has sought the financial equivalent of the stationing of American troops on Korean soil: American backing for direct financial assistance from the International Monetary Fund (IMF) and other major institutional lenders. IMF Director Michel Camdessus' 1994 statement about financial fragility as potentially the first crisis of the twenty-first century now appears unusually prescient.

While most discussion and analysis tends to focus on the economic implications of financial globalization or the political reluctance of the United States to provide direct financial support to troubled countries, relatively little attention has been paid to the political consequences of financial globalization in emerging markets. There has been a lively debate about the economic costs and benefits of financial globalization, but relatively little about its implications for domestic politics. The essays contained in this book are designed to address this deficiency.

Over the course of the last several years, the Watson Institute for International Studies at Brown University has organized several conferences to examine financial globalization. The Institute's mission and scope include the interdisciplinary analysis of contemporary global problems and the development of potential solutions to remedy them. We began studying financial globalization in October 1994 with an analysis of financial fragility in Latin America. William Rhodes, Vice-Chair of Citibank and a member of the Institute's Board of Overseers, convened a panel of financial analysts and scholars to discuss the phenomenon. Rhodes expressed concerns about the lack of transparency in Mexico and the adequacy of global financial regulation, foreshadowing contemporary discussions of global financial instability.

The majority of the essays contained in the present book are derived from a conference that grew out of the October 1994 meeting, co-organized by Leslie Elliott Armijo and myself in November 1995. We deliberately went beyond consideration of economic issues to an examination of the political consequences of financial globalization in emerging markets, specifically for the prospects for democracy. Democratization, or at least movements toward political liberalization, are widespread throughout the world today, and we were interested in exploring the relationships between the two simultaneous global phenomena.

Two keynote addresses brought the perspective of policy immediacy and insightful analysis to our conference proceedings. Jesus Silva Herzog, Mexico's Ambassador to the United States and its Finance Minister during the 1982 debt crisis, opened the conference with an address contrasting the 1980s Latin American and global debt crisis with Mexico's mid-1990s financial crisis. Júlio de Quesada, head of Citibank Mexico, gave the conference his perspective on and described his personal experiences during Mexico's December 1994 financial meltdown. Both the Ambassador and de Quesada participated in the discussions of the papers contained in this edited volume and made a number of important contributions to the enterprise.

Funding for the conference was provided by a number of institutions, in addition to the core support provided by the Watson Institute. Important contributions were received from the International Studies Association, the William and Flora Hewlett Foundation, Northeastern University, and Wellesley College. Leslie Elliott Armijo, who consistently identifies original and innovative topics for research, has done a superb job with this volume. I think it will make an important contribution to our still very preliminary understanding of the political implications of global financial market integration. It is a welcome addition, and I am pleased to be able to bring it to the attention of others.

Providence, Rhode Island   THOMAS J. BIERSTEKER

Preface to the Paperback Edition

It has now been over two years since the final edits to the hardcover edition of this book. Then, the Asian financial crisis was just beginning. Today, in mid 2000, that crisis is mostly over in terms of its threat to the global economy, though several hard-hit countries remain trapped in recession. The big issues of financial globalization and democracy in emerging markets are much the same as before.

Financial globalization, or the international integration of previously segmented national credit and capital markets, continues apace. Net flows to developing countries remain high, averaging almost 5.5 per cent of gross domestic product in the mid and late 1990s, using the definitions of Table 1 of the Introduction. Yet even in advanced industrial countries central bankers deliberating over monetary policy are being compelled by international capital markets to consider exchange rates and external payments positions as factors affecting their domestic monetary policy decisions. For policymakers in emerging market countries, the level of interest rates in the US (a powerful determinant of net capital flows to the developing world) has become a more important parameter in crafting national macroeconomic policy than almost any domestic consideration. If real interest rates in Brazil and Argentina do not remain attractive in comparison to rates in the US, then capital will flee irrespective of any good news on inflation, fiscal deficits, trade, and growth.

This volume's specific concern with the changing forms and instruments of capital flows also remains extremely pertinent. The shifts from public to private sources of finance and public to private borrowers are by now overwhelming and probably irreversible. The shifts among types of financial flows, as among country recipients, can be dramatic and impossible to predict. In the mid 1990s, portfolio investment averaged 40 per cent of net flows and foreign direct investment (FDI) only 28 per cent, while from 1997–99, as a consequence of the Asian financial crisis, portfolio flows fell to only 16 per cent of flows and FDI rose to well over half. This would seem a positive development, as FDI is not volatile and thus less prone to crisis. Less happily, too much of current FDI flows represents mergers and acquisitions (M&A), including via privatization, in which local businesses sell out to foreign owners. For example, almost half of the $75 billion Latin America received in net FDI in 1999 was in M&A (Fernández-Arias, 2000). And as in the past, foreign-owned firms have a much larger average size than locally owned businesses, as well as being more capital-intensive and less likely to provide employment for local workers (Stallings and Peres, 2000). The new flows continue to enhance the bargaining power of capital, especially foreign capital, *vis-à-vis* both elected governments and labor in emerging market countries. Most international market actors, unfortunately, continue to prefer political stability, even under authoritarian auspices, to the uncertainties of democratic transitions.

Nonetheless, the news thus far with respect to democracy in emerging markets is more hopeful than some of us expected. Despite the series of financial crises to hit emerging markets in the 1990s, the global wave of democratization continues. Indonesia, the hardest hit of any of the East Asian countries in the financial crisis of 1997–99, remains in dire economic straits but continues to lurch toward representative government. In 1998 popular demonstrations forced Suharto to step down in favor of his vice president, Habibie. More significantly, in 1999 Habibie lost a democratic election to the candidate of the combined opposition, Wahid. Since then the withering scorn of the global financial press has contributed to continuing investigations into state-sponsored corruption in Indonesia: in early 2000 the elected government even decided to detain Suharto for further questioning. Russia has survived both its financial crash of August 1998 and the subsequent democratic transition from presidents Yeltsin to Putin. Russia's financial crisis may have had a silver lining, as the devaluation contributed to a salutory realignment of prices and stimulus to non-raw material exports. In Mexico in early 2000, campaign managers for Labastida, the presidential candidate of the long-ruling PRI, briefly tried but clearly failed to convince voters and the business community that a victory for the opposition candidate, Fox, would destabilize the economy by provoking capital flight.

At the same time, more subtle questions remain to be answered about the longer run consequences of greater international financial integration for domestic political alignments. All other things being equal, it is still hard to be cheerful about the prospect of multinational firms with greater political access to emerging market governments than at any time since the 1960s. The largely orthodox economic policy changes demanded by foreign institutional investors probably have been good for aggregate economic growth, though there is carefully qualified and partial dissent on this score (Rodrik, 1999; Stallings and Peres, 2000). Since stable political democracy is associated with moderate, rather than high, levels of income inequality, the implications of financial globalization for inequality are much debated. Some neoliberal economic policies demanded by footloose foreign portfolio investors – particularly dampening inflation and cutting government subsidies and employment, very often disproportionately targeted to the middle class – may have raised the relative incomes of the poor (Dollar and Kraay, 2000), which in turn, probably, has augmented their political voice. Other consequences of globalization, such as its implications for employment as noted above, seem to promote greater income inequality, at least for a while (Korzeniewicz and Smith, 2000). Interestingly, in several countries, including Argentina, Chile, Bolivia, Brazil, Poland, Turkey, and South Africa, newly enfranchised masses have given strong political support to democratic governments engaged in stabilization and other reforms. We can at least report the negative finding that there are no obvious recent cases of democratic overthrow in which financial contagion played a direct role. In fact, of the recent cases of democratic backsliding in emerging market countries – including in Ecuador, Peru, Venezuela, and Zimbabwe – only the 1999 Ecuadorean coup was clearly related to an external financial crisis. Yet Ecuador's economic problems easily could be traced to unwise domestic policy choices: its financial crisis was *not* a case of capricious and unpredictable external contagion. Our bottom line on the political consequences of financial globalization thus remains much as it was before the Asian financial crisis of the late 1990s. To the degree that enhanced international financial integration promotes economic growth, its implications for democratization are mostly positive. Yet where financial globalization widens income inequalities or challenges the credibility of fragile democratic transitions, these factors have negative, though seldom fatal, implications for democratic consolidation.

There are, meanwhile, two important ways in which the post-Asian financial crisis debate over financial globalization differs from the discussion just two and a half years ago.

First, there is a severe though underreported split between, on the one hand, most development economists and policymakers in developing countries and, on the other hand, many advanced industrial country policymakers and most private financial actors, including both international bankers and institutional investors. The former group clearly recognizes the phenomenon of *'financial contagion'*, in which countries with good macroeconomic fundamentals are suddenly visited with massive capital flight and an acute liquidity crisis *primarily due to irrationalities and inefficiencies in global capital markets*. The Asian financial crisis showed that even 'well-behaved' countries such as Thailand, Indonesia, and South Korea – all with small government budget deficits, low inflation, strong growth, and unexceptional external accounts – could be suddenly attacked by huge credit outflows. True, problems were discovered after the fact, particularly in the form of weak and under-supervised domestic banking systems. Yet these were not traditional balance of payments crises, akin to the Latin American crises of 1982 and arguably 1994–95. Almost no one had expected the Asian tigers to be vulnerable to rapidly spreading external financial shocks. The dramatic contagion Latin America experienced following the Russian crisis in mid 1998 was similarly unanticipated and, from a domestic macroeconomic standpoint, illogical, since Russia and Latin America had few trade or other economic ties. The main link, it turned out, was via large institutional investors based in advanced countries, who collectively sold their Latin American holdings to recoup their losses in Russia! Nonetheless, the rhetoric of most emerging markets investors and many advanced country policymakers, the second group referred to above, blames externally generated financial crises on *bad public policies* and insufficient political will in emerging market countries. The unwillingness of many advanced country policymakers to acknowledge the systemic contribution to severe financial crises in the late 20th and early 21st centuries increases the vulnerability of emerging market countries to future financial crises, and reduces the likelihood that the international community – and the weak but essential regulatory institutions it contains, such as the multilateral International Monetary Fund (IMF) and the private Bank for International Settlements – will assist developing countries in recovering from the inevitable future financial crises (see Fernández-Arias, 2000; Stiglitz, 2000).

The second new development is more positive from the viewpoint of emerging market countries. A small but influential subset of economic and financial policymakers in the advanced industrial countries has recognized that their home markets are potentially vulnerable to financial contagion. Late 1997 through to late 1998, was the most dangerous period of the Asian financial crisis. These months also saw the near-collapse of Long Term Capital Management, a US hedge fund whose emergency rescue the New York Federal Reserve Bank quickly orchestrated. During this period numerous prestigious economists and former policymakers – including Paul Volcker, Paul Samuelson, and Jagdish Bhagwati – publicly pronounced global capital markets to be inherently crisis prone (Bhagwati, 1998; *Financial Times*, 1998). Out of this turmoil has come a debate over a '*new global financial architecture*', which continues today. Concrete proposals range from the radical libertarian view that the IMF ought to be abolished to utopian calls for a global bankruptcy court, a true international lender of last resort, and multilaterally-agreed controls on short-term capital flows (Blecker, 1999; Eichengreen, 1999). Although the preponderance of negotiating influence clearly rests with the world's major economies, developing countries may find that the new financial architecture, if it is adopted, brings some improvements for them. In general, to the extent that cross-border financial flows come to exist within a reformed international regulatory framework, such changes, whatever their details, may dampen the systemic tendency toward spreading financial crises. Nonetheless, the major goal of most architectural reforms with a real chance of being adopted is to protect the financial systems and economies of the advanced industrial countries, not to maximize productive investment in the developing world nor to shield emerging markets from imported financial crises.

The chapters in this book detail the experiences of several large emerging market countries in the 1990s with simultaneous capital account liberalization and political democratization. The authors illustrate the dilemmas of countries that are highly integrated into international markets and institutions, and vulnerable to changes in international affairs, yet whose governments possess few levers with which to affect the shape or structure of the global international political economy. The major industrial democracies, in contrast, wield enormous influence over the parameters of the international financial architecture within which cross-border financial transactions flow – yet even they find it difficult to act multilaterally. Perhaps one day we will need to devote a volume to discussion of the novel phenomenon of truly cooperative, and globally democratic, regulation of international capital and credit markets. Regretfully, this day is not yet.

Leslie Elliott Armijo
Portland, Oregon

REFERENCES

Bhagwati, Jagdish (1998) 'Yes to Free Trade, Maybe to Capital Controls', *Wall Street Journal*, 16 November.

Blecker, Robert A. (1999) *Taming Global Finance: A Better Architecture for Growth and Equity* (Washington, DC: Economic Policy Institute).

Dollar, David and Aart Kraay (2000) 'Growth Is Good for the Poor', Working Paper, Development Research Group (Washington, DC: The World Bank) March.

Eichengreen, Barry (1999) *Toward a New International Financial Architecture* (Washington, DC: Institute for International Economics).

Fernández-Arias, Eduardo (2000) 'The New Wave of Capital Inflows: Sea Change or Tide?', Working Paper no. 415, Research Department (Washington, DC: Inter-American Development Bank).

Financial Times (1998) 'Personal Views on the World Economy', 7 October.

Korzeniewicz, Roberto Patricio and William C. Smith (forthcoming 2000) 'Growth, Poverty, and Inequality in Latin America: Searching for the High Road', *Latin American Research Review*.

Rodrik, Dani (1999) *The New Global Economy and Developing Countries: Making Openness Work* (Washington, DC: Overseas Development Council distributed by Johns Hopkins University Press).

Stallings, Barbara and Wilson Peres (2000) *Growth, Employment, and Equity: The Impact of the Economic Reforms in Latin America and the Caribbean* (Washington, DC: Brookings Institution Press and Santiago, Chile: United Nations Economic Commission on Latin America and the Caribbean, ECLAC).

Stiglitz, Joseph (2000) 'The Insider: What I Learned at the World Economic Crisis', *The National Republic*, 17 April.

List of Abbreviations

ADR	American Depository Receipt
AMB	Asociación Mexicana de Banqueros (Mexican Bankers Association)
ASEAN	Association of Southeast Asian Nations
ASIDA	American–Soviet Investment and Development Associates
BBC	British Broadcasting Corporation
BIAC	Business and Industry Advisory Committee to the OECD
BIS	Bank for International Settlements, Switzerland
BIT	Bilateral investment treaty
BOLT	Bombay On Line Trading
BPWR	Bangkok Post Weekly Review
BSE	Bombay Stock Exchange
CBR	Central Bank of Russia (Tsentral'nyi Bank Rossii)
CCE	Consejo Coordinador Empressarial (Business Coordinating Council, Mexico)
CCI	Controller of Capital Issues, India
CEPR	Centre for Economic Policy Research
CETES (or *cetes*)	Certificados de la Tesorería (Mexican treasury bonds, denominated in pesos)
CFE	Comisión Federal de Electricidad (Federal Electricity Commission, Mexico)
CMEA	Council of Mutual Economic Assistance (of the Soviet bloc)
Coparmex	Confederación Patronal Mexicana (National Employers Confederation, Mexico)
CVRD	Companhia Vale do Rio Doce (Rio Doce Valley Company, Brazilian state-owned mining firm)
DIEESE	Departamento Intersindical de Estatísticas e Estudos Socioeconomicos (Intersyndical Department for Statistics and Socioeconomic Studies, Sao Paulo, Brazil)
DPR	People's Representative Council (Dewan Perwakilan Rakyat), Indonesia
DRS	Debtor Reporting System of the World Bank
ECLAC	United Nations Economic Commission for Latin America and the Caribbean

EFF	Extended Fund Facility of the International Monetary Fund
EIU	Economist Intelligence Unit
EMC	Emerging Market Country
EMH	Efficient Markets Hypothesis
ESAF	Enhanced Structural Adjustment Fund (of the International Monetary Fund)
ESCAP/UNCTC	Economic and Social Commission for Asia and the Pacific/United Nations Center on Transnational Corporations
EZLN	Ejército Zapatista de Liberación Nacional (Zapatista Army of National Liberation, Mexico)
FDI	foreign direct investment
FEER	Far Eastern Economic Review
FIBV	International Federation of Stock Exchanges (Federation internationale des bourses de valeurs)
FII	foreign institutional investor
FIPB	Foreign Investment Promotion Board, India
FSE	Fundo Social da Emergéncia (Social Emergency Fund, Brazil)
G-7	Group of Seven major industrialized countries
G-10	Group of Ten advanced industrial countries
GATS	General Agreement on Trade in Services
GATT	General Agreement on Tariffs and Trade
GDP	gross domestic product
GDR	global depository receipt
GNP	gross national product
GOI/MOF	Government of India, Ministry of Finance
GOI/MOF/SED	Government of India, Ministry of Finance, Stock Exchange Division
GOLKAR	Functional Groups (Golongan Karya), President Suharto's party machine, Indonesia
Ibope	Instituto Brasileiro de Opinião Pública e Estatística (Brazilian Institute of Public Opinion and Statistics)
ICF	Investor Compensation Fund
IFC	International Finance Corporation, member of the World Bank Group
IMEF	Instituto Mexicano de Ejecutivos de Finanzas (Mexican Institute of Financial Executives)
IMF	International Monetary Fund
INEGI	Instituto Nacional de Geografía y Estadística (National Institute of Geography and Statistics, Mexico)

IOSCO	International Organization of Securities Commissions
ISI	import-substituting industrialization
LDCs	less developed countries
LIBOR	London Interbank Offered Rate
MAI	Multilateral Agreement on Investment
MNC	multinational corporation
MOU	Memorandum of Understanding
MPR	People's Consultative Assembly (Majelis Permusyawaratan Rakyat), Indonesia
NAFTA	North American Free Trade Agreement
NASDAQ	National Association of Security Dealers, Automated Quotations System
NBER	National Bureau of Economic Research
NGO	non-governmental organization
NRI	non-resident Indian (person of South Asian descendent, living outside the sub-continent)
NSDL	National Securities Depository Ltd, India
NSE	National Stock Exchange, India
OAB	Organizacão dos Advogados Brasileiros (Brazilian Bar Association)
ODA	official development assistance
OECD	Organization for Economic Co-operation and Development
OTC	over the counter
PAN	Partido Acción Nacional (National Action Party, Mexico)
PDI	Indonesian Democratic Party (Partai Demokratis Indonesia)
PEMEX	Petróleos Mexicanos (Mexican Petroleum, the state-owned oil company)
Petrobrás	Petroleo Brasileiro S.A. (Brazilian Petroleum)
PKI	Indonesian Communist Party (Partai Komunis Indonesia)
PMDB	Partido do Movimento Democrático Brasileiro (Brazilian Democratic Movement Party)
PND (I & II)	Plano Nacional de Desenvolvimento (National Development Plan, Brazil)
PRD	Partido de la Revolución Democrática (Democratic Revolution Party, Mexico)
PRI	Partido Revolucionário Institucional (Institutional Revolutionary Party, Mexico)
PSE	public sector enterprise
PT	Partido del Trabajo (Labor Party, Mexico)

PVEM	Partido Verde Ecologista Mexicano (Mexican Green Ecology Party)
RET	Russian Economic Trends, a government publication
RETMU	Russian Economic Trends, Monthly Update
RIDBS	Report on International Developments in Banking Supervision
SBI	Bank Indonesia Certificates (Sertifikat Bank Indonesia)
SBPU	Money Market Certificates (Surat Berharga Pasar Uang), Indonesia
SCCI	State Committee for Cooperation and Investment (in Vietnam)
SCHP	Secretaría de Hacienda y Crédito Público (Secretariat of Finance and Public Credit, Mexico)
SEBI	Securities and Exchange Board of India
SEC	United States Securities and Exchange Commission
SEC	Securities and Exchange Commission (Thailand)
SET	Stock Exchange of Thailand
SOE	state-owned enterprise
STF	Systemic Transformation Facility of the International Monetary Fund
Telesp	Telecomunicações de São Paulo (São Paulo Telecommunications, Brazil)
TESOBONOS (or *tesobonos*)	Bonos de la Tesorería (Mexican government treasury bonds denominated in dollars)
TWN	Third World Network
UN	United Nations
USAID	United States Agency for International Development
WB	World Bank
WTO	World Trade Organization

to Kaizad and Zubin

Introduction and Overview[1]
Leslie Elliott Armijo

Recent decades have seen momentous shifts in the forms and quantity of capital transfers from advanced industrial countries, net creditors as a group, to developing countries, net debtors as a group. The 1950s and 1960s were the era of foreign aid, with foreign direct investment also an important source of funds, and the 1970s the heyday of commercial bank lending. The 1980s saw a return of foreign assistance, this time mostly from multilateral rather than bilateral lenders and often associated with painful structural adjustments to the third world debt crisis, which hit hardest in Latin America and Sub-Saharan Africa. The 1990s has seen the rise of the 'new' portfolio flows, as first world mutual fund managers snap up the stocks and bonds of each week's hot new investment destination, from Mexico to the Philippines to such seemingly unlikely destinations as Bulgaria, Kazakhstan, and Algeria. The 1980s and 1990s have also been a period of widespread democratization in developing and transitional economies, from Latin America, to East Asia, to Eastern Europe and Africa.

This book examines the implications of one aspect of the first trend – the *change in the forms of international flows* implied by financial globalization – for the second: *democratization*. The authors suggest that the shift from a preponderance of public to overwhelmingly private sources of cross-border funds means that borrowing countries will find themselves less subject to the overtly political demands of creditor/donor countries but more constrained to implement neoliberal, and perhaps inappropriate, economic policies. A second shift, from the public to the private sector as the direct recipient of capital flows within developing countries, implies that incumbent governments will receive fewer political benefits from capital inflows, while the domestic political clout of big business will increase. A third secular trend, toward more liquid forms of international investment, brings a heightened risk of a balance of payments crisis for the borrowing country – which inevitably will be blamed on its government, responsible or not. None of these probably irreversible changes in the *forms* of capital transfers in global financial markets, unfortunately, is necessarily auspicious for new or fragile democracies, although the contributors to this volume disagree on a number of details. Meanwhile, the larger *quantity* of financial resources being transferred in the 1990s, as compared to the 1980s, is welcome.

The 14 essays in the book explore the consequences of the new forms of foreign capital flows for democracy from a variety of perspectives, both

1

disciplinary (10 authors are political scientists, while three are economists) and analytical. Four theoretical and comparative essays begin the volume. Leslie Elliott Armijo employs a minimalist definition of 'democracy' as procedural political democracy. Identifying six institutional forms of cross-border capital flows (ranging from government-to-government foreign aid to foreign private portfolio investment in the host country's private sector), she traces the implications of each of the six for critical intermediate variables within the capital-importing country: economic growth, the political influence of business, the risk of a balance-of-payments crisis, and pressure on the government for neoliberal economic reforms. Shifts in these intermediate variables, she argues, have important implications for the speed of democratic transitions and the stability of newly-established democracies. She observes that it is ironic that in the 1950s and 1960s, when so many countries were under authoritarian rule, the modal form of cross-border capital flow was government-to-government foreign aid, which strengthens incumbent governments. Most of the commercial bank lending of the 1970s also went directly to incumbent governments, still overwhelmingly dictatorships of one form or another. In the 1980s and 1990s, however, just as the 'third wave' of democracy spread around the world, foreign investment going directly to the private sector in developing and postcommunist countries became the dominant form of cross-border capital transfer, leaving the new, fragile democratic governments comparatively unable to tap foreign resources.

The second essay in Part 1 is by Stefano Manzocchi, who maps the shifts in the major institutional forms of capital flows from developed to developing economies throughout the entire twentieth century. Manzocchi's essay spans the final decades of the era of British imperialism and financial hegemony, the decline of sterling's dominance in the 1920s, the dry spell of the Great Depression, the anomalous period of the Second World War, and the shifting forms of cross-border capital flows since then. His data confirm that the last era in which cross-border capital flows played as large a role in relation to the combined gross national product (GDP) of developing economies was under the classical gold standard prior to World War One. Manzocchi also addresses the 'big' economic question raised by foreign capital inflows, viz., do they, when all is said and done, actually contribute to net investment and economic growth in borrower countries? Manzocchi's answer is a qualified 'yes,' although he feels much surer of the positive macroeconomic effects of certain types of capital inflows, notably foreign direct investment, than of others, notably commercial bank loans. The chapter also flags several related contemporary debates, such as the controversial role of financial liberalization in increasing foreign capital inflows, and of capital flows in equalizing incomes between wealthy and poor countries.

Mary Ann Haley focuses on the heightened volatility of the new portfolio capital flows, noting that many commentators, Armijo included, worry that one of the consequences of higher percentages of short-term, as compared to long-term, investments will be increased pressure on recipient country governments to engage in neo-liberal economic reforms: slashing government budgets for social spending, privatizing radically, and often reducing the role of the state even in essential regulatory functions. Haley agrees. She also doubts that the optimistic 'efficient market hypothesis,' which postulates that liquid international capital markets allocate financing competitively and thus optimally, describes what really occurs among first world institutional investors in emerging markets. Rather, she suggests, institutional investors engage in substantial informal coordination. Moreover, private investors' quite rational preferences are for political stability, not necessarily democracy, in the countries to which they commit funds.

Tony Porter addresses the question of policy making autonomy in capital-importing countries, which he considers an essential component of a sovereign democracy. He argues that the new portfolio capital flows are, in fact, likely to undercut, and rather dramatically, the ability of governments in emerging market countries to forge rational, coherent national economic strategies. Unusually, however, Porter emphasizes not so much the volatility of portfolio capital flows as the more subtle issue of what is (perhaps euphemistically?) called 'regulatory convergence'. He documents the ways in which private institutional investors from advanced industrial countries are attempting to shape the investment environment in capital-importing countries by pressing developing and transitional countries to adopt capital markets regulatory frameworks developed by – and favorable to the interests of – institutional investors from the first world. Porter, that is, is skeptical of the hypothesis that financial regulation ever can be neutral, disinterested, and equally favorable to the interests of all parties. He consequently is disturbed by the absence of emerging market country participants in the transnational fora within which the new global rules of the game are being negotiated.

We might note, as an aside, that the recent history of the 1980s Latin American and third world (or, alternatively, the industrial country banks') debt crisis suggests that international financial arrangements that evolve as a result of bargaining among actors with very unequal power resources are unlikely to be neutral in the ways they apportion cost and benefits. Academic and former banker Ethan Kapstein put it succinctly:

> [T]he policies actually adopted by states during the [debt] crisis reflected not only a general public interest in maintaining a safe and sound international financial system, but the preferences of private banking interests as well ... It should not be forgotten that one important group was largely excluded from the policymaking equation when the crisis erupted, and that group consisted of the poor in the debtor countries. There was nobody to

give them a voice in the creditor governments, money center banks, or multilateral institutions, and one wonders how much they were heard even by their own governments. They would bear the brunt of the austerity measures that followed after 1982, guinea pigs to one economic theory after another ...[2]

How have these issues played themselves out in specific countries? The remaining essays in this collection are case studies of large emerging market countries. The choice to compare only large countries, with populations of over 50 million persons, and 1994 gross national product (GNP) over $100 billion (excepting Vietnam), was made deliberately. All other things being equal, the smaller the country, the more likely it is to be vulnerable to trends in the global economy. If financial globalization affects the chances for constructing stable democracy and achieving economic growth even in large emerging market countries, the Indonesias and Brazils of the world, then it is bound to have significant implications for smaller countries, from Ecuador to the Czech Republic.

The seven countries chosen also illustrate a range of values on both our independent variable, financial ties to the global economy, and our dependent variable, progress towards stable political democracy. Table 1, 'Net resource flows as a percentage of GNP,' shows the recent evolution of the financial profiles of these countries – plus South Korea and China, for comparative purposes – in terms of categories explained more fully in the chapter by Leslie Elliott Armijo. Briefly, 'foreign aid' represents long-term, relatively stable, funds coming from the foreign public sector to the recipient country public sector. 'Foreign direct investment' funds are long-term, stable capital flows coming from the private sector and going to the private sector. The two columns of 'medium and long-term debt' represent private lending, separated highly imperfectly (but as well as available aggregate statistics permit) into flows predominantly going to the recipient country public sector and those probably destined for the local private sector's use. The final two columns track portfolio capital flows, the most volatile form of capital transfers, again separated very provisionally into flows typically destined for the local public versus the local private sectors. Figure 1 shows the evolution of the shares of the six categories of net capital inflows to all developing countries over time.

Table 1 thus suggests that, as of 1994, five of the nine countries profiled were potentially vulnerable to financial crises in terms of the size of net foreign capital flows as a share of gross national product. Mexico, China, Indonesia, Thailand, and Vietnam all had net resource flows of around 5 per cent of their GNPs or more, while Brazil, India, Korea, and Russia seemed comparatively independent, with foreign inflows summing to only 3 per cent of GNP or less. However, a somewhat different list of potentially financially

Table 1   Net resource flows as per cent of GNP

Country	Year	Foreign aid	FDI	Med/lng debt to govt.	Med/lng debt to priv.	Portfolio flows to govt.	Portfolio flows to priv.	Total
Brazil	1970	0.39	1.20	1.27	2.00	0.00	0.00	4.86
	1980	0.37	0.83	1.39	0.10	0.15	0.00	2.83
	1988	−0.10	0.94	1.08	−0.15	0.03	0.08	1.87
	1990	−0.29	0.21	−0.10	−0.03	0.03	0.02	−0.16
	1992	−0.32	0.56	−0.05	0.87	0.14	2.21	3.41
	1994	−0.40	0.57	0.02	0.34	−0.04	2.53	3.01
Mexico	1970	0.39	0.85	0.45	0.16	−0.04	0.00	1.82
	1980	0.36	1.15	2.24	0.90	0.06	0.00	4.71
	1988	0.59	1.56	0.82	−1.64	−0.68	1.25	1.91
	1990	2.19	1.07	1.12	0.72	0.21	3.41	8.72
	1992	0.02	1.35	−0.06	0.14	−1.06	3.28	3.67
	1994	−0.49	2.19	−0.13	−0.38	0.86	3.41	5.46
China	1970	0.00	0.00	0.00	0.00	0.00	0.00	0.00
	1980	0.10	0.00	0.83	0.00	0.02	0.00	0.96
	1988	0.51	1.04	1.52	0.00	0.25	0.19	3.51
	1990	0.42	0.98	1.32	0.00	−0.01	−0.04	2.67
	1992	0.64	2.67	2.14	0.00	−0.05	0.46	5.86
	1994	0.60	6.48	1.15	0.00	0.55	1.11	9.89
India	1970	0.96	0.08	−0.02	0.00	0.00	0.00	1.02
	1980	1.49	0.05	0.34	0.11	0.00	0.00	1.99
	1988	0.76	0.03	1.05	−0.04	0.24	0.26	2.31
	1990	1.29	0.05	0.54	−0.03	0.10	0.38	2.33
	1992	1.44	0.06	0.72	−0.02	−0.08	−0.18	1.93
	1994	0.14	0.21	0.20	−0.15	−0.13	2.27	2.55
Indonesia	1970	4.91	0.86	0.30	1.38	0.00	0.00	7.44
	1980	1.22	0.24	1.02	0.00	0.05	0.00	2.54
	1988	3.59	0.68	−0.89	1.15	−0.19	0.43	4.77
	1990	2.30	1.00	−1.62	3.36	−0.09	3.29	8.24
	1992	2.37	1.34	−0.15	2.15	−0.07	3.09	8.74
	1994	1.00	1.26	0.07	0.61	0.00	1.96	4.89
Korea	1970	2.30	0.73	1.09	0.28	0.00	0.00	4.39
	1980	2.03	0.01	2.02	0.79	0.07	0.00	4.93
	1988	−0.86	0.49	−0.70	−0.13	−0.29	0.27	−1.23
	1990	0.14	0.36	0.25	−0.44	−0.11	0.88	1.07
	1992	0.01	0.24	0.15	0.23	0.44	1.63	2.70
	1994	−0.21	0.25	0.09	0.11	0.46	2.09	2.78
Thailand	1970	0.39	0.61	0.10	0.87	0.00	0.00	1.97
	1980	2.01	0.59	1.72	2.11	0.14	0.00	6.58
	1988	−0.88	1.82	0.39	0.29	0.07	4.32	6.01
	1990	−0.10	2.89	−1.01	3.19	−0.10	3.14	8.02
	1992	−0.12	1.93	0.20	1.06	0.26	2.28	5.62
	1994	0.33	0.45	−0.10	0.29	0.43	8.53	9.93

Table 1   Continued

Country	Year	Foreign aid	FDI	Med/lng debt to govt.	Med/lng debt to priv.	Portfolio flows to govt.	Portfolio flows to priv.	Total
Vietnam	1970	–	–	–	–	–	–	–
	1980	–	–	–	–	–	–	–
	1988	–	–	–	–	–	–	–
	1991	–0.22	0.33	0.52	0.00	0.00	–0.67	–0.03
	1992	2.71	0.24	1.42	0.00	0.00	4.50	8.87
	1994	5.87	0.64	–0.71	0.00	0.00	0.85	6.66
Russia	1970	–	–	–	–	–	–	–
	1980	–	–	–	–	–	–	–
	1988	–	–	–	–	–	–	–
	1990	0.87	0.00	0.66	0.00	0.05	–1.71	–0.13
	1992	1.21	0.14	2.03	0.00	0.00	0.19	3.57
	1994	1.00	0.27	–0.16	0.00	–0.01	–0.06	1.04
All LDCs	1970	0.95	0.42	0.33	0.31	0.00	0.00	2.02
	1980	1.60	0.21	1.47	0.40	0.11	0.00	3.78
	1988	0.92	0.53	0.39	–0.08	0.05	0.31	2.13
	1990	1.27	0.55	0.08	0.19	0.05	0.47	2.61
	1992	1.20	1.00	0.31	0.25	0.10	1.32	4.19
	1994	0.98	1.57	0.08	0.14	0.29	1.50	4.56

Notes:
1. Foreign aid equals sum of grants, multilateral loans, bilateral loans, and IMF loans.
2. Debt to government equals sum of medium and long-term guaranteed debt from foreign commercial banks and other sources.
3. Debt to private sector equals medium and long-term non-guaranteed debt from foreign commercial banks.
4. Portfolio flows to government equals guaranteed bonds.
5. Portfolio flows to private sector equals sum of non-guaranteed bonds, portfolio equity, and short-term debt.
6. Note that total net resource flows, unlike the *World Debt Tables* concept, includes IMF credit and short-term debt.
7. For 1970, 1980 and 1988, where non-guaranteed debt is not broken out into bonds and commercial banks, the latter are assumed.
Source: Computed from World Bank, *World Debt Tables*, 1994–95 and 1996.

fragile countries emerges if one looks not at the quantity of flows, but rather at their composition. Portfolio capital is potentially the most skittish, able to leave the country quickly at the hint of political or economic changes viewed unfavorably by investors. In 1994 Mexico, Thailand, Brazil, India, and Korea received the majority of their net financial resources in the form of portfolio

Figure 1   Types of net foreign capital flows to developing countries

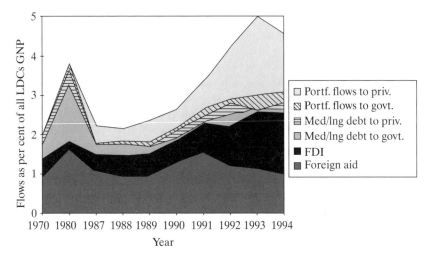

Source: see Table 1.

flows. Indonesia received approximately equal amounts of relatively stable net capital inflows (aid and foreign direct investment) and portfolio capital. Foreign aid dominated flows into Vietnam and Russia, while FDI was overwhelmingly the main source of foreign capital for China. By these two measures of annual flows in the mid-1990s, then, Mexico and Thailand, which show up in the high-risk category of both lists, looked most likely to experience an external financial crisis, while Russia appeared least likely. As it happened, of course, all three countries required large rescue packages (Mexico in 1995, Thailand in mid-1997) or eleventh-hour backstop guarantees (Russia in 1996) in the mid-1990s.[3]

Another way to conceive of external financial fragility is in terms of debt overhang, or the stock of past foreign liabilities remaining. Table 2 reports 1994 figures for the ratio of total medium and long-term debt to GNP, for annual debt service (that is, the principal plus interest payments due in a year) to export earnings, and for the present value to the nominal value of the debt stock (where scores approaching one represent an ever higher share of short-term debt). The ratio of total debt to GNP was huge in Vietnam, and high in Indonesia, but only moderate (ranging from Russia's 25 per cent to Thailand's 43 per cent) in the remaining countries, including both of the Latin American cases. Debt stock was lowest in the two countries included for comparison, Korea and China. In terms of debt service ratios, Indonesia, India, and the two Latin American countries had heavier burdens than the remaining East Asian countries, a function of the latter group's emphasis on export promotion. Russia and Vietnam, which received large shares of concessional loans in the early 1990s, also faced easier debt service. Finally, Thailand had in 1994 the largest share of short-term debt in its mix, while India had the smallest. By Table 2's measures all of the seven countries profiled in this volume, except Russia, looked somewhat vulnerable, while China and South Korea looked less so. Unfortunately, statistics can also be misleading and incomplete. Just as this book was undergoing final revisions, the East Asian financial crisis of 1997 was unfolding. As late as September, South Korea, long the most dynamic Asian tiger economy, looked relatively immune to the spreading 'Asian flu.' Yet in mid-November, the government in Seoul suddenly announced that the country's short-term debt liabilities summed to $60 billion, more than twice the previous official figure, stunning global markets and the International Monetary Fund. Apparently, the assessment of financial fragility is far from straightforward.

The case studies also include countries from several geographic regions, important given the propensity of many foreign investors to generalize

Table 2   Measures of financial vulnerability due to 'debt overhang'

	Total debt/GNP 1994	Debt service/ exports 1994	Present value of debt/ nominal value of debt
Brazil	27.9	31.8	92.6
Mexico	35.2	33.9	91.4
China	19.3	9.3	85.2
India	34.2	26.3	71.4
Indonesia	57.4	30.0	87.2
South Korea	15.3	6.8	91.2
Thailand	43.1	15.6	98.4
Vietnam	161.3	6.1	83.7
Russia	25.4	6.2	92.2
All Developing Countries	37.6	16.6	N/A

Sources: World Bank, *World Debt Tables 1996* (Washington, DC: World Bank, 1996) and World Bank, *World Development Report 1996: From Plan to Market* (New York: Oxford University Press, 1996).

financial crises from one country to its regional neighbors, as happened in Latin America in both 1982 and 1994 as a consequence of troubles in Mexico, and throughout East Asia after Thailand's large and sudden forced devaluation in July 1997. Country-specific information does not, of course, predict this source of external financial vulnerability.

Finally, the seven country cases included here also illustrate a range of domestic political regimes, which is both intervening and dependent variable in this volume. Again as of 1994, India and Brazil were stable if imperfect democracies. Mexico, Thailand, and Russia were in transition to procedural political democracy, while Indonesia and Vietnam had clearly authoritarian governments, Indonesia's of the right, and Vietnam's of the left. Each of the authors considers the implications of foreign capital flows for democratic development in the country he analyses.

The case studies begin with two contributions focusing on Mexico's late 1994 peso crisis, written, respectively, by an economist and a political scientist. William C. Gruben takes up the issue of the degree to which Mexico's serious financial, macroeconomic, and eventually political crisis ought, to be very blunt, to be blamed on irresponsible economic policy management within Mexico (the preferred 'story' of the international investing community, it goes without saying), or instead largely attributed to inherent tendencies of highly volatile portfolio capital flows. Writing with the customary restraint of the central banker he is, Gruben nonetheless opts, on the whole, for the latter explanation of the peso crisis.

Carlos Elizondo Mayer-Serra considers the political implications for Mexican democracy of the international financial crisis. Elizondo notes, on the one hand, that increased integration with the United States market, even before the peso crisis, led to greater external monitoring of Mexican human rights violations and other pressures that arguably were positive for Mexico's long, often excruciatingly slow, transition from a soft, civilian authoritarian regime to mass, multiparty democracy. The economic failures of the governing party in the 1980s, meanwhile, encouraged the rise of opposition parties, both on the left and on the right. On the other hand, throughout 1994, the long dominant Partido Revolucionário Institucional (PRI) gained electoral mileage by hinting that foreign investors might react to a PRI loss with large-scale capital flight. More than one incumbent government, not only in Mexico, has similarly tried to claim that keeping it in office is essential for economic stability. The PRI's implicit strategy backfired, of course, when the feared financial crash arrived anyway, and on the PRI's watch. There have been two interesting consequences since. In the mid-term Congressional elections of 1997, the PRI lost control of the legislature to the combined opposition of four parties, for the first time ever: the PRI's spectacular failure of economic management contributed to the rout. At the same time, however, the left parties had had to promise voters – and foreign investors – that they would continue most of the PRI's free market policies, if elected.

Peter Kingstone's essay on Brazil makes an important point that holds for the biggest of the big emerging markets, that is, the Brazils, Chinas, Russias, and Indias of the world: if a country's domestic market offers sufficiently attractive investment opportunities, foreign investment will come (if it is allowed to) almost no matter what the economic policy regime is. Brazil has hardly ever in recent decades adhered to neoliberal economic prescriptions; its record of multidigit inflation in the 1970s and 1980s, and yawning trade deficits in the 1990s, attests to this. Nonetheless, Brazil has always been rather successful at attracting foreign capital inflows, which have been a boon to successive weak governments, typically unable to impose even relatively small amounts of fiscal austerity on a fairly decentralized federal system. Implicitly, that is, Kingstone suggests an alternative take on Haley's contention that foreign portfolio investors swiftly punish countries for 'bad' scores on a narrowly defined set of cookie-cutter macroeconomic indicators. New, fragile democratic governments in large developing or transitional countries will tend to receive more favorable treatment from global investors than will new, fragile democratic governments in small countries. In other words, not much has changed: a decade or so ago authoritarian governments in larger developing countries could expect the same favorable treatment. Nonetheless, Kingstone also emphasizes that Brazil's external financial crises – albeit mild in comparative perspective – frequently have had negative domestic political repercussions, proving dangerous for incumbent presidents and the political regimes they represent.

The lessons from Randall Stone's chapter on Russia, however, might be read as cutting the other way. Big countries, even with large potential domestic markets, do not always get an easy ride from private foreign investors, particularly portfolio investors who have the option of rapidly withdrawing their cash. Stone's essay provides an analytically interesting comparison of the reactions of suppliers of, on the one hand, government-to-government (multilateral) foreign aid and, on the other, private portfolio investors in Russian government bonds, to distressing macroeconomic news about Russian public finances and macroeconomic prospects. As Armijo's paper predicts, Russia's official creditors – in this case mainly the International Monetary Fund – were significantly more patient with egregious macroeconomic policy failures than were private portfolio investors, because the Western governments that dominate IMF policymaking were extremely concerned that massive capital flight, however deserved, might undercut the already tenuous political position of President Boris Yeltsin. Private investors, however, had no such qualms. As noted above, by most of the readily available comparative quantitative indicators of external financial fragility, Russia, at least as of 1994, was among the least globally integrated of the large emerging market countries. Of course, Russia's vulnerability to external shocks has been multiplied by its chaotic domestic politics and severe domestic macroeconomic problems, including several years of sharply negative growth following the 1990 political transition.

It should be emphasized that Stone sees the 'tyranny' of global institutional investors as positive for Russia democracy: he sees sweeping and rapid market-oriented economic reform as the only path to rescuing Russia's distorted and inefficient economy, which is, in turn, a necessary condition for the population to come to believe in procedural political democracy. That is, Stone argues a version of what Armijo labels the 'optimistic' hypothesis about the effects of portfolio capital inflows.

John Echeverri-Gent's essay on India's stock markets plays off of Porter's thesis that transnational pressures for regulatory convergence may undermine democratic self-governance in emerging market countries. Echeverri-Gent's analysis is that, while the general principle may hold true, the particular circumstances of Indian capital markets regulation led to the effect that foreign pressures in this case were democratizing. The crucial intermediate condition that led to this outcome was that, prior to India's slow but genuine shift toward economic liberalization in 1991 and after, the powerful barons of the Bombay Stock Exchange (BSE) largely had controlled capital markets' regulation entirely by themselves, and had used this power mainly to enrich themselves (that is, to extract monopoly rents). The central government, allied with members of India's seven other regional stock exchanges (whom the BSE had contrived to exclude from the most lucrative trading), was able to use foreign pressure as a lever to break open the stranglehold of the BSE, thus 'democratizing' the regulatory framework for capital markets. Echeverri-Gent acknowledges, however, that another effect of both financial and economic internationalization in India is increased income disparities between already rich and poor Indian states. This outcome strains Indian democracy, both by adding to the already contentious burdens of 'justly' apportioning federal spending among competing states, and by making the relatively disadvantaged more dissatisfied with their lot and thus, potentially, more open to ethnically-based, nondemocratic mass movements.

The next two essays pair two East Asian cases. Indonesia is a long-time recipient of foreign capital flows of various kinds, including foreign aid, foreign direct investment, commercial bank loans, and the new portfolio flows. Jeffery A. Winters sees Indonesia as a strong, clear example of the thesis that foreign capital flows of all types tend, above all else, to support the incumbent government and the type of political system it represents. Despite the popular rhetoric linking market-opening, international trade, and foreign investment with democratization of authoritarian countries, Winters remains deeply skeptical. He provides solid evidence for the alternative thesis that foreign capital inflows have done much to sustain the dictatorial regime of General Suharto. The final versions of this volume's chapters were written, I should note, just as the July 1997 Thai and Southeast Asia financial crisis was breaking. It looked then as though leaders such as Suharto might sustain some damage from the harsh structural adjustments that will be imposed upon their countries. It seemed quite possible that the fallout might help to undermine Suharto's domestic credibility which, like that of the authoritarian leaders in Brazil, Argentina or the Philippines in the 1970s, partly has rested upon his claim to guarantee prosperity.

While Indonesia is a dictatorship of the right, Communist Vietnam is one of the left, currently in the throes of an extraordinarily rapid opening to large-scale foreign capital inflows. Jonathan Haughton takes up the questions of the contributions of foreign investment to Vietnamese economic growth, as well as its implications for political liberalization and the possibilities of an eventual transition to full political democracy. The case of Vietnam is particularly interesting for theory, in that the government has obliged private foreign investors to form partnerships with state-owned enterprises or government ministries, in principle thus capturing at least some of the economic efficiency benefits of private, for-profit investment, while retaining the political benefits to itself of having a large measure of control over the allocation of incoming foreign funds. In fact, Haughton observes, both the economic and political consequences are roughly what Armijo's paper would predict, were its analysis to be extended to this interesting hybrid case. Economically, foreign investment in Vietnam has cemented the economic reforms thus far, by apparently rewarding its market opening with new resources. However, because investment has gone not to the private sector but instead into joint ventures with government companies, private ownership and entrepreneurship per se have not been stimulated, nor has statist inefficiency and corruption been forced to reform by having to compete with private firms. The economic transition thus may have gotten stuck. Haughton also concludes, along with most of the other authors, that, unless foreign investment results in a severe balance of payments crisis, it generally serves to bolster the incumbent government and the larger political regime it represents. Since 1994, both Vietnam and Indonesia have received a comparatively larger share of short-term private capital inflows, one consequence of which has been to expose both countries to some 'contagion' effects of Thailand's mid-1997 financial crisis.

Danny Unger considers the case of Thailand, in the mid-1990s often identified in the financial press as the East Asian junior tiger with the most Latin America-like international capital flows profile. In recent years huge private portfolio flows, largely coming to the private sector, have engendered both trade and budget deficits. They have also encouraged, on balance, political liberalization as private Thai businesspersons translate their newfound

economic bargaining power into political leverage with the civilian government – and its military guardians, who continue to play an active political
role. Whether financial globalization will be as helpful to a further transition
to full democracy, however, remains a very open question. Through early
January 1998, Thailand's economic adjustment to its financial crisis looked
rather better than Indonesia's, at least plausibly because Thailand's greater
political openness provided greater adjustment flexibility. (The same, inci-
dentally, might be said of newly democratic South Korea, where President-
elect Kim Dae Jung already had convinced militant labor unions to accept
some job lossses in return for a promised expansion of the existing small
social safety net.)

We end with two different levels of conclusions. Emerging markets analyst
Walter Molano briefly compares the late 1994 Mexican peso crisis with the
mid-1997 Thai baht crisis, emphasizing elements tracked by the international
investor community. Among his more surprising and intriguing comments is
the observation that the process of adjustment in Thailand is likely to be
more severe than in Mexico precisely because it was the local private sector
(in particular, domestic banks) that borrowed the bulk of the short-term
portfolio capital flows in the years immediately preceding the crisis, rather
than the government, as had been the case in Mexico. As compared to either
Gruben or Elizondo, Molano is also significantly more critical of economic
policy management in Mexico throughout 1994. In her conclusion to the
volume, Leslie Elliott Armijo returns to the hypotheses with which she
began, briefly considering examples of countries where each of the six ideal
types of cross-border financial flows was especially significant.

The essays in this book each deal with one important aspect of financial
globalization – the changing institutional forms of cross-border capital flows
– from slightly different perspectives. All of the authors are broadly in agreement that developing country policy-makers are generally correct to consider
net capital inflows an opportunity to increase domestic savings, investment,
and growth. Most of the authors, however, see relatively few benefits to
capital-importing countries coming from the newer, more volatile private
portfolio capital flows, which have partially displaced foreign aid, commercial bank loans, and even foreign direct investment. Some contributors,
notably Echeverri-Gent and Stone, see a more obvious compensatory silver
lining than others, including Armijo, Haley, Porter, Gruben, and Kingstone.
Virtually all of the case studies demonstrate that real countries are more
complex than abstract theories, as is shown by Unger's insight that a redistribution of economic, and thus political, power away from the state and
towards the local private business community as a consequence of the new
portfolio capital inflows might, on balance, be more likely to promote movement in a democratizing direction in East Asia (with a tradition of comparatively strong, authoritarian, and bureaucratically insulated states) than in

Latin America (with a history of weak states and politically powerful economic elites). The essays, therefore, serve not as the final word on this topic but rather as an opening offering in what should be an ongoing debate about the meaning of financial globalization for emerging market countries and, in particular, for the chances of achieving democracy in those countries.

Notes

1. I join Tom Biersteker in expressing my gratitude to the two keynote speakers at the November 1995 conference that initiated this volume, Jesús Silva Herzog and Júlio de Quesada, and those institutions and persons that made the project possible. I particularly thank the International Studies Association, the Watson Institute for International Studies, Craig Murphy, Chris Bosso, Jean Lawlor, Fred Fullerton – and especially Thomas J. Biersteker. In addition to those authors whose work appears in this collection, I also thank those others who presented or discussed papers at the 1995 meeting, including Lawrence Broz, Vikram Chand, Benjamin J. Cohen, Zhiyuan Cui, Nomsa and Francis Daniels, Denise Dresser, E.V.K. FitzGerald, Peter Garber, Laura Hastings, Joshua Hoffman, Saori Katada, Arvid Lukauskas, Luís R. Luís, Sylvia Maxfield, Gesner Oliveira, Ravi Ramamurti, U. Srinavasa Rangan, Moises Schwartz, Thomas Skidmore, Robert Wade, and Ngaire Woods. Special thanks are due to Timothy M. Shaw, general editor of the International Political Economy series, and to Aruna Vasudevan and Keith Povey for the publishers.

2. Ethan B. Kapstein, *Governing the Global Economy: International Finance and the State* (Cambridge, Mass.: Harvard University Press, 1994), pp. 82–83.

3. In August 1998, as copyediting for this volume was being finalized, Russia's long-feared financial crisis arrived, as the government effectively defaulted on $40 billion of treasury bonds, about a third of which was held by foreigners. The medium-term outlook for both the Russian economy (already suffering from the worst potato and grain harvests in decades) and Russian democracy was grim.

Part I

Democracy and the Evolution of Global Capital Markets

1 Mixed Blessing: Expectations about Foreign Capital Flows and Democracy in Emerging Markets[1]

Leslie Elliott Armijo

Ever tighter and more rapid cross-border financial links gird the globe. High-powered international finance reaches deeply into the same developing countries in which basic local phone service works only sporadically. Many of these countries, moreover, are newly democratic or democratizing, with the attendant explosion in citizen demands of governments for improved jobs, educational opportunities, and better lives. Is the result – large and often volatile foreign capital inflows into democratizing 'emerging market' countries – a fortuitous coincidence of need and supply? Or is it, instead, a perversion of justified popular hopes for accountable government, as public policies become skewed toward the orthodox macroeconomic policies global investors are well-known to favor? Furthermore, do large foreign capital inflows, other things being equal, tend to promote or inhibit democratic transitions and the consolidation of electoral norms?

The forms of cross-border capital flows have altered in recent decades. In the 1950s through the mid-1960s, foreign aid provided more than half of all capital flows between advanced industrial and developing countries. In 1965, for example, foreign aid constituted 64 per cent of net resource flows to developing countries (McCulloch and Petri, 1994). In the 1970s the share of medium and long-term bank loans increased dramatically, supplying about half of net resource flows by the end of the decade. Meanwhile, between 1970 to 1980, total net inflows to developing countries almost doubled, to just under 4 per cent of their combined economies (see Table 1 of the Introduction).[2] Long-term bank lending disappeared abruptly in 1982, in response to Mexico's near default on its external debt. By 1988, foreign aid was again the largest single category of net resource flows (43 per cent), followed by direct investment (25 per cent), and medium and long-term bank loans and trade credit (14 per cent).[3] Total flows plummeted to a little over half of their pre-debt crisis high. Moreover, net transfers (net resource flows minus interest payments on past debt) from advanced industrial to developing countries as a group in the 1980s were approximately nil.[4] Meanwhile, international financial markets evolved dramatically in the 1980s. Jointly known as 'financial globalization,' these changes meant that more money, both absolutely and as a share of world economic output, was more mobile across borders than ever before. The total stock of financial assets traded in global capital markets, the so-called 'eurocurrency assets,' rose from about $5 trillion in 1980 to $35 trillion in 1992. In 1994 the McKinsey Global Institute projected they would reach almost $83 trillion by 2000, about three times the combined gross domestic product of the advanced industrial countries (Woodall, 1995, p. 10). Some commentators argued that, if measured properly, the total stock of outstanding global financial assets was no more overwhelming, as compared to either global output or world trade, than during the turn of the century epoch of British financial hegemony and the gold standard (Bradsher, 1995). However, the volatility of world capital markets in the last decade of the twentieth century unquestionably has had no precedent.[5] In 1973 daily foreign exchange trading was about $10 to $20 billion; by 1992, it was $900 billion; and by mid-1995 it had reached around $1.3 trillion of 'hot money,' backstopped only by the combined foreign currency reserves of government's of the advanced industrial countries, an apparently inadequate $640 billion. Similarly, the ratio of global trade to foreign exchange transactions was about 1:10 in 1982, but as much as 1:60 a decade later (Woodall, 1995, p. 10).

What did these changes mean for developing countries? The largest share of globally mobile capital, of course, flowed among advanced industrial countries, and the largest single destination was the United States, which by mid-1996 owed around $800 billion abroad (Prestowitz, 1996). Nonetheless, after the hiatus of most of the 1980s, large flows again began to go to developing countries. Beginning in the late 1980s, Mexico and other erstwhile pariahs suddenly found themselves again receiving net private voluntary capital inflows again – but this time the forms had altered dramatically. In 1980, portfolio capital flows (defined here to include portfolio equity, bonds, and short-term debt) were only 3 per cent of flows to developing countries, but by 1988 they were 17 per cent and by 1994 had become the largest single category of flows, with 39 per cent. Foreign direct investment, also enjoying a revival, comprised 34 per cent (Table 1). Total net flows, meanwhile, had shot up to 4.6 per cent of developing countries' GDP. The particular profile of the 'new' cross-border capital flows continues to be subject to change: although the figures are not available yet, the consequence of the East Asian financial crises of 1997 will almost certainly be reduced capital flows to emerging markets. What is unlikely to go away is the much larger share, as compared to the other post World War Two decades, of the new (or old, dating back to the late nineteenth and early twentieth century) form of cross-border investments: portfolio flows.

The risks of portfolio capital flows were illustrated by the dramatic events of Mexico's 'peso crisis' in December 1994, when close to a billion dollars exited the Mexican economy in a single day. As had happened with the 1982 debt crisis, in early 1995 the home governments of Mexico's major private creditors, in the interests of preventing a global financial crisis, stepped in with a rescue plan. One consequence of the peso crisis was that the rich countries had to begin thinking about which countries they would bail out should they be threatened with a financial crisis, and whom they would let crash. Presumably most emerging market countries would fall in the latter category – so long, that is, as their troubles did not threaten financial markets in the advanced industrial democracies.[6] Although the potential economic costs of these new, highly liquid, capital flows have been widely discussed (Calvo, Leiderman, and Reinhart, 1993; Fernandez-Arias, 1995; French-Davis and Griffith-Jones, 1995; Folkerts-Landau and Ito, 1995; Nunnenkampt and Gundlach, 1996; Rojas-Suarez and Weisbrod, 1995),[7] the political implications for emerging market countries have been less debated.

This chapter tries to think through the implications of these recent shifts in the institutional form of international financial flows for another global trend of the 1980s and 1990s: the turn from authoritarian to democratic rule in developing and post-Communist countries around the world. Is the relative decline of official development assistance, for example, on the whole 'good' or 'bad' for new democracies like South Africa or the Czech Republic? Why? The second issue of 'financial globalization,' the recent increase in net resource flows as a share of the total economies of developing countries, and the potential for further increases as financial investments become ever more mobile across national borders, I leave for another discussion.

The essay's first major section sets out definitions, first of 'democracy,' then of six ideal types of international capital flows.[8] The second section deductively considers the likely impacts of each of the six broad types of financial instruments on four intermediate variables: (1) the rate of economic growth, (2) the fortunes of four players in the national game of politics in most emerging market countries (foreign governments, the host country government, foreign business, and local big business), (3) the risk of a balance of payments crisis arising sometime in the future, and (4) pressure for neoliberal economic reforms. Section three then links the four intermediate variables with some possible consequences for democratic development.

VARIABLES DEFINED: DEMOCRACY AND INTERNATIONAL FINANCIAL FLOWS

The effects of foreign capital inflows on democracy in emerging market countries are what I hope to explain or predict. This section briefly defines the dependent variable, democracy, and distinguishes a hitherto relatively underexamined source of variation in the independent dimension, foreign capital flows.

Numerous definitions of *democracy* each have their defenders. The most used, and most achievable, is procedural political democracy. Here democracy is defined by wide access (all adult citizens have the vote, with no restrictions on either citizenship or voting imposed by property ownership, race or ethnicity, literacy, or other demographic or economic criteria) and specified, universalistic procedures, including freedom of speech and organization, multiple political parties and candidates, secret ballots, fixed terms of office, and limited authority of elected officials, who themselves are subject to the law of the land. Robert Dahl (1971) aptly suggested defining degrees of democracy along two dimensions: 'participation,' or breadth of inclusion of the population in the franchise and the group of those with potential to lead, and 'contestation,' or degree to which elections offer voters genuine alternatives between viable candidates with differing public policy preferences. Another crucial component of procedural political democracy is a guarantee of basic civil and civic rights, including freedom of expression, association, and religion, equal protection under the law, the right to be charged with a specific crime if arrested and to have an impartial trial within a reasonable time period, and the right to retain one's life and property, except under carefully specified circumstances, as in, for example, the military draft or the government's limited right to seize property for a compelling public purpose under the rule of 'eminent domain.' Finally, it must be true that in a procedural political democracy the elected leaders, assisted often by both appointed advisors and career civil servants, control the major public policy decisions in society; civilian leaders, that is, are not mere figureheads for military authoritarian rulers who exercise the real power.[9]

It should be noted that what the above definition lacks is any limits or comment whatever on the economic conditions that must or should obtain in a 'democracy.' It presumes that neither minimums of economic security nor economic equality are either necessary or sufficient for democratic government. Implicitly, the definition assumes that the one person, one vote rule, combined with the legal imperative of equality before the law, is sufficient to ensure justice in society. Procedural political democracy thus explicitly is a minimalist definition of democracy, requiring only that major conflicts among persons and groups are settled peaceably and through the political process, in theory open to all. All of the advanced capitalist countries, and increasing numbers of developing and postcommunist countries, meet these minimum requirements, at least most of the time. Procedural political democracy thus seems to be an achievable goal. Furthermore, it also serves as an essential, necessary although not sufficient, component of most contemporary definitions of economic democracy.[10] This chapter focuses the bulk of its attention on exploring the possible consequences of foreign capital flows for procedural political democracy. At this point a further dimension must be introduced. Thus far, democracy has been considered only as a static condition. Yet for the vast majority of emerging market countries, the crucial question is not how certain conditions might affect a long-standing and well-established democracy, but rather how they might shape a new or fragile democracy, or influence the possible transition of an existing authoritarian regime in the direction of becoming a future democracy. Reasonably stable and enduring democracies in developing countries, such as those in India, Jamaica, or Costa Rica, have been few. It should be important to review briefly some of what is known about conditions for successful transitions to democracy.

Three observations about transitions to democracy are relevant. First, it is harder for a country to become democratic than to maintain a preexisting democracy. Above all, procedural political democracy requires the consent of all essential political actors – defined as those individuals and groups that can exercise effective veto power over the outcome of democratic decision-making – to abide by the outcomes of elections, parliamentary debates and lawmaking, and like democratic procedures. Adam Przeworski (1991) usefully has formalized these conditions by noting that the rational calculations made by all relevant political actors must suggest to them that the payoffs expected from playing the democratic game, over the medium run, will be greater than those to be anticipated from subverting democracy, even though, and by definition, most players will not achieve their most preferred policy outcomes most of the time. Democracy is about institutionalized uncertainty and continuous compromise; each player's rational calculation must lead to the conclusion that mutual compromise is superior to no-holds-barred conflict, which holds out the possibility of total victory, but also of total defeat (see also O'Donnell and Schmitter, 1986). Once democracy has functioned for awhile, people typically began to attach a positive normative significance to it, and also to see it as the 'normal' state of affairs. After these points have passed, maintaining stable democracy becomes much easier.

Second, heightened economic insecurity usually is not auspicious for a successful democratic transition (Haggard and Kaufman, 1995). It is true that conditions of economic crisis can erode support for authoritarian incumbents. However, in and of itself, there is no reason to believe that a crisis will favor democratic successors over another authoritarian government with a change of personnel. Furthermore, feelings of personal vulnerability are likely to make many key political players more defensive, and thus less willing to compromise, that is, less willing to settle for the second best solutions inherent in the democratic process, than they would be if economic conditions were more settled or promising. Political liberalization that occurs in conjunction with significant economic liberalization, as has happened in Latin America, Eastern Europe, and elsewhere in the 1980s and 1990s, also poses particular problems beyond those associated with making a political transition separately (Armijo, Biersteker, and Lowenthal, 1994). Since new forms of foreign capital inflows to developing countries often are associated with a larger program of market-oriented economic reforms, these problems of transitional incompatibility between political and economic reform can make democratization significantly more difficult. For example, even scholars who believe that economic liberalization ultimately will improve both overall economic growth and increased economic opportunities for all sectors, including the poorest, recognize that the short-term effects of market reforms are likely to involve increased unemployment, structural dislocation, and, quite often, heightened income inequality, whether among quintiles of income earners or diverse geographic regions. Increased insecurity and/or inequality, even if policymakers plausibly expect it to be temporary, easily can provoke societal responses from groups that perceive themselves as losers, ranging from diffuse anti-system radicalism and even violence, to focused xenophobia, nationalist chauvinism, exaggerated protectionism, and religious fundamentalism. The ideas of a Patrick Buchanan or a Jean-Marie Le Pen pose little to threat to an established democracy as in the US or France. It was harder to be quite so confident about, for example, the election of a Vladimir Zhirinovsky or Gennady Zyuganov in Russia in mid-1996, both of whom attacked the incumbent, Boris Yeltsin, for being excessively neoliberal and insufficiently Russian nationalist.

Third, the process of democratization may be conceived of as typically including three stages (O'Donnell and Schmitter, 1986; Przeworksi, 1991). The first, political liberalization, signifies a loosening of overt authoritarian controls on the exercise of basic civil and civic liberties, such as freedom of expression, association, worship, and travel, and perhaps greater tolerance of criticism by the regime, but stops short of formalizing full democratic procedures. The second stage, formal transition to democracy, occurs when a country adopts new laws and procedures marking an official, legal transition to democratic rules of the game. The third stage is that of democratic consolidation, which implies internalization and normative acceptance of the new democratic procedures by all of the major political actors. One of the problems of some democratic transitions, not surprisingly, is that they get 'stuck.' Brazil, for example, spent at least a decade, more or less from the mid-1970s to the mid-1980s, moving from political liberalization to the formal transition to democratic rules. Russia in mid-1997 clearly was somewhere between stages two and three, but probably closer to the former than the later. Transitional political leaders in the Philippines and South Africa, Corazon Aquino and Nelson Mandela respectively, have tried hard to lodge their polities firmly in stage three before the leaders had to leave office. These leaders recognized the overriding importance of creating a shared normative commitment to the politics of institutionalized compromise.

The above definition of *democracy* as procedural political democracy is reasonably well-accepted. That is, the analytical concept is clear, although cross-national measurement is more tricky. The other component to be defined is *foreign capital flows*. Inquiries as to the effects of more or less foreign capital, or its presence or absence in an economy, are fairly standard in the political economy literature. By contrast, the premise of this chapter and this book is that the institutional form of cross-border financial flows makes a difference for political and policy outcomes in the capital-recipient emerging market country – that is, that the *form or quality of the capital flow may be as important in some cases as its sheer quantity.* I define six types of capital flows based on the answers to three questions: Is the source of the capital in the advanced industrial country the public or the private sector? Is the recipient of the foreign capital in the emerging market country the public or the private sector? Third and finally, how intrinsically volatile is the financial instrument employed? Table 1.1 provides a summary description of these six ideal types of international capital flows.

Foreign aid flows from the foreign public to the recipient country public sector and has comparatively low volatility. The category includes both grants and low-interest loans offered by developed country governments – either bilaterally or through a multilateral financial institution such as the World Bank or Inter-American Development Bank – to less-developed countries, almost always directly to their governments.[11] The numbers reported in the book's introduction consider credit from the International

Table 1.1   International investment instruments: ideal types

Financial instrument	Investor	In-country recipient of funds	Volatility
Foreign aid	Public sector	Public sector	Low
Foreign direct investment	Private sector	Private sector	Low
Bank loans to government	Private sector	Public sector	Medium
Bank loans to private firms	Private sector	Private sector	Medium
Portfolio investments w/government	Private sector	Public sector	High
Portfolio investments in private firms	Private sector	Private sector	High

Monetary Fund to be multilateral foreign aid. *Foreign direct investment* (FDI) flows from the foreign private sector to the private sector within the emerging market country in which the multinational corporation becomes, de facto, a local player. FDI also has low volatility. Through FDI multinational corporations set up new businesses or purchase existing firms located in the recipient country. The defining feature of direct investment is that the foreign owner assumes a long-term managerial commitment to the business in which he or she invests. Direct investment need not always mean majority ownership, which developing countries frequently have prohibited; foreign control can be exercised via a plurality of shares. Purchase by foreigners of a dominant interest in a privatized state-owned enterprise, for example, thus constitutes direct investment. The investor is a private corporation based in an advanced industrial country. The in-country recipient of funds is the subsidiary or affiliate of a multinational corporation (MNC), and thus also a private sector entity.[12]

Commercial bank loans to the incumbent government come from the foreign private to the emerging market country public sector, whether directly to the central bank or finance ministry, or to state-owned enterprises, ostensibly operated at some remove from national budgetary accounts, but nonetheless ultimately responsible to the political authorities.[13] Medium and long-term loans should have medium volatility. *Commercial bank loans to local big businesses* originate with the foreign private sector and are spent by the local private sector. In category four, loan recipients are creditworthy large private firms with a high enough international profile to borrow long-term funds directly from multinational banks. Typically, although not invariably, these firms are exporters, thus providing some assurance to the lender that they will have access to the foreign exchange needed to repay the loans.

Portfolio investments in securities of the incumbent government move funds from foreign private investors[14] to the recipient country public sector, as with foreign investment in treasury bonds of the emerging market government or minority shareholding in public sector firms. These securities may be sold directly in international financial markets or to foreign investors who buy them in the capital markets of the capital-importing country. Their defining characteristic is that the funds raised become the responsibility of the emerging market country's government. The sixth and final category, *portfolio investments in securities of local businesses*, refers to the transfer of resources from the foreign private to the local private sector. Securities in this group include both those traded only within the emerging market country and those floated directly in global markets, as with corporate equities or debentures of private firms of developing countries sold on European exchanges in the form of global depository receipts (GDRs) or traded in the US through American depository receipts (ADRs). I include short-term debt with portfolio investments in the local private sector.[15] Portfolio investments with either the public or private sector have the highest potential volatility.[16]

The six ideal types of cross-border capital flows to developing countries just specified have been constructed based on three types of distinctions: the identity of foreign investors (public or private sector), of in-country borrowers (public or private sector), and the hypothesized volatility of the financial instrument or modality (low, medium, or high).[17] In recent years there have been substantial shifts in aggregate flows on all three dimensions. From 1950 through the mid-1960s, foreign aid flows, originating in the public sector of the advanced industrial countries, were substantially larger than flows originating with private investors. By 1970, as shown in Figure 1.1, public and private *sources of foreign funds* were of approximately equal importance. In 1980, which represents the profile of the 1973–81 peak years of multinational commercial bank lending, the foreign private sector contributed about 25 per cent more funds than did foreign aid. Following the 1982 debt crisis, the share of bilateral and multilateral foreign aid again rose, as shown in the data for 1987. However, by 1992 private flows of all types dwarfed official flows, a trend that continued through this writing in late 1997. Figure 1.2 shows an equally pronounced shift in the *recipient sector of capital flows*, as the share of net flows coming to the in-country public sector dropped toward the end of the 1980s, while that of the in-country private sector rose. Figure 1.3's trends in *predicted volatility* reflect, first, the sharp decline in medium and long-term commercial bank lending, second, the recent sharp growth in portfolio flows, now exceeding the magnitude of official loans and grants, and, third, a recent recovery of foreign direct investment in the early 1990s. As compared to earlier postwar decades, that is, trends in the 1990s revealed dramatic movement in the direction of private sector to private sector flows, at least a third of which was in a highly liquid form.

The argument thus far has specified an outcome, procedural political democracy, which I suggest may be affected by the composition of foreign capital flows from advanced industrial countries to emerging markets. I assume for purposes of argument that the sheer magnitude of capital inflows among different hypothetical cases does not differ greatly. Rather, the institutional form of its transfer is what shifts. It is difficult or impossible to suggest logic that would propose a direct link between, for example, foreign direct investment and the strengthening or weakening of democracy in a developing country. The next section, instead, looks at four intermediate dimensions to which the institutional form of cross-border capital flows may have a direct link.

Figure 1.1   Source sector of net foreign capital flows

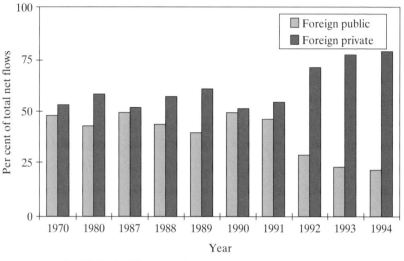

Source: See Table 1 of Introduction.

Figure 1.2   Recipient sector of net foreign flows

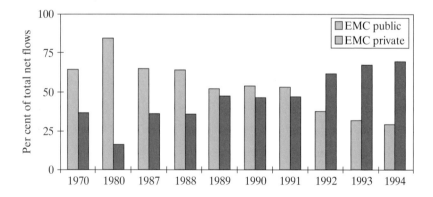

Source: See Table 1 of Introduction.

Figure 1.3 Flows separated by predicted volatility

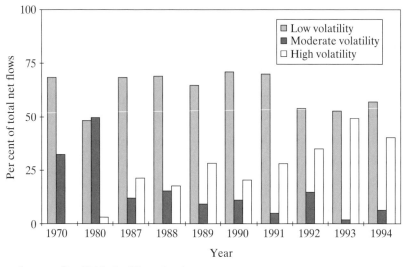

Source See Table 1 of Introduction.

DIRECT CONSEQUENCES OF FOREIGN CAPITAL FLOWS: LIKELY EFFECTS ON GROWTH, POLITICAL RESOURCES, FINANCIAL CRISES, AND PRESSURE FOR NEOLIBERAL POLICIES

Deductive reasoning suggests likely differences among the six types of foreign capital flows in their effects on four important intermediate outcomes – economic growth, the balance of power among nationally relevant political actors, the risk of provoking a balance of payments crisis, and externally imposed pressure for the adoption of neoliberal public policies – each of which, in turn, plausibly is related to democracy. That is, this essay constructs a two-stage argument: first, from alternative instruments of foreign capital flows to the four intermediate variables just listed, and second, from each of these intermediate variables to supportive or inauspicious conditions for democracy. Table 1.2 summarizes the first set of hypothesized links.

The expected relationship between various cross-border financial instruments and *economic growth* turns on the point that the in-country recipients of foreign resources may be either the government or private firms. From a purely economic viewpoint, foreign resources that come directly to governments probably are less efficient in directly producing growth. There is no reason to doubt the conclusions of the extensive literature of the public choice

Table 1.2   International investment instruments: direct implications

Financial instrument	Likely incremental stimulus to economic growth	Political actor whose influence increases (assuming no BOP crisis)	Increased risk of balance of payments (BOP) crisis	Pressure on govt. for neoliberal economic reforms (even if no BOP crisis)
Foreign aid	Low	• Foreign government • Incumbent government	Low	Low
Foreign direct investment	High	• Foreign business	Low	Moderate
Bank loans to government	Low	• Incumbent government	Moderate	Low
Bank loans to private sector	High	• Local big business	Moderate	Low
Portfolio investment with government	Low	• Incumbent government	High	High
Portfolio investment in private firms	High	• Local big business	High	High

school, which argues that rational public sector bureaucrats and managers, as compared to private owners, have fewer incentives to maximize profits and thus efficient operations, but many more incentives and opportunities to reap monopoly rents at the general population's expense (see Bates, 1988; Bates and Krueger, 1993; Meier, 1991). Examples include awarding public sector procurement contracts not to the lowest bidder but rather for a consideration, charging illicit fees for government services that ostensibly are free, and so on. In addition, politicians and the bureaucrats who work for them may choose to allocate a portion of the investment resources that come under their control to alleviate social tensions such as those caused by interregional inequities within the country. That virtually all governments are at least at the margin influenced by political considerations in the allocation of public investment funds suggests that public sector disbursement of international resources is likely to be on average less efficient than private sector investment.

It is, of course, reasonable to counter that the private sector, though likely to run more microeconomically efficient firms, is much less well equipped than the central government to solve collective action problems (see Olsen, 1965). To the extent that society's economic problems are dominated by such typical collective action challenges as environmental degradation, or under-investment in future generations and in infrastructure, resource allocation by the central government may well be more macroeconomically efficient in the long run. Making this judgment about a particular society is an empirical task, and cannot be done on the general, analytical plane on which this essay operates. Possibly different countries have different likelihoods of encoun-tering collective action problems.

Nonetheless, for our present purposes, the point is that resources that come directly to the central government tend to exhibit certain characteris-tics: in brief, the incumbents will employ resource allocation in ways that reflect their public policy priorities, which in turn will be both developmental and directly political. Some expenditures will be directed toward furthering economic growth. Other expenditures, however, are likely to go for other goals, from enhancing equity (arguably laudable, but in the short· run less growth-enhancing than a single-minded focus on profits) to political patron-age. On the other hand, private sector investors will tend to maximize profits, period. Thus, foreign aid, bank loans to the government, and portfolio investment in government securities all might be expected to be compara-tively less efficacious with respect to yielding overall economic growth than foreign direct investment or bank loans or portfolio investments coming to the local non-financial private sector. The judgments in column 1 of Table 1.2 reflect these suppositions.

The second reasonably direct link is that between the institutional form of foreign investments and the *balance of resources and influence among nationally relevant political actors*. A definition may be helpful. National politics may be conceived of as a political 'game' in which various 'players' (social groups and occasionally individuals) jockey for position. Each group's goal is to use whatever politically relevant resources it has available (which may be guns, money, the ability to command votes, ideas, the ability to turn out masses into the street to demonstrate, specialized knowledge, inherited high status, and so on) in order to pursue its preferred public policy agenda (see Wynia, 1990). Thus, for example, organized industrial workers possess the resources of strikes, potential mass action, and a rea-sonably large bloc of votes; maintaining high wages is one of this group's most important policy goals. Capitalists possess the resources of control over funds, which may be channeled to candidates in democratic political systems, or invested abroad, if the business community becomes sufficiently disenchanted with local prospects. Their policy preferences run to lower wages and light government regulation. Interest groups, which may be constituted on the economic basis of class or occupation, or around other identities such as ethnicity or geographical origin, will have competing policy preferences in all political and economic systems. There is nothing *per se* that is insidious or abnormal about the existence of social groups competing to influence public policies, although many political ideologies (from Iberian or Latin American corporatism to Communism) prefer to pretend that society is intrinsically harmonious, and thus intergroup conflict nonexistent or at least illegitimate.

Social groups, or political players, compete over public policy within the framework of political institutions, including both the formal rules of the game (laws and constitutions) and its informal rules (well-understood although unwritten behaviors and practices, ranging from innocuous social conventions to the never-articulated but strictly enforced rule that the dictator-for-life is not to be contradicted on pain of imprisonment or death). Military authoritarianism is one set of rules, which of course exists in many variants, while procedural political democracy, which also has numerous specific incarnations, is another. Both formal and informal rules of the national political game may evolve gradually or instead shift dramatically because of some discrete event, such as a military coup. Circumstances that alter the balance of relative power among political actors constitute one important source of dynamism and change in national political rules, particularly informal ones.

There are *four main political actors* whose influence, overt or indirect, over local policymaking and political choices may be differentially enhanced by diverse forms of foreign capital inflows: foreign governments and international organizations, the incumbent government of the capital-recipient country, foreign business, and local big businesses sufficiently well-known to attract foreign private investors. These obviously are not the only politically relevant players, nor will their initial degree of influence be the same across all emerging market countries. (For example, as of the early 1990s local big business was a more powerful political player in most Latin American than most Eastern European countries, because capitalists had been deemed criminals under Communist rule.) The six types of cross-border financial instruments differentially apportion additional resources among these four political and policy players. Column 2 of Table 1.2 reflects my expectations of marginal increments to the resources controlled by locally relevant political actors. In all cases, I am discussing the pattern of political resources in the absence of a balance of payments crisis associated with the cross-border capital flows.

Foreign governments and multilateral financial institutions (whose policies wealthy foreign governments tend to dominate) enhance their direct influence in local politics through foreign aid. All foreign capital inflows to some extent bolster the *incumbent political 'regime'* (that is, type of political system, as in democratic or authoritarian) and the incumbent 'government' or 'administration' (that is, the set of politicians currently in power). Capital inflows signify the outside world's confidence in the economic management skills of the ruling team. *Foreign business* enhances its direct influence in an emerging market country only through foreign direct investment (FDI). The influence of MNCs is ostensibly strictly economic, but in practice includes the right to have an indirect input into public policy and regulatory decisions that affect them. Once installed within the country, MNCs become local political actors. Foreign investors with a majority stake in a local business enterprise are bound to have preferences on local issues, whether or not the formal rules of the game permit them to participate, as their profits and other legitimate interests will be strongly affected by national economic regulatory policies. Finally, *local big business firms* augment their politically relevant resources when they are able to attract foreign capital flows directly, as in commercial bank loans borrowed directly from multinational banks (category four) or portfolio flows (equity, bonds, or short-term debt) raised by private corporations directly. Where local big business firms have a sufficient international reputation to borrow on their own hook, this enhances their bargaining resources *vis-à-vis* their own governments, putting them in a position analogous to that of private sector entrepreneurs who account for a large share of a country's exports. (Often they are the same people.)

The comments just made apply to cross-border capital flows in the absence of a balance of payments crisis. Following such a crisis, however, the direct influence of all foreign actors in the emerging market country increases, including foreign investors or lenders, international financial institutions, and the home governments of foreign private investors and lenders.

The six types of cross-border capital flows also differ in their degree of potential volatility, that is, in the ease with which the foreign investor can turn around and repatriate his/her/its funds. Consequently these alternative financial instruments imply differing degrees of *balance of payments risk*, as shown in column 3 of Table 1.2. Foreign aid and foreign direct investment have low volatility; they are unlikely to be reversed overnight. Foreign aid flows largely respond to non-economic criteria in any case; it usually takes a very dramatic, and rare, political change within the recipient to have aid flows staunched suddenly. In contrast, the reasons that FDI is of low volatility largely are practical. Factory owners cannot sell out immediately without confronting large losses, particularly in the context of an economic or political crisis. They thus tend to remain in the host country, often attempting to influence public policy choices themselves, whether overtly or covertly.

However, although FDI is unlikely to be volatile in the sense of participating in overnight capital flight, political or economic crises in the capital-importing country can cause potential investors to delay or cancel long-planned inward FDI.[18]

Medium and long-term commercial bank loans (categories three and four) in principle are of intermediate volatility, and thus pose an intermediate risk of external payments crises. Loans for capital projects cannot be called in, barring gross violation by the lender of the terms of the contract, before they mature in six to ten years. Nonetheless, in practice, shorter-term loans, including medium-term trade credit, tend to become linked to the long-term debt. Within six months following Mexico's August 1982 admission of its inability to make its quarterly debt payments, the major commercial bank creditors had generalized the crisis to most other Latin American countries by refusing to renew entirely standard and customary forms of commercial credit, thus provoking liquidity crises and the borrower countries' consequent inability to meet their debt service payments on the longer-term loans.

Portfolio investments (categories five and six) pose the greatest risk of an external payments crisis. Stocks and bonds are designed to be traded regularly, even daily or hourly: this is the reason their prices fluctuate. If they also trade across national borders in sufficient quantities, then the price of a nation's currency can fluctuate with the fortunes of its domestic capital market. Short-term debt is extremely sensitive to interest and exchange rate movements. Thus, a serious balance of payments and currency crisis can accompany a market downturn. A crisis in one country in a region can be rapidly generalized to its neighbors. Finally, if foreign investors (and/or domestic investors intending to move their capital abroad – it makes no difference) also hold large chunks of the government's domestic public debt, then a fiscal crisis ensues as well. Thus Mexico's financial crisis in the months following December 1994 was both a balance-of-payments and a fiscal crisis, because exiting foreign investors held a large share of the public debt.

The final hypothesized direct effect of foreign capital flows, shown in column 4 of Table 1.2, is pressure for developing country policymakers to manage their economies to suit foreign investors, rather than local needs or preferences.[19] *Pressure for neoliberal economic policies* can be expected to vary dramatically according to the type of financial instrument.[20] Both foreign aid and commercial bank loans sometimes went to countries whose economic policy capacities were marginal; donor governments often didn't care, since their major goals were strategic, not economic, and multinational banks during the 1970s lending boom, in retrospect, did not vet their sovereign borrowers carefully (Devlin, 1989; Cohen, 1986). In fact, developing country governments often used aid and loans to delay or avoid painful economic reforms. The pressure for neoliberal economic reforms from these sources of capital inflow typically is low.

Multinational corporations that invest directly in a developing country are more likely than aid donors or bank lenders to care about the host country policy environment. As local actors, however, as well as foreign investors, the policy preferences of multinationals are not likely to reflect a cookie-cutter, one size fits all orthodox mentality. Instead, they tend to prefer a stable regulatory environment. The pressure exerted by foreign direct investors on capital-importing country governments for orthodox economic reform is moderate.[21]

The portfolio investors in emerging markets of the late 1980s and the 1990s differ from their predecessors in two respects. First, the possibility of rapid movement of funds in and out of specific securities, and also in and out of countries and currencies, inspires investors to seek information that will enable them to make profits from rapid arbitrage. Meanwhile, each investor, whether as an individual or institution, must be prepared for rapid movement out of a multitude of idiosyncratic markets. It is very difficult, if not impossible, for investors to have good information on all of them. Thus, summary comparative measures – such as the government budget deficit, trade balance, public debt, growth rates, and inflation – tend to be seized on as a means of selecting among alternative investment venues. Furthermore, comparatively ignorant international investors tend to assume that countries that share similarities of geography, history, or culture (as in 'Latin America' or 'Eastern Europe') follow similar macroeconomic strategies with similar potential for success. Thus, the same herd mentality that caused multinational banks to react to Mexico's de facto default in August 1982 by pulling loans from all other Latin American borrowers was again in effect in Latin America in early 1995 and in East Asia in late 1997, but at an intensified level. From the viewpoint of investors, of course, such analytical shortcuts are entirely rational; it is better to rank possible investment destinations by imperfect data than to invest with no good information at all. From the viewpoint of emerging market countries, on the other hand, such investor behavior ties their hands very rigidly, forcing them into politically (and sometimes economically) risky behavior such as 30 to 50 per cent slashes in already low levels of social spending, often just as democratization finally is giving the poor a voice in politics.[22] This is the 'tyranny of the bond traders,' that moves exchange rates even in the advanced industrial countries.[23]

In addition, global capital markets today contain many decentralized investors, even if one notes the important leadership role of large international institutional investors, as Mary Ann Haley does in her chapter. In this situation, the lowest common denominator of information tends to prevail. Hypothetically, even if a given portfolio investor was aware that a country's heterodox stabilization program, for example, was appropriate given conditions in that economy, he or she might have to divest of that country's treasury securities if the investor suspected that less well-informed investors might flee and drive the value of the country's government debt down anyway. Even in the absence of direct, overt pressure from foreign institutional investors, that is, countries with large quantities of portfolio inflows find themselves under high implicit pressure to adopt neoliberal economic policies.

INDIRECT LINKS: CROSS-BORDER FINANCIAL FLOWS AND DEMOCRACY IN EMERGING MARKET COUNTRIES

The previous section suggested relatively straightforward links between the six types of capital flows and four important intermediate variables – economic growth, the relative power of four important political players, the likelihood of a balance of payments crisis, and external pressure for neoliberal economic policy choices. We now return to our core question: how might the institutional form of cross-border capital flow affect the prospects for a successful transition to, or consolidation of, procedural political democracy?

Let me first make an obvious point: the nature of the incumbent political regime (that is, the type of existing political system) is the most important influence on whether foreign capital inflows promote or retard democracy. *Ceteris paribus*, foreign investment in a democracy will strengthen democracy, while foreign financial resources flowing into a country governed by a dictator will tend to enhance his or her position. Similarly, balance-of-payments crises undermine the credibility of governing incumbents – even if the main borrowers have been private businesses or banks. It makes no sense to discuss the import, for democracy, of any of the six types of financial instruments without also considering the political status quo of the recipient country. The following discussion, summarized in Table 1.3, returns to this point frequently.

I am skeptical about a commonly posited relationship. In my view, forms of cross-border capital flows that *improve economic growth* don't necessarily aid in the promotion of democracy. There is no direct causal relationship between economic growth, on one hand, and the transition to or consolidation of procedural political democracy, on the other hand (see Table 3, row 1).

This is an old argument for political scientists. We can begin with the reason that so many observers have believed that economic growth and political democracy were complementary and mutually reinforcing (see Rostow, 1960). The majority of contemporary liberal democracies are wealthy, industrialized countries. Therefore, it is easy to conclude, changes that move countries in the direction of becoming wealthier or more powerful also help them democratize. However, as Guillermo O'Donnell (1973) conclusively demonstrated for Latin America in the 1950s through the 1970s, it also is possible that progress toward industrialization could lead away from democracy.[24] Many more recent treatments also argue that the relationship

Table 1.3   Intermediate variables: implications for democracy

Intermediate variable	Implications for democracy	
	If incumbents are authoritarians:	If incumbents are democrats:
High economic growth	May delay democratic transition by legitimating incumbents.	Good for democracy.
Foreign government's influence increased	Depends on goals of foreign government.	Depends on goals of foreign government.
Incumbent government's influence increased	Strengthens authoritarian regime.	Strengthens democratic regime.
Foreign business' influence increased	Promotes some political liberalization, but not full transition to democracy.	*Pessimistic hypothesis*: dangerous for weak democratic govts. with leftist policy goals.
		Optimistic hypothesis: protects foolish leftist govts. from policy mistakes that invite military coups.
Local business' influence increased	Promotes some political liberalization, but not full transition to democracy.	Depends on characteristics of local business.
Balance of payments crisis occurs	Discredits authoritarian incumbents with citizenry and international community.	Discredits democratic incumbents with citizenry and international community.
Neoliberal economic reforms occur	May delay democratic transition by weakening pro-democracy actors (organized labor, the poor).	Good in long run. In short/medium run may strain or reverse democratic transition.

between economic or industrial growth, on the one hand, and political democracy, on the other, is highly contingent at best, and may even be negative under some conditions (Haggard and Kaufman, 1992; Haggard and Kaufman, 1995; Armijo, Biersteker, and Lowenthal, 1994).

A comparison of India and South Korea, for example, which had roughly the same per capita income around 1950, suggests that Indian democracy since 1947 did not produce much in the way of rapid economic growth, at least before the 1980s, while Korea's admittedly successful economic strategy did not lead to democracy before the late 1980s (Varshney, 1984). In general, high economic growth under authoritarian political auspices has the effect of legitimating the incumbent non-democratic regime, and thus delaying the democratic transition in the short to medium run. Rapid growth in a democracy similarly validates the current political leaders and their economic policy team.

The second dimension explored in this essay's previous major section linked certain institutional forms of international financial investment to *shifts in the distribution of locally relevant political resources* controlled by key players in the game of national politics. We cannot plausibly argue that an increase in the resources available to player X will either create or destroy procedural political democracy. However, we may be able to assert that, all other things being equal, an increase in the resources available to player X heightens or diminishes the prospects for democracy, particularly under circumstances Y (see Table 1.3, rows 2 through 5).

Increases in the leverage of foreign governments and international organizations, as through a country's acceptance of foreign aid, heighten the impact of the preferences of these foreign actors within the national political game of the emerging market country. Unfortunately, democratization or democratic consolidation is only infrequently a top priority of aid donors. Bilateral aid donors typically rank achievement of their other strategic objectives – such as access to military bases, cementing alliances, commercial reciprocity, or drug interdiction – above democratization. Multilateral financial organizations usually allocate resources according to overt macroeconomic criteria, and sometimes also according to the unacknowledged strategic criteria of their major donor countries, rather than as a reward for or inducement toward democracy. Increased influence in the politics of emerging market countries for foreign governments, even when they these governments are democratic at home, is, at best, a weak recipe for democratization.

Increased influence for the incumbent government promotes democracy only when the incumbents are democratic already. Monies coming directly to the incumbent government augment the resources (often in practice fungible across investment, consumption, and political patronage spending) that ruling politicians can deploy *vis-à-vis* their political opponents. New or weak democratic governments may have a particularly acute need for resources, since previously marginalized classes almost always expect a rapid improvement in their material circumstances, now that an oppressive government has gone. The 1990s shift toward private sector in-country recipients of funds, shown in Figure 1.2 above, thus may be particularly unfortunate for new democracies. However, as noted, all types of capital inflows strengthen governing incumbents to some degree – at least so long as they do not generate a balance-of-payments crisis. What are the consequences of local political influence for multinational direct investors? This is, of course, a highly polemical topic on which much has been written (see Chase-Dunn and Bornschier, 1985). There are two contending expectations. We may call these contrasting predictions the 'pessimistic hypothesis' and the 'optimistic hypothesis.' The pessimistic hypothesis comes in two versions, which are not mutually exclusive. The first version suggests that transnational direct investors will have no patience with democratically elected leftist reformers. Left-leaning governments that promote policies like land reform or preferences for small-scale local production, thus may meet resistance from foreign direct investors in their midst. Foreign direct investment that originally entered the country during previous authoritarian and/or politically conservative times may be especially problematic for a new or weak democratic government in an emerging market country. Democratically arrived at (that is, politically popular) public policies might be excessively economically populist. The foreign businesspersons may feel that the regulatory environment suddenly – and from their viewpoint, unfairly – has been switched under their noses, thus justifying to themselves a decision to retaliate. The political activities of multinationals in host countries have ranged from the relatively innocuous, as in joining or sometimes organizing local chambers of commerce and or other business lobby groups, to the illegal but not unexpected, as in secretly contributing to the campaign funds of pro-business candidates, to the egregiously inappropriate, including involvements in coups and assassination attempts.

A second version of the pessimistic hypothesis reasons from the presence of transnational direct investors to the likely social class structure of a currently authoritarian or semidemocratic country, and concludes that the possibility for a future transition to full democracy has become less likely. Thus, some political sociologists have postulated that full electoral democracy with nearly universal adult participation is most likely to arise in societies that are at certain stages in their economic development, and possess specific sorts of class structures. If this hypothesis is correct, then certain alterations in groups' relative economic power that are non-threatening to an established democracy nonetheless may impede a full democratic transition. Rueschemeyer, Stephens, and Stephens (1992), for example, worry about the domestic political consequences of a developing economy in which multinational direct investors dominate core productive sectors.[25] The three believe a numerically strong and politically assertive industrial working class to be a necessary although insufficient condition for the successful transition to mass democracy. In the absence of effective lower class demands for political participation, they argue, political reform may cease with partial liberalization of overt authoritarian controls on middle class civil liberties, stopping well short of full democratization. For example, they suggest that the particular class characteristics of Latin American industrialization, whose leading actors for well over a century have been foreign direct investors, directly inhibited the formation of strong labor unions, and thus of stable democracies, in most countries there, at least prior to the late 1980s[26] (see also Karl, 1990; Moore, 1966).

Contrasted to these predictions is the 'optimistic hypothesis,'[27] which is the mirror image of the first pessimistic expectation above. Quite so, the optimists argue, foreign entrepreneurs might try to protect their property rights by pressing the government to restore a 'sane' investment climate. However, the intervention of foreign investors on the side of neoliberal policies could end up protecting, rather than undermining, formally democratic rules of the game. That is, foreign business leaders, often allied with local big business, could use their influence to push policymakers to adopt more macroeconomically sensible and sustainable policies. Society as a whole thus might avoid just the sort of economic breakdown that ends with a military coup and the installation of military-technocratic ('bureaucratic-authoritarian'[28]) political regime justifying their withdrawal of political freedoms in the name of restoring economic growth.

The sequences of events imagined in either the first variant of the pessimistic hypothesis, or the sole version of the optimistic hypothesis, of course, only come into play if the elected government wants to enact leftist, populist policies of economic redistribution, social spending, import-substituting industrialization, and the like – particularly if policy-makers are blithely unconcerned with how to pay for their plans. If, on the other hand, democratically chosen policymakers have conservative economic leanings, business actors typically will be more satisfied with the government and less likely to interfere. For reasons outside those analyzed in this essay, neoliberal economic ideas have made a worldwide ideological comeback in the 1980s and 1990s (Biersteker, 1995). If the elected government follows conservative economic policies, then both foreign and most local big businesses can support democracy without contravening their class interests and policy preferences.[29]

Finally, what can we expect if foreign capital inflows augment the resources available to local big capitalists? Emerging market countries differ greatly from one another: blanket predictions would be foolhardy. Nonetheless, deductive logic and a rational choice perspective suggests that big business should, in most developing countries, favor political liberalization but may be ambivalent about a full transition to competitive electoral democracy. A shift away from the arbitrariness of unrepresentative governance to the rule of law reduces the costs of doing business. Protection of individual freedoms protects businesspersons themselves. Press freedom is consistent with good access to timely business data. However, there are good structural reasons why the attitudes of business leaders toward democratic transitions may be ambivalent. On the one hand, entrepreneurs' personal experience of participation in global markets will tend to broaden the knowledge that they have of the larger world: cosmopolitan, educated, high status individuals tend to have been exposed to, and perhaps imbued with, democratic values.[30] On the other hand, successful local business leaders with a presence in global markets will, almost by definition, have been members of the privileged elite in their home countries. Similarly, multinational direct investors, once committed to a country, tend to become de facto members of the incumbent political regime's support coalition. If an emerging market country's current political regime is authoritarian, then the shift to mass electoral democracy almost inevitably will dilute the public policy influence of these same business elites. If we imagine that business leaders as a group are classic 'rational actors,' then their strictly selfish interests should lead them to favor a politically liberalized, semi-authoritarian regime – allowing, say, freedom of the print media but not of radio and television (because the masses don't read); freedom to travel abroad, but not to criticize the government openly at home; and well-codified corporate law, but not the right to strike.[31]

The previous section also ranked the six ideal types of cross-border capital flows according to their *risk of provoking an external payments crisis*. Table 1.3, row 6 suggests that the main consequence of a balance-of-payments crisis is to discredit governing incumbents. Two further observations seem irrefutable.

First, if the political regime itself is weak or fragile, then such crises may also stimulate a political regime change. However, and second, while debt crises certainly are ominous for fragile democracies, it is not safe to conclude that balance of payments crises occurring under the auspices of authoritarian incumbents necessarily are good for democratic transitions.

When an incumbent military regime weakens and topples because political leaders cannot control the recessionary effects of an external financial crisis, then democracy, of course, may result. However, orthodox stabilization or structural adjustment, and the regressive social class and income shifts normally associated with them, may make it difficult for the successor regime to be a full mass democracy. The argument is as follows. Orthodox structural adjustment policies, implying deep recessions and much pain, seem an inevitable consequence of external payments crises in a contemporary emerging market countries. However, social groups whose political resources increase with a transition to political democracy – notably including organized labor and the poor[32] – may be precisely those that tend to lose out economically during standard neoliberal structural adjustments. For example, recessions mean that first private, then eventually public, sector workers lose their jobs – over the protests of their unions, typically, which then are delegitimized and weakened politically as an actor in constructing future political bargains. In addition, the poor, at least those whose livelihood depends on cash employment or casual earnings (as opposed to subsistence farmers), is the group that tends to suffer most during structural adjustment periods.[33] There are purely economic reasons why the poor should suffer more than organized labor, the middle class, or upper-class groups: they lack a diversified portfolio of assets going into the crisis, have little or no safety cushion, and cannot access good information about their options during the lean years.

Loss of relative economic power, however, breeds loss of politically relevant bargaining resources – particularly important during a period of political transition. It is during periods of political transition that the *de jure* and *de facto* 'rules' of the successor political game are being hammered out among all those groups that can, in effect, claim a place at the table. The bargaining weight of a political player is roughly equivalent to the importance and credibility of its threat to withdraw cooperation and sabotage the entire process of political compromise. If unions are discredited, and potentially mobilizable urban slumdwellers are busier than ever in begging and competing against one another for casual employment, then they (usually) become that much less likely to have the status, time, or energy to contest the rules of the successor political game. Therefore organized labor and the poor lose relative influence in the domestic political game.

Meanwhile, groups whose direct public policy influence would be undercut by the shift from policy-making by insider status to majority votes – such as foreign or local big business, as already discussed, or the military, or the urban middle class (particularly where this class is relatively small) – are unlikely to bear the brunt of structural adjustment cuts. That is, they still will be players of some heft during the transition bargaining. The relative balance of bargaining influence among alternative social and political actors that has been constructed during the time of political regime breakdown and renegotiation tends to be perpetuated into the future, at least until the next system-threatening crisis.[34] Of course, many other factors – prominently including the demonstration effect of Latin American and East Asian democratization in the 1980s, and the end of the Cold War and Eastern European democratization in the early 1990s – also play a crucial role in promoting democratic transitions. Nonetheless, the conclusion is that, even if the previous authoritarian regime has been discredited and overthrown, the experience of a balance of payments crisis in an emerging market country is not likely to be particularly conducive to the establishment of democracy.

The last dimension hypothesized to be directly affected by the form of international capital flows is external pressure on the borrowing country for *neoliberal economic reforms*, as shown in Table 1.3, row 7. As noted in this essay's previous section, I expect portfolio types of capital flows to generate the most pressure for preemptive neoliberal policy changes. Neoliberal reforms range from budget-cutting to structural/institutional changes such as shrinking the size of the federal bureaucracy, selling state-owned enterprises ('privatization'), and getting rid of trade barriers. The one-off reform of selling state assets, for example, brings money into the national treasury which can be used to balance the budget, thus attracting capital inflows. Furthermore, the language of market-oriented regulatory changes – 'free' markets, 'liberalization,' and so on – parallels that of democratization. It is no wonder that many thoughtful observers have assumed that free politics and free markets are entirely complementary – or even that they are acceptable substitutes for one another (see Bhalla, 1994).

However, this easy assumption of automatic complementarity appears to be false, except possibly in the long run. Even if we assume, for the sake of argument, that all such 'reforms' actually improve economic performance eventually, there is no linear, necessary connection between market-oriented economic liberalization and the transition to or consolidation of procedural political democracy. A reduction of the state's economic presence typically means not only an end to unnecessary red tape, but also cuts in social spending and the redistributive activities of the paternal state. These social structural shifts are unlikely to promote a transition from authoritarianism to democracy. Under preemptive neoliberal economic reforms we might expect labor unions and the poor to be relatively worse off, at least in the short to medium run, just as we argued they would be following a balance of payments crisis.[35] Moreover, authoritarian leaders, fearing political protests from recessionary reforms and cuts in state spending, may be particularly unlikely to risk political opening while implementing neoliberal economic reforms. Rapid neoliberal reform could make democratic transitions more difficult (Armijo, Biersteker, and Lowenthal, 1994).

At the same time, the consensus of economists, at least those practicing in advanced industrial countries, supports the belief that market-oriented reforms will improve economic growth prospects in the medium to long run (Williamson, 1990).[36] That is, there is also an 'optimistic' hypothesis about external pressure for preemptive neoliberal reforms. Market reforms are sorely needed to turn an authoritarian and inefficient economy around, say some observers, so much so that democracy cannot be safe until tough, and probably politically unpopular, measures are taken to dispossess a huge cadre of rent-seekers within the transitional state. Randall Stone's essay on Russia in this volume makes a strong version of this argument, and Jeffrey Winters' chapter at least raises the possibility that it could apply in Indonesia. If weak or venal domestic leaders are unable to undertake painful reforms, then skittish global portfolio managers (or wealthy locals with the know-how to move their money out through the black market) may, paradoxically, be the common people's best friends. In other words, the credible threat of a balance-of-payments crisis yields better macroeconomic policies, which is good for democratic transitions. In this case, aspects of both the pessimistic and optimistic expectations are both likely to be valid.

*   *   *

I have in this chapter adduced the following rough hypotheses, which the other contributors to the book address in various ways:

1. Economic growth, while desirable in many ways, does not directly bring political democracy, except possibly in the long run. Therefore, assertions that link economic growth with foreign capital flows say little about the consequences for democracy.

2. Foreign capital flows controlled by private, profit-seeking actors, will be allocated more efficiently, on average, than capital flows controlled by governments.

3. The direct beneficiaries of foreign capital inflows will be one or more of four actors: foreign governments, the incumbent government in the capital-importing country, local big business, and foreign direct investors. Different types of cross-border financial instruments add to the politically-relevant resources of those actors that control the flows. None of these actors, except incumbent governments that already are democratic, promotes democracy automatically.

4. Balance-of-payments crises, whatever their causes, are bad for political incumbents. If the political regime (overall political system) itself is fragile, it may be discredited along with the particular office holders.

5. Post-financial crisis periods of structural adjustment often generate socioeconomic changes that disadvantage just those political actors (organized labor and the poor) who can be expected to support and/or benefit from the transition to procedural political democracy with universal suffrage. New rules of the successor post-transition political game may permanently reflect the distribution of political power during the transition.

6. Neoliberal economic reforms instituted in the hope of avoiding a future balance of payments crisis tend to generate inter-group distributional results similar to post-crisis orthodox structural adjustment programs.[37] The final hypothesis is the most important.

7. The most significant factor in determining how capital inflows might affect democracy is the current political situation of a capital-importing country. Foreign capital inflows per se tend to be beneficial for economic development and political incumbents – although some types of capital inflows are easier for a country to digest than others, as this essay has argued. All other things being equal, therefore, foreign investment

received by an authoritarian government strengthens dictatorial rule, while foreign capital inflows into democracies reinforce procedural, representative government.

Thus, if one knew the existing political situation of a country, one perhaps could hazard educated guesses about how a shift in the form of capital inflows might incrementally alter the current national political game. This chapter has presented a deductively derived analytical framework. I should note that it was written in 1994–95, before the effects of Mexico's peso crisis had worked themselves through and in the context of East Asia being seen as relatively stable politically and as having, wisely, specialized in FDI rather than the portfolio equity and bond flows so prominent in the capital accounts of Latin America and, to a lesser extent, Eastern Europe (see Griffith-Jones and Stallings, 1995, and Stefano Manzocchi's chapter in this volume). In my conclusion to this volume, extensively revised in late 1997 and on the basis of the efforts of my fellow authors, I turn to some empirical cases to begin to assess these expectations.

Notes

1. I thank Shahid Alam, Thomas J. Biersteker, Thomas Callaghy, Susan Christopherson, John Echeverri-Gent, David Felix, Mary Ann Haley, Rebecca Hovey, Atul Kohli, Mukul Majumdar, Luigi Manzetti, Sylvia Maxfield, Geraldo Munck, Dale Murphy, Sanjay Reddy, Dietrich Rueschemeyer, Ben Ross Schneider, Moises Schwartz, Danny Unger, Birol Yesilada, Fei-Ling Wang, and the participants in the conference on 'Financial Globalization, Economic Growth, and Democracy in Emerging Market Countries' at Brown and Northeastern Universities (November 1995) for their helpful comments on various versions of this chapter and Chapter 14.
2. The Introduction's Table 1 uses data from the World Bank's annual *World Debt Tables*, but combines the data slightly differently than the World Bank. Use of the World Bank's categories, as in the chapter by Stefano Manzocchi in this volume, does not change the broad trends.
3. A large share of bank loans in the 1980s was not voluntary lending, but instead 'exceptional financing,' in which transnational money center banks agreed to loan countries like Mexico and Brazil 'new money' so they could make interest and principle payments due on past debt – thus saving both debtor country and creditor banks from the pain of a formally declared default.
4. Many Latin American and African debtors had negative net transfers. In 1986, for example, Mexico's net transfers abroad totaled 5.3 per cent of its GDP, while Brazil's summed to 3 per cent (World Bank, 1995).
5. The big question is whether heightened volatility is inevitable, because of advances in computer and telecommunications technologies. Helleiner (1994) argues that financial globalization has only come about because of political choices (including the deceptively passive choice not to regulate) made by the leading industrial capitalist economies. Financial globalization also has been propelled by structural changes occurring within the domestic economies of the OECD countries. Two institutional and regulatory trends that began in the

early 1980s, securitization (the bundling together and resale of in the capital markets of long-term lending commitments formerly held to maturity by banks and other financial institutions) and the large shift of household savings in OECD countries away from bank deposits and toward investments in mutual funds and other institutional investors, have occurred in tandem with the technology-driven inauguration of 24 hour global trading. Domestic and international financial market changes thus reinforced one another.

6. The 1997 East Asian financial crisis was in full swing as this book was in its final editing. US treasury secretary Robert Rubin was busy trying to convince a reluctant US Congress of the necessity of contributing to rescue packages for South Korea and Indonesia, which many members of that body saw as either foreign aid for far-away lands or bailouts of wealthy banks, both highly unpopular causes with constituents. The South Korean package, negotiated by the IMF in December, was for $57 billion, breaking the previous record of $50 billion set in the February 1995 package for Mexico. The general lesson appeared to be that the list of countries whose possible financial crashes the financial authorities in the major advanced industrial countries found threatening had expanded, as the 1997 'Asian flu' seemed even more contagious than the 1995 'tequila effect.'

7. The chapter by Manzocchi in this volume summarizes some of this literature.

8. This essay is not, of course, the first to theorize about the impacts of different institutional forms of foreign capital inflows on recipient countries. Barbara Stallings (1990) suggested that an important influence on the more positive growth experiences of Korea and Taiwan, as compared to Mexico and Brazil, in the 1980s might have been the institutional form of foreign capital inflows. The two East Asia countries relied more on capital from public sector sources and on loans. In contrast, the Latin American countries imported more private capital and direct investment by multinational corporations, both of which compromised host country autonomy. Furthermore, by the 1980s, the two East Asian societies had raised domestic savings rates sufficiently to reduce significantly their overall reliance on foreign inflows. A few years later, Stallings and Stephany Griffith-Jones noted that the institutional forms of capital flows again had shifted. In that paper, they considered both long-term loans and FDI more advantages forms of capital inflows, from the viewpoint of capital importers, than portfolio equity, while noting that, as of 1991–92, Asian developing countries were more fortunate on these grounds than Latin American and Caribbean ones (Griffith-Jones and Stallings. 1995, p. 158).

Jeffery Winters (1994 esp. pp. 446–50) proposed a 'framework for analyzing capital control and end use.' He noted that recipient country governments have low discretion over the investment uses of either portfolio flows or foreign direct investment, medium abilities to control interstate loans (that is, official credits), somewhat greater options for investing private commercial loans as they please, and the greatest degree of discretion over 'state capital,' or revenues raised domestically, through taxes, borrowing and so forth.

Sylvia Maxfield (1995, esp. pp. 12–15) was interested in the degree of influence different types of foreign investors have over the economic policies of recipient governments, positing the greatest leverage for portfolio equity investors, an intermediate amount for long-term bondholders, and the least leverage for foreign direct investors and commercial bank lenders. The determining factors for her were the costs to foreign investors of monitoring recipient country performance and, most importantly, the ease of capital repatriation.

Each of these analysts was concerned with the links between capital inflows and recipient country government autonomy and/or economic growth. None explicitly attempted to pursue the further possible link between the institutional forms of capital inflows and democracy.

9. For an alternative way to think through the meaning of 'democracy' in developing countries, particularly in Latin America, see Karl (1990).

10. Obviously the definition of democracy adopted by Communist countries, or 'peoples' democracies' does not include procedural political democracy as a component. Some theorists commited to economic equality as the foundation of democracy also see procedural political democracy as, at best, a smokescreen for oppression, and, at worst, an instrument of inequality and thus of the lack of democracy (see, for example, MacPhearson, 1966).

11. I exclude military assistance from this discussion for two reasons. Most military aid is in the form of contributions in kind, rather than financial flows. In addition, the rationale for military aid is entirely political and strategic, whereas economic aid may have some investment justifications as well as its overtly political ones.

    For the sake of analytical simplicity, I also exclude that small, albeit growing, portion of concessional foreign lending that flows directly to private sector recipients in the developing country, such as the loans made to local entrepreneurs by the World Bank affiliate the International Finance Corporation (IFC).

12. In some countries MNC investors have been encouraged to enter joint ventures with state-owned enterprises (SOEs). In principle, one could work through the analysis separately, first for MNC investors who formed wholly-owned subsidiaries or joint ventures with a local private partner, and second for MNC–SOE joint undertakings.

13. Due to limitations of the data, the statistics reported in the introduction assume that all 'government-guaranteed loans' are loans directly to the government, which of course overstates the size of my third category, although it is true that governments in capital-importing countries tend to exercise greater oversight over those foreign loans to local private firms that they guarantee. Categories three and four both bundle medium and long-term trade credit ('other guaranteed medium and long-term debt') with commercial bank loans.

14. In fact, some of the largest institutional investors in global markets actually are the pension funds of public sector employees, especially state and local government workers in the US. To the extent that pension fund managers attend only to maximizing profits and minimizing risks, their behavior mimics that of the managers of private sector pension or mutual funds.

15. It is difficult to know whether short-term debt flows are being borrowed by the emerging market country government or the local private sector, except on a case by case basis. Thus, the decision to include all such flows with my category six, portfolio inflows to the local private sector, has the result of overstating the size of this category relative to category five, portfolio flows to the government.

16. While many economists, perhaps a majority, would agree that portfolio capital flows are more volatile than, say, direct investment, opinions do differ. See note 4 to in William C. Gruben's chapter in this volume.

    Sylvia Maxfield (1997) suggests that portfolio investors may differ among themselves in volatility, with those seeking high yields (typically hedge and mutual fund managers) more likely to bolt at the slightest hint of crisis than investors whose principle goals are value and diversification (such as pension fund managers).

17. There is an important caveat. Good, comparable data on all of these categories is difficult if not impossible to unearth: the World Bank's annual *World Debt Tables*, which only started reporting non-debt capital flows such as FDI and portfolio equity in the 1990s, probably is the best source. Particularly difficult to measure with existing data is the distinction between public versus private recipients of commercial bank loans or portfolio flows: that is, easily available data sets do not clearly differentiate between my categories three and four, or five and six.

18. I thank Stefano Manzocchi for this point.

19. In what John Gerard Ruggie (1982) termed the 'compromise of embedded liberalism,' advanced industrial countries during the postwar decades extended to one another the privilege of deviating in their domestic economic regulatory regimes from the market liberalism they all espoused for the international economy. Thomas Callaghy (1989, 1993) points out that this privilege – which might be summarized as the right to selective domestic protectionism along with mostly free access to other rich countries' domestic markets – has never been extended to most developing countries. The exceptions have been those countries, such as South Korea or Taiwan, or Francophone Africa, that had strategic value for the most powerful advanced industrial countries (see also Stallings, 1995).

20. On neoliberal (also known as 'orthodox' or 'neoconservative') economic policies in Latin America, see Pastor (1992) and Foxley (1983).

21. Chase-Dunn and Bornschier (1985) detail some of the ways in which the presence of multinational direct investors skews the host country regulatory environment in a more conservative, neoliberal direction.

22. There also is pressure from global investors for capital-importing countries to construct regulatory frameworks consistent with norms in the advanced industrial democracies. See the chapters by Porter and Echeverri-Gent in this volume.

23. See, for example, the concerns expressed in Cerny, (1993) and Strange (1986).

24. O'Donnell (1973) hypothesized that the breakdown of previously existing democracy in Brazil in 1964, Argentina in 1966, Chile in 1973, and Argentina again in 1976 (after a three-year democratic interlude) came about because these societies already had passed through the 'easy' stage of import-substituting industrialization (ISI), during which period the usually combatitive forces of industrial capital and labor both could become wealthy together. The harder stage of ISI, in contrast, would require diversion of all the surplus created by industrial production into profits and new investment, leaving nothing available for added increments to workers' wages. Consequently, went the argument, authoritarianism was the only economically viable political system, because under electoral democracy, workers would demand concessions that inevitably would produce economic stagnation. Whether or not one accepts O'Donnell's explanation of the phenomenon, Latin America's experience during these decades definitely calls into question the assumption of mutually reinforcing and linear political and economic progress. See also Collier, ed. (1979).

25. Obviously, they are far from the first to raise this concern. However, their recent articulation of these somewhat familiar arguments stands out for its modulated tone, careful historical scholarship, and cross-regional empirical and theoretical investigation.

26. Their argument, while different in many particulars from that of O'Donnell referred to earlier, is not inconsistent with either his empirical observations or his theoretical explanation.

27. I thank Ben Ross Schneider for first bringing the 'optimistic hypothesis' to my attention.
28. The term was coined by O'Donnell (1973).
29. Some businesses, of course, have profits that mainly depend upon monopoly or oligopoly rents deriving from excessive government regulation with particular characteristics that favor their interests. Oligopolists dislike market liberalization at least as much as those who favor government intervention to redistribute income, protect the weak, or solve collective action problems. That is, my assumption of uniform policy preferences across the business community is a simplication of reality. On balance, it is usually true that the business community as a whole will prefer more of the neoliberal policy agenda than many other domestic political actors in developing countries. However, the greater the degree to which the activies of local big business community are fairly characterized by the term 'crony capitalism,' the fainter its likely support for truly free markets. (Of course, local oligopolists probably will dislike the policy agendas of leftist reformers even more.)
30. Individual big business-persons may well prefer mass democracy for altruistic and normative reasons; they also may associate democracy with modernity. There are plenty of empirical examples of such behavior, as in the business tycoons who secretly financed Mohandas Gandhi or Nelson Mandela.
31. The structural position, and consequent political preferences, of ambitious entrepreneurs in post-Communist regimes is more complex. They tend to be strong supporters of political democracy, which they, like many of their fellow citizens throughout the national class structure, rather unanalytically associate not only with political freedoms but also with the capitalist economic prosperity of the Western industrial democracies and Japan. The political attitude of business in many countries in Eastern Europe and the former Soviet Union is further complicated by the connections many new businesspersons have with the old Communist apparatchik class (who often have been the only group with sufficient capital to buy privatized state firms) and/or with criminal organizations (who ran the thriving underground 'capitalist' economy during the Soviet era).
32. Any group whose main political resource is sheer numbers (of potential voters) or good organizational skills (useful for building a strong, grass-roots political party base) benefits from a shift away from authoritarian political rules (which benefit an elite of some kind, whether membership in that elite is defined by heredity, loyal membership in the ruling political party, or control of the means of production) to the political rules of mass electoral democracy. Once again, my argument regarding the importance of 'labor' as a political actor is somewhat different – and rather more simplistic – than that of Rueschemeyer *et al.* (1992). It is not, I think, inconsistent with their analysis.
33. For a game-theoretic treatment of why this should be so, see Sturzenegger (1995). For evidence in the Latin American case, see Oxhorn and Ducatenzeiler (1998).
34. Social science researchers generally assume that human social systems, whether families or national political systems, assume patterns of behavior that, once regularized, tend to persist until upset by some crisis. See Stinchcombe, 1968.
35. An important caveat is that lower-income groups may be disproportionately benefited by an early end to inflation. See the chapter by Randall Stone in this volume and also Armijo (1998).
36. For a more skeptical view of the growth prospects of neoliberal economic reforms, see Przeworski *et al.* (1995).

37. However, preemptive market-oriented reforms (at some point followed by economic growth) might be preferable to waiting for an economic and political crisis before adjusting, thus potentially increasing both their eventual economic and political costs.

Bibliography

Armijo, Leslie Elliott (1998) 'Political Finance in Brazil and India: An Argument about Democracy and Inflation,' Unpublished book manuscript.

Armijo, Leslie Elliott, Thomas J. Biersteker, and Abraham F. Lowenthal (1994) 'The Problems of Simultaneous Transitions,' *Journal of Democracy*, October, vol. 5(4), pp. 161–75.

Bates, Robert H. (ed.) (1988) *Toward a Political Economy of Development: A Rational Choice Perspective* (Berkeley: University of California Press).

Bates, Robert H. and Anne O. Krueger (1993) 'Generalizations Arising from the Country Studies,' in R. H. Bates and A. O. Krueger (eds), *Political and Economic Interactions in Economic Policy Reform: Evidence from Eight Countries* (Oxford: Blackwell).

Bhalla, Surjit S. (1994) 'Freedom and Economic Growth: A Virtuous Cycle?,' paper presented at the South Asia Seminar, Harvard University Center for International Affairs, February.

Biersteker, Thomas J. (1995) 'The "triumph" of liberal economic ideas in the developing world,' in Barbara Stallings (ed.), *Global Change, Regional Response: The New International Context of Development* (Cambridge: Cambridge University Press).

Bradsher, Keith (1995) 'Back to the Thrilling Trades of Yesteryear,' *The New York Times*, 12 March.

Callaghy, Thomas M. (1989) 'Toward State Capability and Embedded Liberalism in the Third World: Lessons for Adjustment,' in Joan M. Nelson and contributors, *Fragile Coalitions: The Politics of Economic Adjustment* (Washington, D.C.: Transaction Books for the Overseas Development Council).

Callaghy, Thomas M. (1993) 'Vision and Politics in the Transformation of the Global Political Economy: Lessons from the Second and Third Worlds,' in Robert O. Slater, Barry M. Schutz, and Steven R. Dorr (eds), *Global Transformation and the Third World* (Boulder, CO: Lynne Rienner).

Calvo, Guillermo A., L. Leiderman, and Carmen M. Reinhart (1993) 'Capital Inflows and Real Exchange Rate Appreciation in Latin America,' *International Monetary Fund Staff Papers*, 40, pp. 108–51.

Cerny, Philip (ed.) (1993) *Finance and World Politics: Markets, Regimes and States in the Post-Hegemonic Era* (Aldershot, England: Edward Algar).

Chase-Dunn, Christopher and Volker Bornschier (1985) *Transnational Corporations and Underdevelopment* (New York: Praeger).

Cohen, Benjamin J. (1986) *In Whose Interest?: International Banking and American Foreign Policy* (New Haven: Yale University Press).

Collier, David (ed.) (1979) *The New Authoritarianism in Latin America* (Princeton: Princeton University Press).

Dahl, Robert (1971) *Polyarchy: Participation and Opposition* (New Haven: Yale University Press).

Devlin, Robert (1989) *Debt and Crisis in Latin America: The Supply Side of the Story* (Princeton, NJ: Princeton University Press).

Fernandez-Arias, Eduardo (1995) 'The New Wave of Private Capital Flows: Push or Pull?,' *Journal of Development Economics*, December.

Fidler, Stephen (1998) 'Chilean lessons for Asian crisis,' *Financial Times*, 14 January.

Ffrench-Davis, Ricardo and Stephany Griffith-Jones (eds) (1995) *Coping with Capital Surges: The Return of Finance to Latin America* (Boulder, CO: Lynne Rienner).

Folkerts-Landau, David and Takatoshi Ito, *et al.* (1995) *International Capital Markets: Developments, Prospects, and Policy Issues* (Washington, D.C.: International Monetary Fund), August.

Griffith-Jones, Stephany and Barbara Stallings (1995) 'New global financial trends: implications for development,' in Barbara Stallings (ed.), *Global Change, Regional Response: The New International Context of Development* (Cambridge, UK: Cambridge University Press).

Haggard, Stephan and Robert R. Kaufman (eds) (1992) *The Politics of Economic Adjustment* (Princeton, N.J.: Princeton University Press).

Haggard, Stephan and Robert Kaufman (1995) *The Political Economy of Democratic Transitions* (Princeton, NJ: Princeton University Press).

Helleiner, Eric (1994) *States and the Reemergence of Global Finance: From Bretton Woods to the 1990s* (Ithaca, NY: Cornell University Press).

Karl, Terry Lynn (1990) 'Dilemmas of Democratization in Latin America,' *Comparative Politics*, October.

MacPhearson, C.B. (1966) *The Real World of Democracy* (New York: Oxford University Press).

Maxfield, Sylvia (1995) 'International Portfolio Flows to Developing/Transitional Economies: Impact on Government Policy Choice,' paper presented at the Study Group on Private Capital Flows to Developing and Transitional Economies, Council on Foreign Relations, New York City, May.

Maxfield, Sylvia (1997) 'Understanding the Political Implications of Financial Internationalization in Emerging Market Countries,' Paper presented at Second Conference on 'The Economic and Political Challenges of Market Reforms in Latin America,' Tower Center, Southern Methodist University, 4 October.

McCulloch, Rachel and Peter A. Petri (1994) 'Equity Financing of Asian Development,' Seminar Paper 94-05, Department of Economics, Brandeis University, May.

Meier, Gerald M. (ed.) (1991) *Politics and Policy Making in Developing Countries: Perspectives on the New Political Economy* (San Franciso, CA: International Center for Economic Growth).

Moore, Barrington (1966) *Social Origins of Dictatorship and Democracy: Lord and Peasant in the Modern World* (Boston: Beacon Press).

Nunnenkampt, Peter and Erich Gundlach (1996) 'The Effects of Globalization on Developing Countries,' paper presented at Conference on 'Globalization: What it is and its Implications,' sponsored by Faculty of Economics, Administration, and Accounting of the University of São Paulo, Brazil, 23–24 May.

O'Donnell, Guillermo A. (1973) *Modernization and Bureaucratic-Authoritarianism: Studies in South American Politics* (Berkeley: Institute of International Studies, University of California).

O'Donnell, Guillermo and Philippe C. Schmitter (1986) *Transitions from Authoritarian Rule: Tentative Conclusions about Uncertain Democracies* (Baltimore: Johns Hopkins).

Olsen, Mancur (1965) *The Logic of Collective Action* (Cambridge, MA: Harvard University Press).

Oxhorn, Philip and Graciela Ducatenzeiler (1998) 'The Problematic Relationship Between Economic and Political Liberalization: Some Theoretical Considerations,' in Philip Oxhorn and Pamela Starr (eds), *Markets and Democracy in Latin America: Conflict or Convergence?* (Boulder, CO: Lynne Rienner, forthcoming).

Prestowitz, Jr., Clyde V. (1996) 'Dole's Supply-Side Delusion,' *The New York Times*, 26 August.

Przeworski, Adam (1991) *Democracy and the Market: Political and Economic Reforms in Eastern Europe and Latin America* (Cambridge: Cambridge University Press).

Przeworski, Adam, Pranab Bardhan, Luiz Carlos Bresser Pereira, *et al.* (1995) *Sustainable Democracy* (Cambridge: Cambridge University Press).

Rojas-Suarez, Liliana and Steven Weisbrod (1995) 'Achieving Stability in Latin American Financial Markets in the Presence of Volatile Capital Flows,' *Working Paper Series 304*, Washington, D.C.: Inter-American Development Bank, Office of the Chief Economist, April.

Rostow, Walt W. (1960) *Stages of Economic Growth* (Cambridge: Cambridge University Press).

Ruggie, John Gerard (1982) 'International Regimes, Transactions and Change: Embedded Liberalism in the Postwar Economic Order,' *International Organization*, 36(2), Spring.

Rueschemeyer, Dietrich, Evelyne Huber Stephens, and John D. Stephens (1992) *Capitalist Development and Democracy* (Chicago: University of Chicago Press).

Stallings, Barbara (1990) 'The Role of Foreign Capital in Economic Development,' in G. Gereffi and D.L. Wyman (eds), *Manufacturing Miracles: Paths of Industrialization in Latin America and East Asia* (Princeton, NJ: Princeton University Press).

Stinchcombe, Arthur L. (1968) *Constructing Social Theories* (New York: Harcourt, Brace & World, Inc.).

Strange, Susan (1986) *Casino Capitalism* (London: Basil Blackwell).

Sturzenegger, Federico (1995) 'Inflation and the Delay of Stabilizations,' in Leslie Elliott Armijo (ed.), *Conversations on Democratization and Economic Reform: Working Papers of the Southern California Seminar* (Los Angeles: Center for International Studies, University of Southern California).

Varshney, Ashutosh (1984) 'Political Economy of Slow Industrial Growth in India,' *Economic and Political Weekly*, 19(34), 1 September, pp. 1511–17.

Williamson, John (1990) 'What Washington Means by Policy Reform,' in *The Progress of Policy Reform in Latin America* (Washington, D.C.: Institute for International Economics, January).

Winters, Jeffrey A. (1994) 'Power and the Control of Capital,' *World Politics*, 46(3), April, pp. 419–512.

Woodall, Pam (1995) 'Survey on the World Economy,' *The Economist*, 7 October, survey pp. 1–38.

World Bank, various years, *World Debt Tables* (Washington, D.C.: The World Bank).

World Bank (1996) *World Development Report 1996: From Plan to Market* (New York: Oxford University Press).

Wynia, Gary W. (1990) *The Politics of Latin American Development*, 3rd edn (Cambridge: Cambridge University Press).

2 Capital Flows to Developing Economies throughout the Twentieth Century

Stefano Manzocchi

The recent surge in capital inflows to developing countries shares several features of the experiences of the late nineteenth and early twentieth centuries, but a number of new characteristics as well. This chapter begins with a survey of international finance at the beginning of this century followed by a review of capital inflows since the 1960s. The final section briefly addresses three issues. First, what has been the role of financial liberalization among the determinants of the recent upswing in capital inflows, and what are its implications for the recipient economies? Second, can we say something on the 'quality' of the new flows? Third, what are the long-run relationships between external finance, growth, and welfare in developing economies?

AN OVERVIEW OF HISTORICAL TRENDS IN EXTERNAL FINANCE TO DEVELOPING COUNTRIES

International lending and borrowing, as they are currently conceived, date back to the birth of the Western financial institutions. Italian bankers of the Renaissance period loaned to other countries, although an overall quantification of such operations is problematic (Kindleberger, 1984). The network of financial flows among different nations was historically centered on a few key trading cities: Amsterdam, Paris and London. Hence, the history of international finance to a large extent overlaps that of the rise and fall of these centres, which provided external finance for trade and investment projects in a large number of nations including western states, colonies and eastern empires. Wars, panics, and crashes often marked the decline of old financial centers, and the rise of new ones.

The history of foreign lending to developing countries is part of this wider picture, with some unique characteristics. First, developing countries (including colonies) have usually been net borrowers from the rest of the world. Second, the record of external finance in developing countries is a sequence

51

of periods of sustained borrowing, debt crises leading to an interruption or even a reversal of the flows, and eventual new surges in capital inflows (Eichengreen and Lindert, 1989; Marichal, 1989). Third, there seem to be complex causal links between the conditions of financial activity in the western centers and the solvency and liquidity position of developing countries. On the one hand, external variables such as international interest rates and commodity prices are often mentioned as crucial determinants of the swings in capital movements to the developing countries (Eichengreen, 1990; Calvo, Leiderman and Reinhart, 1993). At the same time, debt crises in developing countries may have a strong impact on western financial markets (see the description of the 1890 Baring crisis in De Cecco, 1984).

Capital inflows to developing economies during the nineteenth century were mainly associated with the functioning of London as *the* world financial center. Marichal (1989, pp. 27–8) reports that Latin American government issues accounted for the largest share of foreign government securities sold on the London Stock Exchange between 1822 and 1825, at the time of Latin American independence. As early as 1826 Peru suspended payments, followed by Chile, Argentina, Mexico and others. Nonetheless, a new surge in capital flows to Latin America occurred in the 1850s and 1860s, ending with the great depression of the late nineteenth century, 1873–96, when a number of developing country borrowers defaulted again. The securities floated on the London market mainly financed railways and public utilities, although some funds were used for rolling-over old debts or for speculative purposes (Marichal, 1989, pp. 243–255). The final years prior to World War I witnessed a new upturn in capital flows to developing countries, both in absolute and in relative terms, which led to the highest ever stock of gross foreign investment in developing countries, including colonies, as shown in Table 2.1. During this period, net capital outflows from Britain represented as much as 9 per cent of its GDP, while comparable figures for France, Germany and the Netherlands were almost as high (IMF, 1997, p. 113).

Table 2.2 shows that African and Asian countries became important destinations of foreign capital after 1890, while Argentina's 1890 debt crisis may have had a negative effect on flows to Latin America. Note that North America (excluding Mexico) is still the principal destination of portfolio investment abroad. The 1914 financial crisis in London and the start of World War I changed the pattern of world capital movements once again. Net foreign lending to developing countries ended. However, some developing countries, particularly those that benefited from a rise in world commodity prices, became net capital exporters during the war years, as also happened during World War II (for instance, Argentina: see Veganzones and Winograd, 1997, pp. 208, 212–214). In the aftermath of World War I, the world financial community was engaged for a long time in the resolution of the joint problems of the German reparations and of the inter-allied loans

Table 2.1 Gross value of foreign capital in developing countries, 1870–1995
(US$ billions at year end)

	1870	1900	1914	1938	1950	1973	1985	1995*
Total in current prices	5.3	11.4	22.7	24.7	13.6	172	1118	2355
Total in 1980 prices	33.2	108.3	179.2	143.4	46.6	319.1	944	n.a.
Total as a percentage of world GDP (in 1980 prices)	n.a.	10.4	12.5	n.a.	1.6	3.7	7.0	8.5**
Total as a percentage of Asian and Latin American GDP only (in 1980 prices)	n.a.	32.4	45.0	n.a.	7.9	16.5	22.6	44.0***

Notes:
* Includes gross debt outstanding at end-1995, and *net* cumulated direct investment plus other equity flows.
** Total as a percentage of world GDP (current 1995 prices).
*** Total as a percentage of the GDP of all developing countries (current 1995 prices)
Sources: OECD, *External Debt Statistics* (Paris: OECD, 1996) and IMF, *World Economic Outlook* (Washington, D.C.: IMF) various issues, for the data on gross value of foreign capital; A. Maddison, *The World Economy in the 20th Century* (Paris: OECD, 1989) for the data on world GDP in 1980 prices; and World Bank, *World Development Report 1997* (New York: Oxford University Press, 1997), for the data on GDP in 1995.

(De Cecco, 1985). Meanwhile New York gradually established its predominance over London as the world's leading market. International financial activities stagnated until the Dawes Plan of September 1924, which established a schedule to be followed for the war reparations due by Germany to the Western allies, generated the illusion that the post-war reparations problem had been solved. From 1924 through 1929 a wave of foreign lending occurred, centered in New York, as shown in Table 2.3. A sort of 'division of labor' in world financial markets is visible in the data, as loans to Asia and Africa were mainly issued in London while New York lent to Europe and Latin America. However, the global share of capital flows to Africa declined in the 1920s.

The debt crisis of the 1930s followed the October 1929 crash of the New York Stock Exchange. In fact, by that time financial conditions already had deteriorated in some debtor countries as a consequence declining prices for some primary commodities (sugar, rubber, coffee) coupled with bad harvests

Table 2.2   New foreign issues on the London stock exchange, 1870–1914
             (cumulative, millions of British pounds sterling)

	1870–89	*1890–1914*	*1870–89 (%)*	*1890–1914 (%)*
Europe	251	244.7	19.7	9.1
North America	380	997	29.8	36.7
Latin America	240.3	470.6	18.9	17.3
Africa	67.6	345	5.3	12.7
Asia	131	423.8	10.3	15.6
Australia	203	234.5	15.9	8.5
Total	1272	2715	100	100
Total excluding Europe, North America and Australia	439	1239.4	34.5	45.6

Source: M. De Cecco, *Money and Empire* (Oxford, Basil Blackwell, 1974), p. 36.
Used by permission.

in Argentina and Australia, all of which reduced the revenues available for debt service (Kindleberger, 1973). The collapse of the New York Stock Exchange and the restrictive stance of monetary policy in several industrial and developing countries made access to financial markets difficult and expensive for many debtors, both governments and private borrowers, and unleashed a wave of defaults and debt negotiations in the thirties (see Fernandez-Ansola and Laursen, 1995). Evaluated in 1980 dollar prices, the decline in the stock of gross foreign capital in developing countries with respect to the peak of 1914 is quite conspicuous in 1938 and even more dramatic in 1950 (Table 2.1).

The institutional mechanism of foreign lending during the nineteenth and the first three decades of the twentieth century partly explains the high incidence of default before World War II (see Eichengreen, 1991). International capital transfers were mainly accomplished through bond finance. Securities issued by foreign entities were negotiated by banking houses in world financial centers, which lent to the borrower at a discount and then sold the bonds to individual investors. Ultimately, a country's stock of debt was held by a large number of financial institutions and households. Consequently, when a situation of illiquidity occurred (whether it involved an individual investment project or a whole foreign country) it was by no means automatic that a quick and sufficient provision of new funds could be extended to the

Table 2.3   New foreign issues in London and New York, 1924–29
(cumulative, in millions of US dollars)

	London	New York	London (%)	New York (%)
Europe	706	2957	21	45
Canada	265	1231	8	19
Latin America	528	1597	16	25
Africa	437	–	13	–
Asia and Oceania	1365	644	42	11
Total	3301	6429	100	100
Total excluding Europe and Canada	2330	2241	71	36

Source: C. Kindleberger, The World in Depression (Berkeley: University of California Press, 1973), p. 56. Used by permission.

debtor in distress before default had to be declared. Free-riding among a very large number of creditors was a formidable obstacle to the concession of new credit lines. In addition, of course, wide dispersal of creditors meant that the insolvency of sovereign debtors did not threaten the stability of the western financial system (Eichengreen, 1991). However, there were cases when key western financial institutions were shaken by the insolvency of developing country borrowers, as in the 1890 Baring crisis.

The defaults of the 1930s, the protracted negotiations (some of which lingered into the 1950s) and above all the collapse of the world trade and financial system, prevented substantial capital inflows into developing countries for almost three decades. It was only in 1958, when the convertibility of national currencies was reintroduced in Western Europe (full convertibility in Germany and UK, partial convertibility in an other 11 states) that an international financial system slowly reemerged from the ruins. By that time, the American financial institutions had gained an extraordinary advantage over their overseas competitors. The reconstruction of international payments system around the dollar had been completed, as is clearly shown by the experience of the European Payments Union of 1950–58, when payments imbalances among European countries were quoted in dollars (Solomon, 1982). Moreover, the US was the only industrial country with a large and persistent current account surplus, and hence the only one that could afford prolonged capital transfers to the rest of the world. Immediately after the war, the main channels of capital transfers were grants (for example the Marshall Plan) and export credits. American direct investment abroad also recovered in the 1950s, though it was mainly directed to developed countries, especially in Western Europe. Despite the return to convertibility, restrictions on *financial* capital flows were widespread. In the 1960s, for example, the US itself imposed new controls with the Interest Equalization Tax on capital outflows (Tew, 1982).

Capital transfers to the developed countries were revived in the 1960s. Official development assistance (ODA), foreign direct investment (FDI), and export credits were the main components of the flows at the beginning of the decade. By 1970–71, cross-border bank lending was almost as large as FDI (Table 2.4). By the mid-1970s, commercial bank loans plus export credits had drawn equal with foreign aid.

The lending cycle of the 1970s, which ended when Mexico and Brazil announced the suspension of the external debt service in 1982 and 1983, was rather unusual in historical perspective. The boom of the 1970s focused on Latin American, and to a less extent Asian, developing countries. The hike in the international price of petroleum in 1973 generated a huge current

Table 2.4   Resource flows to all developing countries (period averages in percentage terms at constant 1980 US dollar values)

	1960–61[a]	*1970–71*[a]	*1974–77*[a]	*1978–82*[b]	*1983–86*[b]
ODA	56	43	36	28	42
FDI	19	17	14	11	11
Bank sector	6	15	24	36	21
Bond lending		2	2	2	3
Export credits	14	14	12	13	6
Other[c]	5	9	6	10	17
Annual average in billions of constant 1980 US dollars	34.8	53.7	81.0	118.8	83.6

Notes:
[a] From total resource-flows information in dollars at 1983 exchange rates.
[b] From net resource-flows information in dollars at 1985 exchange rates.
[c] Includes grants by private agencies as well as other non-concessionary flows not included elsewhere.
Source: United Nations, *Transnational Banks and the International Debt Crisis* (New York: UN Centre on Transnational Corporations, 1991).

account surplus in oil-producing countries, and therefore the necessity of investing this surplus. Investors in oil-exporting countries had a preference for highly liquid investment. Moreover, there were several constraints to a direct financial relationship between oil-exporting and oil-importing developing countries. Consequently the international banking network intermediated the demand and supply of credit. Existing regulations and controls had been to a large extent already overcome by the emergence of the Eurocurrency market in the 1960s. The collapse of the Bretton Woods system in 1971–73 also helped push commercial banks into a fierce worldwide competition.

The mechanism of syndicated loans centered on large transnational banks. After negotiating the amount and the conditions of the loan with the sovereign borrower, the money center bank would gather a group of smaller banks willing to underwrite the loan. Both sovereign borrowers, who thus could obtain access to foreign credit rapidly and at low cost (world real interest rates remained quite low until 1979), and the organizing banks, who could invest their funds in a period of low demand for credit in the industrial countries and could raise fees and commission income, had good reasons to find this mechanism very convenient. Moreover, economic prospects in developing countries looked promising in the mid-seventies: exports were rising, the growth rate was high, and the aggregate stock of outstanding foreign liabilities was low by historical standards. Therefore, a lending boom occurred in 1974–77 (Table 2.4). Unfortunately, this lending mania left very little room for a careful selection of countries and projects, and the competition among creditors to gain new market shares weakened monitoring of the debtors. By 1978–81, the burden of the debt was already heavy, but no clear signals of distress had emerged (apart from an incipient debt crisis in Poland in 1981). The global banking system was still willing to lend to the developing countries, although part of this lending was devoted to the typical Ponzi game of rolling-over interest and repayments.

The 1982–83 crisis has been widely analyzed (Diaz-Alejandro, 1983; Cohen, 1991; Padoan, 1987). As in the previous episodes, a combination of external developments (the overlending of the mid-1970s; the new stance of US monetary policy in 1979; the fall in the unit price of exports in some heavily indebted countries) and of misguided domestic investment and macro-economic policies was at the origin of the crisis. The scope of the 1982–83 crisis, however, was uniquely wide: almost every debtor country in Latin America and Africa was involved, as well as several low income Asian countries and many Eastern European ones. The ensuing negotiation process reflected the nature of financial instruments involved. Since commercial banks and official agencies (rather than households) were the ultimate creditors of the insolvent countries, a way out of an explicit default was actively pursued by private and official creditors as well as by the IMF. The debt due to official lenders was rescheduled under the terms agreed on by the creditors belonging to the Paris Club (IMF, 1995). A number of operations – including rescheduling, principal and debt-service reduction, and debt-equity swaps – were designed to deal with the liabilities due to commercial banks. Moreover, the contribution of international organizations and creditor governments has been substantial, especially since the rescheduling plan named after US treasury secretary Nicholas Brady and collateralized by American treasury securities was announced in 1989 (see Dooley, Fernandez-Arias and Kletzer, 1996). As a consequence of these operations, generalized default was avoided. Nonetheless, the real amount of net financial resources accruing to developing countries severely contracted after 1982 (Table 2.4). Moreover, a great deal of the capital flows of the 1980s was not the result of voluntary lending by western creditors, but instead represented 'defensive' lending aimed at preventing illiquidity and default in the developing country debtors.

THE SURGE IN CAPITAL INFLOWS OF THE 1990s IN HISTORICAL PERSPECTIVE

The Brady Plan led to a reduction of about 15 per cent of the outstanding foreign liabilities of major debtor countries in the early 1990s. Since there was also an interest rate downturn in industrial countries, international capital began to flow to developing countries (including the transitional economies of Eastern Europe and Central Asia) again.[1] The net amount of external financial resources to developing countries, now known as 'emerging markets' grew by a factor of 1.5 in nominal terms from 1988 to 1993 (Table 2.5).

Although there are controversial measurement issues in this field,[2] a few characteristics of the recent surge are widely recognized. The geographical breakdown of the inflows shows that long term net flows have mainly been directed to three areas (Table 2.6): East Asia, where the rate of growth of net inflows reached 50 per cent in 1992; Europe and Central Asia, where the rapid increase since 1989 is associated with the start of the transition process in formerly planned economies; and Latin America, where the turning point seems to be 1990 (after the Brady Plan had become effective), and where net long term inflows grew by 50 per cent in 1993. Net long term inflows actually stagnated in Sub-Saharan Africa, where they amounted in 1993 to one-third of the value of 1980 *in nominal terms*; in South Asia, where nonetheless the World Bank forecasts are more optimistic for the future; and in the Middle East and North Africa, despite the reconstruction process following the Gulf War.

Overall, the new upturn in capital inflows to emerging markets had through the mid-1990s been restricted to a few regions, consisting mainly of

Table 2.5   Total net capital flows including grants: all developing countries

	(in billions of US dollars)						(percent)					
	1970	1980	1985	1989	1991	1994*	1970	1980	1985	1989	1991	1994*
Net capital inflows plus grants	11.4[a]	89.5[a]	60.8	105.2	147.7	255.3	100[a]	100[a]	100	100	100	100
Grants	1.9	13.2	13.2	19.1	32.5	30.4	16.7	14.7	21.7	18.2	22.0	11.9
Net total capital inflows	9.5[a]	76.3[a]	47.6	86.1	115.2	224.9	83.3[a]	85.3[a]	78.3	81.8	78.0	88.1
I. Long term debt	6.8	71.7	36.4	36.1	47.8	79.5	59.6	79.8	59.9	34.4	32.4	31.1
a) Official creditors	3.4	21.9	20.9	23.3	29.2	23.9	29.8	24.5	34.4	22.0	19.8	9.4
b) Private creditors	3.4	49.7	15.5	12.8	18.6	55.6	29.8	55.3	25.5	12.3	12.6	21.7
i) Bonds	0[c]	2.6[c]	4.9[c]	5.3	12.5	–	0[c]	2.8[c]	8.1[c]	5.0	8.5	–
ii) Commercial banks	0.6[c]	24.2[c]	6.6[c]	0.9	4.0	–	4.8[c]	27.0[c]	10.9[c]	0.9	2.7	–
II Short term debt	–	–	0.6	20.9	23.1	28.1	–	–	1.0	19.9	15.6	11.0
III Portfolio equity flows	0	0	0	3.4	7.5	39.4	0	0	0	3.2	5.1	15.4
IV Net foreign direct investment	2.3	5.3	10.6	25.7	36.8	77.9	23.7	5.9	17.4	24.4	24.9	30.5

[a] Short-term debt is not recorded separately.
[b] Guaranteed and non-guaranteed debt generating flows from private creditors, including bonds, lending by commercial banks and other items (mainly export credits).
[c] Private non-guaranteed flows are excluded.
[d] IMF lending and interest arrears on long-term debt are included.
* Indicates 1994 World Bank estimates.
Source: World Bank, World Debt Tables.

middle-income countries or transitional economies, with the exception of some large low-income countries like China and, more recently, India. Table 2.5 reveals the diminished relative importance of loans from official creditors, which fell from 34.4 per cent in 1985 to only 9.4 per cent in 1994, as well as the large drop in private commercial bank loans after 1980. Categories of capital flows that have grown rapidly since the mid-1980s include portfolio bond flows, portfolio equity investment, and short-term debt – all part of the 'new' portfolio flows of the 1990s – and foreign direct investment, only 5.9 per cent of total flows in 1980, but almost a third of all such flows in 1994. As Table 2.6 makes clear, as of the early 1990s East Asia and the Pacific received the largest share of the new, overwhelmingly private, capital flows, with 45 per cent of all net flows in 1994. Long-term flows to East Asia were skewed towards a relatively greater share of FDI, giving the region almost 78 per cent of all such flows in 1994. East Asia also received about 45 per cent of portfolio equity flows, commensurate to its share of total flows, but only about 18 per cent of portfolio bond flows, as of 1993. As became clear in late 1997, however, financial deregulation in much of the region in the mid-1990s encouraged large, and novel, flows of short-term debt, much of which apparently was not recognized by either national or international regulatory and data collection bodies.

As of 1994, 21 per cent of total net flows went to developing countries in the Western hemisphere, 17 per cent to the transitional economies of East and Central Asia, and 8 per cent to South Asia, whose share had increased from only 5 per cent in 1980 (Table 2.6). Latin America and the Caribbean received 24 per cent of FDI, roughly equivalent to the region's share in total

Table 2.6   Net long-term capital flows to developing countries, by region of destination[a] (in US$ billions)

	1970	1980	1985	1989	1991	1994*
All developing countries	9.0	76.0	47.1	64.5	91.7	197.3
East Asia and the Pacific	1.5	11.9	14.3	23	31.9	89.5
Europe and Central Asia	0.5	16.6	3.5	11.7	16.8	33.4
Latin America and the Caribbean	3.9	29.5	12	5.5	25.5	40.7
Middle East and North Africa	0.8	3.8	8.3	7.9	4.5	9.2
South Asia	1.1	4	4.2	8.2	8.3	15.2
Sub-Saharan Africa	1.2	10.2	4.8	8.2	4.7	9.3

Notes:
[a] Excluding grants.
* Based on 1994 World Bank, *World Debt Tables* estimates.

flows, and 26 per cent of portfolio equity flows, largely corporate debt issues made directly in international markets. The profile of former communist emerging markets showed yet a third pattern. Here the region's share of FDI, only 14 per cent, was a bit below its share in overall capital inflows. Conversely, Eastern Europe and Central Asia received almost a third of portfolio bond flows, but only 6 per cent of equity flows. Larger than proportional foreign aid, both grants and loans, made up the difference.[3] As Eastern European countries move to privatize large state-owned enterprises, the role of FDI and equity flows will increase.

Perhaps the most important trend, however, transcends individual countries or regions, having to do instead with the overall size of the flows in relation to developing countries' economies. Table 2.1, as noted, suggests that the size of the current stock of net foreign-owned assets in developing countries in the 1990s approximates, and perhaps surpasses, that of the pre-World War I standard era dominated by Great Britain. As was the case in the late nineteenth and early twentieth centuries, financial conditions in the western economies have partly triggered the current surge. Consequently, the supply of external resources has been, and will continue to be, strongly affected by the business cycle in industrial countries and the ensuing fluctuations in credit market conditions. If trends in net capital flows to emerging markets are, however, crucially influenced by global (or regional) factors, rather than country specific macroeconomic conditions, then greater openness to external capital flows implies substantial vulnerability for capital-importing countries. I turn to this and related policy-relevant concerns in the essay's final section.

EXTERNAL FINANCE, ECONOMIC REFORM AND GROWTH IN DEVELOPING COUNTRIES: THREE ISSUES RECONSIDERED

This section presents my synthesis of three crucial contemporary debates about cross-border capital flows.

Economic Reform as a Major Determinant of the Surge of the 1990s

Capital flows change direction when the incentives are shifting, and according to them. In the 1960s, financial relations between the developed (largely creditor) economies and the developing (largely debtor) ones were mainly dictated by promising economic fundamentals in developing countries – and of course, by political concerns, as discussed in many of the other chapters in this volume. In the 1970s, the oil surplus provided strong incentives for western banks to lend to developing countries in a period of stagnating economic activity in the advanced industrial economies. In the 1980s the world debt crisis imposed a virtual reversal, with flows from emerging to industrial markets. What is the picture of the 1990s? An important conceptual distinction to be drawn is between the systemic and the country-specific features of the flows. The systemic aspects are more likely to affect the overall *volume* of capital inflows to emerging markets: these include items beyond the control of developing economies, such as the stage of the business cycle and the monetary policy stance in industrial countries, the soundness of the balance sheet of large international financial institutions, and the size of their total outstanding assets in developing countries. The *distribution* of net capital inflows across emerging markets, on the other hand, depends more on country-specific features. For instance, the per capita allocation of net inflows to over the period 1960–82, especially prior to 1972, was significantly affected by a number of country-specific initial conditions, that can be viewed as proxies for the *ex-ante* growth potential in 1960 (Manzocchi and Martin, 1996). In other words, given a pool of external resources available for financing developing countries (the size of which depends largely on systemic factors), the (per capita) distribution of the funds among individual countries is related to their initial level of per capita income, a few proxies for the level of education and health care, and a rough measure of political instability (the number of revolutions and coups). These variables altogether explain about half of the variability of net inflows over 1960–72 and – with the inclusion of a dummy for the Asian economies – over 1973–82 in a cross-section of 33 developing countries, including all major recipients in Latin America and Asia (Manzocchi and Martin, 1996).[4]

The surge of the early 1990s looks different in one important respect: the country-specific elements are not only related to relative factor endowments, but also to the record of economic reform, liberalization, and macro-economic policy in developing countries. When pooled together in a regression, external factors (such as the decline in global interest rates) can explain from 30 to 50 per cent of the time-series variation in capital flows to emerging markets during the recent upturn. The role of external factors appears to be more relevant in Latin America than in Asia (IMF, 1994, p. 53) and in portfolio flows as compared to FDI. The overall trend towards liberalization of the current and capital accounts that has occurred in recent years is also part of the story (Mathieson and Rojas-Suarez, 1993). Evaluating the exact contribution of external trade and financial liberalization poses a problem of empirical analysis, however, as it is difficult to evaluate the relative contribution of changes in the degree of financial integration *vis-à-vis* changes in the *ex-ante* rates of returns in capital-importing countries (Fernandez-Arias and Montiel, 1996). Furthermore, whenever the rise in capital inflows is due to the impulse given by financial deregulation, we are likely to observe the phenomenon of *stock adjustment* in world capital markets. As international investors diversify their portfolios in order to equalize expected returns and protect themselves against country-specific risk, the opening up of previously unavailable investment opportunites will divert some capital from alternative placements and direct it to the liberalizing countries. This is, however, a one-shot reallocation. It may take some time to be completed, but it is not going to be a permanent feature of a recipient country's balance of payments.

Other economic reforms may have a less-transitory impact on a country's capital account, if they are able to affect the ex-ante rate of return in a persistent way. For example, if the prospects for high rates of GDP and export growth, as well as large returns on investment, are permanently raised by reforms, then a sustained inflow of financial resources need not be episodic. Reforms in the 'real' economy (such as trade liberalization; investment and export promotion; measures intended to enhance human capital accumulation through direct government intervention or favorable de-taxation; and fiscal restructuring) are – with some caveats – believed to have a positive impact on long-term capital movements (Rodrik, 1996; Fry, 1997). A more complex picture emerges, however, with respect to financial reform and liberalization. As noted earlier, the predominant impact of financial liberalization is portfolio-adjustment, as leading international investors shift part of their funds into emerging markets. This is the 'expanded opportunities' phenomenon cited by the International Financial Corporation as accounting for the ten-fold growth in stock market capitalization in emerging markets, from $171 billion in 1985 to $1.9 trillion in 1995 (IFC, 1996, p. 7). Nevertheless financial liberalization has, relative to 'real' reforms, a more controversial medium and long-run effect on developing economies.

There are three principal concerns about the impact of financial deregulation in emerging markets. First, financial liberalization can raise the degree of short-termism inherent in an economy. This is due to the increased volatility and speculative nature of financial markets, which may emphasize their bandwagon and herd features at the expenses of *long-term* investment and growth. The so-called Anglo-Saxon model of finance and corporate governance, based on the checks imposed on management by the performance of the company on the stock market, might turn out to be particularly unsuited for emerging markets, where more uncertainty can hinder welfare-improving productive investments. The increase in volatility is likely to be even larger if domestic and external financial liberalization move together, as this 'leads to close links between two inherently unstable markets...the stock and currency markets' (Singh, 1997, p. 779). However, it should be noted that a tightly controlled market is also prone to several dangers, typically related to the abuse of political and bureaucratic influence, as well as the predictable rise in rent-seeking activities.

A second, though closely related, concern with financial liberalization is that it generates an 'excess demand' for prudential regulation and supervision by the emerging market country's monetary and financial market authorities. This problem is most likely to be felt in the commercial banking sector which still accounts for a very large share of financial intermediation in most developing countries (Fry, 1997). Both domestic and external funds are likely to be channeled through commercial banks in developing economies: whenever a surge in capital inflows or an increase in domestic saving raises the resources available for the banks, a deterioration of the quality of the balance sheet can occur if they are not able or willing to asses the riskness of their potential investments but are under pressure to allocate their funds. Note that this problem is even more serious in a situation of rising interest rates, commonly associated with the early phases of financial liberalization: high real interest rates tend to crowd out less risky potential borrowers at the advantage of the risky ones (Rojas-Suarez and Weisbrod, 1995). The recent banking crises in such countries as Venezuela, Mexico, and most recently Thailand, Indonesia, and South Korea illustrate this problem, which is also discussed in Walter Molano's contribution to this volume.

Finally, the medium to long-term consequences for growth and welfare of capital account opening (external financial liberalization) are crucially related to the *credibility and consistency* of the overall economic (and possibly political) reform package. The reason is that, if domestic and foreign agents believe that the measures intended to liberalize the capital account and stabilize macroeconomic policy are not permanent and may be reversed in the future, their behavior – although perfectly rational – will be led by the 'wrong' incentives from the point of view of aggregate domestic welfare in the capital-importing country. For instance, present consumption will be preferred to capital accumulation if a reversal in exchange rate stabilization is predicted; similarly, highly speculative rather than longer-term investment also should be favored.[5] Note that the credibility of a reform must be judged on two different grounds: first, from the viewpoint of the domestic political and social constituency that determines the internal consensus for the reform package; and, second, from the perspective of the international financial 'constituency' that distributes sanctions or rewards according to the perceived economic consistency of the package.

The Mexican (and Argentine) crisis of late 1994 to early 1995, and its aftermath, have shown that the relative role of external and domestic factors must be carefully recognized if one is to make inferences from the past into the future of capital flows to developing countries. The rise in US interest rates during 1994 may have generated financial tensions in debtor countries, but country-specific factors (the behavior of the real exchange rate and of the current account; the dynamics of currency reserves and of domestic liquidity; the extent of banking fragilities) can better explain why only some developing countries were hit by the crisis (Rojas-Suarez and Weisbrod, 1995). Moreover, country-specific fundamentals and not simply 'contagion' (or 'tequila') effects provide the most convincing explanation of the aftermath of the Mexican crisis of 1994. Not all emerging markets, and not even all Latin American ones, suffered the financial turbulence affecting, say, Argentina or the Philippines after the devaluation of the Mexican peso (Sachs, Tornell, and Velasco, 1996). Similarly, more recent experiences, including the downward trend of the Brazilian stock exchange in first half of 1997, or the steep devaluation of the Thai baht in midyear, need not generate widespread contagion effects if fundamentals are sound and economic reform is credible.

The Economic 'Quality' of the Recent Inflows

Section two above showed that the characteristics of the new wave of capital inflows into DCs radically differ from the flows of the 1970s. It is difficult, however, to argue that the financial instruments of the 1990s are absolute novelties, nor that they are intrinsically superior to earlier post-World War II forms of capital transfer. Portfolio bond emissions and FDI both have been popular at various stages in the past. The basic intuition underlying my second statement is that both the domestic and the global economy must be viewed as stochastic environments, where good or bad economic performance is due to a combination of behavior and 'luck' (that is unpredictable events, either favorable or not). Moreover, a peculiarity of financial relations is that they usually involve both conflicting and shared objectives. While the creditor has an interest in sanctioning bad behavior, he has also an obvious interest in avoiding the debtor's economic failure (which would imply no debt repayments, no dividends, capital losses, nationalization or other forms of expropriation). Furthermore, in a stochastic environment the creditor should (but could be unable to) distinguish between the roles of behavior and 'luck' in determining the debtor's performance. Therefore, we can view financial contracts as different systems of reaching a balance between the penalties imposed on the debtor for bad outcomes and the support extended to him in bad situations. For instance, we can think of bank lending as stressing the monitoring role of creditors over the debtor's activities, while portfolio finance underlines the sanctioning role of the markets. Ranking financial instruments according to their inherent quality must take account of this balance.

Let us briefly consider FDI, bond and banking forms of debt finance, and portfolio equity flows. Foreign direct investment is, with some qualifications, a source of external capital whose contribution to economic growth and welfare in developing countries is likely to be relatively larger than that of portfolio equity (Borensztein, De Gregorio, and Lee, 1994; Balasubramanyam, Salisu, and Sapsford, 1996). Both human and physical capital transfers are in principle associated with FDI; hence the constraint on human resources (scientific, technical, managerial) in developing countries should be more easily overcome. At the same time, if FDI is concentrated in the public utility sector or in infrastructure it can produce beneficial external effects for the whole recipient economy. Moreover, *individual* foreign direct investment initiatives should be less volatile than portfolio investment. Note, however, that this is not necessarily true at the *aggregate* level. Classens, Dooley and Warner (1995) find that the distinction between 'hot' and 'cold' flows is largely conventional, as the components of a country's capital account look high substitutable over time. It has also been argued that FDI in emerging markets can be 'incentive-compatible,' as it may lower the incentive to default on external debt on the part of the debtor and the incentive to free-ride on the part of the creditors. (The reasoning is that FDI increases the openness of the developing economy to international trade and production, and therefore raises the penalties associated with insulation in the case of insolvency and default; see Aizenman, 1991.)

At the same time, it would be wrong to treat every kind of FDI as necessarily beneficial for the host economy. The main determinant of FDI in the 'traditional' labor-intensive sectors is the search for lower labor costs, even if this means a frequent relocation of productive capacity (the so-called 'foot-loose' FDI phenomenon). Foreign investment in low value-added sectors can lead to an excessive specialization of the DC in labour-intensive production that may prevent a future upgrading of the domestic industry (the 'lock-in' phenomenon). Moreover, the competition among developing countries to provide favorable locations for FDI can yield welfare-reducing side effects, such as a deterioration of the environmental conditions, a compression of civil and political rights, the systematic repression of social unrest, and a taxation regime that unduly favors capital over labor income (for an introduction to the concept of locational competition and its inherent dangers, see Siebert, 1996).

The mechanism of bond finance was popular during the nineteenth century but was associated with frequent liquidity crises and default in the borrowing countries, as discussed in section one. One difference between the historical and contemporary bond lending booms is that today's international portfolios are to a large extent managed by institutional investors, rather than by individual households. The free-riding problems, in principle, should be partially overcome. As in the past, today's bond issues are sometimes project-specific; hence one may argue that the re-financing of an investment project can be evaluated more carefully by the lender on the basis of the results obtained, and of the future prospects. Moreover, the unwillingness of investors to finance an individual project need not jeopardize the aggregate volume of capital transfers to a particular emerging market country. These conclusions are, however, unwarranted. Small investors tend to delegate monitoring of the debtor's activity to a financial intermediary; this is true both of mutual funds investing in bonds and of bank deposits. Commercial banks are often thought to perform a *better* monitoring of their debtors than other kind of financial institutions, precisely because their involvement with an individual borrower or project is likely to be larger, lasting and more direct. However, in practice, and as demonstrated in the bank lending boom of the 1970s, this involvement of lending banks is a double-edged sword. Close ties between lender and borrower may lead to careful monitoring and avoid the danger of crises due merely to liquidity (as opposed to solvency) problems in debtor countries, but it may also trigger Ponzi games of rolling-over the outstanding service of the debt that may eventually lead to deeper and wider financial crises. In any case, the project-specific nature of bond finance is likely to be an illusion if the lender lacks a constant and complete supervision of the borrower's accounts and, more importantly, if the outcome of one project crucially depends on other complementary invest-ments or on the global economic performance of the developing economy. One benefit of debt finance may be that, if major creditors have a stake in the debtor's economic survival, then syndicated bank lending can *supplement* bond finance in periods of distress, as the aftermath of the 1994–95 crisis perhaps suggests. However, we should not be overly sanguine about the monitoring capabilities of either commercial banks or institutional investors in global bond markets, as the late 1997 East Asian financial crisis made amply clear.

Portfolio equity is, in quantitative terms, the truly new instrument of capital transfers to developing countries. In principle it differs from bond finance, because the burden of the risk associated with the investment is *explicitly* transferred onto the shareholder. However, as noted above, default, the suspension of interest payments, and the reduction in the nominal value of the assets have been historical features of the mechanism of international (sovereign) debt. That is, one can argue that this burden had always been carried to some extent by the creditors. From the capital recipient's view-point, equity markets are even more subject to booms, panics and crashes than bond markets, as the volatility of stock market investment is likely to be higher. Of course it also is true that large investors such as mutual or pension funds might have an interest in stabilizing a market if they face huge capital losses. It has been argued that the existence of a stock market enhances the allocative efficiency of an economy: recent econometric studies have shown that the size and liquidity of the stock market is positively associated with growth in developed and developing countries (Levine, 1996). However, the causal links underlying this relationship are very controversial and appear to be influenced by the characteristics of each individual country or region (Arestis and Demetriades, 1997). From a purely economic point of view, therefore, it is risky to assert that one form of cross-border capital flow is superior to another, although FDI would seem to have some useful advan-tages for the emerging market country.

External Finance and Long-run Growth

Economics textbooks suggest that integration into world capital markets favors economic growth and welfare for several reasons: domestic investment is decoupled from national saving; consumption can be smoothed in the face of country-specific shocks; and world-wide pooling of financial instruments allows more efficient insurance against risk and lower borrowing costs. A widely shared contemporary opinion is that these long-term benefits of capital market integration must be weighed against the short-term difficulties associated with the macroeconomic management of capital movements. Our view is different: there is no general, mechanical outcome of capital market integration that is valid for any economy both in the short and in the long run. On the other hand there can be short-term benefits of capital inflows: for instance, foreign financial resources can help overcome a liquidity shortage in economies affected by a dramatic fall in the real value of monetary balances, as in the recent experience of Eastern Europe (see Manzocchi, 1997). Moreover, capital inflows can provide foreign exchange reserves to finance the net import requirements of a developing economy, especially for machinery and other capital goods. Capital imports can stimulate competition for external funds among domestic borrowers and credit institutions, thus enhancing the efficiency of the domestic financial system.

On the other hand, there is also no guarantee that capital inflows are conducive to higher income growth in the long run. For starters, it is very difficult to come to a satisfactory *empirical* estimate of the *direct* contribution of foreign finance to growth and welfare, as its effects are channelled through investment, trade, and so on. Furthermore, the impact of capital flows on growth necessarily depends on the policies that are implemented by the recipient, both in short term macroeconomic management and in medium and long-term structural reform. Therefore, two different approaches to this issue can be taken: one can look at the general connection between international economic integration and development; or one can try to define an empirical methodology to single out the specific contribution of external capital.

Williamson (1996) provides an updated account of the literature on growth, convergence, and economic integration. Although he argues that convergence in income levels and globalization were correlated both in the late nineteenth century and after World War II, and that there are reasons to believe that causation runs from integration to convergence at least in the former period, he suggests that mass migration and trade were the main engines of the process of equalization of per capita incomes. He estimates that mass migration accounted for 70 per cent of real wage convergence between 1870 and 1910 among those countries that now constitute the OECD, but at that time showed marked income differences. The remaining

30 per cent is explained by other forces like trade integration (Williamson, 1996, p. 295). According to Williamson, the contribution of capital market integration to the catching-up of the backward western economies in the late nineteenth to early twentieth century was rather limited. Of course things might have gone differently in the New World (a net recipient of *both* immigrants and capital flows) and in today's Third World countries (colonies included), but once again it is quite difficult to disentangle the net effect of one single aspect of globalization.

Recent econometric attempts at identifying the specific contribution of external financing to growth in developing countries have turned out to be rather frustrating. The International Monetary Fund (IMF, 1996) recently reviewed the adjustment experiences of eight developing economies from the 1970s through the 1990s, drawing on the empirical and policy indications from a larger set of developing countries. With respect to the role of external finance, the authors argue that no common, clear-cut implications of capital flows for economic recovery can be identified from the experiences of these (or other) countries. Three reasons are suggested. First, the interaction between policies and financing is complex. Second, the level of financing itself is likely to be endogenous, that is, heavily influenced by a country's own prior macroeconomic policies and performance. Third, the impact on investment and growth of a rise in foreign capital inflows very much depends on whether *domestic* saving is crowded-out, and by how much (IMF, 1996, p. 49). Comparative and time series studies yield mixed evidence on these issues (IMF, 1996, pp. 83–4). Nonetheless, some propositions can be advanced. It is quite clear that foreign financial resources, whether in the form of private flows or of official assistance, are welcome if a country is undergoing a process of stabilization, reform, and liberalization. These resources can allow for a continuation of reasonable living standards *and* of sustained investment rates at a time of possible fiscal retrenchment and output contraction. It is also clear, however, that postponing adjustment and stabilization can be especially dangerous under conditions of open capital markets, because it can generate a massive reversal of capital inflows, which raises the cost of the eventual and inevitable adjustment. It is true that speculative movements can lead to abrupt swings in the external payments position of a developing (or a developed) economy even if the macro-economic 'fundamentals' are sound. Still, provided that speculative capital is not predominant, these swings should be temporary and should not outbalance the potential benefits of capital market integration in the long run.

However, as mentioned before, the long-term benefits of capital inflows are by no means mechanical: they crucially depend on whether the *destination* of external financing within the recipient country is investment or consumtion, on the *allocation* of the investment resources to highly profitable projects, on a domestic and international environment conducive to economic growth, and finally on 'luck' (favorable unexpected events) as noted above. All of these conditions must be fulfilled in order for capital inflows to support economic growth and development. For instance, looking at simple univariate correlations, Manzocchi and Martin (1996) find that larger per capita inflows were positively and significantly associated with economic growth in developing countries during the period 1960–72, but that this statistically significant association between growth and capital inflows vanished during the period 1973–82. We show that those developing countries that received more external finance (on a per capita basis) experienced an *increase* in investment rates in the sixties, but an increase in consumption and a *decrease* in investment rates in the seventies.

The counterpart of the foreign capital contribution to growth is the accumulation of an external debt (or in general, of a negative net foreign asset position). The accumulation of external liabilities is viable *if* domestic output and exports are also growing.[6] These are the long-run benchmarks against which the outcome of the recent surge in capital flows to emerging markets eventually will be evaluated. As argued above, sound and credible policies are required to assure that the impact of foreign finance on long term growth in developing countries be positive. Together with liberalization (with the caveats mentioned in the case of financial market deregulation), policies effectively promoting and supporting the accumulation of infrastructure and human capital (education, healthcare, job training and so on) are highly beneficial. Under these circumstances, even *public* borrowing from abroad can raise the overall rate of return of an economy and therefore can be sustainable in the long run.[7] Nonetheless, the behavior of saving and investment rates in the developing countries over the 1970s, although apparently rational in a situation of extremely low global real interest rates, clearly was short-sighted and contributed to the debt crisis of the 1980s. The lesson of historical experience is that, provided external factors matter, the sustainability of external debt as well as the impact of foreign capital on growth in the receiving countries are closely linked to a correct use of the funds. The disposition of borrowed funds within developing countries is, of course, largely a political question. On that I defer to several of my fellow contributors to this book.

Notes

1.   The categories used in this chapter to track the composition of capital flows since 1970 differ somewhat from those used by Armijo in her chapter, and are more similar to categories commonly employed by economists.

2.   To simplify a rather tedious debate, we may say that the four main international institutions collecting information on foreign debt use different sources and definitions: the OECD statistics on ODA are based on donor governments' declarations, and include lending on concessional terms; the Bank for

International Settlements releases data on international lending by private financial institutions of the reporting countries only; IMF statistics are based on balance-of-payments data; and finally, the World Bank Debtor Reporting System (DRS) gathers information from the institutions in the debtor countries. Many inconsistencies arise among the different systems: the choice of the DRS data reflects an overall superior balance between detail and completeness.

3. Data in this and the preceding paragraph are from World Bank, World Debt Tables 1996.

4. Note that this model is not able to provide satisfactory explanations of net per capita flows *after* 1982, possibly because a turning point of the debt cycle from a pattern of 'voluntary' lending towards a situation of involuntary or 'defensive' lending occurred in that year and changed the structure of incentives for international investment in the DCs.

5. Calvo and Mendoza (1996) argue that lack of credibility severely harmed the Mexican reform experiment of March 1988–December 1994.

6. On the experience of the transition economies of Central and Eastern Europe see Manzocchi (1997).

7. See Chapter 1 by Armijo in this volume for an evaluation of the composition of capital inflows according to the (public or private) nature of the borrowers.

Bibliography

Aizenman, J. (1991) 'Trade Dependency, Bargaining and External Debt,' *Journal of International Economics*, 31, pp. 101–20.

Arestis, P. and P. Demetriades (1997) 'Financial Development and Economic Growth: Assessing the Evidence,' *Economic Journal*, 107, pp. 783–99.

Balasubramanyam, V. N., M. Salisu, and D. Sapsford (1996) 'Foreign Direct Investment and Growth in EP and IS Countries,' *Economic Journal*, 106, pp. 95–105.

Borensztein, E., De J. Gregorio, and J. Lee (1994) 'How Does Foreign Direct Investment Affect Economic Growth?,' *IMF Working paper* 94/110 (Washington, D.C.: International Monetary Fund).

Calvo, G., L. Leiderman, and C. Reinhart (1993) 'Capital Inflows to Latin America: The Role of External Factors,' *IMF Staff Papers*, 40 (Washington, D.C.: International Monetary Fund).

—— and E. Mendoza (1996) 'Mexico Balance-Of-Payments Crisis: A Chronicle of A Death Foretold,' *Journal of International Economics*, 41, pp. 235–64.

Claessens, S., M. Dooley, and A. Warner (1995) 'Portfolio Flows: Hot or Cold?,' *The World Bank Economic Review*, 9 (1).

Cohen, D. (1991) *Foreign Lending to Sovereign States: A Theoretical Autopsy* (Cambridge, MA: MIT Press.)

De Cecco, M., (1984) *Money and Empire* (Oxford: Basil Blackwell).

—— (1985) 'Il problema dei debiti internazionali nel periodo tra le due guerre mondiali,' *BNL Moneta e Credito* 36, pp. 31–52.

Diaz-Alejandro, C. (1983) 'Some Aspects of the 1982–83 Brazilian Payments Crisis,' *Brookings Papers on Economic Activity*, 2, pp. 515–42.

Dooley, M., E. Fernandez-Arias, and K. Kletzer (1996) 'Is the Debt Crisis History? Recent Private Capital Inflows in Developing Countries,' *'The World Bank Economic Review*, 1, pp. 27–50.

Eichengreen, B. (1990) *Trends and Cycles in Foreign Lending* (Berkeley, CA: University of California Press).

—— (1991) 'Historical Research on International Lending and Debt,' *Journal of Economic Perspectives*, 5 (2), pp. 149–69.

—— and P. Lindert (eds) (1989) *The International Debt Crisis in Historical Perspective* (Cambridge, MA: MIT Press).

Fernandez-Ansola, J. and T. Laursen (1995.) 'Historical Experience with Bond Financing to Developing Countries,' *IMF Working Paper* 95/27 (Washington, D.C.: International Monetary Fund).

Fernandez-Arias, E. and P. Montiel (1996) 'The Surge in Capital Inflows to Developing Countries: An Analytical Overview,' *The World Bank Economic Review*, 1, pp. 52–77.

Fry, M. (1997) 'In Favour of Financial Liberalisation,' *Economic Journal*, 107, pp. 754–70.

International Finance Corporation (IFC) (1996) *Investment Funds in Emerging Markets*, Lessons of Experience Series 2 (Washington, D.C.: International Finance Corporation).

International Monetary Fund (IMF) (1994) *World Economic Outlook (October 1994)* (Washington, D.C.: International Monetary Fund).

—— (1995) *Official Financing for Developing Countries* (Washington, D.C.: International Monetary Fund).

—— (1996) *Reinvigorating Growth in Developing Countries. Lessons from Adjustment Policies in Eight Economies*, Occasional Paper no. 139 (Washington, D.C.: International Monetary Fund).

—— (1997) *World Economic Outlook (May 1997)* (Washington, D.C.: International Monetary Fund).

Kindleberger, C. (1973) *The World in Depression* (Berkeley, CA: University of California Press).

—— (1984) *A Financial History of Western Europe* (London: George Allen & Unwin).

Levine, R. (1996) *Stock Market Liquidity and Economic Growth: Theory and Evidence*, paper presented at the VIII Villa Mondragone International Economic Seminar, Rome.

Manzocchi, S. (1997) 'External Finance and Foreign Debt in Central and Eastern Europe,' *IMF Working paper* 97/146 (Washington DC.: International Monetary Fund).

—— and Martin, P. (1996) *Are Capital Flows Consistent with the Neoclassical Growth Model? Evidence from a Cross-Section of Developing Countries*, Centre for Economic Policy Research (CEPR) Discussion paper no. 1400 (London: CEPR).

Marichal, C. (1989) *A Century of Debt Crises in Latin America* (Princeton, N.J.: Princeton University Press).

Mathieson, D. and L. Rojas-Suarez (1993) 'Liberalization of the Capital Account: Experiences and Issues,' *IMF Occasional Paper* 103 (Washington, D.C.: International Monetary Fund).

Padoan, P.C. (1987) *The Political Economy of International Financial Instability* (London: Croom Helms).

Rodrik, D. (1996) 'Understanding Economic Policy Reform,' *Journal of Economic Literature*, 34, pp. 9–41.

Rojas-Suarez, L. and S. Weisbrod (1995) 'Financial Fragilities in Latin America: The 1980s and the 1990s,' *IMF Occasional Paper* 132.

Sachs, J., A. Tornell, and A. Velasco (1996). 'Financial Crises in Emerging Markets: the Lessons From 1995,' *NBER Working Paper* 5576 (Cambridge, MA.: National Bureau of Economic Research).

Siebert, H. (1996) 'On the Concept of Locational Competition,' *Kiel Working Paper* 731, Kiel, Germany.

Singh, A. (1997) 'Financial Liberalisation, Stockmarkets and Economic Development,' *Economic Journal*, 107, pp. 771–82.

Solomon, R. (1982) *The International Monetary System 1945–1981* (New York Harper & Row).

Tew, B. (1982) *The Evolution of the International Monetary System 1945–1981* (London: Hutchinson University Library).

United Nations (1991) *Transnational Banks and the International Debt Crisis* (New York: UN Centre on Transnational Corporations).

Veganzones, M. A. and C. Winograd (1997) *Argentina in the 20th Century* (Paris: Organization for Economic Co-operation and Development (OECD) Development Centre).

Williamson, J. G. (1996) 'Globalization, Convergence and History,' *Journal of Economic History*, 56 (2), pp. 277–306.

3 Emerging Market Makers: The Power of Institutional Investors
Mary Ann Haley

The nineteenth century ideal of a world based on the unencumbered operation of a free market once again permeates the public policies and politics of the late twentieth century. International investors are today playing a central role in pushing the gospel of the free market, particularly in the developing countries in Asia, Latin America and Africa. The most effective means of attracting capital into developing countries has shifted rapidly from pledging allegiance to one of the cold war rivals to marketing the nation-state to the world's financiers. Where once a strategic geopolitical position could have ensured a consistent flow of assistance, now an economic policy based on deregulation, privatization, and stabilization is the path to financial success. Moreover, the power of the purse lies more and more with private institutional investors.

However, the neoliberal tenet that the market is an abstract entity which serves as an efficient mechanism for distributing goods within society is called into question by the apparently uncompetitive and inefficient nature of the emerging stock markets. These markets do not function by an invisible hand, but are controlled by the visible hands of institutional investors who concentrate assets and coordination investments among themselves. In addition, in light of the amount of control these institutional investors have over the resources flowing to developing countries, their preferences now serve as guideposts for those countries wanting to attract private capital. Within the most recent wave of global political democratization lies the countervailing force of an inefficient financial market empowering money managers who value stability and growth over political democracy.

PRIVATE INVESTMENT FLOWS AND INSTITUTIONAL INVESTORS

In the decade following the mid-1980s there was a tremendous shift in the composition of capital inflows into developing countries. Official development finance was rapidly replaced by private investments as the primary source of capital for developing countries. Although official development financing increased from $33.4 billion to $53.9 billion, or 61 per cent, between 1983 and 1993, private financing increased almost 300 per cent, from $35.6 billion in 1984 to $159.2 billion in 1993. In the near future, 90 per cent of the capital flowing into developing countries may be from private investments (IFC 1995, p. 6). The World Bank, IMF, and similar institutions contributed less than 15 per cent of all international financing to developing economies in 1993, down from almost 30 per cent in 1989. By far the fastest growing category of private investment has been portfolio investments. Total portfolio investment, or stocks and bonds, increased from $32.6 *million* in 1984 to almost $89 *billion* in 1993. In 1993, portfolio equity comprised 31 per cent of the total net resource flows to developing countries (see also Chapters 1 and 2 in this volume). [1]

ARE EMERGING MARKETS 'EFFICIENT'?

This rise in portfolio equity investments to developing countries, prompts us to ask how these funds from advanced industrialized countries are allocated among the emerging markets. As the origins of capital inflows shift from public to private sources, one could expect dissipation of distributional control as market mechanisms take the place of aid agencies.

Economic liberals such as Friedrich Hayek (1944) and Milton Friedman (1962) argue that the best and fairest way to allocate goods is to allow the market to operate unimpeded by human intervention. If accompanied by proper laws allowing free access and fair competition, supply and demand will sort out inefficiencies. As more and more developing countries have adopted the idea that impartial market mechanisms are better suited to allocate resources than public enterprises, the focal point of development debates has been how best to implement economic reforms which will realize this neoliberal ideal. A large part of these economic reforms has been the development and implementation of a financial infrastructure grounded in this free market ideal. The rush to establish emerging securities markets has been a subset of this trend. However, the level of efficiency and subsequent fairness of these developing stock exchanges remains in question.

Financial theorists, it has been said, fall basically into two camps, those that believe that financial markets are efficient and those that don't. In 1973 Burton Malkiel published *A Random Walk Down Wall Street*, giving the world what has become known as the efficient markets hypothesis (EMH). The much debated EMH suggests that within securities markets information is disseminated and assimilated almost immediately, causing the price of the security to reflect and continually incorporate all available public and private information. The implications of this assumption are that any type of analysis, from stock charts to earnings estimates, is useless. In other words, 'a blindfolded chimpanzee throwing darts at the *Wall Street Journal* could pick a portfolio of stocks that would perform as well as those carefully selected by the highest priced security analyst' (Malkiel 1983, p. 44). Others have offered various refinements to the random walk hypothesis (Grossman and Stiglitz, 1976; Mader and Hagin, 1976; Diamond and Verrechhia, 1981; Garber, 1991). These modifications have engendered more sophisticated versions of the original hypothesis which take into account certain anomalies, such as the 'tulip mania' (Garber, 1991), in which investors bandwagon around certain investments whose intrinsic value might suggest greater caution, or the presence of volatility in certain stocks (Mader and Hagin, 1976).[2]

Others, however, have refuted the notion that markets are efficient and have offered evidence suggesting that the use of econometric, technical, and fundamental analyses can help detect such things as undervalued stocks, cyclical pricing, and correlations between pricing and other factors.[3] Through the detection of such market anomalies, one can exploit market opportunities and theoretically do better than the chimpanzee. In fact, the market in emerging country securities displays many characteristics of inefficiency.[4]

This chapter suggests that international portfolio flows into emerging markets do not fulfill two of the primary conditions necessary for an efficient market.[5] First, the EMH assumes there are a sufficient number of investors in the market to warrant competition and render it impossible for any one investor to manipulate the market. Second, in a fair and efficient market investors have access to roughly the same information and react similarly and 'rationally' within the confines of profit-maximization. Neither of the assumptions describes the reality of contemporary emerging market investing.

In addition, if by an 'efficient market', we mean a market in which funds are allocated to investments offering them their highest rate of return, then we must recognize that from the viewpoint of the advanced industrial country investor, investments in advanced industrial countries and in emerging markets are substitutes for one another. If the rate of return in the US goes up then, obviously, the *relative* rate of return in Mexico, if it remains unchanged, will fall. While such investor behavior may be 'rational' and even 'efficient', it is so from the viewpoint of the *investor* but not necessarily from the perspective of the EMC. These 'push' factors are very important among the factors determining net flows into EMCs. The argument that the shift in financial flows, in particular the growth of portfolio capital, has had a positive impact on economic policies in developing countries, implies that certain economic conditions within a country will attract investments, or that 'pull' factors matter. Although 'pull' factors were once thought to be the main determinant of country choice, this assumption has been challenged recently by theorists claiming the predominance of 'push' factors, or factors external to a country which encourage an increase in portfolio flows regardless of internal changes. If push factors are the main determinants of portfolio inflows, then policy choices within developing countries should be less constrained and the argument that foreign portfolio investors positively influence economic reforms in emerging market countries becomes less plausible.

There are several reasons to believe that 'push' factors are the most prevalent determinant of portfolio flows to developing countries. There is a correlation between source country regulations and the amount of capital that has flowed into the emerging markets.[6] A recent study indicating a correlation between US and Mexican long-term financial assets provides further evidence that external factors may have a strong impact on emerging market capital inflows.[7] Another analysis finds that emerging market country fund investments are related more to US market performance than emerging market stock valuations.[8] In all of these cases, these advocates of the 'push' hypothesis find a weak relationship between economic conditions in emerging market countries and the prices of emerging market stocks.[9]

In addition to the correlations found between external factors and investment in emerging stock markets, certain investor strategies for allocating equity investments to developing countries lead to the conclusion that developing countries can do little to influence the inflows into their countries. Portfolio allocations are chosen based on the risk tolerance and investment goals of the investor. Often, the first step in professional asset allocation is to decide how money will be divided between particular investment instruments. These decisions are usually made by the first level of money managers within a bank, pension fund, or even at the individual level. Emerging markets are considered foreign stock, and fall into the category of a high-risk international investment. External factors such as the source country's interest rate expectations are taken into account during this first-level allocative phase of investor strategy. If the US market is bearish due to high interest rates for instance, emerging markets may present portfolio managers with international diversification and a high growth alternative. Professional portfolio investors most frequently decide which portion of their portfolio to allocate to the investment category of 'emerging markets' based on predetermined formulas for international diversification and the performance of the domestic markets in developed economies. Thus, a portfolio strategy is developed in which the desired share of foreign equity in the total portfolio is established before decisions are made about specific country allocations. For instance, one study suggested that a portfolio with less than 20 per cent invested in the Emerging Markets Index[10] is suboptimal (Hartmann and Khambata, 1994, p. 100). As defenders of the 'push' thesis suggest, this percentage can change depending on factors exogenous to the appeal of specific emerging market countries, thus affecting the overall amount invested in the emerging markets.

Although 'push' factors probably determine the size of the pie, 'pull' factors presumably determine how it will be sliced. 'Pull' factors such as economic reform and political stability are the elements through which developing country governments can impact capital inflows. Here, the specialized role of the emerging market mutual fund manager becomes crucial. Behind the bulk of portfolio equity investments and bond purchases, and now a fair amount of foreign direct investment, are institutional investors: the money managers of mutual funds, pension funds, insurance companies, banks, brokerage firms, and large multinational corporations. Estimates indicate that as much as 90 per cent of portfolio assets invested in emerging market equities involve institutional investors; the capital flowing to these investors continues to increase (Howell, 1993, p. 78). Mutual funds, managed by the large brokerage firms, increased their contribution to the emerging markets from $6 billion in 1988 to $81.5 billion in 1993 (IMF, 1995, p. 18). Similarly, pension fund contributions to the emerging markets rose from just $500 million in 1990 to $18 billion in 1993 (Lee, 1995, p. 15).

Most institutions, including pension funds, insurance companies, and banks, however, do not control their individual investments into emerging markets. Due to the high cost of travel, data collection, and transaction fees, it is frequently more cost-effective for institutional investors to use specialists within the field of emerging markets to choose the countries and sectors in which to invest. This phenomenon has created a group of individuals with enormous power over private resource flows to developing countries: the emerging market mutual fund managers.

In Chapter 1 of this volume, Leslie Elliott Armijo cites the possibility that institutional investor pressure for neoliberal economic reform may force incumbent governments to choose policies that could be problematic for political democracy. What is perhaps understated in Armijo's work is the level of coordination and potential power of institutional portfolio investors. In her analysis, democratic processes are most affected by capital inflows through the benefits that accrue to the recipients of these funds. Any systemic changes in the selection process of, and/or control over, recipients are compressed into this framework. I would like to suggest that it is not only the laws of supply and demand that are impacting democratic processes, but also the conventions and preferences of institutional investors.

EMERGING MARKETS, FUND MANAGERS, POWER CONCENTRATION, AND INVESTMENT COORDINATION

One way to examine the decision rules governing the channeling of money into emerging market mutual funds managers is to examine the portfolio holdings of what was in 1996 the largest emerging markets fund: Templeton Developing Markets. Mark Mobius, manager of the various Templeton emerging market funds, commanded a mammoth presence in the emerging markets arena. Referred to as the 'reigning king of emerging-markets funds' and an 'emerging markets guru' by the *Wall Street Journal*, Mobius was responsible for over $10 billion of emerging market fund assets at the end of 1996 (Dow Jones and Company 1996, p. 2). Table 3.1 lists the shares of one of Mobius' funds held by investment banking and other securities-related firms, giving a preliminary indication of the reliance of other institutional investors on specialists such as Mobius.

Another dimension of the concentration of power appears when one examines the clumping of assets within one of the main vehicles for emerging market investors: the emerging market fund. In its 1997 database of mutual funds, Reuters lists 56 European and US funds that fall into the category of emerging market funds.[11] The top 50 of these funds total $13 billion in assets.[12] Within this particular fund universe, five emerging market institutional investors controlled 72 per cent of these assets: the Templeton fund alone held a 32 per cent share of these funds (see Table 3.2). Such funds wield considerable influence. Thus, for example, in May 1996 the International Finance Corporation's *Monthly Review of Emerging Stock Markets* reported that both the Chilean and Colombian markets had been affected (Chile downwards, Columbia upwards) by the comments of a representative of Merrill Lynch, the smallest of Table 3.2's big five (IFC 1996, pp. 18, 22). Region-specific funds show similar concentration. For

Table 3.1   Institutional investors' holdings of Templeton developing markets fund

Investor	Industry	Shares held
Alex Brown & Ass.	Securities	7 178
American National Bank & Trust	Banking	2 036
Bank One Investment	Investment Bank	11 892
Barclays Bank	Banking	173 226
Baring Private Investment Trust	Securities	747 632
Bear Stearns & Co.	Securities	12 639
Chase Manhattan	Banking	42 000
Chicago Trust Co.	Banking	67 000
A. G. Edwards & Sons	Securities	10 271
Franklin Resources	Securities	110 300
Mercury Asset Mgt	Unit Trust	982 008
Norwich Union	Banking	979 335
Smith & Williams Growth Trust	Unit Trust	198 915
Treadneedle Investment	Offshore Fund	850 000
Valley Forge Asset Mgt	Securities	168 080

Note: Second quarter filings, 1996.
Source: Bloomberg data files, June 1996.

Table 3.2   Concentration of emerging markets funds

Management group	Percentage of assets of top 50 funds
Templeton	32
Fidelity	13
Morgan Stanley	13
Montgomery	9
Merrill Lynch	5
Total	72

Source: Reuters money network research data on CD-ROM, June 1996.
Note: Second quarter, 1996. Top 50 emerging market funds, excluding regional and country specific funds, but including both equity and income funds.

example, of the 26 emerging Asia funds listed, three institutions controlled 59.7 per cent of assets, totaling over $9 billion. Similarly, three institutions controlled 59.3 per cent of the assets in 19 Latin American regional funds.[13]

In addition to the concentration of assets within a few emerging market funds and the resulting power accruing to the managers, there is evidence to suggest that the decisions of these managers have been coordinated. To test whether or not institutional investors could function coherently as political actors in developing countries, it was necessary to show that in making investment decisions these investors were not simply reacting independently to the same macroeconomic and risk statistics, but were influenced by principles, norms, and/or information exchanges between investors.[14] If this were the case, then developing countries' economic and political destinies could not be said to be solely subject to the dictates of an invisible hand. The test reported here assumes that, if fund managers from a certain geographic area systematically coordinate their decisions with one another (but systematically differ from fund managers located elsewhere), then one has uncovered prima facie evidence of non-market coordination.

I suggest that if investors show any signs of grouping around a norm, that is if individual institutional investors are not making independent decisions, then this indicates a departure from a competitive and efficient market.

Results

I looked at the portfolio allocation of 18 emerging market funds, 8 US-based and 10 European, using 1996 second quarter reports.[15] As Figure 3.1 indicates, there are considerable differences between fund allocations to certain countries, particularly the larger emerging market countries: Brazil, Hong

Kong, Malaysia, Mexico, and Thailand. The less-noticeable differences are in the smaller emerging market countries and are highlighted in Table 3.3. Both are discussed below.

Figure 3.1 and Table 3.3 highlight some of the large differences between US and European institutional investors' geographic distribution choices for emerging market mutual fund portfolios. US investors seem to have shied away from investments in India, Singapore and Peru entirely during this time period. Of the funds included in this analysis, no US fund reported any of these three countries in their top-ten holdings. Possible explanations are that European funds, primarily based in London, have many more historical ties to India and Singapore. Peru, a much smaller market, may be an anomaly, or low US investment here may simply have reflected its status as a pariah among US investors due to the large amount of 1970s debt overhang. In the latter half of 1996, Peru picked up significantly within US holdings, because of the successful debt restructuring through Brady bond issues. Conversely, European-based funds show no top-ten holdings for Greece, Portugal, Taiwan or Venezuela, but allocated larger proportions of their portfolios to

Figure 3.1   Average country allocations: European and US emerging markets compared

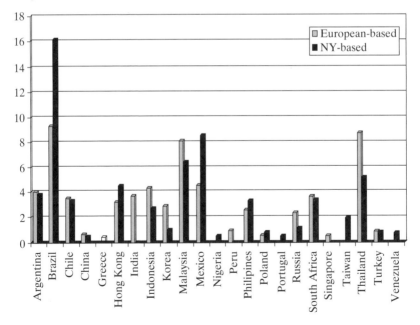

Source: Second quarter filings, 1996.

Table 3.3   Differences in country allocations by location of emerging market fund

European-based funds per cent more than NY funds		NY-based funds per cent more than European funds	
Korea	186	Greece	100
Russia	107	Portugal	100
India	100	Taiwan	100
Peru	100	Venezuela	100
Singapore	100	Mexico	87
Thailand	68	Brazil	75
Indonesia	61	Poland	56
China	31	Hong Kong	43
Malaysia	27	Philippines	30

Source: Second quarter reports, 1996.

Malaysia, China, Indonesia, and Thailand.[16] Another important difference was US investors' significantly larger allocations to Brazil and Mexico and their significantly smaller distributions to Korea and Russia. That US funds would prefer the larger Latin American countries over Southeast Asia is not surprising given the historical and geographical ties between the Americas. It is also not surprising that European funds, primarily out of London, would gravitate to Southeast Asia given their colonial history there. Although preliminary, these differences emphasize the possibility that a fund manager's subjectivity may influence country allocation and that market mechanisms are not the only determinant of emerging market equity flows.

There was much higher correlation within US funds (.54) than between US and European funds (.18). The average correlation among funds based in Europe (.36) was much lower than among US funds. One of the apparent reasons for this was that not all the funds traded on the same exchange. One of the funds, Credit Lyonnais Emerging Market Fund, traded on the Singapore exchange, although its parent company was French. The average correlation for European funds increased (to .40) when Credit Lyonnais was excluded. Tellingly, the highest correlation between funds was between the Montgomery Emerging Markets Fund and the Montgomery Emerging Markets Institutional Fund, not surprising given that the funds shared a common manager. A quick look at Japan's foreign stock holdings provides additional evidence that the operations of the supposedly impersonal global marketplace remain rather more subjective and culture bound than is often recognized. The portfolio breakdown here differed significantly from that of both the European and US funds.[17] Figure 3.2 shows the geographic allocations of Japanese funds, which were, in comparison to the US-based funds,

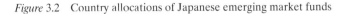

Figure 3.2   Country allocations of Japanese emerging market funds

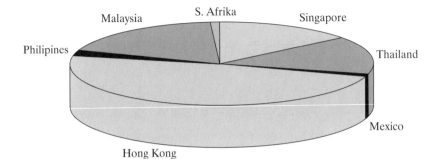

Note: Fourth quarter, 1995.

Source: Data provided by Kazu Kijima of Shoken Toshishintaku Kyokai, an association of Japanese investment trusts.

heavily weighted toward Asia and away from Latin America. Fund location matters in the allocation of capital to emerging markets.

PREFERENCES OF INSTITUTIONAL INVESTORS: STABILITY OVER DEMOCRACY

US President Bill Clinton, in his second inaugural address, proclaimed that today 'democracy and open markets are on the march together.'[18] In a brief survey of some of the key participants in this 'march' international institutional investors, a different picture emerges. Stability and a consistently investor-friendly financial infrastructure are two of the primary criteria investors seek when investing in emerging markets, often at the expense of political democracy.

How emerging market fund managers choose where to invest can be a complex process. Once the decision has been made to allocate to the emerging markets, the 'pull' factors are assessed. Macroanalysis, or the top-down approach, surveys the macroeconomic and political risk factors of countries and determines investment allocations accordingly. Microanalysis, or the bottom-up approach, focuses on company and industry statistics. It would typically include such indicators as the price-to-earnings ratio and an assessment of corporate management. Macro-factors are the main determinants of country choice. The preferences of emerging market investors can be derived from a variety of sources. Two of the most prominent of these sources are investor advisory publications for emerging markets and direct statements from emerging market fund managers. The examples that follow, though anecdotal, are cumulatively quite revealing.

In his 1995 publication, '*The Handbook of Emerging Markets*,' Robert Lloyd George listed several 'requirements needed for a successful emerging market' (George, 1995, p. 13). In order, the first three of these are political stability, sound currency, and low inflation. The next seven elements focus on legal, accounting, and transparency issues for foreign investors. Using these guidelines, George advises investment in Asia because of its population size, political stability, and low inflation. He also highlighted the advantages of privatization to international investors by listing three of its achievements. The first, the reduction of government deficit, falls perhaps most clearly into the category of economic reform. The second and third advantages, however, have more direct consequences for political democracy. The creation of first-time shareholders was important to George because this new class would 'tend to vote for pro-business and conservative policies' while the third advantage was that privatization 'diminishes the power of trade unions' (George, 1995, p. 17). George clearly illustrates a common preference for political conservatism over workers' rights.

Another publication, *New World Business*, offered investors an analysis of what makes an emerging market successful. Published by Euromoney Publications and Worldlink in association with several large banks, this edited volume began its overview of emerging markets with a comparison of alternative economic reform strategies. Comparing shock therapy to gradual reform, Fiona Jebb applauded the successes of China's gradual reform measures and the country's emphasis on economic, not political, reform. She questioned whether 'democracy is a help or a hindrance to economic reform processes' (Jebb, 1995, p. 10).

Another source of advice to investors interested in the emerging markets is the academic business journals. Writing in the *Columbia Journal of World Business*, Mark Hartmann and Dara Khambata listed three categories of risk/return determinants in the emerging markets: changes in economic policy, external factors, and political risk. The first category highlights the importance of a government's ability to implement long-term economic reform and liberalization of foreign portfolio investment. They cite Nigeria's inability to implement its Structural Adjustment Program quickly as a reason for a 56 per cent decline in its equity markets in 1986. However, 'once these reforms had been successfully implemented, the stock market rose, ending the year with a 40.9 per cent return' (Hartmann and Khambata, 1993; p. 92). What the authors fail to mention is the manner in which many of these reforms were implemented. Under the military rule of President Ibrahim Babangida, there was mounting domestic opposition to the reforms, accompanied by increased pressure from the international financial institutions. In order to implement reforms the regime 'resorted to repression...[and] the human rights cloak worn by the regime at its inception in 1985 became increasingly ill-fitting' (Herbst and Olukoshi, 1994, p. 494). Hartmann and Khambata also note that the 'long-term nature of equity investment implies a necessity for political stability' (1993; p. 93).

A second means of assessing the preferences of top emerging market managers is through their direct statements. Clinton's inaugural statement echoes the neoliberal tenet that democratization and open markets are natural partners. Meanwhile, a common hope of policymakers in new democracies has been that once a country adopts a constitution and holds elections, foreign investment will follow. Top investment managers may find such sentiments naïve. Mark Mobius, for example, recommends that investors look for good economic indicators and ignore the absence of democracy, citing Singapore as an example of a good investment location, despite its absence of 'Western-style democracy' (Mobius, 1995, p. 122). Mobius also offers guidance to investors in prominent business publications. In an interview with *Fortune*, he suggested that buying into a country when it is in turmoil might be the best strategy, because other investors might be avoiding it for this reason. 'Buy when blood is running in the streets' he urged.[19] On another occasion, he recommended investing in Nigeria despite unrest stemming from a military takeover. 'Sure Nigeria is a mess' Mobius said cheerfully, 'but we have a saying that by the time you see the light at the end of the tunnel, chances are it's too late' (cited in Cox, 1997, p. 2).

Yet another example of a leading investor's ambivalent attitude towards democracy was evident in the remarks of Rimmer de Vries, Senior Vice President and Chief Economist for Morgan Guaranty Trust, who noted worriedly:

> [An] additional deterrent to foreign...investment...in heavily indebted LDC's [less developed countries]...is heightened uncertainty associated with transition to more representative forms of government, whether in Latin America or the Philippines. The new democracies have sought to revise laws and practices put into place by dictatorial regimes in the 1960s and 1970s and, in so doing, have opened protracted debates of private property rights and the participation of foreign capital. (de Vries, 1990, p. 97)

De Vries cited Brazil as the 'most lamentable case' because of the drafting of its new 1988 constitution, which had 'greatly upset the business climate' and noted the counter-example of military-ruled Chile in the 1970s and early 1980s, a country that, in his opinion, had made all the right decisions to enhance its investment potential (de Vries, 1990, p. 97). Not surprisingly, foreign direct investment in Chile increased from $70 million in 1983 to over $1 billion in 1988, two years prior to its 1990 transition to democracy (Wallace, 1990; p. 100).

In addition to these emerging market fund managers, other players in the emerging markets investment field have been explicit in their preference for stability. A fund manager for one of the largest insurance companies recently wrote, '...The operative word here is, of course, stable. Just how much stability is there in a private power project in an emerging country? Many lenders look to sovereign governments to ease their anxieties...' (Perry, 1994; p. 24). Finally, in one of the most publicized expressions of preference for stability over democracy, a prominent political scientist working as an investment consultant for Chase Manhattan outlined an alarming set of prescriptions for the government of Mexican President Ernesto Zedillo in the tense days following the peso devaluation of December 1994. Riordan Roett's injudicious letter to Chase's clients seemed to advocate armed repression of the Chiapas rebels, fixing elections, and stricter control over labor unions (Cockburn and Silverstein, 1995). At the very least, we can conclude that the global private investment community is quite wary of democratic transitions, fearing that their consequences will include political instability and poorer macroeconomic policy decisions.

CONCLUSIONS

In this chapter, I have argued that the shift in the composition of global capital flows towards flows controlled by private institutional investors has ushered in a new regime of power that is organized by the perceptions and goals of a few large emerging market managers. I have found that these institutional investors are relatively few in number, show signs of coordination and have the capacity, singly and as a unit, to impact the capital flows to developing countries. This power, a distortion to a fair and efficient market system, carries with it the ability to reward and punish developing countries according to their ability to implement and maintain economic reforms beneficial to foreign investors. Moreover, emerging market fund managers frequently value stability over political democracy. Investors, attracted to those countries that rapidly implement and maintain intense economic reforms while simultaneously controlling political opposition to these measures, may continue to find political democracy not only unnecessary, but perhaps even contrary to their interests.

Notes

1. Figures in this paragraph are from IFC, 1995, and World Bank, 1995.
2. Garber (1990) argues that in the case of the tulip mania the market as a whole did not actually exhibit irrational pricing. For a survey of rational herding literature, see Devenow and Welch (1995). Mader and Hagin (1983) defend the random walk hypothesis by disputing studies that show predictabililty in price change volatility.

3. Any type of stock selection analysis is an argument against the random walkers. For critiques of the random walk theory, see Fosback (1995) and Bernstein (1995).
4. See Howell (1993, pp. 81–82) for a model formulated to take advantage of emerging stock market inefficiencies.
5. Other factors contributing to inefficiency are the relative illiquidity of emerging stock markets, the lack of a well-developed legal system to enforce market rules and the looser accounting standards often present in these markets. See Kumar (1994).
6. For example, the United States' Securities and Exchange Commission (SEC) Rule 144A has loosened restrictions for developing-country borrowing, thus increasing the portfolio outflows for the US to these countries.
7. McLeod and Welch (1991), as cited in Maxfield and Hoffman (1994).
8. Hardouvelis, La Porta and Wizman (1994).
9. On push factors, see Hardouvelis, La Porta and Wizman (1994), McLeod and Welch (1991), and Tesar and Werner (1993).
10. This is the International Finance Corporation's Composite (IFCC) index. For a list of countries, see IFC (1996).
11. This does not include all emerging market funds available to investors. It does, however, represent a significant number of both major and minor funds within the US and Europe.
12. These funds are specifically mandated for investing in emerging market countries. Other funds, such as international funds and global funds, may invest in emerging market countries but invest in other countries as well – thus making it difficult to break down the amounts flowing specifically to emerging market countries. However, it should be noted that many of the global and international funds are run by the same institutions and research departments that control the emerging market funds. Information from Reuters 1996.
13. The institutions controlling the largest portions of the Asian funds were, in order, T. Rowe Price (26 per cent), Merrill Lynch (21.6 per cent) and Fidelity (12.1 per cent). For Latin America, the major investors are Merrill Lynch (27 per cent), Fidelity (16.5 per cent), and BEA (15.8 per cent). The figures come from Trustnet, an investment advisory service. Country funds were not included in this analysis.
14. For more information on how coordination or market inefficiencies function, see Devenow and Welch (1995), Hirschleifer (1994), and Haley (1996).
15. My methods were as follows. First, the geographic allocations of 18 emerging market mutual funds were compared. The funds were divided into two groups, those based in the US and those based in Europe. All funds based in the US are traded on the New York exchange and nine of the 10 European funds are traded on the London exchange. These funds, all under the investment category of 'emerging markets' growth funds, are equity funds with the same investment objectives. The portfolio compositions analyzed are all from 1996 second quarter semi-annual reports which come out at the end of June.

    Two tests were performed to see if fund location influenced the country allocation of the funds. The first test was simply a comparison of the mean allocations per country by location. For instance, if country A received a greater average allocation from US-based funds, this would indicate that the location of the fund might have impacted the portfolio choices of the managers. Next, the average of correlations on country allocations between all of funds should be approximately equal to the average of correlations on country allocations between funds traded in New York or those traded outside of New York.

Similarly, the average of country allocation correlations between funds traded in New York should be approximately equal to those funds traded outside of New York. This second test compares the average correlations between fund locations.

16. It should be noted that this does not necessarily mean there was nothing allocated to these countries since the figures are based on the top ten holdings. If all holdings were included these percentages would change slightly.

17. These figures represent Tokyo's total investments, not just those of their emerging market funds.

18. 4 February 1997.

19. *Fortune*, Vol. 130, 31 October 1994, p. 54.

Bibliography

Bernstein, Peter (ed.) (1995) *The Portable MBA* (New York: John Wiley).

Bloomberg c/o Technimetrics, Inc. (1996), on-line financial services data.

Claessens, Stijn and Sudarshan Goopta (eds) (1993) *Portfolio Investment in Developing Countries* (Washington, D.C.: The World Bank).

Cockburn, Alexander and Ken Silverstein (1995) 'The Demands of Capital', in *Harper's Magazine*, 290 (1740), May, pp. 66–67.

Cox, James (1997) 'The king of the emerging markets funds', reprint of article originally published in *USA Today*, posted by Lipper Analytical Services on Templeton's website: *www.franklin-templeton.com*.

Devenow, Andrea and Ivo Welch (1995) 'Rational Herding in Financial Economics', Finance Working Paper, The Anderson Graduate School of Management at the University of California, Los Angeles.

de Vries, Rimmer (1990) 'Foreign direct investment in heavily indebted developing countries: a view from the financial community', in Cynthia Day (ed.), *Foreign direct investment in the 1990s: A New Climate in the Third World* (The Netherlands: Martinus Nijhoff).

Diamond, Douglas W. and Robert E. Verrecchia (1981) 'Information aggregation in a noisy rational expectations model', *Journal of Financial Economics*, 9(3), pp. 221–36.

Friedman, Milton (1962) *Capitalism and Freedom* (Chicago: University of Chicago Press).

Fosback, Norman G. (1995) *Stock Market Logic* (Dearborn, Mich.: Dearborn Financial Publishing, Inc).

Garber, Peter (1990) 'Famous first bubbles', *Journal of Economic Perspectives*, 4(2), pp. 35–54.

George, Robert Lloyd (1993) *The Handbook of the Emerging Markets: A Country-by-Country Guide to the World's Fastest Growing Economies* (Chicago: Probus).

Grossman, Sanford J. and Joseph E. Stiglitz (1976) 'Information and competitive price systems', *American Economic Review*, 66(2), pp. 246–53.

Haley, Mary Ann (1996) 'Freedom and Finance: Portfolio Flows and Democratization in the Emerging Markets', Paper presented at the Western Meetings of the Political Science Association, San Francisco, April.

Hardouvelis, Gikas, Rafael La Porta, and Thierry Wizman (1994) 'What moves the discount on country equity funds?', in Jeffrey A. Frankel (ed.), *Internationalization of equity markets* (Cambridge, Mass.: National Bureau of Economic Research (NBER), pp. 345–97.

Hartmann, Mark and Dara Khambata (1993) 'Emerging stock markets' *The Columbia Journal of World Business* 29(2) (Summer); pp. 83–103.

Hayek, Friedrich (1944) *The road to serfdom* (Chicago: University of Chicago Press).

Herbst, Jeffrey and Adebayo Olukoshi (1994) 'Nigeria: economic and political reforms at cross purposes', in Stephan Haggard and Steven B. Webb (eds), *Voting for Reform* (Oxford: Oxford University Press).

Hirschleifer, David (1994) 'The blind leading the blind: social influence, fads and informational cascades, Finance Working Paper at the Anderson School of Management, UCLA.

Howell, Michael J. (1993) 'Institutional investors and emerging stock markets', in Stijn Claessens and Sudarshan Goopta (eds), *Portfolio Investment in Developing Countries* (Washington D.C.: World Bank).

International Finance Corporation (1995 and 1996) *Emerging Stock Markets Factbook* (Washington, D.C.: International Finance Corporation).

—— (1996) *Monthly Review of Emerging Markets* (Washington, D.C.: International Finance Corporation), May.

International Monetary Fund (1995) *Private Market Financing for Developing Countries* (Washington, D.C.: International Monetary Fund).

—— (1994) *Balance of Payment Statistics Yearbook* (Washington, D.C.: International Monetary Fund).

Jebb, Fiona 1995 'The challenges of economic change', in Lance Knobel (ed.), *New World Business* (London: Euromoney Publications and World Link), pp. 8–10.

Kumar, P. C. (1994) 'Inefficiencies from financial liberalization in the absence of well-functioning equity markets', in *Journal of Money, Credit and Banking*, 26(2), May, pp. 341–4.

Lee, Shelly A. (1995) 'A world of opportunity', *Pension Management*, 31 (6), June, pp. 14–33.

McLeod, Darryl and John H. Welch (1991) 'North American Free Trade and the Peso', *Federal Reserve Bank of Dallas Working Paper*, no. 9115.

Mader, Chris and Robert Hagin, (1983) *Dow Jones – Irwin Guide to Common Stocks* (Homewood, Ill.: Dow Jones-Irwin).

Malkiel, Burton (1973) *A Random Walk down Wall Street* (New York: W. W. Norton).

Malkiel, Burton G. (1982) *The Inflation Beater's Investment Guide* (NewYork: W. W. Norton).

Maxfield, Sylvia and Joshua Hoffman (1995) International portfolio flows to developing/transitional economies: impact on government policy choice', Paper presented at the Workshop on 'Financial Globalization and Emerging Markets: Policy Autonomy, Democratization and the Lessons from Mexico', Watson Institute of International Studies, Brown University, 18–19 November.

Mobius, Mark (1995) *The investor's guide to emerging markets* (Burr Ridge, Ill. and New York: Irwin Publishing).

Moran, Theodore (ed.) (1986), *Investing in development: new roles for private capital?* (Washington DC: Overseas Development Council).

Perry, Christopher (1994) 'Hot new funds look for high yields', *Infrastructure Finance*, 3(3) (June/July); pp. 19–24.

Reuters (1996) *Reuters Money Network Research Data*, Research data base on CD-Rom, 30 June.

Spragins, Ellyn E. and Daniel McGinn (1995) 'Spanning the globe', in *Newsweek*, 3407 (13 February); p. 52.

Tesar, Linda and Ingrid Werner (1993) 'US Equity Investment in Emerging Stock Markets', in S. Claessens and S. Goopta (eds), *Portfolio Investment in Developing Countries* (Washington, D.C.: The World Bank).

Trustnet (1996) Website for unit trust information, *www.trustnet.co.uk*, London, UK.

Wallace, Cynthia Day (1990) *Foreign direct investment in the 1990s: a new climate in the third world* (The Netherlands: Martinus Nijhoff Publishers).

World Bank (1996) *World Debt Tables* (Washington, D.C.: The World Bank).

4 The Transnational Agenda for Financial Regulation in Developing Countries
Tony Porter

Often global finance is portrayed as involving on the one hand individual states, the locus of political authority, and on the other hand billions of dispersed intangible private financial transactions, the locus of market forces. This *states versus financial markets* dualism underestimates the important political role played by international institutions in bringing about and regulating the globalization of finance. Analyzing the impact of these international institutions on citizens and governments is an important part of better understanding the relationship between financial globalization and democracy in emerging markets.

Because of this chapter's international focus, its treatment of democracy differs in a key respect from that in other chapters. When we shift to the international level, an approach to democracy that stresses such criteria as the competitiveness of party systems or the existence of well-defined civil liberties becomes inadequate. In part this is because these indicators of democracy are properties of states and therefore much less relevant in analyzing the functioning of international institutions. Relatedly, but even more importantly, if the sole mechanism for citizens' expression of their political preferences remains the nation-state, then the migration of decision-making to the international level can restrict the range of issues which are legitimately the subject of public debate. As Held (1995, p. 16) has put it, democratic theory's traditional assumption that there is an asymmetrical and congruent relationship between political decision-makers and the recipients of political decisions may no longer be valid.[1] In looking at the international level, then, we need to add a concern about whether international institutions, in a process exogenous to conventional democratic decision-making, are excessively limiting the scope of that decision-making – a concern which cannot be addressed by simply focusing on the process by which decisions are made at the domestic level.

In this chapter I choose as well to examine two other ways in which the strengthening of the international institutions regulating private cross-border financial flows can affect democracy by setting boundaries on the scope of democratic deliberation and decision-making. The first of these is the tendency in the international institutions regulating global finance to treat issues with public policy implications as merely technical. Technical complexity, simply because of challenges in grasping the issues at stake, can make it difficult for citizens and political leaders to monitor and influence a decision-making process. This is reinforced by a normative proscription: technical issues are seen as properly the preserve of experts and best kept insulated from political interference.[2] The second is the emergence of private international institutions which exercise the type of rule-making and market-shaping authority which would conventionally be associated with states (see Cutler, Haufler, and Porter, eds. forthcoming). Such a shift from the public to the private can make it appear that citizens and political leaders have no need or right to be involved in the decisions being made or to hold decision-makers accountable, even if such decisions would have been seen as part of a public policy process in previous historical periods or in other settings.

The above concerns, while relevant to citizens and political leaders in all countries, are especially important for the developing countries in which emerging markets are located, because the resources that come more into play when boundaries around the scope of democratic deliberation constrict are so unequally distributed internationally. A migration in decision-making from the state to an international institution is of concern not just because of the potential autonomy and remoteness of the institution, but also because international relations has traditionally been the location in which might makes right, and in which the most powerful states unabashedly seek to promote their interests, relatively unconstrained by the moral and legal obligations associated with democracy. International institutions can be a vehicle for the practice of power politics. A shift in the other boundaries can similarly benefit those powerful states which enjoy a disproportionate share of the world's private organizational capacity and technical and legal expertise.

While there are good reasons to take seriously the above concerns about the relationship between the international institutions regulating private cross-border financial flows and democracy, it is also possible that this relationship is neutral or beneficial. Three reasons not to be concerned suggest themselves. First, the international institutions may be so weak that they are irrelevant. Second, even if these institutions play a significant role there might be more opportunity for democratic input than would be suggested by the above paragraphs. These institutions may simply aggregate the preferences of their member states, allowing citizens to transmit their preferences to these institutions and offsetting concerns about the migration of decision-making up from the state. Citizens may even be able to band together with like-minded counterparts in other countries and may be better able to influence policy at the international level than the domestic, particularly if their government is unreceptive to citizen input. The codification of expectations which comes with the institutionalization of authority at the international level may increase transparency and therefore the ability of citizens and political leaders to monitor and participate in decisions. Codified expectations may also constrain power politics. A third reason to dismiss concerns about international institutions would hold if the matters with which they deal are indeed not public policy issues, either because they are properly private or because they are purely technical. Some would argue that technical rules have a mutually reinforcing relationship with international market forces and as such they expand the potential for the commercial initiatives of private citizens, an expression of freedom, and weaken the inherently oppressive interference of states.

Based on such considerations, three types of evidence are needed to assess the impact of the international institutions which regulate private cross-border financial flows on democracy. First, we need to assess the degree to which there is independent policy-making capacity lodged in international institutions. If there is none then they can either be treated as irrelevant or as simply expressing the underlying policies of their member states. Second, we need to examine the opportunity for citizens and political leaders to monitor and influence the policy-making process at the international level, paying special attention to the role and influence of representatives of developing countries relative to those of developed countries. Third, we need to assess the degree to which decisions made in international institutions are, in effect, matters of public policy as opposed to matters of concern only to experts or private parties. The next three sections examine three key issue areas: bank regulation, securities regulation, and the liberalization of financial services trade and investment flows. I then briefly consider the degree to which public policy-making capacity has been displaced by private international institutions.

INTERNATIONAL BANK REGULATION

The strengthening of international bank regulation has been primarily carried out through the Basle Committee on Banking Supervision (see Basle Committee, various years, and Porter, 1993). The Basle Committee, consisting of bank regulators from the G-10 countries plus Luxembourg, was set up by the G-10 central bank governors[3] in 1974 in response to bank crises involving inadequate control and monitoring of international transactions. Broadly speaking, the accomplishments of the Basle Committee are of two types. The first is the establishment of a division of labor and agreed general principles for the regulation of multinational banks. The adoption of consolidated supervision in a 1983 Concordat required a home regulator to obtain information on, and supervise, all the operations of the banks headquartered in its jurisdiction. This concordat clarified the division of responsibilities among regulators and reduced the ability of banks to escape regulation by shifting funds to more lightly regulated jurisdictions. This policy was reinforced in 1992 by the adoption of a set of standards for adequate supervision and by commitments by home and host regulators to refuse entry by banks into markets that did not meet these standards.

The second major accomplishment of the Basle Committee was to agree upon a fairly complex and specific set of common standards for bank capital in July 1988. These standards were based on risk-weighted capital–asset ratios which enhance stability of banks by (a) limiting the growth of loans and other assets by requiring banks to maintain a certain level of capital relative to those assets;[4] (b) shifting more of the responsibility and cost for monitoring riskiness to shareholders by increasing the amount of their capital that is available to offset problems with solvency; and (c) forcing banks to hold more capital to offset the greater riskiness of some types of assets. These standards have been implemented in all countries with significant international banking activity. It is now widely recognized and accepted by the Basle Committee itself, however, that the original capital standards were too crude. The Committee is therefore is developing a new policy which allows banks to use data generated by their own internal risk-management systems in the determination of the minimum levels of capital which they must maintain. This revolves around the concept of 'value-at-risk': the bank's estimate of its maximum loss over a given time period. Required capital levels will be a multiple of this value-at-risk. The multiple will be increased for banks which underestimate their value-at-risk over time. Banks can choose to be regulated under conventional capital adequacy standards if the development of internal risk-management systems is too costly or difficult.

There are a number of ways in which the Basle Committee displays a substantial autonomous policy-making capacity at the international level. First, the policies that it has developed are not insignificant: many banks have experienced difficulty in complying with the Basle Committee's standards and substantial alterations in national regulations have been required, but nevertheless compliance has been widespread. Indeed, there is widespread acknowledgement that the Committee has had significant success in arresting the downward trend in bank regulatory standards, often thought to be irreversible in our contemporary period of high capital mobility and jurisdictions competing to entice banks with light regulations. Second, despite its lack of formal organizational structure, certain features of the Committee's process, most notably its secrecy, its esprit de corps, and the high degree of technical complexity of its work has allowed it to insulate itself from political oversight. For instance, a General Accounting Office team mandated by the US Congress was unable to get access to a significant number of Basle Committee documents (Porter, 1993). Third, in more than two decades of operation the Committee has initiated numerous highly technical policy studies which have in turn fed into revisions of its existing policy – an important sign of autonomy in policy-making.

The emerging process of international bank regulation organized around the Basle Committee displays features which are problematic with regard to democracy. First, it is clear that the developing countries are marginalized in the Basle Committee's process. The Basle Committee, the membership of which is restricted to the G-10 countries plus Luxembourg, has fostered the creation of groups of bank supervisors from countries outside the G-10. These include the Offshore Group, consisting of smaller banking centres such as the Bahamas and the Cayman Islands, many of which had been seen as lightly regulated jurisdications which banks could use to escape regulations. There were also, as of 1994, seven other regional supervisory groups covering emerging markets around the world such as the Group of Banking Supervision Officials in Arab Countries. While there is some two-way communication between these groups and the Basle Committee, descriptions of the emerging market groups make clear that their primary purpose is to discuss the implementation of procedures developed in the Basle Committee itself. Tacit threats to exclude foreign banks from the markets of Basle Committee members have contributed to the spread of compliance with the Committee's standards beyond its membership. The Basle Committee's secrecy and the high degree of technical complexity of its work make it difficult for concerned outsiders to monitor its policy process.

Lack of democracy in the formulation of international bank regulations would not be problematic if its work was merely technical or of concern only to its G-10 regulators but there are several indications that this is not the case. First, the agreement on capital adequacy further reduced the availability of credit from commercial banks, already restricted in response to the debt crisis. Banks were generally required to hold substantially more capital for key claims against all less developed country (LDC) governments and banks as compared to claims against OECD governments and banks. This OECD/non-OECD distinction has been criticized by offshore regulators (Basle Committee, 1994, p. 106).[5] Second, the ability of offshore financial centers to attract business by offering lighter regulation, a development strategy for some developing countries, has been ended. While there is little disagreement that there was a need for stronger regulation, offshore regulators have criticized the tendency of home regulators to reject strengthened offshore regulatory regulations merely because they are different. (Basle Committee, 1994, p. 105). Third, the extension of the capital adequacy agreement to cover new kinds of risk, and the move to allow the use of more sophisticated hedging strategies and risk-assessment techniques, increases the competitive advantage of banks from markets in which knowledge of those strategies and techniques are more developed. It also increases the attractiveness to banks of sophisticated markets with derivatives that can be used for such hedging, markets which are located in the G-10 countries.

Fourth, the stability of the banking system has emerged as a major constraint for emerging market states attempting to deal with surges in cross-border capital flows and the present Basle standards appear to offer little assistance in this regard (IMF, 1995, pp. 8, 120–7). The present direction of the Basle Committee's policies – which focuses on the solutions offered by, and health of, the world's most sophisticated derivatives markets and banks – inadequately addresses the risks present in emerging markets. For instance almost all Mexican banks met current Basle standards before the late 1994 crisis. Fifth, the standards promoted by the Basle Committee may be poorly suited to the needs of microfinancing institutions, a type of community banking involving very small loans to the poorest people, mostly women, in developing countries, despite the growth of these institutions in size and recognition. For instance, an officer of BancoSol, one such microfinance institution located in Bolivia, notes that Basle-mandated capital levels for the banks serving wealthier clientele can be reduced by having loans secured by home mortgages, but BancoSol serves a client base that cannot offer traditional guarantees. While BancoSol has demonstrated that the solidarity group guarantee and sequential lending produce extremely low default rates the national regulator considers such loans to be secured only by personal guarantees (Krutzfeldt, 1996, pp. 3–4). Sixth, and finally, the Basle Committee has drawn on its regulatory capacity, at the behest of the United States which was concerned about the drug trade, to contribute to control of money laundering. Simultaneously, the committee explicitly considered and rejected the extension of its work to cover tax-evasion related problems, a project which would have been particularly useful to developing countries (UNCTAD, 1993; Freeland, 1994, pp. 231–40).[6]

Even those expressing concern about these six issues do not generally intend to suggest that developing countries would be better off without the enhanced capacity for international cooperation on bank regulation that the Basle Committee represents. Taken as a whole, however, the six concerns indicate that the lack of democracy in international bank regulation has negative consequences for developing countries relative to an alternative scenario in which institutional mechanisms existed for those developing countries to play a bigger role in shaping the regulatory agenda.

INTERNATIONAL SECURITIES REGULATION

The leading forum for the negotiation of global securities regulation is the International Organization of Securities Commissions (IOSCO) in Montreal, the membership of which includes 115 state and non-state securities regulators.[7] Promotion of emerging markets has always been an important focus of IOSCO's work, especially between 1974, when it was founded as the Inter-American Association of Securities Commissions, and 1983 when it adopted its present name and global aspirations. Presently its Emerging Markets Committee is primarily responsible for emerging market issues, although the work of IOSCO's most important body, the Technical Committee, also is significant. The Emerging Markets Committee's mission is formally defined as being 'the development and improvement of efficiency of emerging markets by establishing principles and minimum standards, preparing training programs for the personnel of members, and facilitating the exchange of information, transfer of technology, and expertise' (IOSCO, 1994, p. 10).The most concrete accomplishment of IOSCO is the establishment of principles for the proliferating bilateral memoranda of understanding for sharing information between regulators and preventing cross-border fraud (Porter, 1993). In 1994, IOSCO initiated a programme of surveillance of its members' commitments to information-sharing.

International securities markets have always tended to rely more heavily on private self-regulatory arrangements than is the case for international banking. The International Federation of Stock Exchanges (known by its French acronym FIBV) sees itself as working with the regulators at IOSCO but at the same time as countering excessive state regulation by fostering private self-regulatory initiatives (FIBV, 1995; Millspaugh, 1992). The FIBV also works on common concerns with its regional counterparts, the African Stock Exchange Association, the Federacion Ibero-Americana de Bolsas de Valores, the Federation of European Stock Exchanges, and the East Asian and Oceania Stock Exchange Federation. These organizations are also concerned with promoting the advantages of organized exchanges as compared to over the counter (OTC) markets. The shared commitments which the FIBV represents are remarkably formalized, including 22 statutes; 19 internal rules organized into 5 articles; 'General Accepted Principles with Respect to Securities Trading' which were adopted in 1988 with which all members must comply; 'Generally Accepted Principles of Securities Business Conduct 1992'; and six organized committees and subcommittees. The role of the FIBV in emerging markets is in a statement by captured its President, Jean-François Théodore, '1994 was the right year for the FIBV to take the lead in applying the framework of regulated markets to emerging ones...Many of the emerging stock exchanges were seeking the international recognition provided by an admission to the FIBV' (FIBV, 1995, p. 5).

While institutional arrangements for the international regulation of securities markets are not as developed as for banking there is nevertheless a growing institutional capacity as represented by the work of IOSCO and the FIBV. Like bank regulation it is clear that the process is effectively controlled by regulators from the developed markets. In IOSCO, despite a formal structure in which all member countries are treated as equals, most new initiatives originate in the Technical Committee, which is dominated by regulators from developed markets. The US Securities and Exchange Commission (SEC) has played a particularly prominent role. For instance, the memoranda of understanding (MOU) principles that have been codified at IOSCO are essentially a summary of the common principles of a series of bilateral MOUs which the US SEC initiated (Porter, 1993). An effort to coordinate rules on securities prospectuses, which has been less successful, followed a similar pattern, with it being envisioned that negotiations initiated among the US, the UK and Canada would set out a model which could be further multilateralized.[8] In the case of the FIBV the process is similar to that for banking regulation: the FIBV's regional counterparts in emerging markets primarily implement standards and practices established in the FIBV.

International securities regulation tends to be more open than banking regulation, as is the case traditionally at the domestic level as well. Nevertheless obstacles exist for concerned citizens and political leaders wishing to monitor the policy process. For instance, securities regulators deliberately adopted MOUs rather than treaties in part to avoid the surveillance by legislators that comes with the latter. Once established, the MOUs' information sharing frameworks can be the basis of a sustained cooperative but confidential relationship between regulators. The highly technical language in which international securities regulations are developed and negotiated, as in banking, acts as a further barrier to the flow of information.

Imbalances between emerging and developed markets in the policy process are hardly surprising given the smaller size and shorter history of emerging securities markets. Indeed, to the extent that regulators from developed markets are merely sharing valuable and universal lessons, or that they are developing regulations that only affect their own jurisdictions and constituencies, then it is only proper that they retain control of the process. However, while this is the case in part, there are also reasons to be concerned at the effect on emerging markets of their subordinate position in these arrangements.

A first reason to be concerned is that regulatory infrastructure and practices for globalized securities markets are being constructed in relative isolation from other policy processes. This may be fine for developed markets that are integrated into well established social and political institutions. It can be problematic, however, when market practices are transferred internationally into emerging markets where such institutions may not exist. An example is the lack of coordination between banking and securities regulators at the Basle Committee and IOSCO, on the one hand, and the trade negotiators who produced the North American Free Trade Agreement

(NAFTA) on the other (Porter, 1997). The only additional international regulatory capacity put into place by the NAFTA, the Financial Services Committee, was relatively inactive and primarily concerned with the resolution of disputes under the agreement rather than the stability of financial systems and firms. However, it was to be expected that the liberalization of access to Mexican financial markets that came with the NAFTA, combined with the new respectability and prominence bestowed on them by the agreement, would lead to dramatic financial inflows. The bulk of these inflows were portfolio investments, organized by firms that had been accustomed to relying on the transparency of US securities markets and these markets' ability to support diversified portfolios and rapid high-volume trading as a way of controlling risk. These features of US markets were not present in Mexico. This contributed to the markets' excessive optimism initially, and then to excessive pessimism once the December 1994 crisis had started, leading to financial volatility with disastrous consequences for the Mexican economy. Additionally, the vulnerability of the banking sector, which became painfully evident once interest rates were raised to defend the peso, was not considered in the negotiation of financial liberalization under the NAFTA.

This Mexican example refers to the danger of separating a financial regulatory policy process and a trade liberalization process, but there are other risks for emerging markets associated with an excessively narrow focus in international securities regulation. Traditionally in countries with financial systems in which competitive securities markets played a big role, the negative social consequences associated with such markets have been addressed by regulation, facilitated by a democratic deliberative process. A key example is the New Deal financial regulation in the US which responded to excessive concentrations of economic power that had been associated with US securities markets in the 1920s (Roe, 1994). More recently such centralized regulatory initiatives have been regarded with scepticism in the US, but this does not mean that mechanisms for offsetting the negative social consequences of securities markets do not exist. Instead this function has been accomplished by the rapid expansion of rights, via the so-called 'rights revolution,' which has involved a substantial limitation of the rights of shareholders and the expansion of rights of other 'stakeholders' in corporations. This system of individual rights enforceable through the court system is well-suited to the US culture but would be less likely to succeed in less litigious and individual rights-oriented cultures. The current narrowness of the international securities regulation policy process tends to encourage the expansion of US-style securities markets in developing countries without the corresponding mechanisms for offsetting the negative social consequences of those markets.

There is another way in which the current process for international securities regulation may underestimate the disadvantages of competitive securities markets for developing countries. Even in the United States a vigorous debate in the United States over the potential negative impact of competitive capital markets on 'short-termism' – the short time horizons for investment and on corporate governance in general – has engaged major political and academic figures (Jacobs, 1991; Porter, 1992). No such debate has occurred with respect to international financial regulation despite the possibility that a greater reliance on intrafirm and tacit institutional linkages between firms might be justifiable on efficiency grounds in emerging markets.[9] The narrow focus on international securities regulation contributes to this lack of debate.

Emerging markets can also be disadvantaged by the adoption of increasingly complex market-based solutions for coping with risk (such as ever more complex derivatives) because these will inevitably confer an advantage on firms based in national markets that have specialized in these techniques.[10] The negotiations in IOSCO over capital adequacy standards for securities firms are deadlocked over this issue as neither the more market-based jurisdictions (the US and the UK) nor the universal banking countries that rely on internal risk-management techniques, were willing to adapt to the other's system. The prominence of the developed countries in this conflict does not indicate that such conflicts are irrelevant for the emerging markets – rather it indicates the difficulty for the emerging markets of formulating and promoting a position in matters that are highly technical, in fora that are dominated by the developed markets, and in an issue area where their own institutions are in a process of rapid change. Ironically the US has been glacially slow in altering key features of its domestic regulatory regime (such as prohibitions on inter-state branching and links between banks and securities firms) despite their negative effects on foreign firms. The SEC has recently expressed concern about the effects of foreign ownership of US securities firms (Acworth, 1995, p.1). Similarly, the international promotion of strengthened insider trading regulations, an apparently technical regulatory initiative, can be seen as conferring a direct commercial benefit on the securities firms that sell the information that the state forces out of informal intra-corporate networks into markets (Haddock and Macey, 1987, pp. 311–39).

THE LIBERALIZATION OF FINANCIAL SERVICES TRADE AND INVESTMENT FLOWS

A third international financial regulatory arena comprises initiatives to liberalize global trade in financial services. A key change in the organization of international financial markets since World World II has been the increased ease with which firms and flows can cross borders. In part this is driven by the increased technological and organizational capacity of market actors. Many states have also unilaterally increased foreign access to their domestic financial markets in order to attract financial flows or to increase efficiency and reduce costs in their financial systems through exposing domestic firms to competitive pressures. With respect to international institutions and emerging markets, however, the most significant sites for negotiating these changes have been the North American Free Trade Agreement, the Uruguay Round of the General Agreement on Tariffs and Trade (GATT) and an emerging set of arrangements for regulating foreign investment flows. I begin by summarizing provisions of these agreements and then assess their relationship to democracy and emerging markets.

The NAFTA

The NAFTA, which formally came into being on 1 January 1994, is especially important because it represented the most ambitious attempt yet to integrate developed and emerging markets, and because of its role in the most severe crisis to date related to such integration, the peso crisis that began in December 1994 (see Gruben, Elizondo, and Molano in this volume). Moreover, US negotiators hoped that the NAFTA's unprecedented strengthening of investment provisions would become the model for other financial services negotiations, including those in the Uruguay Round.

The NAFTA expanded financial liberalization by guaranteeing the better of most-favored nation status or national treatment to financial firms, by expanding the right to sell financial services across borders, and by reducing restrictions on foreign ownership of banks. Signatories renounced the use of requirements on foreign investments to source locally, have nationals on boards of directors, meet export targets, or restrict repatriation of profits and capital. Mexico also modified its long standing position on national sovereignty with respect to expropriation, a position for which it had been the leading advocate in previous North–South negotiations, by agreeing that expropriation must be compensated promptly at 'fair market value' in convertible currency, precluding the use of arguments about rectifying past exploitative practices (Gantz, 1993, pp. 335–48).

One of the most remarkable features of the NAFTA is the provision, in Chapter 11, of the right for private investors to use binding arbitration to collect damages from or reverse decisions of states that do not comply. For the first time Canada and Mexico committed themselves to use the International Center for the Settlement of Investment Disputes at the World Bank, the dispute resolution process favored by the United States. Provisions for prudential regulation, including a new Financial Services Committee, appear to be surprisingly minimal given the increased systemic stress arising from heightened integration (Porter, 1997).

NAFTA's significance goes beyond its three current members because of the stated goal of bringing in other countries in the hemisphere and because

Mexico's key commitments on financial services were extended to the North American subsidiaries of non-NAFTA firms. This reinforces the degree to which it had already been seen as setting a new standard for emerging markets in joining the Organization for Economic Cooperation and Development and accepting that organization's commitments to the liberalization of capital movements (Poret, 1994, pp. 39–42).

Financial Services and the Uruguay Round

The commitments made to liberalization under the financial services negotiations in the Uruguay Round and subsequently in the World Trade Organization (WTO) are weaker than in the NAFTA but this is offset by the greater number of participants in the WTO. As with the NAFTA, the WTO commitments revolve around national treatment and most-favored nation principles. As with the NAFTA, the right of service providers to establish offices in host countries was expanded along with the strengthening of the rights of foreign investors in general. The General Agreement on Trade in Services established the right to the free flow of capital across borders where such a flow is an essential component of the provision of a service (Footer, 1993, pp. 356). Additionally the considerable strengthening of the dispute resolution process in the WTO (the shift towards requiring unanimity to stop rather than initiate a complaint, the establishment of shorter and more clearly defined schedules, and the creation of a quasi-judicial appellate body to hear appeals) will benefit financial sector participants affected by violations of WTO rules (Shell, 1995; Young, 1995).

Despite these similarities in the expansion of market access there are a number of ways in which the Uruguay Round financial services commitments are weaker. Unlike the NAFTA in which all services are included unless otherwise specified, the Uruguay Round commitments only apply to those specified in the agreement. Each country determined which of its services it wished to include. The greater disparity and numbers of participants in the Uruguay Round negotiations makes bargaining over these offers more difficult than was the case with the NAFTA (Broadman 1993). Like the NAFTA there is a 'prudential carve-out' in the Uruguay Round commitments which allows a country to control financial flows where the stability of its financial system is threatened. The effect of this on the liberalizing force of the agreement as a whole remains to be seen.

Commitments made during the Uruguay Round were provisional and it was clear at the Round's conclusion that further negotiation would take place. In July 1995 a new set of commitments were made, but the US decided not to participate in this package, claiming that it had not received adequate concessions from its negotiating partners, and indicating that the commitments it had made would not be applied to newcomers to its markets nor to new activities of foreign financial firms. This abandonment of the most-favored nation principle, combined with the apparent US intention to use bilateral bargaining to achieve its goals, led to widespread criticism of its conduct as destructive of fundamental WTO principles (Securities Regulation and Law Report, 1994; Yerkey, 1995; Banker 1993; *The Economist*, 1995).[11] The July 1995 commitments of other countries came into force in September 1996. Negotiations began on a subsequent package in April 1997 with the goal of having a final agreement, to include the US, by the end of that year.

The investment provisions in the Uruguay Round were weaker than in the NAFTA. There is no provision for dispute resolution between private investors and states and the standards for compensation of foreign investors are not as strong.[12] The prohibitions on restrictions on investment flows are not as broad as in the NAFTA or the investment agreements discussed in the next section, covering only investment measures directly related to trade and not other investment measures such as local equity participation or technology requirements. Only direct investment was addressed by the Uruguay Round, unlike the NAFTA which covers virtually all types of cross-border investments including portfolio flows (Osty and Winham, 1995, p. 78).

Investment Agreements

The outlines of an emerging multilateral regime for regulating cross-border investment flows are evident in the series of bilateral and regional investment treaties that now total more than 600 (Osty and Winham, 1995, p. 77) and most of which involve one industrialized and one developing country. The most comprehensive effort to date is the Multilateral Agreement on Investment negotiations in the OECD. The bilateral arrangements were initiated by the Europeans; it was not until the late 1970s that the US began developing its own program (Shenkin, 1994, pp. 573–82). The European agreements generally include reciprocal national and most favored nation treatment for existing investments and guarantee at least full compensation for nationalization. As of 1992 there were more than 400 of these European agreements. The US bilateral investment treaty (BIT) program seeks to go beyond the European one by covering the establishment of new investments and all investment measures. As of 1992, however, only 25 of these US BITs had been signed (Shenkin, 1994, p. 579). Despite this small number, they are significant because they are seen by the US government as expanding the basis in international law for an investment treaty along the lines preferred by the US (DeLuca, 1994). Both the Association of Southeast Asian Nations (ASEAN) and the Organization of the Islamic Conference have signed similar regional investment treaties (Shenkin, 1994). All these investment treaties generally provide for arbitration between investors and states at the

International Center for Settlement of Investment Disputes at the World Bank, creating considerably expanded rights for private investors relative to states. The US is aggressively using the BIT strategy in order to shape the investment climate in the former Soviet bloc countries (Comeaux and Kinsella, 1994; and Lewisa, 1991).

In 1995 the industrialized countries, led by the European Union, began to more vigorously campaign to bring investment into the WTO. Alarm was expressed at the EU initiative by non-governmental organizations and developing countries, most notably India and Brazil, both because of the perceived negative impact that a strengthened agreement would have on the capacity of southern states to foster development, and because of concerns at the degree to which the negotiation process is dominated by the North.[13] In part because of US and EU concern at the resistance that investment negotiations would meet in the WTO, the primary forum for creating a new Multilateral Agreement on Investment (MAI) has since 1995 instead been the Organization for Economic Cooperation and Development, comprising the world's 28 most industrialized states. Once negotiations are completed non-OECD countries will also be able to sign the MAI. The agreement will govern investments in both tangible and non-tangible assets, will include most-favored nation and national treatment provisions, has strong provisions regarding compensation for expropriation and the free repatriation of profits, permits the unrestricted transfer of key personnel by corporations across borders, and provides for binding arbitration between states and investors that can be initiated by investors.[14] In the end, that is, even the modest efforts of middle income developing countries such as India and Brazil to influence the negotiating process in the multilateral forum of the WTO seems to have backfired. The advanced industrial countries simply moved negotiations to a venue they controlled.

DEMOCRACY AND THE LIBERALIZATION OF FINANCIAL SERVICES TRADE AND INVESTMENT

Some serious deficiencies of process and content can be noted with regard to democracy and the financial services and investment negotiations just summarized. With regard to process, two key shortcomings can be noted. First, there is an emerging tendency for a like-minded group of industrialized countries to negotiate agreements and then to seek to expand their reach by bringing in developing countries to endorse a *fait accompli*. This is evident in the bilateral investment treaty process in which the industrialized countries, drawing on previous bilateral treaties as a model, gradually created an established way of treating investment by adding bilateral treaties with one developing country after another. Similarly, the NAFTA brought Mexico, formerly a leader in the developing countries' campaign to establish their sovereignty over foreign investment, into a three-way negotiation with two industrialized countries, the US and Canada. Once established, the NAFTA was envisioned as being expanded to include all of Latin America. Finally, the MAI has been negotiated first among the OECD's wealthy membership. Once it is complete developing countries that hope to attract and retain foreign investment will be expected to sign on. The architects of the MAI also hope that its reach can be expanded by having it serve as a model for subsequent investment negotiations in the WTO. A similar process was seen in the discussion of bank regulation and the role of the Basle Committee. In contrast to a multilateral negotiation which included developing countries from the start, this process makes it difficult for developing countries to influence negotiations because they have no formal mechanism to affect the direction of negotiations at the critical early stages, and because there is a reduced opportunity for them to work together to offset positions taken by industrialized countries.

A second deficiency in the process by which financial services and investment liberalization has been negotiated is the much greater access to the negotiations enjoyed by corporations relative to other non-government organizations and citizens more generally. This is most evident in the MAI which has been absent from public or parliamentary debate but has been developed in close consultation with the international business community. As an OECD director noted, 'This community's views are directly fed into the OECD's deliberations by the Business and Industry Advisory Committee to the OECD (BIAC), whose experts have been regularly consulting with us as negotiations proceed' (Witherell, p. 40). By contrast, one Canadian non-governmental organization, frustrated at the lack of public discussion of the negotiation, suggested that the world's richest countries and biggest corporations have 'been working secretly on the Multilateral Agreement on Investment (MAI),' a treaty that would give multinational corporations so much power that Parliament might not even matter any more (Council of Canadians, p. 1).

As with banking and securities regulation, lack of democracy in the process by which new policies are established might not matter if the subject of the negotiations had little public policy relevance because it was merely technical or of concern only to a small group of private citizens. There are good reasons, however, to doubt that this is the case. Many of the concerns raised above with respect to international securities regulation apply here as well. Treating the financial system as involving tradable financial services for which barriers should be reduced can obscure other relevant public policy issues, including the need for regulation to enhance the stability of the system and of firms, the impact of financial liberalization on the distribution of wealth, and the danger of excessive concentration and restrictive business practices that can come with the entry of large foreign firms into emerging markets. The emerging arrangements for regulating investment flows are prohibiting many public policy tools, such as local content requirements or rules requiring the transfer of technology, that had in previous periods been seen as legitimate ways of offsetting the historic and contemporary advantage of multinationals from developed countries relative to economic actors in developing countries. Individual investors and corporations are enjoying an unprecedented expansion of rights, including the right, in arbitration procedures, to deal with states as equals, the right for certain corporate employees to move freely across borders, and greatly expanded rights to move funds across borders and to purchase assets in foreign countries. These are increasingly integrated into the trade regime while other rights, such as those of labor, are excluded.[15]

There are well-developed arguments that existing and expanded liberalization of financial markets and investment flows either will not contribute to the potential problems cited in the previous paragraph, or will ameliorate rather than exacerbate those problems. An adequate assessment of the literatures that applaud and criticize financial liberalization goes beyond the scope of the present chapter. Here I simply indicate that all these debates are not fully resolved and that the character of the present international policy process through which liberalization is being promoted, with its separation of liberalization into distinct and autonomous negotiations dominated by developed countries, tends to suppress rather than encourage such debate, and thereby reduce the likelihood that negative effects of liberalization on developing countries will be identified and addressed.

PUBLIC POLICY AND PRIVATE INTERNATIONAL INSTITUTIONS

At the beginning of this chapter three ways in which the scope of democracy could be restricted in a policy process were identified. The first of these was the migration of policymaking up from the state, the traditional locus of democratic deliberation, to international institutions in which power differentials outweigh democratic procedures. The second was the treatment of public policy issues as merely technical and therefore not properly subject to democratic monitoring and input. These two have been addressed in the sections above. In this section I will briefly address a third way in which the scope of democracy can be restricted: the treatment of public policy issues as private matters.

Private international institutions play a large and growing role in the organization of private cross-border financial flows. They range from large formal organizations like the FIBV which seek to produce regulations that parallel and overlap inter-state institutions, like IOSCO, to smaller more informal institutions, such as the syndicates that organize large bank loans and bond issues. Some private institutions seek to directly influence the policy process, like the Business Industry Advisory Committee involved in the investment negotiations at the OECD, while others influence it more indirectly, perhaps by providing mechanisms for firms and investors to bypass regulations.

While a comprehensive analysis of the scores of such private institutions which are significant in global finance goes beyond the scope of the present chapter, I will briefly examine three to give a sense of their institutional capacity.

The Group of Thirty, established in 1978, bills itself as a 'private, independent, nonpartisan, nonprofit body' (G-30, 1994, p. 3). Its 1994 30-member composition is typical. Chaired by Paul Volcker, former Chairman of the US Federal Reserve Bank, it includes top private bankers representing such institutions as Deutsche Bank, Goldman Sachs, Yamaichi Securities, central bankers and finance officials representing the Bank of England, Banque de France and Banca d'Italia, and academics (Peter Kenen, Paul Krugman and Sylvia Ostry). It seeks to influence the development of financial markets by issuing reports and running seminars and also has played a more practical role in spearheading efforts to improve clearance and settlement practices in the world's securities markets.

For commercial banks the most prominent transnational association is the Institute of International Finance. The roots of this association lie in the debt crisis: the organizing committee that founded it was established by representatives of 30 banks in October 1982. By 1990, it had a staff of 40, a $5 million budget, and 147 full member banks and financial organizations from 39 countries, representing over 80 per cent of international bank exposure in the developing world (Sarver, 1992, pp. 433–7). Its primary function has been to share information about sovereign borrowers, but it has more recently begun developing positions on regulatory matters.

Within the International Chamber of Commerce, a third private transnational organization, there are Commissions on Financial Services Banking Technique and Practice, Taxation, and International Trade and Investment Policy. The Commission on Financial Services was formed in 1991 and 'examines such questions as debt provisioning, banking supervision, liberalisation of financial markets and securities and capital markets'. It has 109 members from 29 countries and includes four working parties (debt provisioning, regulatory aspects of international portfolio management, international aspects of payment systems, and netting). The Commission on International Trade and Investment Policy, chaired by Arthur Dunkel, former GATT Director General and now on the boards of Nestle and Credit Suisse Holding, is promoting international investment treaties.[16]

These brief descriptions of the activities of these private international institutions indicates that they can play an important role in the policy-making processes which I have been examining in previous sections. The existence of such organizations might be taken to be beneficial to emerging markets, because they represent the type of democratic involvement in the policy process which, I have argued, has been inadequate. There are, however, three reasons why this is not likely to be the case. First, to the extent that policy originates in such institutions, then it is removed from any expectation that it should be subject to public scrutiny. Second, these institutions often explictly represent the interests of financial firms or other market actors and cannot be expected to consider the public interest in emerging markets where that diverges from the interests of the institution's member firms. Third, and relatedly, there are far more financial services firms based in developed markets than in emerging markets, and thus the marginalization of developing country firms in these institutions is likely to be no less problematic than the marginalization of developing country regulators in public international institutions.

These concerns would be offset by the involvement in financial regulation of citizens other than financial firms and interest associations. There are, however, no international nongovernmental organizations comparable to environmental and human rights ones such as Greenpeace, the World Wildlife Fund, or Amnesty International. There are no electronic or hard-copy publications that report from an independent, lay, or critical perspective on negotiations comparable to the *Earth Negotiations Bulletin* for environmental and social issues, or *Nuclear Proliferation News* for nuclear proliferation issues. Non-governmental organizations other than industry associations are not very involved in negotiations or in domestic hearings, a contrast to these other issue areas as well. The comparison with these other policy areas is relevant because, like financial policymaking, their impact on citizens can be both significant and diffused, leading to classic collective action problems. There is also a contrast with the organizations that organize official flows such as the IMF and World Bank, in relation to which non-governmental organizations are comparatively well-organized and vocal.

As noted previously, many liberals argue implicitly or explicitly that shifts in authority from the public sector to the private sector will strengthen individuals against the state, and thereby enhance democracy. Sceptics would express concern about concentrations of private economic power and the usurping of authority that is properly public by private actors. This raises long-standing fundamental debates about democracy that are hardly resolvable in the present chapter. It can be pointed out, however, that these debates themselves are also a fundamental *part* of the democratic tradition and their absence in the study and practice of international financial regulation is troubling.

CONCLUSION

This chapter has highlighted the degree to which regimes for regulating private financial flows have grown in strength and complexity as part of the ongoing globalization of finance. The Basle Committee, IOSCO, the FIBV, the NAFTA, the Uruguay Round financial service commitments, and the investment arrangements have all grown both intensively (in their strength and number of commitments) and extensively (in the number of participants). The vitality of these policy processes signifies the degree to which decision-making authority is migrating to the supranational level.

All of these policy processes display three types of shortcomings with respect to democracy. First, the type of information that would be needed for concerned citizens and political leaders to monitor and influence policy processes is often lacking. This is evident in the secrecy of the Basle Committee, in the decision of securities regulators to rely on informal memoranda of understanding to avoid the involvement of legislatures, and in the confidentiality with which the Multilateral Agreement on Investment has been negotiated.

Second, a common tendency is for like-minded developed countries to get together and establish new regulatory arrangements, and then to promote the spread of these arrangements to emerging markets. The institutional arrangements through which emerging markets are integrated into this policy process are designed more to facilitate this transfer of regulations than to provide a mechanism for developing countries to collaborate in addressing common problems associated with private cross-border financial flows or to jointly respond to the initiatives of the developed countries. This is evident in the relationship of the Basle Committee to the Offshore Group and the regional groups of developing country bank regulators, in the control exercised by IOSCO's Technical Commitee over IOSCO's policy process, in the relationship between the FIBV and its regional counterparts in emerging markets, in the NAFTA's beginning with two developed countries and one developing one, in the sequential inclusion of developing countries in the emerging regime constituted by the bilateral investment treaties, and in the location of the Multilateral Investment Agreement negotiations in the OECD.

Third, the breaking of the various international policy processes that are regulating private cross-border financial flows into discrete and narrowly focused fora make it difficult to identify and address larger issues and problems for emerging markets regarding financial liberalization in general, or regarding the relationship between financial liberalization and other policy concerns. In the developed countries very well established mechanisms exist for handling such issues and relationships, some of which are private, such as firms that contribute to market transparency by providing information, and some of which are public, such as a strong tradition and set of institutions that foster democratic debate and integrate relevant policy issues. This chapter has indicated that such deficiencies with regard to democracy, which might not be of concern if the issues were merely technical or of concern to a small number of private citizens, have negative consequences for emerging markets relative to a conceivable alternative set of arrangements which would be more democratic. Some of these consequences are very concrete, such as the contribution of the separation of regulatory and liberalization policy processes to the Mexican crisis that began in 1994 or the mismatch between the Basle Committee's bank regulations and the needs of the microfinance industry in developing countries, while others are more speculative, such as the consequences of introducing competitive securities markets into countries that lack mechanisms, such as a legal system which can enforce stakeholders' and other citizens' rights, to offset those markets' negative social effects. It has been argued that, even in the case of more speculative consequences, greater democracy in international policy processes would be useful in better assessing their significance.

The need for more democracy in the international arrangements for regulating private financial flows can be defended on the grounds of the general ethical superiority of democracy and on its practical benefits for the policy process. Unfortunately there has been little discussion of these issues in the literature on the globalization of finance in general or in the regulation of emerging markets in particular (but see Pauly, 1995; Underhill, 1995). Just raising these issues is a first step in addressing them. Hopefully as the arrangements continue to evolve, such continued discussion will contribute to reducing the gap between the growth in authoritative supranational decision-making and the institutional preconditions for democratic input and debate.

Notes

1. Held (1995, p. viii) argues that globalization is 'a daunting challenge facing democratic theory and practice today'.
2. It should be noted that the question of limits on the legitimate scope of democratic deliberation is not a trivial issue – on the contrary it has been central historically to the debate over the nature of democracy and thus a key part of democratic deliberation itself. This is most evident for the frontier between public and private, which has been crucial in assessing democracy for both liberal and radical theorists of democracy. For liberals a shift in the frontier towards the private threatens to expand excessively the influence of the state over the individual, or the majority over the minority, and to erode the very freedom that democracy is supposed to bring about. The constitutive principles and rules of a democracy, by setting permissible limits to the domain of public policy, are therefore crucial. Critics of this liberal view fear that an

expansion of the private sphere will unduly restrict the range of issues over which citizens can express, or perhaps even imagine, their preferences, as key economic, social, and cultural structures are arbitrarily sequestered. A similar debate has occurred with the frontier between the technical and the political and between the legal and the technical, most notably in the Frankfurt School, but more recently in the work of post-structuralists such as Michel Foucault and Chantal Mouffe. The dominant approach in international relations theory, realism, has also regarded with scepticism liberal aspirations to replace political conflict with technical solutions, and the shortcomings of liberal theories such as functionalism and regional integration theory based on the growth of technical cooperation are well-known.

3. The G-10 traces its origins back to 1962 when 10 wealthy IMF members plus Switzerland agreed to provide additional funds to the International Monetary Fund (IMF) beyond their quotas, the General Arrangements to Borrow. The G-10 arrangement allowed them to exercise more control over this lending then if it had simply been processed through standard IMF channels. The Bank for International Settlements provides the Secretariat and meeting venue for the G-10 and its committees.

4. Because capital – most of which is equity – is more expensive than deposits as a source of funds, capital standards restrained the strategy of rapid growth and high volume that had been followed by most international banks.

5. For a full description of the weights and the definitions of capital see the agreement itself (Committee on Banking Regulations and Supervisory Practices [the Basle Committee's previous name], 1988).

6. A Basle Committee official has noted of money laundering that 'a few years ago, it would have been difficult to conceive that the Basle Committee, which deals with concerns about the prudential soundness of banks, would have become involved in this topic at all. However, the Committee's higher profile became a target for the US Congress, who directed the US members of the Committee to bring the matter to our table. Initially there was some reluctance to deal with it, because there were questions of legal competence for at least some of the Committee member institutions' (Freeland, 1994, pp. 237–8).

7. On IOSCO in general see IOSCO's annual reports, as well as Millspaugh (1992), pp. 355–77, Porter (1993) and Underhill (1995).

8. These Multijurisdictional Disclosure System negotiations turned out to be more complicated than their sponsors had realized. The UK dropped out and the effect of the agreement between Canadian and US regulators on securities markets was unimpressive. See Porter, 1993.

9. On the efficiency advantages of bank-led systems see Mayer, 1990.

10. On the reliance of Mexico on derivatives as a solution to its current problems see BNA, 1995.

11. More recent information on the WTO negotiations on financial services can be found at the WTO website: www.wto.org.

12. On this and the next two points see Shenkin (1994), pp. 541–606, especially p. 565 and p. 580.

13. Third World Network, package of materials sent over the internet by Martin Khor, Director of the Third World Network (TWN) on 9 November 1995. See for instance 'WTO Should Not Negotiate Foreign Investment Treaty – NGO Statement on the Foreign Investment Issue in WTO,' a statement signed by 32 NGOs. The TWN can be reached on the internet at twn@igc.apc.org or twnpen@twn.po.my.

14. On the MAI see Witherell, 1997. For a highly critical analysis see Council of Canadians, 1997.
15. Some developing country governments have been vehemently opposed to bringing labor rights into trade negotiations for fear that it would undermine their competitive advantage in cheap labor. Whether this position is beneficial for the citizens of these governments is a matter of dispute.
16. The information in this paragraph is based on information sheets provided by the International Chamber of Commerce.

Bibliography

Acworth, William (1995) 'Foreign Ownership Brings Mixed Results, SEC Says,' *International Banking Regulator*, 95 (27), 10 July.

BNA (1995) 'Mexican Stock Exchange Accelerates Plans for Currency Futures Market,' *BNA's Banking Report* 64 (18), 1 May, pp. 881–2.

Banker (1993) 'The US Waves the Protectionist Stick,' *Banker*, 143 (814), December, p. 8.

Basle Committee, various years, *Report on International Developments in Banking Supervision* (RIDBS) (Basle, Switzerland: Basle Committee).

Basle Committee (1994) *Report on International Developments in Banking Supervision* (RIDBS) (Basle, Switzerland: Basle Committee), no. 9, September.

Broadman, Harry G. (1993) 'International Trade and Investment in Services: A Comparative Analysis of the NAFTA,' *International Lawyer*, 27 (3), pp. 623–46.

Comeaux, Paul E. and N. Stephen Kinsella (1994) 'Reducing Political Risk in Developing Countries: Bilateral Investment Treaties, Stabilization Clauses, and MIV and OPIC Investment Insurance,' *New York Law School Journal of International and Comparative Law*, 15 (1), pp. 1–48.

Committee on Banking Regulations and Supervisory Practices [Basle Committee's previous name] (1988) 'International Convergence of Capital Measurement and Capital Standards,' (Basle, Switzerland: Committee on Banking Regulations and Supervisory Practices), July.

Council of Canadians (1997) 'When Corporations Rule the World,' *Action Link* (July update), p. 1.

Cutler, A. Claire, Virginia Haufler, and Tony Porter (eds) *Private Authority in International Affairs* (SUNY Press, forthcoming).

DeLuca, Dallas (1994) 'Trade-Related Investment Measures: US Efforts to Shape a Pro-Business World Legal System,' *Journal of International Affairs*, 48 (1), Summer, pp. 251–77.

The Economist (1995) 'Double Trouble,' 17 June, p. 79.

Fédération Internationale des Bourses de Valeurs (FIBV) (1995) *Annual Report and Statistics* (Paris: FIBV).

Footer, Mary E. (1993) 'GATT and the Multilateral Regulation of Banking Services,' *International Lawyer*, 2 (2), Summer, pp. 343–67.

Freeland, Charles (1994) 'The Work of the Basle Committee,' in Robert C. Effros (ed.), *Current Legal Issues Affecting Central Banks* (Washington, D.C.: International Monetary Fund).

Group of Thirty (G-30) (1994) *Annual Report* (Washington, D.C.: G-30).

Gantz, David A. (1993) 'Resolution of Investment Disputes under the North American Free Trade Agreement,' *Arizona Journal of International and Comparative Law*, 10 (2), pp. 335–48.

Haddock, David D. and Jonathan Macey (1987) 'Regulation on Demand: A Private Interest Model, with an Application to Insider Trading,' *Journal of Law and Economics*, XXX, October, pp. 311–39.

Held, David (1995) *Democracy and the Global Order: From the Modern State to Cosmopolitan Governance* (Palo Alto, CA.: Stanford University Press).

International Monetary Fund (1995) *International Capital Markets: Developments, Prospects, and Policy Issues* (Washington: IMF), August.

International Organization of Securities Commissions (IOSCO) (1994) *Annual Report* (Montreal, Canada: IOSCO).

Jacobs, Michael T. (1991) *Short-Term America: The Causes and Cures of Our Business Myopia* (Boston, MA.: Harvard Business School Press).

Krutzfeldt, Hermann (1996) 'The Experience of BancoSol,' in Craig F. Churchill (ed.), *An Introduction to Key Issues in Microfinance: Supervision and Regulation, Financing Sources, Expansion of Microfinance Institutions* (Washington, D.C.: Microfinance Network), February.

Lewis, Eleanor R. (1991) 'The United States–Poland Treaty Concerning Business and Economic Relations: New Themes and Variations in the US Bilateral Investment Treaty Program,' *Law and Policy in International Business*, 22 (3), October, pp. 527–46.

Mayer, Colin (1990) 'Financial Systems, Corporate Finance, and Economic Development,' in Glenn R. Hubbard (ed.) *Asymmetric Information, Corporate Finance, and Investment* (Chicago and London: University of Chicago Press).

Millspaugh, Peter E. (1992) 'Global Securities Trading: The Question of a Watchdog,' *George Washington Journal of International Law and Economics* 26 (2), pp. 355–77.

Ostry, Syliva and Gilbert R. Winham (1995) 'Post-Uruguay Round Trade Policy,' in Sylvia Ostry and Gibert R. Winham (eds), *The Halifax G-7 Summit: Issues on the Table* (Halifax: Centre for Foreign Policy Studies).

Pauly, Louis W. (1995) 'Capital Mobility, State Autonomy and Political Legitimacy,' *Journal of International Affairs*, 48 (2), Winter, pp. 369–88.

Poret, Pierre (1994). 'Mexico and the OECD Codes of Liberalisation,' *The OECD Observer*, no. 189, August/September.

Porter, Michael E. (1992) *Capital Choices: Changing the Way America Invests in Industry* (Washington, D.C.: Council on Competitiveness).

Porter, Tony (1993) *States, Markets and Regimes in Global Finance* (Basingstoke, U.K.: Macmillan).

—— (1997) 'NAFTA, North American Financial Integration and Regulatory Cooperation in Banking and Securities,' in Geoffrey R. D. Underhill (ed.) *The New World Order in International Finance* (Basingstoke, U.K.: Macmillan).

Roe, Mark J. (1994) *Strong Managers, Weak Owners: The Political Roots of American Corporate Finance* (Princeton, N.J.: Princeton University Press).

Sarver, Eugene (1992) *Eurocurrency Market Handbook*, 2nd edn (New York: New York Institute of Finance).

Securities Regulation and Law Report (1994) 'US to Seek Bilateral Deals in Asia for Financial Services Bentsen Says,' *Securities Regulation and Law Report*, 26 (3), 21 January, pp. 71–2

Shell, Richard G. (1995) 'Trade Legalism and International Relations Theory: An Analysis of the World Trade Organization,' *Duke Law Journal*, 44 (5), March 1995, p. 27.

Shenkin, T. S. (1994) 'Trade-Related Investment Measures in Bilateral Investment Treaties and the GATT: Moving Toward a Multilateral Investment Treaty,' *University of Pittsburgh Law Review*, 55 (2), Winter, pp. 541–606.

Underhill, Geoffrey R. D. (1995) 'Keeping Governments out of Politics: Transnational Securities Markets, Regulatory Cooperation, and Political Legitimacy,' *Review of International Studies*, 21, pp. 251–78.

United Nations Conference on Trade and Development (1993) *International Monetary and Financial Issues for the 1990s*, Research papers for the Group of 24, Volume III (New York: United Nations).

Witherell, William H. (1997) 'Developing International Rules for Foreign Investment: OECD's Multilateral Agreement on Investment,' *Business Economics*, XXXXII (1), January, pp. 38–43.

Yerkey, Gary G. (1995) 'United States Steps Up Effort to Open Foreign Markets to US Banking Services,' *BNA's Banking Report*, 64 (10), 6 March.

Young, Michael K. (1995) 'Dispute Resolution in the Uruguay Round: Lawyers Triumph over Diplomats,' *International Lawyer*, 29 (2), Summer, pp. 389–409.

Part II
Country Cases

5 Mexico: The Trajectory to the 1994 Devaluation

William C. Gruben

Among the most striking responses to the Mexican financial crisis that began in December 1994 was surprise. The devaluation surprised US markets (Fidler and Bardacke, 1994; Lustig, 1995; Torres and Campbell, 1994; Tricks, 1994). The subsequent financial meltdown seemed to surprise Mexican policy-makers.[1] Moreover, not only were there superficial reasons to be surprised – Mexico in December had not yet released information on the sudden outflow of foreign currency reserves that had begun in November – but there were also deeper reasons. Mexico largely followed the same monetary policy rules in 1994 that it had been pursuing throughout the 1990s, but with very different results.

This discussion examines factors that led to the devaluation, considers why it surprised markets, and addresses financial market behavior in the wake of the devaluation. To provide a context for considering what led to the devaluation, I discuss Mexican and US policy in light of the so-called impossibility theorem. According to the impossibility theorem, governments cannot simultaneously and continuously pursue the three objectives of free capital mobility, fixed exchange rates, and an independent monetary policy.

The impossibility theorem means that – if Mexico pegs its exchange rate to the dollar – the central bank of Mexico must either pursue US monetary policy or impose so many capital controls that monetary independence will not make a difference.

A problem with the impossibility theorem is the functionality of the term continuous. If it is impossible for a country to pursue continuously and simultaneously the three objectives of monetary independence, a pegged exchange rate, and free capital mobility, for how long can these three objectives be pursued without yet being thought continuous?

In the early 1990s, some of Mexico's institutional characteristics could have suggested that Mexico might reasonably follow a somewhat independent monetary policy for a while, but it was difficult to know how much and for how long. Even though Mexico's exchange rate was pegged to the US dollar before the December 1994 devaluation, Mexico nevertheless gave itself room to maneuver. In pegging the peso to the dollar, Mexico was announcing its intent to cede some control over its monetary policy to the United States. Pegging can signal that non-inflationary policies will be in place. Pegging sends this signal because, if Mexico ran a persistently more expansionary monetary policy than the United States, the resulting reductions in foreign reserves would ultimately make it impossible for Mexico to defend the peso and a devaluation would ensue. Indeed, it is for this reason that programs like Mexico's are referred to as exchange-rate-based stabilization policies.

It is important to understand the special flexibilities built into Mexico's exchange rate pegging arrangement. Although Mexico did control its exchange rate according to clear rules, Mexico permitted it to fluctuate within a band, instead of fixing its exchange rate hard and fast to the dollar. Moreover, the weak-side edge of the band devalued at 0.0004 pesos per dollar. With a band, Mexico's central bank could run expansionary or contractionary monetary policies different from those of the US central bank – provided that the resulting movements in the exchange rate remained within the band. Thus, while pegging to the dollar meant Mexico was surrendering much monetary policy independence, the combination of the band and the daily devaluation meant that Mexico was not surrendering all of its monetary independence.

To the extent that Mexico had the capacity for monetary independence for one reason or another, a noteworthy characteristic of this independence was its term-structure. Gruben, McLeod, and Welch (1995) show that movements in U.S. short-term interest rates appear not to influence Mexican short-term or long-term interest rates, but US long-term rates seem to influence Mexican long-term interest rates.[2] Insofar as these results mean financial integration between the US and Mexico is limited, for whatever reason, Mexico may have perceived itself able to pursue a relatively independent monetary policy in the short run.

Nevertheless, Gruben, McLeod, and Welch's (1995) result that US long-term rates influence Mexican long-term interest rates signifies that, even under its pegged-cum-band exchange rate regime, Mexico's monetary policy could not remain independent for very long. In the face of an increase in US long rates, for example, Mexico's rates would have to rise quickly or the country would face large capital outflows. Political factors probably accounted for much of the accretion of day-to-day changes in capital outflows that ultimately motivated the Mexican devaluation of December 1994. However, during much of the second half of 1994, Mexican monetary policy was not consistent with reversing these outflows.

Before turning to a more detailed discussion of the trajectory of events that triggered and then compounded Mexico's financial crisis, one additional peculiarity of Mexican monetary independence deserves preliminary mention. In 1994, Mexico markedly increased the share of its debt that was accounted for by dollar-indexed bonds – known as *tesobonos*. The shift out of peso-denominated debt into dollar-indexed debt seems to have had important implications for the credibility of Mexico's exchange rate regime. Because at least temporary increases in inflation almost inevitably follow a devaluation, the real value of peso-denominated debt falls after a devaluation, offering an incentive to devalue. But for reasons that will be detailed subsequently, the real value of dollar-indexed debt would typically increase after a devaluation. As a result, the markets appear to have viewed these bonds as signs of commitment not to devalue.

Increasing the share of *tesobonos* as a portion of total debt – which in 1994 meant replacing peso-denominated bonds (*cetes*) with *tesobonos* – can be seen as permitting a slightly more expansive monetary policy, temporarily. Such a move in monetary policy might otherwise raise investor concerns about the increasing likelihood of devaluation, but econometric results due to Gould (1994) suggest that the punishment that a devaluation would impose on the real value of Mexican *tesobono* debt offsets those expectations. Thus, raising the share of *tesobonos* in total debt outstanding may temporarily have seemed to have increased the opportunities for monetary independence, despite what the *tesobonos* came to signify in the wake of the initial devaluation.

As a final detail in considering the events leading to and following from Mexico's initial devaluation it should be noted that exchange rate devaluation is usually a matter of choice. A central bank can typically maintain a pegged exchange rate if it is willing to pay the price. The price is contraction in the monetary base or, equivalently, a persistently high or rising interest rate. Sometimes, the consequences of such policies are seen as too serious to endure.[3] In effect, some other policy takes precedence over the policy of a pegged exchange rate. But if tensions between Mexico's exchange rate policy and other goals became intolerable in late 1994, tensions existed well before then.

TENSIONS WITHIN MEXICO'S EXCHANGE RATE-BASED STABILIZATION PLAN

Incomes Policies

Although there is little evidence that countries begin them with the intention of a finally destabilizing devaluation, exchange rate-based stabilizations are difficult to pursue effectively over protracted periods. The ultimate collapse of programs like Mexico's is not unusual, even when care is taken to address their typical problems by using exchange rate pegging as only a part of the overall program. But in Mexico it was hoped that, this time, the effort would be successful because of the program's special structure. Banded exchange rate pegging was an important element of a broader program that included reduced government spending, tax reform, deregulation, privatization, and significant trade liberalization – including rapid reductions in tariffs and quotas, and entry into the General Agreement on Tariffs and Trade (GATT) and later into the North American Free Trade Agreement (NAFTA). Fiscal stabilization preceded the exchange rate-based stabilization efforts. The history of exchange rate-based stabilization in the southern cone countries had suggested that a single nominal anchor – such as the exchange rate – could be inadequate to motivate quick disinflation. Policy incredibility (that firms would not believe the exchange rate regime would persist) as well as backward indexation and nonsynchronized price setting could lead to persistent inflation (Calvo and Végh, 1992). Accordingly, an important component of Mexico's stabilization policy was the *Pacto*. Under this government-organized accord, representatives of the business community agreed to limit price increases, the government made commitments about the exchange rate and public sector prices, and labor representatives agreed to limit wage increases.

Although there are historical exceptions, exchange rate-based stabilization programs that also include incomes policies – like the *Pacto* – fairly commonly result in a specific dynamic of consumption and investment patterns, current account movements, and exchange rate pressures. Although the typical trajectory (Calvo and Végh, 1992; Kiguel and Liviatin, 1992) begins with marked reductions in inflation, the real exchange rate rises because an inflation rate differential remains between the pegging (typically developing) country and the country (typically a developed country) to whose currency the developing country's currency is pegged. The real exchange rate rises because this inflation rate differential is not fully offset by nominal exchange rate movements. As a result, the trade and current account balances deteriorate. In the early stages of the program, capital inflows finance the excess of consumption and investment over domestic production, allowing a boom to ensue. Ultimately, however, the inflows reverse. With this reversal, the growing current account deficit can no longer be financed. The consumption boom ends and a bust begins.

In recognition of this instability, one strand of the literature suggests that exchange rate pegging ought to be a temporary stabilization tool, ultimately followed by a managed float (McLeod and Welch, 1992). Reflecting the same concerns, another narrative suggests that if pegging is done at all, the exchange rate crawl should be partially indexed to a measure of domestic prices (Kamin, 1991). Ultimately, it has been argued, 'as useful as exchange rate pegging is at the outset, it is equally important to eliminate it as soon as possible' (Dornbusch and Werner, 1994, p. 281).

Trade and Capital Flows

Despite the special characteristics of Mexico's exchange rate stabilization, incomes policy, and trade liberalization programs, the ensuing economic trajectory was typical of heterodox programs. Consistent with the intentions of such plans, inflation fell markedly – from 159.2 per cent in 1987 to 8 per cent in 1993. By the third quarter of 1994, the annualized inflation rate had declined to 7 per cent. Mexico's trade liberalization was a part of this disinflation effort. Oligopoly typifies the organization of domestic markets in Mexico, so that the imposition of price controls could mean the risk of product shortages. Mexico used trade liberalization to enforce price discipline – so as to hold down inflation and to lower the likelihood of product shortages. Domestic producers would have more difficulty raising their prices if they tried it while foreign competitors were in the market. The tensions within Mexico's exchange rate policy played a disinflationary role in the context of trade liberalization. Recall that the government consistently depreciated the peso more slowly than the rate of inflation – or than the difference between the US and Mexican inflation rates – so that real exchange rate appreciation was chronic. This tension is typical of exchange-rate-based stabilization programs, and its operation in Mexico followed the usual pattern. Since real exchange rate appreciation meant that foreign products were increasingly cheaper than Mexican products, this exchange rate policy motivated domestic producers – at least of tradable goods – to resist the temptation to raise prices. But many producers, – especially those who sold such non-tradable products as buildings and various services – did not resist the temptation. As a result, despite nominal devaluations, the real exchange rate rose.

Partially because of this tension between inflation and the pace of nominal exchange rate depreciation, the nation's merchandise trade balance grew increasingly negative. As may be expected in an economy that had reoriented itself towards a market system – and had deregulated, privatized, and generally rationalized its policies towards the private sector – a significant portion of Mexico's current account deficit reflected purchases of capital goods. The increased productivity and efficiency that these purchases imply resulted in steady increases in exports. But the capital imports' share of total imports was still only 16.9 percent in 1993, versus 71.1 per cent for intermediate goods, and 12.0 per cent for consumer goods.

The trade and current account deficits were possible because the rationalization of Mexico's fiscal, monetary, and exchange rate policies had helped to stimulate large inflows of foreign investment funds through early 1994. These flows also gave Mexico the reserves it would need to defend the peso later, if exchange rate pressures required it. Increased capital inflows are common to chronic inflation countries that introduce exchange rate-based stabilization programs. The great bulk of these flows into Mexico involved portfolio investment – inflows typically for the purchase of bonds and stocks – rather than foreign direct investment.[4] While portfolio investment permitted Mexican enterprises to fund privately-owned toll roads, the recently privatized telephone company, and some manufacturing operations, the focus of this investment on the production of non-tradables made inflows and outflows susceptible to concerns of devaluation risk.

But to the extent that capital is not perfectly mobile, Mexico's chronically low saving rate meant that the country's investment and growth were more susceptible to external financial events. There is much to suggest that capital flows into Mexico did not occur solely because of Mexico's policies. During the early 1990s, foreign capital began to flow into Latin America generally, despite wide differences in macroeconomic policies and economic performance among countries there. An important reason appears to be low US interest rates, suggesting that increases in US interest rates might have the opposite effect.[5]

CENTRAL BANK POLICY AND THE FINANCIAL SECTOR

One reason tensions surfaced between Mexico's exchange rate regime and other policies is that international elements of Mexico's disinflation programs – trade liberalization, real exchange rate appreciation, and a trade deficit financed by foreign capital inflows – collectively weakened Mexico's financial sector.

Three factors joined to impose pressures on Mexico's financial sector. First, differences between the pricing performance of the non-tradeables and tradeables sectors damaged the latter. The increased international competition held down prices in the tradeable goods sectors. But even with the *Pacto*, prices of non-tradable products – including real estate and some services – rose relative to prices of tradables. This disparity imposed profit squeezes on tradeables firms because they often used non-tradeables as inputs, and because non-tradeables producers could bid up wages of workers for whom tradeables firms had to compete. The direct effects of trade liberalization and real exchange rate appreciation had, of course, also imposed cost-price-squeeze pressures on some of these firms. These pressures were expressed in increasing loan defaults by tradeables firms.

Second, to maintain inflows of foreign capital, real interest rates began to increase starting in 1992, even though nominal rates were falling at this time. During the early 1990s, Mexico's commercial banking system did not, at least by developed country standards, behave very competitively.[6] Spreads between cost of funds and loan rates were large. So were return on assets, return on equity, and other income statement ratios (Mansell Carstens, 1993; Gruben, Welch, and Gunther, 1994). Bank lending rates were typically very high by developed country standards, in any case. But increases in real rates made it particularly difficult for some firms to compete with foreign producers from countries where financial costs happened to be lower.

Third, to take advantage of the consumption boom of the early 1990s, Mexico's financial institutions had issued many more credit cards – to the wrong borrowers. By the standards of developing companies, the reporting of consumer credit histories was relatively sketchy and unorganized in Mexico. Defaults became common.

These factors converged to pressure Mexico's banking system.[7] Just between the fourth quarter of 1992 and the third quarter of 1994, the percentage of nonperforming loans rose from 5.6 per cent to 8.3 per cent.[8] Moreover, between December 1991 and September 1994, the ratio of high-risk assets to bank net worth rose from 51 per cent to 70 per cent. Banking system problems like these take on special significance anywhere a central bank is both the monetary authority and, as in Mexico, the administrator of the deposit insurance system. As Heller (1991) argues, to the extent that a central bank is not only the nation's monetary authority but also is responsible for the health of the banking system, policy tensions may exist. Even though central banks are typically committed to the restraint of monetary expansion, and Mexico's is, an incipient banking crisis may create incentives to expand credit to the banking system.

It is here that the tensions expressed in the impossibility theorem appear, since it holds that free movement of capital, independent monetary policy, and a pegged exchange rate are sooner or later incompatible. Mexico followed a sterilization rule for its inflows of foreign reserves. To impose a monetary stabilization rule atop the exchange rate-based stabilization, accumulations of foreign currency reserves were sterilized via offsetting reductions in domestic credit the central bank created for the financial system. Conversely, outflows of foreign currency reserves were sterilized through offsetting increases in domestic credit.[9]

Recall that a central bank can always maintain a pegged exchange rate, but sometimes the price is an otherwise undesirably tight monetary policy. When foreign currency reserves flow out – even if purely political episodes are the motivation – this can signal that a monetary contraction or interest rate increase is in order.[10] Such policies may be inconsistent with the expansion of domestic credit as an offset to capital outflows, even if the policy is purely an act of sterilization.[11]

THE CURRENCY CONFIGURATION OF MEXICAN SHORT-TERM DEBT

Mexico had simultaneously issued short-term peso-denominated debt (*cetes*) and short-term dollar-indexed debt (*tesobonos*), but, as 1994 progressed, Mexico radically altered the currency configuration of its short-term debt so as to strengthen the peso. In January 1994, the dollar value of *cetes* outstanding was $12.9 billion compared with $302 million in *tesobonos*. By November, *cetes* outstanding had fallen to $7.27 billion while *tesobonos* had risen to $12.9 billion.

An interesting characteristic of these debt issues, as demonstrated econometrically (Dornbursch and Werner, 1994), is that the changes in spreads between their interest rates are not affected by changes in factors normally associated with exchange rate expectations. Dornbusch and Werner (1994) argue that changes in spreads between the interest rates of *cetes* and *tesobonos* are not explained by changes in the real exchange rate or in Mexico's trade balance because the government managed the composition of its domestic debt so as to respond to cost differentials. That is, as exchange rate risk rose, Mexico shifted its composition of short-term debt towards *tesobonos* and away from *cetes*. The authors argue that this shift reflects government responses to cost differentials. As rates on *tesobonos* fell relative to rates on *cetes*, the government replaced *cetes* issues with *tesobono* issues.

If one advantage of a shift towards *tesobonos* was to save on interest expenses while gaining foreign exchange by selling debt to foreigners, it was not the only advantage. Mexico's increased issuance of *tesobonos* may also be seen as making its exchange rate regime more credible by imposing a clear and obvious fiscal penalty for devaluation. Ize and Ortiz (1987) note that devaluation is tantamount to a default on domestic debt because, by raising the price level, the government erodes the debt's real value. Accordingly, a large overhang of domestic debt may be seen as a motivation to devalue – particularly when the debt is held by foreigners. While this motivation may exist when a nation's domestic debt is denominated in the home currency, the motivation erodes if – as with the *tesobonos* – the debt instrument is indexed to the dollar. A shift out of *cetes* and into *tesobonos* is a shift out of an instrument for which outstanding real debt falls with devaluation and into an instrument for which devaluation means a real debt increase. This statement holds whenever the subsequent rate of inflation does not match or exceed the rate of devaluation by the time the debt matures.

The *tesobono* shift's role in enhancing credibility that the exchange rate regime will persist may be indirectly measurable. Insofar as agents recontract for higher wages or higher purchase or selling prices now in anticipation of a generalized bout of price increases – so that present prices reflect expectations of future price increases – and insofar as a devaluation may be seen as triggering a future generalized bout of price increases, the implications of a shift into *tesobonos* as a commitment technology for the exchange rate regime may be expressed in current price increases.[12] Preliminary econometric research by David Gould (1994) shows that even when monetary base growth and other factors linked to inflation are included in a model of Mexican consumer price changes, a negative and significant relation exists between consumer inflation and the share of Mexican short-term debt that is indexed to the dollar. That is, with this credibility enhancement in place, the market seems to reduce its expectation of the devaluation and so of the inflation that typically follows devaluation.[13] It does not seem unreasonable to conjecture that this credibility enhancement could also have been seen as a potential enhancement for transitory monetary independence.

THE TRAJECTORY OF A FINANCIAL CRISIS

The implications of the general dynamics of heterodox exchange rate-based stabilization programs, of the role of domestic credit expansion in addressing systemic bank crises and in triggering currency collapses, and of the use of *tesobonos* as a commitment technology become more dramatic when we consider the roles they played in Mexico in 1994.

Recall that typical patterns of exchange rate-based stabilization programs include falling inflation, rising real exchange rates, consumption booms, capital inflows in the early stages that fund increasingly negative balances of trade and current account and, finally, capital outflows that ultimately induce currency collapses. Recall also that a typical characteristic of a currency collapse is not the impossibility of maintaining a pegged exchange rate, but a policy priority rearrangement in which the exchange rate is subordinated. Finally, note that the intention of this paper is not only to explain why the choices were made that triggered the devaluation, but to explain why its aftermath was explosive despite prior claims that 'the Mexican government would not lose credibility from a devaluation, because it would be recognized as a constructive response to a crisis' (Werner, 1994, p. 310).

I noted earlier that one reason Mexican bonds and stocks attracted US and other foreign investors was low US interest rates. During the first quarter of 1994, United States monetary policy began to tighten, raising US interest rates and attracting capital back to the United States. While the increase in US rates signified that factors pushing capital towards Mexico were diminishing, political events in Mexico weakened the country's pull effects for capital. Chiapas rebels may not have threatened the nation's stability, but the assassination of Mexican presidential candidate Colosio in March 1994 was another matter to investors. After rising earlier in the year, reserves fell profoundly just after the assassination, but stabilized in April. To hold foreign capital in the country, Mexico raised interest rates significantly, signaling that exchange-rate preservation remained important. But US interest rates were also rising, and they continued to do so throughout the year. The exchange rate moved toward the weak edge of the band, but remained within it.

It is in this context of rising US rates at a time when increasing financial problems offered motivations to lower or at least hold Mexican rates that the value of the *tesobonos* as a commitment technology can be appreciated. Instead of offering a commitment technology based on the accumulation of larger foreign currency reserves to defend the peso, when real rates were already at high levels, the issuance of *tesobonos* might be thought a reasonable substitute – at least temporarily.

When the Colosio assassination triggered a capital outflow, Mexico sterilized by raising domestic credit. At the same time, Mexico stepped up its substitution of dollar-indexed *tesobonos* outstanding for peso-indexed *cetes* outstanding. By mid-year *tesobonos* outstanding began to exceed *cetes*, and the substitution increased through the rest of the year.

In the third quarter, Mexico began to relax its interest rate pressures. Interest rates remained considerably higher than they had been at the beginning of the year, but they were not high enough to restore reserves to the levels of the first quarter – not, at least, when US rates were also rising.

Nevertheless, reserves remained relatively stable during the third quarter. One reason may be that, as the summer ensued, it became more obvious that substitute Institutional Revolutionary Party presidential candidate Ernesto Zedillo was likely to defeat the other candidates, whose abilities or policies might have inspired more investor uncertainty about future growth. Then, in August, he did win. But Gould's (1994) results on the negative influence of *tesobonos'* share of total short-term debt on inflation rates suggest that an exchange-rate commitment technology also helped to stabilize foreign currency reserves. The third quarter ended with foreign currency reserves as high as those with which it had begun. As 1994 ensued, the differential between Mexican and US interest rates began to fall – much as one might expect, other things equal, as a reasonable policy response in the face of mounting problems in the Mexican financial system.[14] Nominal *cetes* rates fell absolutely in August and remained below their spring and summer highs until the devaluation.

In the fourth quarter, another political event transpired that was followed by capital outflows from Mexico – but an economic event at the same time makes interpretation difficult. After the assassination of Institutional Revolutionary Party official José Francisco Ruiz Massieu, his brother was appointed to investigate the case; in November he resigned, alleging that powerful officials were stymieing his investigation. Meanwhile, on 15 November, the Federal Open Market Committee of the US Federal Reserve System met and decided on policies that would lead to a 75 basis point increase in the federal funds rate – its most restrictive monetary policy action since 1990. In sterilizing the subsequent outflow of foreign capital, Mexico's central bank again increased domestic credit to the banking system.[15] Such measures can be expected to hasten the conditions linked to currency collapses. Mexican interest rates were not pushed up sufficiently to maintain reserves.

Perhaps as a result of the fiscal implications that the large overhang of *tesobonos* offered in the event of a devaluation, the exchange rate continued to show what could be interpreted as signs of credibility.[16] But this *tesobono* commitment technology had been imposed in a period of increasing risk to the financial system and of the additional trade balance pressures partially induced by the commencement of NAFTA in January 1994. Taken collectively, these factors meant that Mexico could be risking a financial crisis if it devalued the currency and allowed interest rates to go where they would or if it defended the currency by raising interest rates.

On 20 December, the *tesobono* overhang that had suggested exchange rate credibility now signified financial market as well as currency collapse. When the Mexican government surprised US markets by announcing that the peso would move from 3.47 pesos per dollar to 3.99, it also announced that the exchange rate pegging regime – in which the peso would devalue against the dollar at a rate of .0004 pesos per day – would persist. The band would simply be lowered.

But instead of settling markets, the announcement incited massive capital flight, apparently surprising Mexican government officials. Large increases in interest rates ensued. Perhaps the fiscal implications of the *tesobono* overhang – with a maturity schedule in which the value of *tesobonos* falling due within the first six months of 1995 exceeded the value of Mexico's foreign exchange reserves – were calculated by financial markets. But given the moderate magnitude of the initial announced devaluation, the pure act of abridgment of such a commitment seems to have played an important role in and of itself.

CONCLUSION

Of the many problems Mexico faced in 1994, three were paramount. First, the controlled rate of depreciation of the peso was inconsistent with the persistent inflation rate differential between the United States and Mexico. Mexican rates of inflation had converged towards US inflation rates, but the accretion of differences from past years had resulted in a very high real exchange rate. Second, capital outflows drew down foreign exchange reserves that Mexico was using to defend the peso. To a significant degree, however, this phenomenon materialized as a result of the third and final principal problem. Third, in the conflict between greater monetary tightness to support the exchange rate and less tightness to avoid further financial sector problems and a downturn in the economy – the latter won out. While Mexico wished growth, it was caught in an episode of US monetary tightening that only *de facto* monetary independence would have permitted it to avoid following with a vengeance – and in financially destabilizing episodes of political unrest.

Despite evidence that some monetary independence was available transitorily, as the short run grew into a longer run, independence and dependence collided with a result long since posited by the impossibility theorem. But while these factors are consistent with an ensuing devaluation, they alone are not consistent with the explosion that took place in financial markets following the initial devaluation.

The crisis' explosiveness seems linked to reactions to the term structure and volume of Mexico's short-term dollar-indexed debt, even though there is little evidence to suggest that the *tesobono* debt was seen as problematic before the devaluation. Indeed, it had served as a positive commitment technology.[17] That the *tesobono* maturity schedule signified obligations in early 1995 that were well in excess of Mexican dollar reserves to cover them may have triggered the anticipation of a financial musical chairs game in which each investor began to fear that her or his *tesobonos* would be the one left out of convertibility.

Notes

1. Officials of the Mexican government spoke and acted as if they expected the devaluation to have a stabilizing influence. When they presented the devaluation, they announced that the nation's erstwhile crawling exchange rate peg would remain in place, and that the devaluation would signify only a change in the weak or soft edge of Mexico's exchange rate band.
2. More specifically and technically, Gruben, McLeod, and Welch (1995) show that three-month US Treasury bill rates do not Granger cause and are not Granger caused by three-month Mexican treasury bill (*cete*) rates, and that three-month US Treasury bill rates do not Granger cause and are not Granger caused by Mexican Brady par bonds. However, 30-year US treasury bonds do Granger cause Mexican Brady par bonds. Mexican Brady par bonds may be seen as long-term bonds. These results suggest that financial integration between Mexico and the United States is significantly abridged in the short term but not in the long run.
3. It may be useful to recall how raising interest rates affect exchange rates. Raising Mexican interest rates encourages foreigners to purchase Mexican financial assets, other things equal. When US citizens or funds buy Mexican financial assets, they typically trade dollars for pesos. This process increases the demand for pesos and so bids up the exchange rate. As a result of these exchanges, the central bank of Mexico accumulates dollar reserves. If pressures to devalue arise, the central bank of Mexico can use these dollar reserves to buy up pesos – raising their dollar price. Moreover, squeezing monetary growth and raising interest rates lowers Mexican inflation. Insofar as dollar prices of Mexican goods rise faster than dollar prices of US goods, both Mexican and US buyers are discouraged from buying Mexican products and encouraged to buy US products. The resulting trade deficit increase means declining demand for pesos – as fewer Mexican products are bought – and rising demand for dollars, as more US products are. Pressure to devalue the peso arises. The devaluation lowers the dollar price of Mexican products and raises the peso price of Mexican products, erasing the deficit. A tight monetary policy that includes

raising interest rates dampens Mexican inflation, squeezes the differential between Mexican and US inflation, and lowers pressure to devalue.

4. Eichengreen and Fishlow (1995) argue that portfolio equity flows' increased share of total capital flows in the 1990s has given rise to large increases in recipient country instability. Their work is typical of a strand in the literature that offers bases to argue for the control of capital flows, a policy measure to which Mexico's crisis has attracted much attention. However, Claessens, Dooley, and Warner (1995) offer econometric time series evidence to suggest that capital volatility is not a function of capital market category – whether it be portfolio capital, foreign direct investment, short-term or long-term capital. In their casting, all capital flows can be hot flows. In an inquiry into what countries sacrifice when they impose capital controls, Gruben and McLeod (1995) find that the contribution of portfolio equity flows to growth in an 18–country sample is not statistically significantly different from the contribution of foreign direct investment, and that both types of capital flows generally contribute significantly to growth. Gruben and McLeod (1995) also find, however, that capital flows to Mexico were so large during the 1990s that they ultimately contributed very little – on a dollar per dollar basis – to real GDP growth compared to what typically occurs in developing countries in response to capital inflows.

5. For fuller discussions of external factors leading to such flows, see Calvo, Leiderman, and Reinhart (1993); Chuhan, Claessens, and Mamingi (1994); and Dooley, Fernandez-Arias, and Kletzer (1994). The bulk of capital flows to Latin America in the early 1990s went to Mexico.

6. With the exception of union-owned Banco Obrero and US-owned Citibank, the entire Mexican commercial banking system was nationalized in 1982. With a series of consolidations, the original 53 nationalized banks were pared to 18. These 18 institutions were privatized, one by one, in 1991 and 1992.

7. For a fuller development of the links between Mexico's banking problems and the subsequent exchange rate crisis, see Calvo and Mendoza (1995).

8. In the United States, once a loan goes into arrears, the entire remaining loan balance is considered in arrears. In contrast, Mexico's calculation procedure does not consider the entire remaining loan balance to be in arrears. For example, in Mexico, if a loan is three months in arrears, only the balance that had been contracted to be paid during those three months is calculated as in arrears. Any loan balance scheduled to be paid thereafter is not yet calculated as in arrears. Other things equal, then, US protocols would sometimes result in higher past-due loan ratios than Mexican protocols.

9. The Banco de México (1995) notes that 'the increase in domestic credit in 1994 occurred in response to reserve declines' and that reserves 'did not fall because domestic credit was expanded' (p. 64, author's translation).

10. Kamin and Rogers (1996) offer econometric evidence to suggest that when interest rates did rise, they rose only moderately less than could be predicted by the authorities' standard reaction function. Kamin and Rogers argue that, to have maintained the peg, the authorities would have had to intensify their responses to exchange market developments. That is, policy-makers would have had to alter their reaction regime, and they would have had to at a time when concerns for the health of the banking system would have suggested a relaxation of monetary policy.

11. While this is not the place to discuss the merits and liabilities of currency boards, one discipline they impose is that when foreign exchange reserves flow out, the resulting reduction in the stock of money is not offset. Although such boards may be seen as having significant liabilities, Argentina's peso (which is

disciplined by a currency board) maintained its nominal value through the difficult mid-1990s while Mexico's did not.

12. Brown and Whealan (1993) offer econometric evidence to suggest, for example, that present oil prices reflect agent expectations of futures prices.

13. Lustig (1995, p. 379) notes that 'this dollarization of internal debt probably explains the surprising stability of international reserves before such adverse events as the increase of foreign interest rates and domestic political unrest' (author's translation). Moreover, the Banco de México (1995, p. 69) states that 'the issuance of *tesobonos* was carried out in order to reduce exchange market pressures' (author's translation).

14. Recall that inasmuch as a central bank can always preserve a pegged exchange rate through a sustained high interest rate or a contraction in monetary base, interest rates insufficient to prevent declining reserves suggests that other policies must dominate a commitment to a pegged exchange rate. Garber and Svensson (1994, p. 29) note that one of these policies may be 'the preserveation of solvency of a banking system'.

15. The capital outflows were not well-known, however, and a number of analysts have complained that something kept Mexico during the latter portions of 1994 from releasing data on central bank holdings of foreign reserves.

16. Interest rates typically reflect nervousness about devaluations. Consider, for example, the movement of yields on the 28-day *cete* auction for the following dates: 9 November, 13.49 per cent; 16 November, 13.45 per cent; 23 November, 13.95 per cent; 29 November, 13.85 per cent; 7 December, 13.30 per cent; 14 December, 13.75 per cent.

17. Calvo and Mendoza (1995) and Sachs, Tornell, and Velasco (1995) address other aspects of the sudden and explosive nature of Mexico's financial crisis that clearly deserve attention. Calvo and Mendoza argue that this phenomenon reflects, among other things, a trade-off between diversification and information that investors face when information is costly to acquire.

In Calvo and Mendoza's paradigm, as investment opportunities expand across countries, the payoff to purchasing information about a particular country declines. It becomes rational for investors to become sensitive to even 'small' bad news, especially when it follows previous bad news, even if none of the news is related to fundamentals. In sum, the reduced incentives to acquire much information about Mexico in particular and Latin America in general motivated a herd behavior that triggered the *tequila effect*.

Sachs, Tornell, and Velasco (1995) argue that, while real disequilibria and reserve erosion laid the groundwork for the crisis, the timing and magnitude of the crisis came from a self-fulfilling panic after the government ran up its short-term debt and ran down gross reserves. That is, like Calvo and Mendoza (1995), Sachs, Tornell, and Velasco (1995, p. 7) do not believe that the crisis was fully consistent with fundamentals. Instead, they conclude, 'the panic was self-fulfilling in that expectations of a run on both pesos and *tesobonos* by other agents led each individual investor to engage in the same kind of speculative behavior'.

Bibliography

Banco de México (1995) *Informe Anual 1994* (Mexico City: Banco de México).
Brown, S. P. A., and Kelly Whealan (1993) 'Oil Price Expectations and US Oil Conservation,' paper presented at the North American meetings of the International Association for Energy Economics, October.

Calvo, Guillermo A., Leonardo Leiderman, and Carmen M. Reinhart (1993) 'Capital Inflows and Real Exchange Rate Appreciation in Latin America,' *IMF Staff Papers*, 40, March, pp. 108–51.

—— and Enrique G. Mendoza (1995) *Reflections on Mexico's Balance of Payments Crisis: A Chronicle of a Death Foretold* (College Park, Md.: Center for International Economics, University of Maryland).

—— and Carlos A. Végh (1992) 'Inflation Stabilization and Nominal Anchors,' *IMF Paper on Policy Analysis and Assessment*, December.

Chuhan, Punam, Stijn Claessens, and Nlandu Mamingi (994) 'Equity and Bond Flows to Asia and Latin America: The Role of Global and Country Factors' (The World Bank).

Claessens, Stijn, Michael P. Dooley, and Andrew Warner (1995) 'Portfolio Capital Flows: Hot or Cold,' *The World Bank Economic Review*, 9 (1), pp. 153–74.

Dooley, Michael P., Eduardo Fernandez-Arias, and Kenneth M. Kletzer (1994) 'Recent Private Capital Inflows to Developing Countries: Is the Debt Crisis History?' *National Bureau of Economic Research Working Paper Series*, no. 4792, July.

Dornbusch, Rudiger and Alejandro Werner (1994) 'Mexico: Stabilization, Reform, and No Growth,' in William C. Brainard and George L. Perry (eds), *Brookings Papers on Economic Activity*, 1 (Washington, D.C.: The Brookings Institution), pp. 253–97.

Eichengreen, Barry and Albert Fishlow (1995) 'Contending With Capital Flows: What is Different About the 1990s?' *Council on Foreign Relations Working Paper*, December.

—— James Tobin and Charles Wyplosz (1995) 'Two Cases for Sand in the Wheels of International Finance,' *The Economic Journal*, January, pp. 162–72.

Fidler, Stephen and Ted Bardacke (1994) 'Nervous over Deficit and Dissidence: Stephen Fidler and Ted Bardacke Assess the Devaluation Yesterday of the Mexican Currency,' *Financial Times*, 21 December, p. 5.

Garber, Peter M. and Lars E. O. Svensson (1994) 'The Operation and Collapse of Fixed Exchange Rate Regimes,' *National Bureau of Economic Research Working Paper*, no. 4971, December.

Gould, David M. (1994) 'Forecasting Mexican Inflation,' Federal Reserve Bank of Dallas, August (unpublished manuscript).

Gruben, William C. and Darryl McLeod (1996) 'Capital Flows, Savings, and Growth in the 1990s,' paper presented to the Latin American and Caribbean Economics Association sessions of the Allied Social Sciences Association meetings, San Francisco, January.

—— John H. Welch, and Jeffrey W. Gunther (1994) 'US Banks, Competition, and the Mexican Banking System: How Much Will NAFTA Matter?,' *Federal Reserve Bank of Dallas Working Paper*, no. 94–10, May.

—— Darryl McLeod and John H. Welch (1995) 'Propagation Mechanisms Between US and Mexican Financial Markets,' paper presented at the meetings of the Council on Foreign Relations, New York, March.

Heller, Heinz Robert (1991) 'Prudential Supervision and Monetary Policy,' in *The Evolving Role of Central Banks* (Washington, D.C.: International Monetary Fund).

Ize, Alan, and Guillermo Ortiz (1987) 'Fiscal Rigidities, Public Debt, and Capital Flight,' *IMF Staff Papers*, pp. 311–32.

Kamin, Steven B. (1991) 'Exchange Rate Rules in Support of Disinflation Programs in Developing Countries,' *International Finance Discussion Paper*, no. 402. Board of Governors of the Federal Reserve System.

—— and John H. Rogers (1996) 'Monetary Policy in the End-Game to Exchange-Rate Based Stabilization: The Case of Mexico,' Board of Governors of the Federal Reserve System, *International Finance Discussion Paper*, no. 540.

Kiguel, Miguel and Nissan Liviatan (1992) 'The Business Cycle Associated with Exchange Rate-Based Stabilizations,' *The World Bank Economic Review*, 6, May, pp. 279–305.

Lustig, Nora (1995) 'Mexico y la crisis del peso: lo pre-visible y la sorpresa,' *Comercio Exterior*, 45, May, pp. 374–82.

Mansell Carstens, Catherine (1993) 'The Social and Economic Impact of the Mexican Bank Reprivatization,' paper presented at Institute of the Americas, La Jolla, C.A., January.

McLeod, Darryl and John H. Welch (1991) 'North American Free Trade and the Peso,' *Federal Reserve Bank of Dallas Working Paper,* no. 9115.

Sachs, Jeffery, Aaron Tornell, and Andrés Velasco (1995) 'The Mexican Peso Crisis: Sudden Death or Death Foretold?,' paper presented at the conference 'Speculative Attacks in the Era of the Global Economy: Theory, Evidence, and Policy Implications,' Center for International Economics, University of Maryland at College Park, December.

Torres, Craig and Paul B. Campbell (1994) 'Mexico Reverses Currency Policy: Peso Falls 12.7 Percent,' *Wall Street Journal*, 21 December: A3.

Tricks, Henry (1994) 'Mexican Markets Panic After Peso Devaluation,' *Reuter European Business Report* (Reuters Ltd), 21 December.

Wall Street Journal (1994) 'Mexico Drops Effort to Prop Up Peso, Spurring 15% Fall and Eroding Credibility,' 23 December: A3.

Werner, Alejandro (1994) 'Comments and Discussion,' in William C. Brainard and George L. Perry (eds), *Brookings Papers on Economic Activity*, 1 (Washington, D.C.: The Brookings Institution).

6 Mexico: Foreign Investment and Democracy
Carlos Elizondo Mayer-Serra

The goal of this book is to assess the effects of foreign capital inflows on macroeconomic policy-making and democracy. The case of Mexico is particularly interesting for two reasons. First, from 1990 to 1993 net capital inflows to Mexico summed to $52.8 billion, more than to any other developing country. China with $49.2 billion, and Argentina with $24.5 billion, were the next most popular destinations (de la Dehesa, 1994, p. 5). A significant percentage of the inflows to Mexico were portfolio investment,[1] which made capital flows particularly sensitive to any event that could impact short-term profits. These enormous flows were possible thanks to a process of macroeconomic reform, widely perceived as creating the basis for long-term growth, and financial liberalization. By 1994, however, foreign flows had started to contract as a result of both international conditions, mainly a rise of US interest rates, and domestic ones, mainly the uncertainties regarding the political stability of the country (Krugman, 1995, pp. 28–44). By December 1994, capital flight had become unsustainable, forcing the new government to devalue the peso. The devaluation triggered a deep financial crisis not only in Mexico but in other emerging markets, that could only be controlled thanks to a US-sponsored international financial aid package amounting to over $50 billion.

A second reason making Mexico an interesting case study is the nature of its political system. In Mexico, democratization has gone far more slowly than in most of Latin America. Unlike Argentina, Chile, Brazil, Uruguay, and many other new democracies in the region, Mexico's prior system was not a military regime but rather an inclusive, civilian, authoritarian political system that has been dominated by a single party since 1929 (Purcell, 1975, pp. 3–11; O'Donnell, 1977). Mexico, of course, is formally a democracy: it has regular elections, a party system, and an elected president and national legislature. After the 1917 Revolution, however, peasants, workers other 'popular' sectors (ranging from bureaucrats and taxi-drivers to street vendors and the urban poor), as well as businessmen, were organized from the top through corporatist political institutions that served not only as a system of interest representation, but also as a way by which the state attempted to control these actors. Mexico's gradual democratization during the 1980s and 1990s has proceeded during the same period that the country has experienced three major external financial crises in 1982, 1985–86, and 1994–95, and years of recessionary structural adjustment.

This chapter makes four central arguments. First, the economic opening during the *sexennio* of President Carlos Salinas (1988–94) led to some democratization in Mexico's overall political system, although this outcome was not necessarily sought by the government nor conducted within the ruling political party, the Partido Institucional Revolucionario (PRI). Second, from the *destape* (unveiling) of PRI presidential candidate Luís Donaldo Colósio in late 1993 onwards, the Mexican economy (and, consequently, also the popularity of the incumbent government) became increasingly dependent on a net capital account surplus to finance the large current account deficit. Therefore, foreign investors, as well as Mexican owners of capital who had the option of capital flight, came to have increased structural power throughout 1994.

Third, purchasers of Mexican treasury securities and other portfolio assets in 1994, like financial investors everywhere, sought assurances from the Mexican government of both pro-business economic policies and political stability. However, investor preferences in Mexico in 1994 had some unusual components. For example, investors did not display a strong preference for neoliberal policies. They were not particularly worried about avoiding the traditionally dangerous combination of overvaluation and large trade and current account deficits, since these two problems were not the result of an underlying large public sector deficit. Moreover, most investors believed that political stability was more important to Mexico's future economic prospects than specific new neoliberal economic policies. In addition, many or even most investors in Mexico's capital markets had come to believe that some democratization, in particular more transparent and honest balloting procedures, would be more effective in maintaining political stability than would be maintenence of traditional authoritarian controls on leftist and lower-class protests, such as those that emerged after the 1988 presidential election. In other words, in Mexico in 1994 the 'structural power of capital' was, on balance, a force promoting cautious but genuine political democratization. Of course, the majority of Mexican business leaders took comfort in the fact that the polls suggested that the PRI would win the presidential election.

Fourth, the democratization that occurred prior to the 1994 election gave both a secure democratic victory and considerable popular legitimacy to Ernesto Zedillo, chosen to succeed Colósio as the PRI candidate following the latter's assassination in March 1994. Once the newly democratic rules of the game, giving the opposition fairer access to the media and campaign finance, were in place, the PRI found that it could not rescind them, even if it should wish to. With the coming of the financial crisis in December 1994, and the subsequent painful economic adjustment and contraction of the

Mexican economy, voters in the local elections of 1995 and 1996 to defect in substantial numbers to the major opposition parties. In the key midterm elections of July 1997, the PRI lost its majority in the lower Chamber and the PRD candidate, Cuauhtémoc Cárdenas, won Mexico City's first ever mayoral election.

PRIVATE BUSINESS AND MEXICAN DEMOCRACY

The tension between democracy and private property is an old theme of political theory. A democracy implies the risk of having property rights, at any level, altered by a majority. To avoid this risk, most liberal democracies originally limited the right to vote to property holders (Schlatter, 1951, pp. 162–237). The process towards universal suffrage has varied greatly among countries, but the ubiquitous underlying conflict has been how and whether to protect property holders from the tyranny of the majority. After intense political pressures, the masses have achieved the right to vote – but only after taming their demands in order to satisfy investors and avoid economic stagnation (Przeworski, 1986, pp. 7–46).

Capitalists can always move their assets abroad to protect them if democratic pressure implies too high taxation or a risk of expropriation. This gives them structural power[2] to limit state interference in property rights. Resources can be moved, and this limits the capacity of each national state to regulate private property. The ease with which resources can be moved from one country to another is a crucial variable explaining the constraints to manage the economy faced by a government. In Mexico, a country with a shared border of more than 3100 kilometers with the United States, the veto power of domestic capitalists historically has been high. This border has made Mexican control over capital exports virtually impossible, regardless of the policy objectives of the state elite.

Consequently, Mexican financial markets historically have been extremely liquid.[3] A significant proportion of financial savings are deposited abroad, and there have been few exchange controls. For Mexican savers the dollar is not only a means of exchange, but also a store of value.[4] This preference for liquidity and for holding US dollars is the result of two factors. The first is historically feeble property rights. The Mexican government has strong constitutional powers to expropriate, as it did to foreign oil companies in 1938 and Mexican commercial bankers in 1982. Second, numerous devaluations of the peso, and various periods of high inflation, have taught investors of the importance of having the possibility of a quick 'exit' from peso assets. In fact, capital 'exit' has remained legal for most of the post-revolutionary regime. Even during the most acute period of government-business conflict, during the sexenio of President Lázaro Cárdenas (1934–40), exchange controls could not be introduced. In Cárdenas' words: 'Exchange controls can only work in highly disciplined countries where customs rules are well organized and borders can be effectively watched; exchange control in Mexico would surely be undermined by the black market' (Maxfield, 1990, p. 72).[5] Moreover, powerful businessmen in Mexico traditionally have enjoyed privileged access to policy-making. For example, the popular sectors were controlled by an inclusive authoritarian state that from 1940 to 1970 followed an economic policy that tended to favor the most important business groups.

When the administration of President Luis Echeverría (1970–76) pursued policies that threatened business interests, large businessmen organized themselves through the creation of the CCE (Consejo Coordinador Empresarial, or Business Coordinating Council), an umbrella group of the most important business organizations. The political opposition of business, plus severe capital flight, contributed significantly to the incapacity of Echeverría to control the economy. The 39 per cent devaluation of the peso on 1 September 1976 was the most evident signal of this.[6]

José López Portillo, Echverría's successor, initiated his *sexennio* (1976–82) with a new agreement with businessmen. Thanks to oil revenues, the pact worked initially. However, by the end of his administration, a new conflict with the business community had arisen as Mexico came near to defaulting on its foreign debt. Carlos Tello, appointed President of Mexico's central bank on 1 September 1982, publicly and undiplomatically blamed this failure on Mexican big business, particularly on the commercial banks. That same day Lopez Portillo's government nationalized the banks and imposed exchange controls. As usual they were quite ineffective,[7] as capital seeped across the long and porous border with the United States.[8] A run against the peso ended in devaluation and the partial confiscation of deposits denominated in dollars, which were paid at an exchange rate fixed by the government. Businessmen, who for decades had been content to pursue their interests quietly and through personal contacts with the federal executive, this time opted for a more open participation in politics to confront the government. After 1982, some of them chose to participate with the PAN (Partido de Accion Nacional), in order to compete electorally against the PRI (Elizondo, 1996, pp. 41–58).

Another element of the implicit economic model that cracked open in 1982 had been a persistent tendency to currency overvaluation. Overvaluation of the peso followed by an abrupt devaluation has been one of the most visible economic fiascoes of Mexican government economic policy making of the past 20 years. The roots of an economic policy that favored overvaluation can be found in the logic of the so-called 'stabilizing development,' the economic policy followed from 1958 to 1970 that allowed the Mexican economy to grow 6.7 per cent a year with and average inflation of 2.5 per cent. A cheap dollar partially financed by agricultural exports

financed import-substituting industrialization (Reynolds, 1970; Solis, 1991).
However, what initially had been an economically sound strategy to finance
industrial development, became politically very difficult to alter as interests
reoriented themselves to benefit from this strategy, particularly industrialists, financiers, specialized workers in capital-intensive industries geared to
the domestic market, and the middle class. Savers also became used to a predictable value of the dollar. This strategy operated at the expense of peasants
and the unemployed, but the upper income groups had more political clout.[9]
Consequently, Mexican presidents knew the political cost of a devaluation
that would upset the most important political groups in Mexico. In López
Portillo's words: 'Devaluation ... is the most serious political problem a
President of the Republic has to face. ... This phenomenon of economic
adjustment that seems to be normal in other nations, in Mexico, was truly a
national tragedy.'[10]

    After the financial crash of 1982, President Miguel de la Madrid (1982–88)
had to face critical conditions. Businessmen – in particular financiers – and
many Mexican savers had lost confidence in the government, now preferring
to retain their capital abroad. Foreign reserves were depleted, inflation was
over 100 per cent, the public sector and many large firms were highly
indebted, and the central government faced a deficit of nearly 17 per cent of
GDP. De la Madrid's response was a drastic contraction of the economy and,
in 1986, decisions to enter the General Agreement on Tariffs and Trade
(GATT) for the first time and to begin privatization. The economy did not
grow during his sexenio. Meanwhile increased political openness allowed the
growth of a leftist opposition to current Mexican government policies, a phenomenon that worried both the Mexican business community and the PRI.

    In the 1988 presidential elections the PRI candidate, Carlos Salinas, won
only a narrow victory over his challenger, Cuauhtémoc Cárdenas, head of a
broad opposition coalition on the moderate left that by the 1990s had taken
the name Partido Revolucionario Democratico (PRD). Political tensions
rose, as many Mexicans refused to consider Salinas' election legitimate.
Cárdenas' disappointed and disillusioned supporters demonstrated in the
streets of Mexico City. Nevertheless, most businessmen, including many of
those that sympathized with the 1988 PAN presidential candidate, Manuel
Clouthier, supported the government (or at least remained silent). Contrary
to the expectations of those businessmen supporting the PAN, the elections
of 1988 showed that most Mexicans were unwilling to support the PAN in
1988. As most Mexicans voted for the PRI and for the Cárdenistas (in what
proportion it is difficult to know), businessmen realized it was better to trust
the Salinas government which seemed to be a better alternative than an
unpredictable populist coalition.

    Large businessmen realized that Salinas gave them access to policy-
makers[11] and was prepared to go further than expected in major economic

issues, as for example with respect to privatization, deregulation and trade liberalization. The Salinas government even softened the PRI's stand on issues previously considered unchangeable, such as the laws regulating the relationship between government and the church. Consequently, most prominent businessmen began to believe that it was time to build a new relationship, one that has increasingly implied being directly involved in PRI activities. By the time of the elections of 1994, most major businessmen openly supported the PRI presidential candidates in a more explicit alliance than in the past. Foreign investors were less open, but equally supportive.

An interesting side consequence of the newly overt relationship between Mexican business leaders and the PRI has been their greater readiness to fund the PRI openly. Business participation in the PRI initially was promoted by the government as a way to rob the PAN of its 'natural' support. Once the relationship with businessmen was radically transformed into a more or less open alliance between government and the more important businessmen, the political role of these businessmen changed. The government expected businessmen to financially support the party, especially as elections become more competitive and state resources were increasingly more difficult to channel into the PRI. Funding the official party was a cost many businessmen were not eager to pay, but it was difficult to avoid in a political system where power was so concentrated, the party system so dominated by one party, and benefits were likely to be expected from the new government.[12] However, the 1996 electoral reforms formally limited private funding of campaigns, and controls over party spending began to be implemented.

The significance for democratization was that, as businessmen started to participate in the PRI, democratization became a less menacing process for them. By the mid-1990s, the PRI and the PAN, the two parties where businessmen participated, clearly led the polls[13] and eventually received more than three quarters of the total votes of the presidential elections of 1994. Contrary to 1988, democratization during the Salinas administration seemed to many business leaders, domestic and occasionally foreign, to be a relatively painless procedure, in that it apparently did not imply the risk of empowering a party that opposed economic reform.

THE POLITICS OF THE 1994 DEVALUATION

Fighting inflation through an almost fixed exchange rate during the Salinas administration (1988–94) led the government to promote the opening of the economy,[14] and the partial liberalization of the financial markets enabled the administration to finance the current account deficit and the overvaluation of the peso. The strategy worked initially because markets believed it would be successful, and therefore poured resources in to Mexico. Controlling inflation and stabilizing the exchange rate were the initial economic, and thus political, successes of Salinas. This monetary and exchange rate policy increased private consumption of dollar-intensive goods at a subsidized rate, ensured high dollar-equivalent interest rates to savers, and reduced the unfair inflationary tax.

Of course the strategy had costs. Once a band of devaluation of a currency is imposed it is very difficult to abandon it while it works, as there is a risk that, when pulling out of it, what has been gained in terms of stability, and therefore of popularity, will be lost. International confidence was also built on the predictable value of the peso, and any abrupt devaluation would destroy it. Each time the Salinas administration felt investors' confidence was diminishing, which could undermine the exchange rate policy that anchored the whole program, its response was a new dramatic coup towards liberalization, such as selling the state-owned banks, proposing NAFTA (the North American Free Trade Agreement) to the United States, and removing barriers to foreign portfolio investment in government bonds. These liberalizing policies were perceived by foreign and domestic investors as creating the conditions for stable economic growth. Moreover, as foreign investors started to participate in the Mexican economy, the government increased its leverage with domestic investors. Although foreign direct investment increased, the lion's share of foreign capital flows was portfolio investment in financial instruments.

By the end of 1992, however, the capacity to continue with bold structural initiatives that could have created new incentives to invest in Mexico and made the economy more efficient was diminished, as the short-term political agenda gained priority. Many key decisions – including reforming the labor law, making PEMEX (the national oil company) and the Comisión Federal de Electricidad (the national electricity company) more efficient or perhaps privatizing them, drastically reforming social security, maintaining a more competitive exchange rate,[15] and opening the banking sector to foreign entrants – were not implemented. Any of these measures would have led to a larger share of direct foreign investment, and therefore to less potential volatility.

Between late 1988 and 1992, President Salinas conducted economic reforms despite the opposition of important segments of his party. This was possible thanks to the concentration of power of the Presidency. By the end of 1992, however, Salinas seems to have felt that he had to avoid confronting opponents of his economic policies within the PRI. The President needed to ensure a positive political environment to promote the candidate that would likely become his successor, according to the then prevailing rules of the Mexican political system. The President perceived that any dramatic neo-liberal reform initiative could have led to a nationalistic reaction that might have been used by those opposing his political project. Potential presidential candidates had also to ensure their own role was not questioned, which created incentives to cover up any policy disagreements they might have had. The leitmotif of this game was freezing conflicts and potential problems.

The increased private capital inflows during the Salinas administration had mixed implications for Mexican democratization. As Leslie Elliott Armijo suggests in her conclusion to this book, portfolio investment flowing to a PRI administration certainly gave resources to Salinas, which had been used to ensure governability after the difficult 1988 elections. However, such a large inflow also made investors more aware of the threats to Mexico's political stability. Although democracy implied uncertainty, the lack of credible elections was even more uncertain. Moreover, the US Congress in late 1993 voted, in effect, to accept Mexico as a member of NAFTA. Although NAFTA did not formally include democratic provisions, it did impact the margin of maneuver of the Mexican government, increasing the costs of authoritarian solutions. Critics of NAFTA were keen to point out any violation of human rights, and President Clinton wanted to avoid a weak Mexican flank.

International markets, in particular financial markets, demand information regarding the political stability of the country. Transaction costs are relatively low, so any event that can potentially lead to lower profits is quickly reflected in the market. Mexico became, therefore, a more monitored country than in the past. As a consequence of the larger amounts of foreign capital inflows coming to Mexico in the early 1990s, domestic political conflicts not only had to be solved effectively, but without reference to the 'menace' of Soviet influence, within the norms expected in the more developed countries.

During the Salinas *sexennio*, 1993, the year of the unveiling of his successor (the *destape*), was also the year of NAFTA. After two years of delay there was finally a chance that NAFTA could be approved by the United States Congress. For all of these reasons, no new radical measures that could lead to a nationalistic reaction within the PRI were implemented. The value of the peso was defended and the economy was put into a halt by means of high real interest rates in order to avoid a devaluation that would have increased the difficulties of getting NAFTA through the US Congress, as it would have infuriated trade union leaders who felt Mexican wages were already too low.

In the past, once the *destape* took place, elections had been less important, allowing the sitting government some margin of maneuver. For example, in early 1988 then President De la Madrid had started economic shock therapy, which included a devaluation that gave Salinas the capacity to start his administration with a stable economy, *before* the elections.[16]

However, in 1993 and after, the PRI's fate in elections was too uncertain for the outgoing president to risk taking economic measures sure to be unpopular with some key electorates. Instead, the Salinas government sought to prolong the propitious economic conditions for one more year in order to give Colósio a better chance in the elections. In any case, the genuinely competitive nature of the approaching elections themselves also helped to promote the confidence of foreign investors, thus closing the circle. Salinas thus switched to expansionary short-term policies that made a booming economy possible. By early 1994, thus, outgoing President Salinas was playing a delicate game: he was following economic policies that some of his economic advisors must have known could not be sustained, for reasons that were essentially political.

Meanwhile, opposition parties and movements maneuvered for advantage. For example, the opening of the economy probably helped some of the anti-government political movements of 1994. The EZLN (Ejército Zapatista de Liberación Nacional) launched its uprising on 1 January 1994, correctly calculating that, because of NAFTA and the need to calm foreign markets, the government would have to react with unusual restraint. The Zapatistas, therefore, recognized that they required the support of domestic and foreign press to have some success.[17]

Then, on 23 March 1994, PRI presidential candidate Luís Donaldo Colósio was murdered. Since Mexico and Mexicans had prided themselves for decades on being almost unique in Latin America for the peaceful way in which political conflicts were resolved, the assassination threatened to touch off a major political crisis. Anecdotal evidence after Colósio's murder suggests that domestic capitalists were more likely to export their capital than foreigners.[18] Without the higher stability of foreign investors and the support of international financial organizations, maintaining the value of the peso at that moment would have been much more difficult.[19]

Why did foreign investors (backed by the US government) maintain their faith in the Salinas administration's economic program? Many observers believed that Mexico's basic economic strategy was sound (see also Gruben in this volume). Although there were important political reasons not to devalue, many high level bureaucrats and local and foreign investors believed the model could be sustained, as the economic imbalances were not perceived as serious.[20] Mexico was then widely seen as a case study of proper economic management – the best example of how the 'Washington consensus' policies (Williamson 1990) could work – and financial markets were eager to pour resources into the Mexican economy. Although, for example, the current account deficit started to increase well beyond government projections, it never became, at least openly, a serious problem that required a significant change of policy. In the words of *The Economist* (1995), Mexico 'had a big current-account deficit, but since this reflected private (as opposed to public-sector) decisions about saving and investment, it seemed to pose no danger.' Most observers believed the market would adjust automatically to any change in investor's preferences. Paul Krugman (1995, p. 36) put it thus, 'Views contrary to the immense optimism of the time were treated not so much with hostility as bemusement. How could anyone be so silly as to say those gloomy things?'

Within Mexico, criticism was also relatively subdued. The most important opposition party, the PAN, agreed with most of the government's economic policies, claiming, in fact, that Salinas was just stealing the economic program they had defended for decades. They also lacked expertise to discuss the details of the program, as most sophisticated economists were working for the government or in institutions close to it. The PAN in 1994 therefore chose to concentrate its attention on the electoral agenda and to confront the government on charges of corruption. The PRD by definition opposed most government policies. However, its criticisms were too crude and all encompassing for them to be taken seriously within the government. As elections drew near, even the PRD diminished its criticism, at least in front of investors, of an economic policy that was still perceived as successful by a significant proportion of voters. Thus for a variety of reasons, both political and economic, many people favored the model, a major component of which was maintaining an overvalued exchange rate, supported by large foreign capital inflows under increasingly short term conditions. Moreover, while the majority of the federal governments's short term debt as of early 1994 was in the form of peso-denominated bonds known as *cetes*, during the course of that turbulent year, the government was obliged by market conditions (assuming that they wanted to sustain the exchange rate) to transform most of its internal debt into a dollar-denominated instrument, the *tesobonos*, redeemable in pesos at the market exchange rate of the day. Investors accepted this new paper.

As the August presidential elections approached, most analysts concurred on the need to seek a more open political system that could better accommodate the demands of a more complex society.[21] An illegitimate triumph of the PRI would have been unsatisfying and potentially destabilizing. For financial markets the uncertainties associated with a political system in the midst of a profound transition were serious.[22] To confront this fear, some businessmen made an effort to collaborate in the legitimization of the process. For example, Coparmex (Confederación Patronal Mexicana, or the National Employers Confederation), a business organization closer to the PAN than to the PRI, organized and promised to finance a quick, unofficial, post-election count with the aim of giving certainty to the electoral process (Rebello Pinal, 1994).

At the same time, there was no doubt that the business community preferred that the PRI win the election, nor were at least some of its spokespersons above using the threat of financial instability as an implicit campaign theme. For example, Roberto Hernández, President of the AMB (Asociación

Mexicana de Banqueros) and of Banamex-Accival, the most important financial group, declared four weeks before the elections that in his view democracy implies uncertainty. This uncertainty, he affirmed, had impacted financial markets, pushing interest rates up. His conclusion was clear: only if Zedillo won interest rates could go down. In his words, Zedillo is 'the candidate that gives us certainty.'[23] Roberto Hernández's message was correctly seen by the press as a warning of the risks, in terms of financial stability, of voting against the PRI. Potential financial instability, therefore, became an element in favor of Zedillo, as voters valued the stability of the peso and Zedillo was able to portray himself as the only one capable of managing it.[24]

Ernesto Zedillo won the August 1994 elections based on a promise: that he knew how to manage the economy.[25] Zedillo became the symbol of continuity for what was by then perceived by investors and important sectors of the electorate as a successful program of economic reform. As institutions were weak, the technocratic elite that was competing under the PRI banner became politically that much more attractive.[26] The country's great dependence on foreign resources, coupled with the feeble institutionalization of economic reform, favored the electoral chances of the PRI, or in any case a conservative transition. Investors and the business community at large, both foreign and domestic, as well as many middle and even lower class voters perceived financial stability as very important, but fragile. As the presidential election approached, it was difficult for the leaders of the leftist PRD to construct an economic program attractive to their political supporters that would not be perceived as risky by investors and therefore be likely to undermine economic stability. Even the candidate of the rightist PAN was less attractive than the PRI's Zedillo, as the latter was perceived as more capable of ensuring continuity and of having the technical capacity to manage the economy.

Although the economic uncertainty in 1994 did not promote the fortunes of the PRD or the PAN, I have argued that on balance it did help to democratize and open up the formal rules of the national electoral game. On the one hand, markets were nervous, fearing that the PRI might lose, or (even worst in their view) that the PRD might win. At the same time, the strong economy during the Salinas administration had won great popular support for the PRI. Polls suggested that the PRI would win handily, unlike the party's close call in 1988. Furthermore, what the domestic, and especially the foreign, business community most feared was political instability. A fraudulent election in 1994, for Salinas' successor, could have sparked a social reaction difficult to channel through existing political institutions, which many ordinary Mexicans increasingly perceived as undemocratic. Therefore, the business community strongly opposed political repression, which would, they thought, increase political instability. Instead investors hoped for, and expected, a peaceful, but essentially conservative, transition to full democracy.

CONCLUSIONS

Portfolio investment is extremely volatile, and obviously risky. Many governments, however, believe they can control the beast. As long as capital
imports are booming, they can reap enormous political and economic
benefits. In the case of Mexico, capital came because the government was
implementing what was seen as an appropriate economic reform that would
enable the country to achieve growth with stability, although, as argued
above, there were signs that the economy was not as healthy as assumed by
government officials and investors. However, the pressures faced by a political system in the midst of a gradual democratic transition, while simultaneously having to cope with the demands of liquid investors, were enormous.
Moreover, political events uncommon in Mexico for decades frightened
investors. These included the assassination of PRI presidential candidate
Colósio in March, and another prominent political murder on 28 September
of José Francisco Ruiz Massieu, General Secretary of the PRI, after the election but before Zedillo's inauguration.

The new administration, elected under the banner of economic continuity,
could not manage these pressures and had to devalue. On 19 December, just
18 days after the Zedillo team took office, they devalued the peso by 15 per
cent. However, the clumsy way that the devaluation was conducted, with no
structural adjustment plan attached and with open differences within the
government regarding whether to fix or float the peso thereafter, led to a
new attack against the peso and a serious financial crisis.[27] The combination
of the devaluation, the international aid package of February 1995, and a
very contractionist monetary policy that led the economy into a profound
recession in 1995 and early 1996, led Mexico's current account deficit to virtually disappear. However, illusions regarding the virtues of Mexico's economic reform were seriously damaged. If before the devaluation foreign
investors had made economic growth possible, now they demanded clear
prospects of growth before investing.

The floating of the peso also increased the uncertainties of domestic and
foreign investors who had been convinced to invest in Mexico during the
Salinas administration, in part because there was predictability in the
exchange rate. Stability was lost, and financial markets, in spite of an orthodox monetary policy, were extremely volatile for more than a year, apparently under the influence of very short-term speculative capital. To confront
the crisis, the Zedillo administration sought to deepen economic reform, and
airports, more highways, satellites, electric power plants, and petrochemical
plants were slated for privatization. In early December 1995, social security
was reformed.[28] As of this writing in mid-1997, the privatization process of
ports, warehouses, and railways has already begun. The telephone long-
distance market was liberalized in 1997, and the domestic market was slated

to follow soon. The transportation, distribution and storing of natural gas had also been deregulated, allowing private investors,[29] and the financial sector was being liberalized even more quickly than envisaged by NAFTA legislation.[30]

However, the crisis had undermined the popularity of economic reform within Mexico. Former President Salinas left office with great popular support. His administration was associated with successful economic reform. Now he is seen as the example of corruption, and economic reform is being linked to corruption, recession, and rising inequalities. There have been, as a result, two important consequences for Mexican democratization: one within the PRI itself, and another in the political system as a whole. During its first three years, the Zedillo government had a significant margin of manuever, since no clear alternative economic strategy was visible. However, Zedillo encountered more resistance to economic reform coming from within the PRI than in the past. Congress, for example, in an unusual step, introduced some qualifications to the legislation that was proposed by the government to liberalize the banking sector.[31] Modifications in the new social security legislation were also introduced by Congressional dissidents from Zedillo's own party, the PRI.

Because of the economic crisis, the legitimacy of the new president, despite relatively clean and credible elections, was severely undermined, not only with the population in general, but with the business community. Government and business could no longer agree on the basic elements of the program to confront the financial crisis. The *pacto* schemes, in which government officials, businessmen, and trade union and peasant leaders agreed upon major economic policy issues, were suspended for more than a year. When renewed, they did not have a positive impact on financial markets. To confront this crisis of legitimacy, the government negotiated a further incremental political reform with the main opposition parties to ensure more credible elections and a more open political environment. Participants were the PAN, the PRD, and the small PT (Partido del Trabajo). The constitutional reforms needed to create a new electoral law were approved by the four parties with representation in Congress. In the discussion regarding the details of the new electoral law this consensus was broken, but the four parties continued to agree on the most important details of the reform. In mid-1997, congressional and some local elections took place. The new law gave the opposition parties relatively equal access to television and public resources. In the cleanest and fairest elections in Mexican history Cuauhtémoc Cárdenas, reborn moderate and moral leader of the PRD, won election as mayor of Mexico City, after more than 60 years of appointed Mexico City mayors. Even more dramatically, the PRI lost control over the lower chamber of Congress to the combined opposition for the first time since 1929, the year when the PRI, under another name, had been born.[32]

With the July 1997 elections, Mexico's long process of democratization seemed to be finally coming to an end. As the people of Mexico City voted for the PRD candidate, the financial markets celebrated with euphoria. Elections were clean and accepted as legitimate by the major opposition parties. Financial markets seemed happy with a new distribution of power, even if it had tilted in favor of the PRD. In any case, the PRI retained secure dominance in the Senate. Although investors face some risks that the PRD, should it come to power, might implement a more left wing economic program, most investors today are less worried about the consequences of a genuine democratic transition than they are about the possible political instability that might result from fights within the PRI or from fraudulent elections.

It is still too soon to know whether this positive relationship between democratization and financial markets will remain. Negotiating the budget will be a difficult test. With no majority in the lower chamber after the July 1997 elections and a PRI likely to be less disciplined and deferential to the president, future reforms will be less probable and in any case much slower. However, with the strong structural power they gained through the last decade of economic reform, financiers seem to know that even left wing parties will have to accept the restrictions imposed by the markets. Apparently, many investors, both foreign and domestic, have realized that the economy can profit from the political stability derived from a more institutionalized and democratic environment.

Notes

1. From 1991 to 1993, portfolio investment in Mexico went from $12.74 to $28.91 billion, falling to $8.18 in 1994. In 1991 Mexico captured 54.5 per cent of all portfolio investment directed to Latin America, though this amount fell to 18.6 per cent in 1994. From 1991 to 1994 the percentage of the current account deficit financed by direct investment amounted to 57.5 per cent in Argentina, 46.8 in per cent Brazil and 24 per cent in Mexico. Data are from INEGI (no date); México: Presidencia de la República (1994); GEA Económico (1995 p. 20) and Baring Securities 1995, Table 3, n.p.
2. Structural power is understood as the crucial role played by those that control private capital. How they use their capital, whether they invest or consume it, and in which particular way they invest it, affects the growth of the economy and therefore everybody's material situation.
3. They still are. The IMEF (Instituto Mexicano de Ejecutivos de Finanzas) asserts that by September 1995, '80 per cent of the national financial savings are constituted of resources placed in terms lower than one year and the largest part is concentrated in terms that expire in 28 days' [author's translation], Zúñiga (1995).
4. For an analysis of the implications of the dollarization of savings in developing countries, see Yotopoulos (1995).
5. Cárdenas' argument is very similar to the defense of freedom of exchange by Miguel Mancera, president of the Banco de México, in April 1982. Structural conditions, particularly the long and porous border with the United States,

rather than the links between bankers and government officials emphasized by Maxfield (1990), seem crucial to explain freedom of exchange. See also Maxfield (1991).

6. On 31 August the 1976, the government announced the end of the fixed exchange rate and in a few days the exchange rate increased from 12.5 to 20.5 pesos per dollar. After more turmoil, five weeks later the government allowed the peso to float freeely (Ortíz and Solís, 1984).

7. The establishment of exchange controls implied that banks could not sell foreign currency and could buy only by order of the central bank. Credits and deposits in foreign currency were also suppressed. However, creative transfer pricing by firms, plus a vigorous parallel exchange market just across the border in the US quickly undermined the Mexican government's efforts at control (Pérez López, 1987, pp. 111–21).

8. Moreover, money that went out and earned a profit as a result of the devaluation was not taxed for this capital gain. Although this taxation is contemplated in the tax law, it is impossible to collect without United States' help, and banking secrecy makes this extremely unlikely. See the chapter by Porter in this volume on the different preferences of advanced industrial and developing countries with respect to the evolving international regime in cross-border bank regulations.

   In fact, to promote the return of flight capital from the 1980s, the government in the 1990s has consecutively legalized tax evasion. Since May 1990, the government has charged capitalists returning an almost symbolic tax equivalent to 1.0 per cent of money brought back if the 'exit' was before that date. *El Financiero*, 22 April 1994. The SCHP (Secretaría de Hacienda y Crédito Público) announced in October 1995, a new fiscal pardon for resources maintained abroad before 30 September 1995 (*Reforma*, 19 October 1995).

9. An undervalued peso penalized agricultural exports. Capital-intensive industries that imported capital goods were more attractive than labor-intensive industries, due to the size of the domestic market, could only grow through exports.

10. President José López Portillo, quoted in *Excelsior* (9 April 1982).

11. According to A. Swardson and M. Hamilton (1995, p. 4): 'Heads of the major mutual funds had [finance minister Pedro] Aspe's home telephone number and they used it.'

12. The study of business involvement in PRI politics is still underdeveloped. For a brief discussion see Elizondo (1995).

13. Polls were used systematically for the first time in Mexico. Most of these polls showed the advantage of the PRI and the distant third place of the PRD.

14. For more details, see Elizondo (1997).

15. For many economists this was not a serious problem.

16. Which were, however, almost lost, as political life in Mexico had changed more than what the government then acknowledged.

17. The EZLN leadership also knew the fragility of the peso. Just days after Zedillo took office, on 8 December 1994, they announced an end to their temporary ceasefire, staging a 'troop movement' on 19 December 1994, which precipitated the devaluation.

18. The author advised a Mexican security firm from 1993 to 1994. During this period I had several interviews with important fund managers of New York. My statements regarding their reactions and their political perceptions are based on this experience. After the murder of Colosio, foreign funds were not major sellers through this security firm.

19. The same day that Colósio was murdered, US President Bill Clinton offered a credit of almost $6 billion. The Treasury Minister Lloyd Bentsen and other officials also gave their public support. International financial organizations and foreign bankers approved the program and offered help in avoiding a stock market crash. The invitation for Mexico to be part of the Organization for Economic Cooperation and Development, which came sooner than originally expected, also had a positive impact in terms of investors' confidence. *El Financiero*, 25 March, 29 March, and 18 April 1994.

20. Many, in fact, still believe that the mistake *was* devaluing.

21. For an example of the discussions that took place at this time, see Aguilar Camín *et al.* (1994).

22. Financial markets seemed most frightened by the end of March, not only because of the uncertainty surrounding the electoral process following Colósio's murder, but also because the United States raised short-term interest rates after February 1994. This affected emerging markets, including Mexico. Nevertheless, results from the elections in August brought back some certainty. The interest rates for *cetes* of 28 days maturity show this clearly. They were 9.45 in February, 9.73 in March, 15.79 in April, and reached 17.07 in July. However, they fell to 14.46 in August, 13.76 in September, and 13.74 in November (Cámara de Diputados, 1995).

23. *Reforma,* 22 July 1994.

24. It is worth noting that in contrast to arguments made by analysts such as Delia Boylan (1995), Mexico's lack of an autonomous central bank clearly went against the interests of the opposition parties. On the one hand, the Banco de Mexico helped the government to avoid higher interest rates, even at the cost of losing international reserves, making possible a significant expansion of the economy in the last semester of 1994. On the other hand, in the absence of a strong and credible central bank, the economic risks of a defeat of the PRI became stronger.

25. According to an exit poll overseen by Warren Mitofsky, 62 per cent of voters thought that the most important personal asset of Zedillo was his experience, which was linked, at least in PRI propaganda, to his capacity to manage the economy. Nonetheless, the most visible element in explaining the triumph of Zedillo, was party identification: 65 per cent voted for him because they always vote for the PRI. See Mercado Gasca and Zuckermann Behar (1994).

26. A similar logic seems to have been behind the electoral success of President Carlos Saul Menem in Argentina. For several years the Treasury Minister, Domingo F. Cavallo, became an essential figure in inspiring confidence as well. Mexican Finance Minister Pedro Aspe played a similar role during the Salinas administration.

27. On 19 December 1994 the government accepted a maximum 15 per cent devaluation. Two days after, the government decided to abandon that limit and the exchange rate increased from 3.4662 pesos to the US dollar on 19 December to 5.1000 on 26 December a nearly 40 per cent devaluation. During the first days of 1995 the peso–dollar exchange rate continued to rise, reaching nearly 8 pesos per dollar by the third week of March. The peso stabilized around 6 in mid-April.

28. *El Financiero* (10 December 1995).

29. The new regulation was established on 8 November 1995 (*Reforma*, 1996).

30. NAFTA imposed a limit of 15 per cent of total shareholdings by foreigners in any given financial institution. As a result of the crisis, this has been raised to 20 per cent in brokerage houses and 25 per cent in banks. Moreover, in

NAFTA no foreign bank could have more than 4 per cent of the total market share of all banks, a figure now raised to 6 per cent (*El Financiero*, 1 February 1995).

31. The Federal Executive sent a bill to Congress to reform the laws which regulate financial groups, credit institutions and the stock market, in order to enlarge foreign capital participation in the Mexican financial system. In a meeting without precedent in Mexico, senators and deputies (from the PRI, PAN and PRD) got together with prominent bankers. Even though national bankers gave their support for the proposed reforms, and expressed confidence on the fact that corporate control of these institutions would not be entirely held by foreigners, legislators revealed their worry that banks would end up under the control of foreigners. They proposed the establishment of "locks". The most important one limits foreigners to purchasing banks whose net capital does not exceed 6 per cent of the net capital of the entire banking system (*El Financiero*, 11, 12, 14, 21, 25, 28 January 1995; *Reforma*, 11, 21, 25 January 1995).

32. For local elections in 1995 the PAN obtained 37.4 per cent of votes, the PRI 44.1 per cent and the PRD 12.4 per cent. However, if one compares federal election results from 1994 to July 1997, it is evident that the PRI has lost approximately 10 percentage points of the total vote. The PAN just rose 1.5, while the PRD has risen approximately 7 points, gaining most of what the PRI has lost. Of the 500 seats of the lower chamber the PRI got 239, PAN 122, PRD 12, PT 6, and PVEM (Partido Verde Ecologista Mexicano, or the Green Ecology Party) 8. As for the Senate, the PRI obtained 13 seats, out of 32 elected (adding up to a total of 77), the PAN 9 (with a total of 33), the PRD 8 (summing up 13), and the PVEM 1.

Bibliography

Agenda del Economista (1995), no. 9.

Aguilar Camín, Hector, Jorge Alcocer, Rolando Cordera, and Carlos Monsiváis (1994) 'México ante la adversidad,' *Nexos*, 197, May.

Banco de México, Instituto Nacional de Geografía y Estadística (INEGI), no date. Data files of the INEGI, México, D.F.

Baring Securities (1995) *The Mexico Crisis: Analysis and Implications for Financing: Preliminary Views*, January.

Boylan, Delia (1995) 'Holding Democracy Hostage: Central Bank Autonomy in the Transition from Authoritarian Rule.' annual meeting of the American Political Science Association, Chicago.

Cámara de Diputados (1995) *Agenda del Economista*, México, D.F.: H. Cámara de Diputados y El Colegio Nacional de Economistas, no. 9, Septiembre–Octubre.

de la Dehesa, G. (1994) 'La reciente afluencia masiva de capital privado hacia los países en desarrollo, ¿ es viable?' Conferencia Per Jacobsson, Madrid.

The Economist (1995) 'The Mexico Syndrome, and how to steer clear of it,' 18 March pp. 73–5.

The Economist, 18 March.

Elizondo, Carlos (1995) 'Privatizing the PRI: Shifts in the Business–PRI Relationship.' Mexico, unpublished manuscript.

—— (1996) 'Constitutionalism and State Reform.' in Monica Serrano y Victor Boulmer Thomas (eds), *Rebuilding the State Mexico After Salinas* (London: Institute of Latin American Studies).

—— (1997) 'Tres Trampas: sobre los orígenes de la crisis económica Mexicana de 1994,' *Desarrollo Económico, Revista de Ciencias Sociales*, 36(144), Instituto de Desarrollo Económico y Social, Argentina, enero-marzo, pp. 953–70.

El Financiero (1995), 10 December.

Grupo de Economistas y Asociados (GEA) (1995) *GEA Económico* (México, D.F.: GEA), no. 49, January, p. 20.

Krugman, Paul (1995) 'Dutch Tulips and Emerging Markets,' *Foreign Affairs*, 74(4), pp. 28–44.

Maxfield, Sylvia (1990) *Governing Capital: International Finance and Mexican Politics* (Ithaca, N.Y.: Cornell University Press).

—— (1991) 'Bankers' Alliances and Economic Policy Patterns: Evidence from Mexico and Brazil,' *Comparative Political Studies*, 23(4), pp. 419–58.

Mercado Gasca, Lauro and Leo Zuckermann Behar (1994) 'La encuesta a la salida de las casillas,' *Nexos*, September.

México: Presidencia de la República (1994) *Sixth Annual Government Report 1994/ Carlos Salinas de Gortari* (México, D.F.: Presidencia de la República).

O'Donnell, Guillermo A. (1977) 'Corporatism and the Question of the State,' in J. M. Malloy (ed.), *Authoritarianism and Corporatism in Latin America* (Pittsburgh: University of Pittsburgh Press, Pitt Latin American Series).

Ortíz, Guillermo and Leopoldo Solís (1984) 'Estructura Financiera y Experiencia Cambiaria: México 1954–1977,' *Documentos de Investigación del Banco de México, Subdirección de Investigaciones Económicas*, #1, March.

Pérez López, Enrique (1987). *Expropiación bancaria en México y desarrollo estabilizador* (México, D.F.: Editorial Diana).

Przeworski, Adam (1986) *Capitalism and Social Democracy* (Cambridge: Cambridge University Press).

Purcell, Susan Kaufman (1975) *The Mexican Profit-Sharing Decision: Politics in an Authoritarian Regime* (Berkeley, CA: University of California Press, 1975).

Rebollo Pinal, Hermínio (1994) 'Mesa de Negocios,' *El Financiero* (Mexico City, 22 July 1994)

Reforma [newspaper] (1996) *Anuario Reforma–1995* (México, D.F.: Reforma), 6 January.

Reynolds, Clark (1970) *The Mexican Economy: Twentieth-Century Structure and Growth* (New Haven: Yale University Press).

Schlatter, Richard (1951) *Private Property: The History of an Idea* (London: George Allen).

Solis, Leopolodo (1991) *La realidad económica mexicana: retrovisión y perspectivas* (Mexico City: Siglo XXI).

Swardson, A. and M. Hamilton (1995) 'Investment Funds Link Economic Series: The Americas, a Changing Neighborhood,' *The Washington Post Foreign Service*, no. 2, 21 August.

Williamson, John (1990) *Latin American Adjustment: How Much Has Happened?* (Washington: Institute for International Economics).

Yotopoulos, Pan R. (1995) 'La reputación asimétrica, devaluaciones y la enfermedad de no crecimiento de los países en desarrollo: A propósito de la crisis del peso,' *Investigación Económica*, no. 214, pp. 277–90.

Zúñiga M., Juan Antonio (1995) '80% del ahorro financiero, en depósitos a menos de un año; la mayoría, a 28 días: IMEF.,' *La Jornada*, 10 Octubre.

7 Brazil: Short Foreign Money, Long Domestic Political Cycles

Peter R. Kingstone

Financial globalization and foreign capital flows have come to occupy great attention in Latin America in the mid-1990s. In political terms, the increased importance of foreign capital has held out both promises and threats for Latin American democracy. On the one hand, foreign investment and financial liberalization have held out the possibility of financing new growth and replacing the now exhausted sources of state financing for industry. Similarly, these new inflows of capital have also helped support financially strapped governments, allowing them to maintain key services and political support while substantially cutting overall spending. On the other hand, substantial and sometimes rapid capital inflows also posed risks – as the Mexican peso crisis and resulting 'tequila effect' dramatically revealed. When financial flows reverse their direction, the resulting payments problems can force politically difficult choices over who should bear the costs.

While Mexico has commanded a great deal of attention in the mid-1990s as a result of the peso crisis, the issues noted above apply to Brazil as well. Brazil liberalized its trade and financial system later and more slowly than countries like Mexico, Argentina, and Chile. However, this liberalization, beginning in 1990, has attracted greater and greater inflows of foreign capital, both direct and portfolio investments. This is especially true since 1994 when then Finance Minister, Fernando Henrique Cardoso, successfully stabilized inflation through the *Real* Plan.[1]

As dramatic as this new visibility of foreign capital in the region may be, it does not represent a sharp break with the past. After all, foreign capital has played a positive and vital role in economic and political development ever since Latin America increasingly integrated into the global economy in the nineteenth century. British capital financed infrastructure development and early industrialization in the late nineteenth century and early twentieth century. Foreign direct investment was critical for Brazil's growth in the 1950s through its miracle years of the 1960s and 1970s. International lending financed large scale state led expansion in the 1970s.

At the same time, foreign capital has also had a negative impact. In fact, almost all of Brazil's regime breakdowns in the twentieth century happened in conjunction with balance-of-payment crises. In 1930, the 'Coffee and Milk' (*Café com Leite*) Republic collapsed under the weight of a convertibility and balance-of-payment crisis (Skidmore and Smith, 1992, p. 164). In 1964, Brazil's democracy collapsed anew in the context of increasing political polarization, spiraling inflation, and a balance of payments crisis (see Wallerstein, 1980; Sola, 1982; Stepan, 1978). In 1985, the military government gave way to democratic rule in a context of brutally spiraling debt, inflation, and balance-of-payment problems.[2]

This paper argues that we can understand the broad implications of foreign investment for democracy in Brazil in the 1990s in terms of a pattern of long cycles of political instability in Brazilian politics. Brazil's history suggests a pattern in which foreign capital begins this cycle as an important and useful source of financing. In the beginning of the cycle, foreign capital has provided funds for development and has allowed governments to forestall distributive conflicts by purchasing political support from key domestic groups. Historically, the cycle has ended when capital outflows (for varying reasons) placed increasing pressure on governments to make difficult choices about who should bear the costs of economic adjustments. The resulting distributional conflicts undermined successive regimes as critical social groups sought anti-regime solutions to their concerns. Thus, foreign capital became a dangerous source of pressure on a polity with historically weak political institutions: an electoral system that historically has produced perverse incentives for politicians, political parties with limited legitimacy and shallow roots in society, and a society with only a weak normative commitment to democracy.

In this regard, Brazil in the 1990s shares much in common with these earlier periods. The government of Fernando Henrique Cardoso has relied on foreign financing to ease its financial difficulties, to finance renewed growth, and to limit conflicts over distribution of resources and the costs of economic reform. However, in relying on foreign capital, the Cardoso government has created or sharpened new lines of conflict that could pose significant challenges to the country's weak institutions should Brazil face balance-of-payment problems in the future.

FOREIGN CAPITAL AND DEMOCRACY

As the other chapters in this book show (both Armijo's theoretical argument and the specific country studies), there are a variety of ways that foreign capital can either advance or hinder democracy depending on the particular political circumstances. Thus, we should be sceptical of perspectives that argue that foreign capital is inherently bad or that increases in the influence of capitalists inherently threatens democracy.[3]

What Brazil's long cycles of instability suggest is that weak political institutions with fragile legitimacy matter most for the Brazilian context. As observers from Robert Dahl (1961) to Adam Przeworski (1986) have reminded us, democracy is a set of rules and procedures for resolving conflicts. It becomes stable because a wide set of actors (especially elite actors) accept the outcomes of decisions about policy/conflicts made within the rules.[4] However, as Przeworski further notes, there must be some limits on the losses actors, especially elites, may suffer if they are to accept democratic decisions as binding. If actors come to believe that the existing regime does not adequately protect their interests, then they face strong incentives to look for alternatives.[5]

One important limit to this problem is if actors develop a normative preference for democracy that commits them to the regime.[6] This view, as expressed by Dankwart Rustow (1970) and again by Guillermo O'Donnell (1986), suggests that actors may come to value democracy over continuous struggle to impose a preferred regime, even if they can conceive of an alternative where they believe they may do better (Rustow, 1970; O'Donnell, 1986). Under these conditions, democracy may stabilize as groups eschew extreme positions and tactics in favor of preserving democratic procedures.[7] In such a case, one might expect a polity to successfully weather a balance of payments crisis.

This paper argues that Brazil's history reveals the absence of that normative commitment to democracy, although that may be slowly changing in the 1990s. In earlier periods, groups backed democracy until economic crises generated intense conflicts over the distribution of the costs of the crisis. As foreign capital withdrew in response to the crisis, the state lost the capacity to pay off support groups, many of which had supported the regime primarily on instrumental grounds. Thus, foreign capital did not express inherently a preference for authoritarianism over democracy, nor did it necessarily subvert democratic politics. Rather, the withdrawal of foreign capital led to balance of payment crises which forced the government to confront hard choices with poor institutional tools and weak legitimacy to manage the resulting distributional conflicts. In that context, key social groups (especially industry and bankers) sought out alternative regimes to protect their interests.

Brazilian elites have shown a greater normative commitment to democracy in the 1990s than they have in the past. However, the form of foreign capital inflows has changed as well in ways that has intensified the risks of a balance-of-payments crisis. Specifically, while FDI and international lending have returned to Brazil, the country has grown more dependent on portfolio investment. Historically, foreign banks, international lending institutions, and MNC's have tolerated a great deal more uncertainty and policy mistakes than portfolio investment does. In fact, portfolio investment tends to take much shorter positions in the market and is designed to withdraw rapidly in response to changing market conditions. Thus, Brazilian elites today may be more committed to democracy, but the possibility of a rapid outflow of capital also is much greater.

FOREIGN CAPITAL, BALANCE-OF-PAYMENTS CRISES, AND LONG CYCLES OF INSTABILITY

To illustrate the argument about the risks of foreign capital in general and with reference to the context in the 1990s, it is worth briefly reconsidering three crucial cases of regime breakdown in twentieth century Brazil: the 1930 coup, the 1964 coup, and the end of military rule in 1985.[8] In each of these three instances, balance-of-payment crises resulting from the withdrawal of foreign capital precipitated or accompanied political crises over economic policy. As capital withdrew and the balance of payments worsened, key social groups defected from the support coalition in search of alternatives. In the absence of strong institutions that could credibly mediate conflicts, each of the regimes quickly fell.

THE 1930 COUP AND THE *MIL REIS* CONVERTIBILITY CRISIS

In the period leading up to the coup of October 1930, Brazil had a nominally democratic regime informally labeled the Republic of *'Café com Leite'* (coffee and milk). The label referred to the implicit agreement between two of Brazil's leading states, São Paulo (coffee) and Minas Gerais (milk) to share the national presidency between themselves. State elites controlled national voting to insure safe transitions from one president to his chosen successor. Overall, Brazil's republic was a fragmented, highly decentralized, weak federal system in which a variety of elite groups acquiesced in, though increasingly resented, the dominance of two state elites, most importantly São Paulo and the coffee growers.

Over the early twentieth century, opposition emerged among political liberals (basically urban liberals in São Paulo and Rio de Janeiro), quasi-fascist military modernizers, and 'outsider' state elites excluded from the presidency. Brazil experienced very little industrial development at that time and as a consequence did not produce any notable working class movement or party. Although this political system generated increasing opposition over time, it took a crisis to bring that opposition together.

The Great Depression provided the catalyst needed to break the fragile support base of the Republic. In the period leading up to the crisis, Brazil's economic growth rested on two pillars: British investment and lending, particularly in infrastructure, and coffee exports. By 1929, Brazilian debt exceeded $1 billion, but rising coffee export revenues through the 1920s maintained a positive balance of payments until the crisis (Marichal, 1989, p. 219). Coffee exports climbed from 56 per cent of all exports in 1919 to 75 per cent in 1924, while exports' share of GNP climbed to over 12 per cent in the same period (Baer, 1983, pp. 40–1). Thus, coffee growers were the key supporters of the Republic, both politically and economically.

The country's difficulties actually began in 1927 as increasing coffee harvests led to declining global prices and as a result growing balance-of-payment concerns. The major contraction of world trade beginning with the 1929 crash delivered another shocking blow to the already weakening position of coffee growers and government revenues. The value of Brazilian exports fell from over $440 billion in 1929 to $180 billion in 1932. Foreign capital inflows came to a virtual halt while President Washington Luís' decision to maintain the full convertibility of the *Mil Reis* and a fixed exchange rate led to a rapid exhaustion of all gold and British Sterling reserves. Within a very brief period of time, the Republic's most important political supporter had suffered a major blow while Brazil faced a staggering debt and balance-of-payments crisis.

Washington Luís might have survived his decision to back British investors' preferences for full convertibility had he made different choices about how to manage the presidential succession, but as a *Paulista* (native of São Paulo) he chose to push another *Paulista*, Júlio Prestes, for the presidency. A substantial coalition of liberals, outsider state elites, and the Minas Gerais elite supported Getúlio Vargas in the 1930 elections. Although Vargas lost, liberals, military modernizers, and state elites outside of São Paulo organized an armed uprising to challenge the outcome. However, it was the key defections of São Paulo coffee growers and the senior military over Washington Luís' decision to maintain the convertibility of the currency that probably sealed the fate of the Republic. Angry coffee growers defected as Washington Luís maintained his fixed exchange rate policy, lowered coffee export prices even further (to attract more foreign buyers), suspended a surplus harvest purchase program, and refused to extend credit to financially strapped coffee farmers (Skidmore, 1967, p. 11). The senior military withdrew support (and in fact actively forced Washington Luís from office) because they felt they could not ask common soldiers to fight to defend a regime which had imposed such high costs on society (Skidmore, 1967, p. 6).

Thus, the 'Old Republic' came to an end. A regime which had rested on fragile support from a variety of elite groups had maintained that support by limited power sharing, promotion of its key support group (coffee growers), and reliance on coffee export revenues to finance large scale consumption of foreign goods and loan payments for infrastructure development. When the crisis hit, the government protected currency stability at the expense of its ability to finance protection and promotion of the interests of key constituencies. Washington Luís then delivered the mobilizing linchpin for opponents by refusing to share power with rival elites. In angry response, those rival elites brought down the regime.

BETWEEN A ROCK AND A HARD PLACE: THE 1964 COUP

Even more than the 1930 coup, the coup of 1964 illustrates the danger of weak political institutions. The economic 'crisis' that prevailed in the years leading up to the coup was not as severe as the situation in the 1980s. Inflation rose to a peak at 140 per cent per year in 1964 just before the coup, a level well below those recorded in the 1980s (although without a system of indexation, the inflation rate of the 1960s had a brutal impact). GDP growth had slowed, but remained positive as did real profit and real wages growth (Wallerstein, 1980, pp. 17–19). Furthermore, neither the terms of trade nor the current account deficit deteriorated to an unresolvable point under João Goulart (1961 to 1964) (Castro and Ronci, 1991, pp. 156, 161).[9] In short, the critical factors were the exhaustion of foreign reserves and the perceptions of crisis[10] among key actors (notably domestic business elites and foreign creditors) coupled with the inability to impose or demand sacrifices from important social groups.

The period leading up to the coup was one of rapid industrialization following a strategy of import substitution. Both labor and business supported the regime in exchange for rising real wages and protected profits and credit. Unfortunately, like many other Latin American nations at the time, this strategy was not self-financing, particularly due to the high costs of importing capital goods for industrial expansion. Brazilian governments, from Getúlio Vargas (1950–54) to Juscelino Kubitschek (1955–60) borrowed abroad to finance their development programs. They also confronted steadily rising inflation rates throughout the 1950s. Neither president had the political will or capacity to implement a stabilization plan, although both faced growing pressure from foreign creditors to do so (see Wallerstein, 1980, and Sola, 1982). Vargas ended his life in a context of growing conflict over satisfying his different constituencies. His inflammatory suicide note pointed the finger at foreign companies and domestic elites with ties to foreign interests.

Kubitschek's choices had even graver consequences for the Republic. Kubitschek engineered a complex and costly bargain in order to promote 50 years of development in five years. He assured labor rising real wages and provided subsidies, extensive credit, and substantial market protection to industry. Coffee producers received price supports, while members of Congress received both patronage resources and access to bureaucratic posts for patronage purposes (Nunes and Geddes, 1987). In exchange, Kubitschek was able to invite foreign direct investment, especially for key areas like automobiles. He was also given room to create new, politically insulated, technocratic bureaucratic agencies to help advance his development schemes (Nunes and Geddes, 1987). However, his plan required a massive expansion of long-term borrowing, and a subsequent turn to short-term loans when worried foreign creditors cut off long-term funds (Wallerstein, 1980, p. 30).

When the International Monetary Fund (IMF) demanded an orthodox stabilization program in 1958 in exchange for new long-term loans, Kubitschek did not have the political capacity to implement one. Although Kubitschek faced rising inflation, a worsening balance of payments situation, and growing unease among international creditors, stabilization violated Kubitschek's implicit agreements with key members of his political base. On the one hand, he could not impose costs on either business or labor by limiting imports, credit, and subsidies, or by allowing wages and working-class consumption to be squeezed. On the other hand, he faced three weakly organized, fractious and fragmented, and highly clientelistic political parties in Congress that simply would not back stabilization or any related policy such as fiscal, administrative, or land reform (all of which Goulart later attempted without success). Unable to ask any group to make sacrifices, especially in the absence of political parties with which he could effectively bargain, Kubitschek plunged Brazil into deeper financial difficulties and left the growing balance-of-payment crisis for his successors.

His successors, Jânio Quadros[11] and João Goulart, made several attempts at stabilization without success. As stabilization efforts continued to founder in Congress, both business and labor groups intensified their struggle over resources in a context of slower growth. Strikes and government interventions in labor conflicts increased sharply (Stepan, 1978, p. 112). Government deficits grew, both in response to decreasing government revenues and to escalating prices. Perhaps most importantly, by 1964 Brazil had exhausted its reserves in a context of high short-term debt payments as well as payments on imported goods (Wallerstein, 1980, p. 31).

Goulart's policy choices were sharply constrained. Facing growing political polarization, party fragmentation in Congress, and intransigent foreign creditors (especially the IMF), Goulart lost the capacity to finance a strategy that paid off all constituency members. Badly cross-pressured, Goulart ultimately moved further and further to the left in search of political support. In that context, the business community in particular sought out the military to restore order.[12] The outcome of their appeal for help is of course well-known.

Scholars have debated the inevitability of the coup. Some like Stepan (1978) suggest that Goulart's specific tactical choices produced the coup and that the political and economic context did not make one necessary. Others like O'Donnell (1972) or Cardoso (1973) locate its causes in the structural requirements of the economy. In either case it remains true that the democratic regime that ended rested on pay-offs to all key constituencies that exceeded the government's revenues. In order to finance them, successive governments had to borrow money abroad. When the entry of foreign capital slowed and then stopped, it placed a strain on the Brazilian government's capacity to meet its foreign obligations. Unfortunately, the organization of the regime and the weakness of its political institutions prevented successive presidents from bargaining cost sharing or allocating agreements. As the financial situation deteriorated, key actors on both the left and the right defected from the regime.

DEBT, DECAY, AND THE FAILURE OF MILITARY RULE

Clearly, military rule in Brazil rested on force, but it also rested on a narrow mandate from middle-class and business-class supporters: that mandate was to restore order and growth. To the extent that elites and the middle class acquiesced in routinized, bureaucratized military rule, it was because the military suppressed the dual threats of revolutionary behavior and financial chaos. Although they succeeded in meeting both of those demands in their first ten years of rule, their downfall rested on the narrowness of the mandate that allowed them to rule in the first place. Specifically, when the oil shock of 1973 hit Brazil, the military did not have a mandate to impose the cost of adjustment on the privileged members of their support coalition. Thus, rather than attempt adjustment to significant oil price increases, the military sought to grow out of the problem. The legacy of that decision remained as a heavy burden for democratic Brazil in the 1990s.

After a three year austerity program from 1964 to 1967, and with inflation down to 20 per cent per year, the military began to promote industrial expansion again based on three pillars: encouragement of foreign direct investment; extension of credit to domestic businesses and facilitation of borrowing abroad; and state investment in and promotion of key areas. Thus, the military deepened and modified the import substitution strategy rather than abandon it. State priorities for growth were identified in two national development plans (PND I in 1970, and PND II in 1974). Foreign financing was widely available, especially for the state, after 1973 when international banks sought to recycle petro-dollars.

When the 1973 oil shock hit, Brazilian technocrats argued that Brazil could grow out of the crisis. Consequently, the second national development plan proceeded without any suggestion that resources might become scarce and that the government might have to establish priorities for growth. Like Kubitschek before them, the military solved its resource dilemma through foreign borrowing. Brazilian debt increased from over $12 billion in 1973 to over $50 billion by 1980. While the government encouraged exports, export earnings did not increase fast enough to offset rising oil prices. Thus, even though export revenues increased from just over $6 billion in 1973 to over $20 billion in 1980, the import bill rose from just over $6 billion to over $22 billion by 1980. By the time the second oil shock hit in 1979, Brazil's growth rate had slowed significantly and inflation had begun a slow, but steady rise.

Business protests killed an effort in 1979–80 to finally attempt an orthodox adjustment (that is, essentially an austerity plan designed to reduce credit, subsidies, and consumption). Instead, Delfim Netto, the architect of Brazil's miracle in the late 1960s and early 1970s, was brought in to work his expansionary magic again. He failed, and by 1982 he was forced to finally promote an orthodox adjustment. However, by that time, inflation was rising dramatically and had a substantial inertial component that derived from the complex indexation system that the military had introduced in 1967. In addition, by the time the military acted the condition was far worse than it had been ten years earlier.

Between 1980 and 1982, Brazil experienced a real deterioration in its current account and the relation between debt and export earnings. After implementing an orthodox adjustment package, the country experienced some improvement in its current account, but continued to experience net capital outflows, spiraling inflation, and to add to its difficulties, recession. From 1983 to 1985, Brazil maintained inflation rates above 200 per cent per year while idle capacity in industry exceeded 30 per cent (Dinsmoor, 1990, p. 92).

Not surprisingly, new labor movements had arisen to challenge military rule (Keck, 1989), but the business community had joined them as well by the early 1980s (Frieden, 1991, pp. 129–32). By the mid-1980s, the military had lost all their original allies by violating the terms of their rule. The military had received a mandate to restore economic growth, but as their policy imposed higher and higher costs on privileged members of their support coalition, they lost the mandate for continued rule. Ultimately, a badly demoralized military allowed a civilian alliance within the Electoral College to vote it out of office. Thus, once again, a Brazilian regime with a limited legitimacy, grounded in instrumental concerns, used foreign financing to avoid imposing costs on key members of its support coalition. However, as in 1930 and in 1964, eventually the tension between meeting foreign obligations and paying off domestic supporters overwhelmed institutions with limited legitimacy. Unlike the two previous regime breakdowns, the military left its financial chaos for a democratic regime to address.

FINANCIAL GLOBALIZATION AND THE POLITICS OF ADJUSTMENT IN THE 1990s: INAUSPICIOUS BEGINNINGS

The 'New Republic' emerged in 1985 under inauspicious circumstances. The civilian president, Tancredo Neves, died before taking office, leaving his far less popular or credible vice-president, José Sarney, to govern. The party system, which had had few parties under military rule, almost immediately fragmented as opposition groups that had cooperated against the military previously now competed against each other. To add to his difficulties in governing, Sarney inherited the financial woes of the military regime, and acquired a cumbersome constitution in 1988 that compounded the nation's financial disarray.

Although the military's harsh austerity program from 1983–85 helped improve the current account deficit,[13] Brazil's external finances remained precarious. Over the course of the crisis in the early 1980s a large number of banks had become reluctant to lend further to Brazil. Foreign direct investment also sharply slowed down. As a result, Brazil became increasingly dependent on IMF lending, short-term lending, and growing domestic borrowing as a substitute for foreign funds. Thus, between 1985 and 1988, Brazil faced continuing net capital outflows and a heavy debt burden on its economy (Table 7.1).

The Constitution, debated and negotiated in 1987 and adopted in 1988, exacerbated the government's financial problems in a number of ways. The most important of these was a measure that transferred roughly 25 per cent of the federal government's revenues to the states and municipalities without accompanying spending obligations (Dinsmoor, 1990, pp. 106–7, see also Kingstone, 1994). In turn, these new resources helped contribute to politically motivated, massive public spending by the state and municipalities. Payroll expenses had risen 71 per cent in real terms between 1982 and 1988, consuming 70 per cent of federal revenues. While federal employment rose

Table 7.1   Brazil: external debt, 1979–87 (US$ millions)

	1979	1981	1983	1985	1987
Disbursed external debt	60 419	80 373	97 488	106 473	123 962
Long-term	51 785	65 052	80 636	90 848	106 086
Short-term	8 634	15 321	14 204	11 017	13 868
Debt/exports	361.2	313.6	412.1	385.3	441.4

Source: James Dinsmoor (1990) *Brazil: Responses to the Debt Crisis* (Washington D.C.: Inter-American Development Bank), p. 30.

to 700 000 jobs, with an additional 860 000 in parastatals, the problem in the states and municipalities was even worse. State and local employment had climbed to 4.5 million jobs by 1988. The same political patronage logic that drove constant public sector hiring also drove constant, real wage increases. This dynamic played an important role in increasing public sector debt (Gall, 1991).

Unfortunately, Sarney had very weak political tools to confront the deteriorating financial situation. Sarney's party, the PMDB (Brazilian Democratic Movement Party), had begun its life as the only officially sanctioned opposition party under military rule. as such, it had acted as an umbrella for every group in society opposed to the military. With democracy restored, the PMDB splintered rapidly so that by 1990, 26 parties competed for the presidency while nineteen sat in Congress. More importantly, their behavior in Congress revealed that they were perhaps even less coherent or cohesive than the parties of the earlier democratic period (Mainwaring, 1991, 1993). Thus, while the PMDB remained the largest party, Sarney had little choice but to explicitly buy support for any policy he tried to pass.

The consequence of this tremendous political weakness emerged clearly in Sarney's repeated efforts to stabilize Brazil's runaway inflation. His most important effort was a heterodox policy called the Cruzado plan, named for the new currency introduced as part of the effort to break the inertial element of the inflationary spiral. However, Sarney's administration politically manipulated the implementation of the Cruzado plan to shift resources to consumers – a naked attempt to buy electoral support, but ultimately one that added substantial fuel to inflation (Sola, 1988). By 1989, Sarney's Finance Minister, Maílson da Nobrega, publicly admitted defeat on inflation, saying that the patient needed surgery but that it kept getting an anesthetic instead (Gall, 1991, p. 42).

CARDOSO, THE *REAL* PLAN, AND BRAZIL'S TURNABOUT

By the end of 1996, Brazil's situation appeared different. After one impeached president and one weak interim president, Fernando Henrique Cardoso won the 1994 presidential elections in a context of budget surpluses, healthy foreign reserves, and inflation below 2 per cent per month. Although Brazil had not changed much politically, enough changes had occurred that Brazil received the stamp of approval of the international financial community. Not surprisingly, new capital inflows began, particularly in conjunction with Cardoso's tenure as Finance Minister in 1994 and as president beginning in 1995.

Cardoso's successes rested on two sets of important contributions from his predecessors in office. Fernando Collor (1990–92) ended his presidency in disgrace, impeached on corruption charges. However, before his rule ended, he had effectively destroyed the base of Brazil's old development model – a condition Cardoso needed for his later policies. Collor campaigned as an outsider attacking elite privilege and he governed that way as well (see Schneider, 1991; Kingstone, 1994). Using slash and burn tactics, Collor substantially deregulated the economy, began a large-scale privatization program, eliminated virtually all obstacles to foreign commerce, substantially cut public spending, fired civil servants, limited patronage spending, and implemented a gradual, coherent tariff reduction program (Haggard and Kaufman, 1995, pp. 209–10; Kingstone, 1994). By cutting public spending, limiting patronage spending, and ending inflation indexation of the government's debt, Collor eliminated the budget deficit. Collor ruled by intimidating elites through his direct appeal to the poorest masses rather than by purchasing elite support. However, elites had warned Collor that he could get elected by the masses, but he had to rule with them.[14] In December of 1992, they finally removed him, but by then he had significantly damaged the old bases of Brazilian political economy.

Under Itamar Franco – Collor's Vice President and successor – the economy behaved erratically in response to considerable confusion over the policy direction. The inflation rate reached 50 per cent per month and both growth and capital flows remained volatile in response to rapid shifts in expectations and evaluations of government performance. Facing a rapidly decaying economy, Franco appointed Fernando Henrique Cardoso as his Finance Minister in 1994.[15]

Cardoso, as a finance minister, managed to force through a key Constitutional reform: a temporary emergency measure (the Social Emergency Fund, FSE) diverting funds from the states and municipalities to the federal government.[16] This became a crucial piece of Cardoso's stabilization plan, the *Real* plan, named for the currency it introduced (see Baer, 1995; Oliveira and Toledo, 1995; Sachs and Zini, 1995; Bresser Pereira, 1996; Martone, 1996). Like the *Cruzado* plan before it, the *Real* plan was a heterodox shock that attacked inertial components of inflation. However, this plan differed from past experiments in ways that reflected substantial learning from past errors.

The *Real* plan sought to avoid three types of errors committed in previous experiments (Oliveira and Toledo, 1995). First, its design incorporated fiscal and monetary austerity, a structural reform to correct institutional sources of fiscal imbalances, and a policy to coordinate contracts and incomes. Second, it provided clear rules well in advance to avoid sudden changes or other surprises that would increase the uncertainty associated with stabilization. Finally, its design minimized government interventions such as wage and price controls (such as the *Cruzado* plan used) or asset seizures (as in the Collor plan) (Bresser Pereira, 1994). The *Real* rested on two other critical policies. First, Collor's tariff reduction schedule concluded in 1994 reducing high rates of protection to an average of only 14 per cent. As a consequence, domestic businesses could not maintain high prices in the face of import competition. This checked speculative price increases which might have fueled inflation. Second, the *Real* was anchored by an exchange rate band that kept the value of the currency close to one dollar per *Real*. The overvaluation of the *Real* fueled a consumption boom while also drawing in large amounts of new foreign capital, largely portfolio investment, although direct foreign investment increased as well.

The results came rapidly. Between February 1994 and October 1994 when presidential elections occurred, the rate of monthly inflation fell from 50 per cent to under 2 per cent. Not surprisingly, the Finance Minister turned presidential candidate, Fernando Henrique Cardoso, won handily in the first round of voting. Cardoso entered office in January 1995 with high public support, tremendous credibility, and high public expectations of success in passing constitutional reforms.

Between January 1995 and this writing, mid-1997, Cardoso registered a number of crucial successes, despite significant legislative travails (Kingstone, 1994). Brazil had successfully weathered the 'tequila effect' that swept the region in the wake of the 'peso crisis.' A combination of very healthy reserves, a lower degree of financial liberalization than countries like Argentina and Mexico, and series of measures designed to curtail consumption (especially of imports) all worked to halt Brazil's loss of reserves by mid-1995. In the wake of the 'tequila effect,' Cardoso had passed Constitutional reforms making rules for foreign investment more flexible, resumed privatizations, and continued to trim government spending. By mid-1997, Cardoso looked guaranteed to pass a constitutional amendment allowing reelection of the president and looked certain to win. Finally, inflation continued to register some of the lowest rates in over 35 years. Not surprisingly, between mid 1994 and mid 1997, foreign capital began to flood into the country.

SHORT MONEY, LONG MONEY, AND EVERYTHING BETWEEN

By 1996, Brazil was the leading destination for foreign capital in Latin America (see Table 7.2). The total inflow of external resources increased from just under $18 billion in 1992 to $43 billion in 1994 to just under $80 billion in 1996 (Banco Central do Brasil, 1997a). Of Armijo's six categories of foreign capital (see Chapter 1 in this volume), Brazil drew substantial sums from all but foreign aid. Brazil had drawn over $24 billion in portfolio investments, almost all in stocks, and almost all in the small number of Brazilian blue-chips, primarily large parastatals. Multinational companies brought in over $9 billion in direct foreign investment, and the Brazilian

Table 7.2   Brazil: foreign capital inflows, 1992–96 (US$ millions)

	1992	1993	1994	1995	1996
Total inflows	17 791	32 667	43 073	53 885	78 999
Portfolio equity	3 863	14 971	21 600	22 559	24 684
FDI	1 325	877	2 241	3 285	9 580
Debt financing*	12 603	16 823	19 232	28 041	44 735

Note: * Debt financing includes medium and long-term debt, trade credits, portfolio bonds, and short-term debt.
Source: Brazilian Central Bank *Bulletin*, April 1997.

government and the private sector combined to draw in almost $30 billion in currency loans, including over $18 billion in bonds, commercial paper and fixed interest rate notes (Banco Central do Brasil, 1997a).[17]

It is impossible to make simple claims about the impact of financial integration given the mix of sources and uses of foreign capital. Overall, the variety of sources of foreign capital provided a complex mix of benefits and potential risks for Brazilian democracy. However, the general trend is consistent with the argument in this chapter: new capital inflows have tended to benefit the country by providing funds for renewed growth and providing external savings to compensate for public sector deficits and low and declining private domestic savings. However, the new inflows have also deepened the country's dependence on foreign capital, increased the vulnerability to balance-of-payments problems, and generated new potentially damaging lines of conflict. The hypothesized impact of these different forms is summarized in Table 7.3.

Consistent with the argument of this paper, foreign capital entering between 1994–97 has tended to play a positive role. The continuing increase of direct foreign investment, rising from just over $3 billion in 1995 to over $9 billion in 1996, with projections of as much as $16 billion in 1997, helped maintain moderate, but steady growth. Growth rose and declined sharply in 1995, the year of the 'tequila effect,' but stabilized at 4.2 per cent for the year. Growth for 1996 and projections for 1997 hovered around 3.5 per cent. Portfolio investment, new foreign commercial loans and a variety of papers, helped introduce new financing to Brazilian firms after a decade of watching credit become scarcer and scarcer. As a consequence, investment rose sharply even though government credit and domestic private credit remained scarce (FIESP, 1997). In addition, the new inflow of investment capital tended to diminish the concentration of investment in São Paulo as other regions, encouraged by the Federal government competed to attract new investments.

Table 7.3 Types of inflows into Brazil, 1990s, and hypothesized risks and benefits

Type of capital	Benefits	Risks
Portfolio investment in private sector	Financing for firms Helps support growth	Volatility Inequitable access to financing
Portfolio investment in public sector	Financing for public sector firms Budgetary flexibility for government Resources for patronage	Volatility
Commercial lending to private sector	Financing for firms Helps support growth	Growing indebtedness Public sector assumption of private debt
Commercial lending to public sector	Budgetary flexibility for government Resources for patronage	Growing indebtedness Impact on public savings of debt-servicing costs
Foreign direct investment	Growth Increased competitiveness	Displacement of local producers Unemployment Rapid shift from local production to imports

Finally, the inflow of capital has helped the government finance its deficits and given the Cardoso government substantial room to provide ample patronage to its coalition members. This, combined with Cardoso's distinct political skills, has facilitated the government's passage of several key elements of its reform package. In fact, one of several crucial differences between Cardoso and Collor has been Cardoso's willingness and ability to dispense substantial amounts of patronage to maintain his coalition (Kingstone, 1994).

SHORT-TERM PROBLEMS – LONG-TERM CONSEQUENCES

Despite the immediate benefits of the new capital inflows, Brazil faced a significant underlying risk to its new dependence on foreign capital. Specifically, the government's continuing failure to pass constitutional reforms to social security (*Previdencia*), civil service, and especially the fiscal system meant that it depended on capital inflows to offset its fiscal deficits.

The fiscal disorder also meant that the government had no choice but to rely on the exchange rate as the anchor for the currency. Thus, in the short term, the possibility of an outflow of capital threatened to undermine the *Real* and probably the government with it.

Cardoso's inability to pass constitutional reforms through Congress (much like his predecessors) forced him to use a range of measures to protect the balance of payments. Most importantly, the administration maintained the *Real* at an overvalued rate (estimates ranged from 10 to 20 per cent overvalued). In addition, to curb Brazilians' appetites for imports, the administration raised interest rates sharply in the first half of 1995 and allowed them to drop slowly through the next two years. The administration also introduced a host of import barriers, including tariffs, non-tariff barriers, as well as restrictions on import financing. As a counter against short-term speculative capital, the administration levied taxes on foreign money entering on a short-term basis.

The combination of measures successfully protected the *Real* through this writing in mid-1997. However, they had a number of immediate effects with longer-term consequences. First, high interest rates slowed economic growth. Brazilian economists of widely differing ideological persuasions agreed that 3.5 per cent GDP growth was insufficient to contain the country's rapidly increasing public sector indebtedness or reduce the unemployment rate of roughly 16 per cent.[18] Moreover, the interest rate policy protected the *Real*, but at the expense of domestic industry: industry posted record numbers of bankruptcies from 1994–97, while most domestic firms rightly complained about the impossibility of obtaining credit to finance competitive improvements. Second, the overvalued exchange rate punished exports and encouraged imports. The country ran a current account deficit of $12 billion in 1995, $5.5 billion in 1996, and an estimated $13 billion in 1997. The 1997 deficit came as a particular shock given the government's efforts to introduce new export incentives and financing. One particularly serious problem was that the combination of the overvalued *Real* and high domestic interest rates favored imports over local production (even if price and quality was competitive) because of the opportunities to profit financially through interest rate arbitrage.

The drag on economic growth coupled with the favoring of imports over exports as well as domestic production had the effect of provoking a wave of denationalization. Domestic producers needed constitutional reforms in order to permit lower interest rates, a renewal of credit for industry, a change in the tax system to remove uncompetitive taxes, and to allow for a small devaluation of the *Real*. Without them, they faced extraordinary competitive pressure from imports and from multinational firms with a range of advantages, including greater economies of scale and much easier access to much lower cost capital. This competitive pressure presented Brazilian industrialists with a series of exit options: selling their firms to MNCs, merging with MNCs, or becoming licensed distributors for MNCs and diminishing or eliminating domestic production. As of 1997, there is no conclusive data about this trend, but certain sectors, such as auto parts, machine tools and equipment, and consumer electronics have already displayed this trend quite sharply (Kingstone, 1994).

This new context in the make-up of Brazilian industry has created new potential lines of conflict. One significant line of differentiation lay between those firms with access to international credit or portfolio investment and those without – a function primarily of size. Brazilian stock market capitalization had reached $100 billion by 1996 with roughly 35 per cent foreign participation. However, 80 per cent of new investment went to the 10 largest blue-chip stocks, mostly parastatals such as Telesp, Pétrobras, and CVRD (privatized in 1997). Beyond those ten firms, the stock market proved an inadequate source of financing for private industry. In fact, interviews with representatives of the business community in 1997 revealed a sharp disagreement: representatives of the São Paulo exchanges complained that they could issue a lot more paper but Brazilian firms were not taking advantage of the opportunity while domestic producers complained that the investors were not truly interested in most domestic stocks.[19] The same split replicated itself with respect to access to foreign commercial banks. MNC's and large Brazilian companies with well established export records had an easier time obtaining credit at rates as low as Libor plus a quarter per cent. Smaller Brazilian firms and those with little export history had to rely on domestic interest rates that sharply exceeded international levels (as high as 30 per cent real rates in 1995, and falling to 10–15 per cent by 1997).

A second line of potential conflict lay between domestic producers and MNCs. Foreign direct investment entering into Brazil in the period 1994–97 was of several different kinds. Some, as in the auto industry, represented an expansion of existing capacity. Some came as purchases of newly privatized industries. However, a large amount of FDI simply displaced local production. The favored investment route for new MNCs came through mergers and acquisitions which allowed MNCs to obtain a position in the market and an existing distribution network without the risk of significant investments in new capacity. The sector most clearly affected by this trend was auto parts: for example, between 1995 and 1997, Metal Leve, Cofap, and Freios Varga, three of Brazil's most highly regarded domestic firms were either acquired outright or merged. One clear trend was a shift in influence away from Brazil's most highly regarded industrialists to MNCs and financial sector leaders.

A further line of potential conflict lay in the high rate of unemployment. Cardoso repeatedly made the case to the public that the rate of unemployment reflected improvements in technology that were unavoidable if Brazil wanted to compete with the world. However, the unemployment rate also reflected *Real* related policies such as high interest rates, as well as the tendency for MNC investment and imports to simply displace domestic producers. Although labor groups remained largely quiet (and unsuccessful when they weren't) from 1995–97, unemployment remained one of the public's principal concerns and one of the greatest causes of discontent with an otherwise highly credible government.

One crucial source of potential conflict lay in the poorest category of Brazilians, what Brazilians refer to as Class 'D'. This large mass of Brazilians had been the greatest beneficiaries of Cardoso's price stabilization. Researchers have estimated that the income of this lowest income category increased by 12 per cent (Martone, 1996, p. 60) between 1994 and 1996, and other research estimated that the *Real* plan had lifted at least five million people above the poverty line in the same period.[20] These income improvements drove the burst of new consumption that pushed items like televisions and cement to record highs. Interviews with business representatives during June 1996 suggested that many members of the business community saw this class of consumers as the most important political base for the stability of the *Real* and the pursuit of associated reforms.[21]

The potential for conflict with this group, which represents at least a large plurality of Brazilians, lies in the possibility of the return of inflation. This group would suffer the most from any return of inflation and politically is least able to protect itself through legitimate political participation. One clear political danger this group represented lay in their volatility as a voting bloc. Brazilian voters have had very weak party identification and loyalty, and particularly low income voters have demonstrated that their potentially rapidly shifting views can dramatically alter the outcome of elections. This was the case in the direct presidential elections for Fernando Collor de Mello and Fernando Henrique Cardoso, both of whom poor voters supported. Should inflation return or a balance of payments crisis impose harsh costs on this group of voters, it is not clear what political options (or regimes) they may support.

One final consideration is the political class, at all levels of government. Brazilian politicians are intensely patronage-dependent. State governors, mayors, and members of the Federal legislature have supported a wide array of leaders and programs as long as they have obtained access to resources. In the 1990s, patronage resources have helped protect the Cardoso administration from a variety of potential corruption scandals, from those relating to the banking crisis to a vote buying scheme connected to the reelection amendment of 1997. Failure to provide patronage played a role in the impeachment process of Fernando Collor. Most of Cardoso's legislative successes have turned on his ability to provide generous sums of patronage resources. On the other hand, all of his, and his predecessors' legislative failures stemmed from legislators protecting access to patronage. Thus, like the poor, a balance-of-payments crisis could lead to sharp restrictions on the availability of patronage with unpredictable, but plausibly very negative, results.

WEAK INSTITUTIONS, BALANCE-OF-PAYMENTS CRISES, AND DEMOCRATIC CONSOLIDATION

As of mid-1997, Brazilian democracy looked secure for the short term at least. Despite a constant stream of corruption accusations and investigations (none of which had tainted the president) and an often violent conflict over land distribution, elite Brazilian actors (including business leaders, the Church, the Organization of Brazilian Lawyers (OAB), and the press) explicitly endorsed and supported democracy. Furthermore, there is no better way to dull potential conflicts than to succeed economically. As of mid-1997, few commentators found significant fault with the progress Cardoso had made on stabilizing the currency (although there were many critics on the most advisable way to assure Brazil's resumption of growth).

However, even if Cardoso managed to avoid a rapid outflow of capital or a balance-of-payments crisis in the short term, his administration had left Brazil highly dependent on foreign capital in the long term. Total external debt rose between 1992 and 1997 from $110 billion to $177 billion, divided equally between public sector and private sector debt. In addition, $26 billion of portfolio investment flowed into Brazil in 1996. The rate of inflow increased by 35 per cent in the first trimester of 1997 over the same period in 1996 (Banco Central do Brasil, 1997b). Thus, should a balance of payments crisis occur in the longer term, Brazilian politicians will face very difficult choices about how to distribute the costs of adjustment. The discussion above suggests that the new inflows have foreign capital have generated new, potentially intense lines of conflict. It is in that context that Brazilian regimes have repeatedly collapsed throughout the twentieth century.

It is in that context also that the weakness of Brazil's political institutions matter. As of 1997, Brazil continued to have one of the most poorly institutionalized party systems in Latin America. Scott Mainwaring and Timothy Scully labeled Brazil's party system 'inchoate,' meaning that parties exhibited little regularity in electoral competition, had very weak roots in society, were accorded little legitimacy by voters, and had organizations with very little relevance (Mainwaring and Scully, 1993, pp. 6–16). Similarly, work by Mainwaring (1993, 1991) and Power (1991) has demonstrated the wide range of perverse elements in Brazil's electoral system that contribute to the weakness of the political system. Those features include complex and unstable bargaining, tremendous dependence on patronage, cynical disaffected voters, and the difficulty of maintaining any kind of policy or program oriented coalitions.

The resulting venality cuts both ways. Opportunistic politicians, a large majority of Brazil's political class, sell their support and therefore may support the government at a price. This permits presidents who are willing to bargain and have resources to bargain with to construct coalitions for their policies. However, when resources dry up, as they did in 1964, presidents may find themselves unable to construct any legislative coalition. The venality and opportunism takes its toll in another way. In the 1990s a large number of politicians, including President Fernando Collor, have lost office (although most have been acquitted of charges and/or pardoned) in corruption scandals. Public confidence in Congress, political parties and politicians remained low in Brazil. Large per centages of Brazilians, especially among lower income groups, believe the military governed better than the democracy.[22] Elite groups, such as business, have routinely expressed frustration with their inability to influence Congressional behavior. Interviews with representatives of the business community and polling in June 1996 suggest that some support existed for a soft coup (a *Fujimorização*).[23]

CONCLUSION

The *Real* plan has lured in significant quantities of foreign investment, particularly portfolio investment of short term nature. In the short term, government has benefited by having some budget flexibility to purchase support for their program, but at the cost of greater debt and real vulnerability to capital outflows. Business benefits only if the macro-economy truly stabilizes and growth resumes without inflation. If not, then they have simply paid the costs of stabilization for elusive stability.

The eventual pay-offs to government, business, and the poor all depend on the success of macroeconomic stabilization and the willingness of foreign capital, particularly short term portfolio investment, to stay in the country. If that occurs, Brazilian governments may not face the kinds of difficult choices about the distribution of costs that they have faced, without great success, in the past. Macroeconomic stability in turn may help to deepen the growing normative commitment of elite groups to democracy. Optimistically, we might imagine that political parties may become more coherent over time as they mature in a stable democracy.

However, if capital withdraws and stabilization fails, the pessimistic scenario remains plausible. As of the end of 1995, Brazil's weak political parties continued to make bargaining over reforms extremely difficult. The government's declining fiscal performance, growing indebtedness, and deteriorating current account point to the continuing threat of balance-of-payments problems. A defection of key elite groups from democracy is not a necessary result of this scenario. However, Brazil's pattern of long cycles of instability coupled with the persistence of weak political institutions and dependence on foreign money makes it plausible.

Notes

1. One indicator of Brazil's success in drawing new foreign capital, especially portfolio investment, is that in January 1996 the Brazilian stock market provided the highest return in the world (*Jornal do Brasil*, 1996).

2. See Stepan (ed.) (1989) for descriptions of the political, economic, and morale crisis that hit the military in the 1980s. Frieden (1991, pp. 129–32) provides a good account of the vocal attack of the business and financial community on the military regime as external funding dried up.

3. For example, the dependency literature, argues that the introduction of foreign capital inherently leads to unequal distribution of wealth, inappropriate investments, regional disparities of wealth, as well as the loss of an autonomous capacity to domestically generate technology and capital (see especially Cardoso and Faletto, 1979). Cardoso argues later (1973) that foreign capitalists and their domestic capitalist allies wield enormous influence on politics to the detriment of democracy. Guillermo O'Donnell (1973) argued in earlier work that capitalists, especially multinationals preferred authoritarianism to democracy because they needed to repress workers' demands in order to create a favorable investment climate for high value-added capital goods. More recently, Rueschmeyer, Stephens, and Stephens (1992) have argued that specific classes have relatively fixed preferences for varying regime types, with business inherently preferring authoritarianism. Although the latter volume provides substantial evidence in support of this conclusion, I think the evidence is still unconvincing.

   Other investigators have assessed the political role of business more positively. For example, Leigh Payne (1994) has convincingly demonstrated that Brazil's business class has strong elements that favor democracy both on normative and instrumental grounds. This represents a shift over time that suggests that the political and economic context may shape preferences in different ways. This same variation in preferences and sensitivity to political context emerges in Jorge Dominguez' (1982) discussion of domestic capital's shifting attitude towards multinationals in response to changing circumstances. Finally, there is a substantial literature that casts doubt on the existence of any systematic relation between regime type and growth or specific requirements of growth. For example, Collier (1979) significantly undermines O'Donnell's thesis relating bureaucratic authoritarianism to specific policy requirements. Along different lines, Remmer (1986) and Skidmore (1977) suggest that there is no clear relationship between regime type and the capacity to either control inflation or promote growth. Thus, it is neither true that capitalists necessarily fare better under one regime type than another, nor is it true that they necessarily prefer one type to another.

4. It is worth remembering that, although Dahl's (1961) classic, *Who Governs*, is widely considered one of the most important defenses of pluralist democracy, he reaches some disturbing conclusions about American democracy. Most importantly for the purposes of this paper, Dahl concludes that democracy is

stable in America largely because of politicians vested interests in democratic procedures. Overall, the American population is largely apathetic and tolerant of some very undemocratic attitudes.

5. This important observation is in both Przeworski (1986) and Rustow (1970).

6. In this, my argument diverges from Przeworski (1986) who focused primarily on individual calculations of the likelihood of alternative organizations defeating the existing regime. Thus, each actor must make a calculation as to the likely rewards and penalties he or she faces as a consequence of his or her choice. If actors come to believe that the existing regime cannot long survive, then they face a strong incentive to defect and therefore not suffer penalties under the new regime. For Przeworski, lack of legitimacy is not a causal factor but a signal that the existing regime may be eroding. However, if legitimacy entails a normative commitment to a set of institutions, then presumably actors are more likely to accept outcomes because the procedures for decision-making are credible and valued in and of themselves. If support is purely instrumental, then we should expect actors to defect for purely instrumental reasons. This, I argue, is the problem in Brazil, where support turns overwhelmingly on instrumental grounds, and thus defection also occurs relatively easily on purely instrumental grounds.

7. This same argument appears in Sheahan (1986) in reference to economic policy. Sheahan observes that a range of crucial choices in economic policies involve crucial trade offs between equity and efficiency – a trade off around which Latin American economic policy has shifted repeatedly from extreme to extreme. To stabilize democracy, Sheahan argued that policy-makers have to find some middle ground between the two. It is ironic, however, that Sheahan made this case before neoliberal economic reform swept the region. As of this writing in mid-1997, it appears as if the forces pushing towards equity are reviving, raising some questions about the long-term viability of neoliberal reform.

8. The only other regime transition in the twentieth century is the transition from the *Estado Novo* to the second Republic beginning in 1945. That transition was relatively easy (easy enough that Getúlio Vargas ran for president five years later). Foreign capital played no role in that transition.

9. Goulart did inherit an already dangerous short-term debt load from the previous administrations.

10. This is David Collier's (1979) important modification of O'Donnell's bureaucratic-authoritarianism argument. In that volume, a series of contributors, including O'Donnell himself, systematically disproved the O'Donnell thesis about stages of industrial growth and the need to forcibly remove labor from the government's support coalition in order to move to a more advanced phase of import substitution industrialization. Collier, in concluding the book, argued that O'Donnell's model could be strengthened by moving away from the structural argument to one which focused on elite perceptions of crisis.

11. Quadros ruled less than one year. After failing to pass a stabilization plan early in his term, Quadros resigned in what is frequently considered a gamble to force the Congress to increase his powers. They not only did not increase his powers, but they reduced the power of his successor, João Goulart.

12. Stepan (1978) reviews newspaper editorials from before the crisis that starkly reveal the sense that Brazilian institutions had reached their limit and the sense that the political forces unleashed had acquired a threatening revolutionary quality.

13. Falling oil prices and interest rates as well as increasing export revenues played a critical role in helping Brazil out of the immediate crisis in 1982, in addition to the military's harsh, but effective austerity program.

14. This position was widely expressed in the press and in editorials after his election. Collor's campaign style was explicitly and virulently anti-elite, to the point that most poor voters thought that Collor would represent them better than Lula, the labor leader. A good measure of how effective Collor's campaign was in fact how scared elites felt after the election.

15. Franco's government began with a cabinet of unknowns and a policy framework that quickly left observers frustrated and nervous. Franco's own tendencies favored Brazil's traditional economic policy of import-substituting industrialization (ISI). However, as inflation raced up again and Franco's attempts at a social pact failed, he essentially withdrew from governing and allowed Cardoso full authority to act.

16. The way Cardoso passed the FSE is a telling indicator of the difficulty of governing within Brazil. In order to preclude an attempt by legislators to fail to provide a quorum for a vote (the Congress' favorite mechanism for derailing Constitutional reforms in 1993), Cardoso appeared on television appealing for popular support and threatening to resign if the Congress did not show up and pass the measure. Even so, Cardoso was forced to water down his proposal before the Congress approved the FSE – the only Constitutional reform passed in 1993.

17. Unlike Mexico in 1994, the Brazilian Federal government and Central Bank had few outstanding debt obligations directly to foreign portfolio investors, as Brazil did not place a significant amount of government bonds or other papers in foreign markets. However, in order to sterilize the massive inflow of dollars, the government did issue a vast quantity of domestic debt paper, primarily National Treasury bonds and notes, jumping from a total of $11 billion in 1993 to $84 billion in 1995 and over $120 billion by April of 1997. Clearly not all of this was driven by the need to sterilize the inflow of foreign capital. Meanwhile, a large share of the foreign capital entering through portfolio equity flows went to state enterprises, whose shares long have been among the most actively traded in Brazil's capital markets.

18. See for example the discussion among four prominent economists, Casseb *et al.*, 1997. The unemployment figure used here is the *DIEESE* unofficial rate – a more reliable figure than the government's official rate of roughly 5 per cent.

19. Author interviews, São Paulo, June 1996.

20. The study showed that the per centage of people living in poverty in six urban centers declined from 42 per cent of the population to 28 per cent (Rocha, 1996).

21. Author interviews, São Paulo, June 1996.

22. See Lamounier and Marques (1992) for a detailed discussion of public attitudes towards democracy and various political institutions, as well as rankings of past leaders. Although somewhat out of date by 1996, the findings still reveal disconcertingly low rates of belief in democracy. A more recent poll conducted throughout the region, found support for democracy, but continuing skepticism about Brazil's specific version of it (Latin American Newsletters, 1996, p. 3).

23. That is, a quiet centralization of power and closing of the legislature by an elected incumbent president, like that engineered by Peruvian President Alberto Fujimori in the early 1990s. The opinions expressed come from interviews by the author in São Paulo, June 1996, and a poll conducted by and published in the magazine *Istoé*, June 1996, p. 26.

Bibliography

Baer, Werner (1983). *The Brazilian Economy: Growth and Development* (NewYork: Praeger).

Banco Central do Brasil (1997a) *Boletim*, April.

Banco Central do Brasil (1997b) *Notes for the Press, Foreign Sector* (Brasilia: Banco Central do Brasil), June.

Bresser Pereira, Luiz Carlos (1996) *Economic Crisis and State Reform in Brazil: Toward a New Interpretation of Latin America* (Boulder: Lynne Rienner).

——— José Maria Maravall, and Adam Przeworski (1993) *Economic Reforms in New Democracies* (Cambridge: Cambridge University Press).

Cardoso, Fernando Henrique (1973) 'Associated-Dependent Development: Theoretical and Practical Implications,' in Alfred Stepan, (ed.), *Authoritarian Brazil: Origins, Policies and Future* (New Haven, Conn.: Yale University Press).

——— and Enzo Faletto (1979) *Dependency and Development in Latin America* (Berkeley: University of California Press).

Casseb, Cassio, José Roberto Mendonça de Barros, Delfim Netto, and Luiz Gonzaga Belluzo (1997) 'Balança Mensal,' a monthly discussion among economists appearing in the Internet edition of *Jornal do Brasil,* Rio de Janeiro, *http://www.jb.com.br*, 1 July.

Castro, Paulo Rabello and Marcio Ronci (1991) 'Sixty Years of Populism in Brazil,' in Rudiger Dornbusch and Sebastian Edwards (eds), *The Macroeconomics of Populism in Latin America* (Chicago, Ill.: University of Chicago Press).

Collier, David (1979) 'The Bureaucratic-Authoritarian Model: Synthesis and Priorities for Future Research.' in David Collier (ed.), *The New Authoritarianism in Latin America* (Princeton, N.J.: Princeton University Press).

Dahl, Robert (1961) *Who Governs? Democracy and Power in an American City* (New Haven, Conn.: Yale University Press).

Dinsmoor, James (1990) *Brazil: Responses to the Debt Crisis* (Washington, D.C.: Inter-American Development Bank).

Dominguez, Jorge (1982) 'Business Nationalism: Latin American National Business Attitudes and Behavior Towards Multinational Enterprises,' in Jorge Dominguez (ed.), *Economic Issues and Political Conflict: U.S.–Latin American Relations* (London: Butterworth).

Frieden, Jeffry (1991) *Debt, Development, and Democracy: Modern Political Economy and Latin America, 1965–1985* (Princeton, N.J.: Princeton University Press).

Gall, Norman (1991) 'The Floating World of Brazilian Inflation,' Instituto Fernand Braudel, São Paulo, Brazil, September.

Haggard, Stephan and Robert Kaufman, (eds) (1995) *The Political Economy of Democratic Transitions* (Princeton, N.J.: Princeton University Press).

Industrial Federation of São Paulo (FIESP) (1997) *Caderno Estatistica*, May. World Wide Web publication.

Jornal do Brasil (1996) 'Bolsas no Brasil dão o maior lucro do mundo,' *Jornal do Brasil* internet edition, *http://www.jb.com.br.*, 11 February.

Keck, Margaret (1989) 'The New Unionism in the Brazilian Transition,' in Alfred Stepan (ed.), *Democratizing Brazil: Problems of Transition and Consolidation* (Oxford,: Oxford University Press).

Kingstone, Peter (1994) 'Shaping Business Interests: The Politics of Neoliberalism in Brazil, 1985–1992,' Ph.D. dissertation. University of California, Berkeley.

——— (1996) 'Constitutional Reform and Macro-Economic Stability: Implications for Democratic Consolidation in Brazil,' paper prepared for delivery at the International Studies Association, San Diego, Calif., 17–20 April.

Lamounier, Bolivar and Alexandre Hubner Marques, (1992) 'A Democracia Brasileira no Final da 'Decada Perdida',' in Bolivar Lamounier (ed.), *Ouvindo O Brasil: Uma Análise da Opinião Pública Brasileira Hoje* (São Paulo, Brazil: Editora Sumaré).

Latin American Newsletters (1996) *Special Report on Democracy*, SR-96–01 (London: Latin American Newsletters), February.

Mainwaring, Scott (1991) 'Politicians, Parties, and Electoral Systems: Brazil in Comparative Perspective,' *Comparative Politics*, October, pp. 21–44.

—— (1993) 'Presidentialism, Multipartism, and Democracy: The Difficult Combination,' *Comparative Political Studies*, 26, pp. 198–228.

—— and Timothy Scully (1995) *Building Democratic Institutions* (Stanford, Calif.: Stanford University Press).

Marichal, Carlos (1989) *A Century of Debt Crises in Latin America: From Independence to the Great Depression, 1820–1930*. (Princeton, N.J.: Princeton University Press).

Martone, Celso (1996) 'Recent Economic Policy in Brazil Before and After the Mexican Peso Crisis,' in Riordan Roett (ed.), *The Mexican Peso Crisis: International Perspectives* (Boulder, Col.: Lynne Rienner Press).

Nunes, Edson de Oliveira and Barbara Geddes (1987) 'Dilemmas of State-Led Modernization in Brazil,' in John Wirth Edson de Oliveira Nunes, and Thomas E. Bogenschild (eds), *State and Society in Brazil: Continuity and Change* (London: Westview Press).

O'Donnell, Guillermo (1986) 'Introduction to the Latin American Cases,' in Guillermo O'Donnell, Philippe C. Schmitter, and LaurenceWhitehead (eds), *Transitions from Authoritarian Rule: Latin* America (Baltimore, Md.: Johns Hopkins University Press).

—— (1973) *Modernization and Bureaucratic-Authoritarianism: Studies in South American Politics* (Berkeley, Calif.: Institute of International Studies, University of California).

Oliveira, Gesner and Celso Toledo (1995) 'The Brazilian Economy under the Real: Prospects for Stabilization and Growth,' paper presented at the Latin American Studies Association, Washington, D.C., 28–30 September.

Payne, Leigh A. (1994) *Brazilian Industrialists and Democratic Change* (Baltimore, Md.: Johns Hopkins University Press).

Power, Timothy J. (1991) 'Politicized Democracy: Competition, Institutions, and "Civic Fatigue" in Brazil,' *Journal of Interamerican Studies and World Affairs*, 33 (3), pp. 75–112.

Przeworski, Adam (1986) 'Some Problems in the Study of Transitions to Democracy,' in Guillermo O'Donnell, Philippe C. Schmitter, and Laurence Whitehead (eds), *Transitions from Authoritarian Rule: Comparative Perspectives* (Baltimore, Md.: Johns Hopkins University Press).

Remmer, Karen (1986) 'The Politics of Economic Stabilization: IMF Standby Programs in Latin America, 1954–1984,' *Comparative Politics*, 19 (1) (October).

Rocha, Sonia (1996) 'Renda e Pobreza: Os impactos do Plano Real,' Texto para discussão no. 439, Rio de Janeiro: IPEA (Insituto de Pesquisa Econômica Aplicada), December.

Roxborough, Ian (1992) 'Inflation and Social Pacts in Brazil and Mexico,' *Journal of Latin American Studies*, 24 (3), (1992) pp. 1–26.

Rueschmeyer, Dietrich, Evelyne Huber Stephens, and John D. Stephens (1992) *Capitalist Development and Democracy* (Chicago, Ill.: University of Chicago Press).

Rustow, Dankwart (1970) 'Transitions to Democracy: Toward a Dynamic Model,' *Comparative Politics*, 2 (3), April, pp. 337–64.

Sachs, Jeffrey and Alvaro Zini (1995) 'Brazilian Inflation and the *Plano Real*,' paper presented at the Latin American Studies Association, Washington, D.C., 28–30 September.

Schneider, Ben Ross (1991) 'Brazil Under Collor: Anatomy of a Crisis,' *World Policy Journal* 8 (2), Spring, pp. 321–47.

Sheahan, John (1986) 'Economic Policies and the Prospects for Successful Transition from Authoritarian Rule in Latin America,' in Guillermo O'Donnell, Philippe C. Schmitter, and Laurence Whitehead (eds), *Transitions from Authoritarian Rule: Comparative Perspectives* (Baltimore, Md.: Johns Hopkins University Press).

Skidmore, Thomas (1977) 'The Politics of Economic Stabilization in Post War Latin America,' in James Malloy (ed.), *Authoritarianism and Corporatism in Latin America* (Pittsburgh, Penn.: University of Pittsburgh Press).

——— and Peter Smith (1992) *Modern Latin America* (Oxford: Oxford University Press).

Sola, Lourdes (1988) 'Heterodox Shock in Brazil: Técnicos, Politicians, and Democracy,' *Journal of Latin American Studies*, 23, pp. 163–95.

——— (1982) 'The Political and Ideological Constraints to Economic Management in Brazil, 1945–1964,' Ph.D. dissertation, Oxford University.

Souza, Maria do Carmo Campello de (1989) 'The Brazilian 'New Republic''. Under the "Sword of Damocles",' in Alfred Stepan (ed.), *Democratizing Brazil: Problems of Transition and Consolidation* (Oxford: Oxford University Press).

Stepan, Alfred (ed.) *Democratizing Brazil: Problems of Transition and Consolidation* (Oxford: Oxford University Press).

——— (1978) 'Political Leadership and Regime Breakdown: Brazil,' in Juan J. Linz and Alfred Stepan (eds), *The Breakdown of Democratic Regimes: Latin America* (Baltimore, Md.: The Johns Hopkins University Press).

Wallerstein, Michael (1980) 'The Collapse of Democracy in Brazil: Its Economc Determinants,' *Latin American Research Review*, 15 (3), pp. 3–40.

Weyland, Kurt (1995) 'How Much Political Power do Economic Forces Have? Conflicts over Social Insurance Reform in Contemporary Brazil,' paper presented at the Latin American Studies Association, 28–30 September.

8 Russia: The IMF, Private Finance, and External Constraints on a Fragile Polity

Randall W. Stone

In the years since the collapse of the Soviet bloc, a vast new territory has become integrated into the world economy, international capital movements have threatened governments throughout Central Europe and Eurasia, and multilateral lending agencies have gained striking influence over economic policies. As of this writing, the International Monetary Fund has signed conditionality agreements with every country of the former Soviet Union and Eastern Europe except Bosnia, Serbia, Tadzhikistan, and Turkmenistan. Indeed, critics of unbridled capital markets and the 'Washington Consensus' that supports them – including Leslie Elliott Armijo, Mary Ann Haley, and Tony Porter in this volume – worry that international institutions and international investment may so constrain economic policies during the transition that weak democratic institutions are swept away by popular discontent. This chapter takes a different view. I argue that the policies urged by international financial institutions are in fact the ones best suited to consolidating democracy in post-Communist countries, because inflation has such disastrous consequences. Unfortunately, however, the multilateral lending agencies are not very effective at constraining Russia's economic policies. Instead, the most binding constraint on government policies comes from international capital markets; but the lessons that they teach are often learned too late, and the compulsion that they exert comes on the heels of economic disaster. In the Russian case, the consequence of flouting IMF advice has been $110 billion of legal and illegal capital flight since 1992, a 220 000 per cent increase in the price level, and widespread disillusionment with democracy – an institution which appears to the average person to make the rich richer and the poor poorer. Indeed, Russia emerges from the transition as the most unequal post-Communist society. In the Baltic States and Central Europe, where the IMF wielded more influence, economic growth has been stronger and a more secure basis has been built for democracy.

THE STRATEGY OF TRANSITION: INFLATION AND DEMOCRACY

Critics of austere, anti-inflationary policies in post-Communist countries point to the apparent success of gradual reform in China, and to the enormous human costs and political instability associated with neoliberal policies in Latin America.[1] The image that captures the imagination is Adam Przeworski's 'J-curve,' which describes a trade-off between the short-term and long-term pain of the transition (Przeworski, 1991, p. 163). As countries enter the reform process, they take austerity measures that reduce output, cut social transfers, and create unemployment, moving down into the 'valley of the transition.' The more rapidly this is done, the more quickly comes the recovery – but at what cost? What if the misery of the transition is so intense that popular patience is exhausted, and democratic institutions are swept away? Perhaps a flatter 'J-curve' would be preferable, which reduces the depth of the recession, and spreads the transition over a longer period of time.

The evidence of the last seven years is that there is, in fact, no such trade-off (Hellman, 1997). Instead, the post-Communist countries that succeeded in quickly bringing inflation under control suffered a smaller drop in output than those that continued to endure the ravages of inflation. In addition, they maintained a much less skewed distribution of wealth and income. Meanwhile, they attracted foreign investment and began to grow, laying the groundwork for long-term political stability. Economies that failed to tame inflation declined more precipitously, and continued to decline long after the reforms had been completed in more successful countries. One could argue that Eastern Europe fared better than the former Soviet Union on both the inflation and growth fronts because it enjoyed a more advantageous starting point; however, the relationship between inflation and growth is clear among the countries of the former Soviet Union, as well. High inflation is correlated with lower growth in the following year.[2]

Stopping inflation is more urgent in post-Communist countries than in the developing world, for three reasons. First, the policies that lead to high levels of inflation – loose credit, budget deficits, and government subsidies – warp the incentives of firms, preventing rapid industrial restructuring. Firms make choices about whether to make costly investments in future competitiveness or to engage in lobbying activity, and when the latter is relatively inexpensive and lucrative, they fail to restructure. This is particularly costly in post-Communist countries, because the structure of production inherited from central planning is highly inefficient. The evidence indicates that controlling inflation makes a substantial contribution to industrial restructuring (Berg, 1994). Countries that succeed in controlling inflation and restructuring industry, in turn, experience higher rates of growth.

Second, inflation undermines the confidence of international investors. Recent research shows that the most important determinant of capital flows to developing countries, after the rate of return, is the domestic inflation rate (Maxfield, 1997; Sobel, 1997). International investment provides needed foreign exchange, and in many cases access to foreign technology and management expertise. Foreign investment takes on critical significance for post-Communist countries, because it determines the success of privatization programs and represents the best hope for industrial restructuring. In the most successful Central European countries, foreign direct investment has made a substantial contribution to export-led growth, and has turned a number of centrally-planned dinosaurs into modern, competitive firms. In countries like Russia, on the other hand, potentially lucrative investments long remained mired in political risk and economic uncertainty, and investment surged only after inflation was finally tamed in 1995 (Halligan and Teplukhin, 1996; Watson, 1996).

Third, high inflation leads to a skewed distribution of wealth, because inflation creates opportunities for non-productive activities that generate a great deal of profit, usually at the expense of the state. For example, Russian banks accumulated most of their present wealth by taking subsidized credits from the Central Bank of Russia, investing in foreign currency, and repaying the credits after the ruble fell (Treisman, 1998). Similarly, high rates of inflation and access to subsidized credits for the privileged few led to the pervasive pattern of 'insider privatization' that has tarnished the legitimacy of Russian reform. Although most of the shares in enterprises were distributed to their workers, managers ended up with controlling interests because they were able to buy up shares with cheap credits and repay the loans with deflated currency. Workers, on the other hand, had higher discount rates because they did not have access to subsidized credits, and they sold. While elites with political access make fortunes in inflationary times, ordinary citizens without recourse to arbitrage opportunities suffer from inflation because their savings are eroded and their wages and pensions fail to keep pace with rising prices.

In the post-Communist context, therefore, the first step towards establishing political legitimacy for reform is to freeze inflation. The failure to restructure industry and attract foreign investment will trap post-Communist countries in a spiral of economic decline, which poses severe challenges to the legitimacy of a democratic order. The corrosive influence of inequality is even more insidious. Economic reform always entails winners and losers, but at least rapid reform keeps the winnings and losses within bounds. An extended transition transfers most of the dwindling wealth of society to a narrow and largely criminal elite which is closely linked to the government – a prospect that is profoundly disheartening to democrats.

WHAT WOULD WE LIKE THE IMF TO DO?

The politicians who set monetary and fiscal policies face a dilemma of dynamic inconsistency: *ex ante*, a policy-maker prefers to be able to commit to an anti-inflationary policy for all future periods; yet, *ex post*, the policy-maker prefers to renege (Kydland and Prescott 1977; Barro and Gordon 1983). Inflation rates depend upon the expectations of private agents such as wage setters, investors, and currency traders, so the policy-maker would like to be able to commit to an anti-inflationary strategy to reassure markets. The dilemma is that there are many temptations to renege on such commitments. Economic models often invoke the idea that 'surprise' inflation has macroeconomic benefits, while political models point to imminent elections and the disproportionate power of narrow interests (Alesina and Perotti, 1995; Alesina and Rosenthal, 1995). The temptation to pursue inflationary policies compels private agents to hedge their bets, driving the inflation rate higher than it would be if policymakers were able to pursue a strategy of full commitment.

The consequence is that inconsistent authorities cast about for ways to tie their hands. The classic solution is to delegate monetary policy to an independent central bank, but this may not be feasible for countries that are still in the process of building democratic institutions. The same short-term considerations that drive politicians to promote inflationary policies will also compel them to undermine the independence of the central bank. In principle, however, the IMF can substitute for entrenched domestic institutions by monitoring compliance with stabilization programs and offering rewards and punishments that tip the balance of incentives in favor of the full-commitment equilibrium (Dhonte, 1997; Swoboda, 1992; Jones, 1987).[3]

It is ultimately international capital markets that enforce the bargain. As the volume of international transactions increases, national governments become increasingly subject to the power of markets.[4] As barriers to capital flows fall, exit becomes less costly for private agents, and governments concerned about promoting welfare and productivity are compelled to provide more hospitable conditions for capital. The IMF plays an important role, however, because capital markets consist of dispersed actors who are unable to coordinate their actions (Lipson 1986). Investors can punish bad economic policies without coordination, simply by diving for cover. It is more difficult, however, for decentralized actors to reward good policies, because a sound investment climate is a state of mind that has to be painstakingly constructed. The fund is able to negotiate with governments and make judgments that become focal points for coordination. Investors benefit from following IMF signals, because stabilization agreements help to separate reliable from unreliable governments, and the threat of IMF sanctions for non-compliance helps to protect the value of their investments. In return, the impact of the fund's resources is vastly magnified by world capital markets, which are opened up by the IMF seal of approval. Under favorable circumstances, a virtuous circle can arise, in which IMF intervention, government policies, and international investment reinforce each other.

The evidence is mixed, however, about the implementation of IMF-sponsored stabilization programs. A recent survey of 45 stand-by and Extended Fund Facility programs conducted by the IMF concluded that only 17 remained on track, and most of these had required waivers or extensions of key fiscal conditions (Bennett, Carkovic, and Dicks-Mireaux, 1995, pp. 28–9). Econometric studies have failed to show that signing IMF programs leads countries to take the steps necessary to improve macroeconomic policy, reduce inflation, or improve current account deficits (Spraos, 1986; Killick, 1984; Kirkpatrick and Onis, 1985).[5] Furthermore, a growing case-study literature points to the overwhelming importance of domestic politics in determining the outcome of stabilization programs, suggesting that the effectiveness of international intervention may be very limited (Haggard, 1986; Nelson, 1990; Kahler, 1992; Haggard and Kaufman, 1992). Indeed, in arguing that the impact of IMF programs on domestic politics has been exaggerated, Karen Remmer suggests that 'standby arrangements have not caused more regime instability because the risky cures recommended by the IMF simply have not been administered' (Remmer, 1986, p. 10).

The implementation of IMF programs is problematic, but domestic constraints are only a part of the problem; more fundamental is the fund's own credibility problem. IMF lending decisions are not informative signals, because they are not costly: the fund does not have to worry about default.[6] Therefore, the IMF seal of approval is only valuable if conditionality is backed by rigorous enforcement. The IMF, however, is not an autonomous actor, analogous to an independent central bank. Rather, IMF policy is closely held by the fund's executive board, which is appointed by the donor countries. A coalition of a few large donors can set policy under the IMF system of weighted voting, and all new agreements, loans, and disbursements must be cleared by the Board. Consequently, the autonomy of the IMF staff varies in inverse proportion to the international significance of the case at hand. The fund has a relatively free hand in negotiating with small developing countries, but in important cases the negotiations are dictated by the interests of the donor governments. International strategic concerns and trade policies override the stabilization agenda.[7]

If economic stabilization is essential to consolidating democracy in post-Communist countries, and if the IMF is unable to exert a strong influence in the most important cases, what does this mean for Russian democracy? The inflationary crisis is now past, since stabilization finally took hold in 1995. The legacy of the inflationary transition, however, is a very authoritarian form of democracy and a weak base of legitimacy for democratic institutions. While the IMF exerted some influence over Russian policies, it was unable to deter flagrant violations of its stabilization programs, in large part because the Russian government had too much influence in Washington. At several turning points in the story, capital flows applied the discipline to Russian policy-makers that the IMF could not, eventually paving the way for successful stabilization of the ruble. The price of the extended transition was staggering, however, and the human costs were much greater than they need have been.

SIX ATTEMPTS TO STABILIZE RUSSIA

In comparison with the East European countries, Russia has been very unsuccessful in controlling inflation; in comparison with the abysmal records of the other countries of the former Soviet Union, Russia's performance is about average. The Russian government has imposed discipline on monetary and fiscal policy for short periods, and pulled back from the precipice of hyperinflation; yet as quickly as they took hold, efforts to restrain demand have evaporated and inflation has surged forward. Table 8.1 compares

Table 8.1   Inflation in the states of the former Soviet Union

	1993	1994	1995	1996
Armenia	10 896	1 885	32	6
Azerbaijan	1 294	1 788	85	7
Belarus	1 994	1 959	244	39
Estonia	36	42	29	15
Georgia	7 484	6 474	57	14
Kazakstan	2 169	1 160	60	29
Kyrgyz Republic	767	96	32	35
Lithuania	189	45	36	13
Latvia	35	26	23	13
Moldova	836	116	24	15
Russia	842	203	131	22
Tajikistan	7 344	1	2 135	41
Turkmenistan	–	1 328	1 262	446
Ukraine	10 155	401	181	40
Uzbekistan	885	1 281	117	63
Mean	3 209	1 120	297	53
Median	1 089	401	60	22

Note: Inflation at end of period.
Source: Kapur and van der Mensbrugghe, (1997) 'External Borrowing by the Baltics, Russia and other countries of the former Soviet Union: Development and policy issues,' International Monetary Fund *Working Paper*, WP/97/72, p. 36. Used by permission.

Figure 8.1   Monthly inflation in Russia

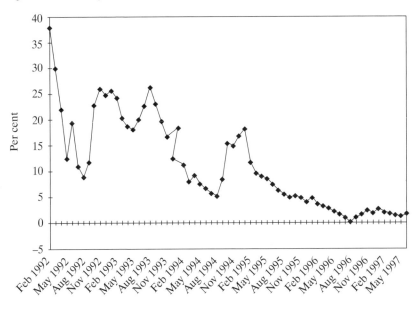

Source: Russian Economic Trends.

Russia to its neighbors in the former Soviet Union; Figure 8.1 illustrates the rollercoaster of inflation and contraction in Russia.

The Shadow Program, January 1992

Russia's first agreement with the IMF, the 'Shadow Program,' committed Russia to a decisive plunge into shock therapy.[8] Real money balances declined sharply, inflation fell rapidly from a monthly rate of 245 per cent in January to 12 per cent in May, and enterprises began to feel the pressure of scarcity. The budget showed a small surplus for the first quarter, and the ruble appreciated against the dollar. If the policies of the first few months had been continued, Russian inflation might have been under control by the years' end. The opportunity was missed. Opposition gathered quickly, and one should not underestimate the political constraints or the uncertainty of the early days of reform, but never again would the political risks involved in stabilizing the economy be so low.

The Russian Congress of Peoples' Deputies granted Yeltsin broad authority to rule by decree and initiate reform, but the logic of institutional incentives gradually asserted itself. Powerful lobbies coalesced around agriculture, sectoral interests, and the military. Concentrated interests demanded more spending for their constituencies, and the diffuse interest of economic stabilization was poorly represented. Furthermore, the Soviet-era constitution left legislative institutions that lent themselves to the centralization of power. An unworkably large Congress of Peoples' Deputies was the supreme legislative authority, but delegated its powers between sessions to the Supreme Soviet, which it elected from its own membership. Speaker Ruslan Khasbulatov soon found that the best way to win support in the Congress was to appeal to economic populism, and he stepped up the pressure on the government to change its course. Yeltsin's economic convictions wavered, and he began to distance himself from his own government in April.[9] Policy shifted dramatically in May, with a jump in the money supply of 27.5 per cent. The Russian inflation rate spiked upwards in June, and the ruble resumed its long slide against the dollar as the market responded to signs that Russian commitment to restraining demand was flagging.

Meanwhile, in the midst of an election campaign, the Bush administration sought to deflect criticism of its policy towards Russia by cobbling together a $24 billion relief package from the Group of Seven leading industrialized countries. Since new direct government aid was scarce, however, the G-7 turned to the IMF as the one source of aid unconstrained by the need for legislative ratification.[10] The package included a $4 billion stand-by arrangement with the IMF, a $6 billion fund from the IMF to stabilize the ruble, and a $500 million loan from the World Bank. Yeltsin, however, struck a hard bargaining posture, asking for a two-year moratorium on Russian debt and demanding that IMF conditionality be waived because 'Russia is unique and its reform is unique.'[11]

IMF negotiators refused to agree to a loan unless Russia rededicated itself to financial stabilization. They demanded a monthly inflation target no higher than 3 per cent, with strict limits on the money supply and Federal spending. Negotiations broke down, and the IMF decided to postpone a stand-by arrangement ten days before the G-7 meeting. The Bush administration intensified its lobbying campaign, urging the IMF to soften its usual requirements. An agreement with Russia was the only promising item on the G-7 agenda, since the United States and the European Union remained far apart on the Uruguay Trade Round, and macroeconomic coordination was as inaccessible as ever because of the respective domestic preoccupations of Germany, the US, and Japan. Finally, on the weekend before the summit was to begin, the IMF Managing Director, Michel Camdessus, flew to Moscow to smooth over differences. The commitments that Russia undertook under the new agreement were predictably watered down. Russia consented to cut its budget deficit and control inflation, but its goal for monthly inflation remained a generous 7–9 per cent. There was agreement on a credit ceiling and spending guidelines, but instead of strict targets, the IMF announced a vague promise of 'new measures' to 'strengthen the economic reforms and the stabilization program.' Discussion of reducing subsidies and liberalizing energy prices was put off indefinitely. The IMF's bargaining position was dramatically weaker than if it had been able to wait to disburse the first tranche on its own preferred terms. The fund lent Russia a first tranche of $1 billion immediately, but the remaining tranches of the loan and other elements of the $24 billion package depended upon further negotiations.[12]

The First Stand-by Agreement: July 1992

No sooner was the ink dry on the agreement than Russia took steps to undermine it. The first and most disastrous step was Yeltsin's appointment of Viktor Gerashchenko – with the reluctant acquiescence of his acting Premier, Yegor Gaidar – as Chairman of the Central Bank of Russia (CBR).[13] Gerashchenko, an opportunistic Soviet-era official, argued that it was his responsibility to assure adequate liquidity in the money market and protect industry from the rigors of reform; in short, to abort stabilization. One of his first official acts was to resolve the problem of inter-enterprise arrears by flooding the market with subsidized credits. In order to sustain an international ruble zone, he granted unrestricted credits to the former Soviet republics. The CBR increased its total level of credit by over 50 per cent per month in June, July and August, and the money supply grew 300 per cent by September. Meanwhile, in spite of commitments to rein in the budget deficit, government spending steadily rose from 25 per cent of GDP in the first quarter to 39 per cent in the second, 42 per cent in the third, and 46 per cent in the fourth, driven by subsidies to enterprises and price supports (Russian Economic Trends (RET), 1993, 2(1), p. 12, RET, 1993, 2(3), pp. 9–10). The deterioration of fiscal and monetary policy in the wake of the agreement was not lost on the public. The Supreme Soviet had the government very much on the defensive, and much of the press had already determined that stabilization had failed.

Capital markets quickly moved to punish the prodigal government by fleeing the ruble. Figures 8.2 through 8.5 at the end of the chapter, and particularly Figure 8.5, illustrate the ruble's dramatic collapse. The exchange rate fell from 135 rubles to the dollar in June to 241 in September, 338 in October, and 419 in November. Figures for capital flight are unreliable for 1992, but the gross capital drain from Russia, including legitimate and illegitimate transfers and unremitted earnings from foreign trade, has been estimated at nearly $2 billion per month.[14] After stabilizing in May, the demand for dollars on the Russian market surged 31 per cent in June and 38 per cent in July. Private savings were rapidly 'dollarized,' since foreign currency represented the most effective hedge against inflation: dollar deposits in

Russian banks rose from 34 per cent of M2 in April to 119 per cent of M2 in November (Aslund, 1994, pp. 192–3). Investment continued to fall, and enterprises accumulated vast stocks as a hedge against inflation. The inflation rate jumped from a low of 9 per cent in August to a roaring 23–26 per cent per month that was sustained from October through February. As the Russian stabilization program collapsed, the IMF froze the additional tranches of its loan under the stand-by arrangement. Since much of the $24 billion international aid package had been linked to agreement with the IMF, this meant that half of the package cobbled together by the Bush administration was suspended. Circumstances conspired, however, to bring Russia back to the top of the US agenda and to undermine the IMF strategy.

The Congress of Peoples' Deputies ousted Yegor Gaidar as Acting Premier in December 1992, but the new government headed by Viktor Chernomyrdin proved to be surprisingly friendly to the stabilization agenda. Reform might be an issue without a political constituency, but it possessed two strong, silent allies: galloping inflation and a retreating ruble. Russia flirted with hyperinflation in December, when the weekly inflation rate reached 10 per cent. The ruble fell almost 40 per cent in January on the news of Gaidar's departure, and capital streamed into Western investments at a rate of $1.5 billion per month. The demand for dollars doubled every month in January, February and March. Events on the capital markets tipped the balance once again in favor of the reformers, and Yeltsin appointed a vigorous, young economist named Boris Fedorov as Finance Minister. Fedorov launched a systematic assault on commodity subsidies, import controls, the lax credit policies of the CBR, and the federal budget deficit.

As winter gave way to a frosty spring, however, the opponents of reform began to regain momentum. Khasbulatov launched a noisy campaign to 'impeach' Yeltsin, which in Russian usage meant a two-thirds vote of the Congress to remove him from office. The government's allies narrowly defeated the measure in March, but only by agreeing to hold a politically risky national referendum on the president and his economic reform program. The drama in Moscow sent Western leaders scrambling to show their support for Yeltsin before the referendum on 25 April, particularly in view of the imminent summit meeting between Clinton and Yeltsin in Vancouver. In advance of the summit, President Clinton publicly called upon the IMF to forgo its tough conditionality and lend Russia $13.5 billion per year.[15] He further signaled the seriousness of his intentions by launching an effort to rally the Western allies behind a new $30 billion package of aid.[16] The Paris Club of official creditors responded by granting Russia a 10-year deferment on $15 billion of former Soviet debt, and when Clinton met with Yeltsin over the next two days, he offered $1.6 billion in new direct aid.[17] Clinton used personal calls to the Japanese Prime Minister, Kiichi Miyazawa, to press Japan to drop its refusal to aid Russia due to the Kurile

Islands dispute, and Miyazawa surprised Japanese opinion by giving in, opening the way for Yeltsin to come to the G-7 summit in Tokyo.[18] After strenuous US lobbying, the G-7 countries announced a $28 billion package that relied heavily on contributions from the international financial institutions.[19]

The impact of Clinton's lobbying campaign was felt most directly in the halls of the IMF. Under severe pressure from the US and other governments, the fund announced on 10 April that it would change its approach to Russia and offer up to $4.5 billion without the usual conditions concerning inflation and the budget deficit.[20] On the eve of the Russian referendum, the fund announced a new program for the former Soviet-bloc countries called the Systemic Transformation Facility, designed to help ease the pain of economic transition without imposing strict conditions. A total of $4 to $6 billion would be available, of which $3 billion was allocated for Russia. At the same time, Michel Camdessus announced that the Fund intended to lend Russia up to $30 billion over the next four to five years.[21] Yeltsin won the referendum resoundingly, but by then the fund had committed itself to a much softer bargaining position. Final agreement on the terms of the STF came in May, and the Fund promised to try to reach a stand-by agreement in the fall with stricter conditions if the stabilization program remained on track. This additional agreement would provide up to another $10 billion, including the $6 billion fund discussed the previous year to stabilize the ruble.

The fund made a determined effort to enforce its 1992 agreement with Russia: it suspended the stand-by agreement, triggering clauses in several other international agreements, and withheld financing for at least six months. The outcome, on the other hand, did little to reinforce the fund's credibility. Faced with an intransigent fund – and armed with a convenient domestic emergency – Yeltsin appealed to Clinton, and had the rules changed. In effect, the fund was compelled to overlook Russian behavior in the previous year, and agree to provide the remaining $3 billion promised under the original 1992 agreement under revised terms. This reinforced Russian confidence that the fund's conditions could be flouted in the future.

The Systemic Transformation Facility: May 1993

The IMF offered Russia terms so gentle that they were without precedent, including an inflation target of 10 per cent per month, or almost 300 per cent per year. Nevertheless, the fund declared Russia off track and suspended the agreement after only four months. On the other hand, offering a new loan in 1993 gave the fund leverage to bargain for conditions governing Russian budget deficits, credit ceilings, and interest rates; for a policy down payment; and for a reform of the regime covering the CBR. As with previous agreements, the provisions that could be carried out before the money changed hands were implemented, but the long-range provisions were not. The most significant achievement of the 1993 agreement was the nudge that it gave to the balance of power between the CBR and Boris Fedorov's Ministry of Finance. CBR Chairman Gerashchenko remained the major obstacle to stabilizing the ruble; as a principle source of political favors, he was perhaps the only official in Moscow who enjoyed the strong support of both Ruslan Khasbulatov and Viktor Chernomyrdin. Fedorov's objectives of reaching an agreement with the IMF and restraining the CBR coincided, and his strategy demonstrates what a wily negotiator can achieve in the midst of a two-level game (Putnam, 1988). As a condition for disbursing the first tranche of $1.5 billion, the IMF insisted that CBR credit come under a more restrictive set of rules (a condition supported by Fedorov), and Fedorov convinced key Gerashchenko allies to accept this deal. Premier Chernomyrdin and Gerashchenko signed an agreement in May committing the CBR to credit ceilings and targets for interest rates (Fedorov, 1994; RET, 1993, 2(3), p. 5). At the same time, Russia agreed with the IMF to reduce money and credit growth to 4–5 per cent per month by the end of the year.

Fiscal policy had tightened significantly by the time of the agreement. Fedorov aggressively sequestered funds that had been appropriated by the Supreme Soviet for the military industries, investments, and social services – a policy for which he was widely vilified and occasionally praised (*Segodnia*, 1993a). He engineered an impressive contraction of government spending from 42.5 per cent of GDP in 1992 to only 27 per cent of GDP in the second quarter of 1993, and briefly brought the budget back into surplus. As soon as the agreement with the IMF had been signed, however, the Chernomyrdin government moved to relax budget discipline, and soon found itself in a bidding war with the Congress of Peoples' Deputies for the allegiance of strategic lobbies and regional leaders. Figure 8.4, at the end of the chapter, illustrates the rapid deterioration in fiscal policy that resulted.[22] Subsidies to industry doubled in the third quarter, and total government spending expanded by 120 per cent. In nominal terms, Federal spending on subsidies and price supports in the fourth quarter of 1993 exceeded Russia's gross domestic product for all of 1992 (RET, 1993, 2(3), pp. 9–10, RET, 1994 3(1), pp. 9–11). Meanwhile, the confrontation with the Supreme Soviet had been building to a climax. Its appetite for government spending unsated, the Supreme Soviet passed 432 amendments to the budget for 1994, amassing a deficit estimated at 25 per cent of GDP (*Segodnia*, 1993b). Yeltsin vetoed the budget, and the impasse lasted through the summer.

In the fall of 1993, Yeltsin executed a fateful about-face in his economic policy, which turned his conflict with the Supreme Soviet into a constitutional crisis. Swelling government spending created a surge of inflation, which reached 26 per cent in August. For Yeltsin, this appears to have been a telling argument: the economy simply could not be stabilized without controlling inflation, and two years of experience confirmed his ministers' arguments that inflation really could not be controlled without cutting government spending.[23] Currency traders were responding to the desperate state of Russian finances by fleeing the ruble: demand for dollars surged 165 per cent in August. Meanwhile, legitimate and illegitimate forms of capital flight reached new heights, as Russia exported nearly $12 billion of capital during the summer. Capital flight in August reached 60 per cent of Russia's international reserves, and 15 per cent of the month's GDP. Yeltsin felt compelled to change course.

On 21 September, Yeltsin set aside the constitution, dissolved the Supreme Soviet, and called new elections for December which would also serve as a referendum on a new constitution. The parliament resisted; Yeltsin besieged the building, and finally, on 5 October, stormed it with shock troops. After the defeat of the Supreme Soviet, the way was cleared for new parliamentary elections and a sharp turn towards stabilization, but at grievous cost to Russian democracy. The legitimacy of the new state had been founded on the Supreme Soviet's brave defiance of the military coup against Gorbachev in 1991, and now Yeltsin had turned the same military on the parliament that he had once led against it. If consolidating democracy means, above all, establishing routine, institutionalized means of resolving conflicts, building confidence that such means will be used rather than force, and linking the reputation of leaders to their adherence to democratic norms, the fall of 1993 represented a severe setback for Russian democracy.

The clash in 1993 had another important consequence for Russian political institutions: it allowed Yeltsin to consolidate his power by writing a new and much more authoritarian constitution. The constitution inherited from the Soviet period had many failings, but it provided for a separation of powers between the legislative, executive and judicial branches of government. The Supreme Soviet had to confirm the members of the government, pass the budget, and approve major pieces of legislation. Yeltsin ruled by using numerous extra-constitutional expedients, but the Supreme Soviet was a real alternative center of power, and it imposed serious constraints upon his policies. The 1993 Constitution, on the other hand, provided for a form of government that has been called 'superpresidentialism' (Linz, 1993). It allows the president to issue legislation by decree, requiring a two-thirds majority of the new Duma to override Presidential orders, and allows the president to dissolve the Duma if it fails to pass a major piece of legislation or rejects a Government appointment three times. Since 1993, this has allowed Yeltsin to rule with vastly reduced legislative restraints, making him perhaps the most powerful democratically elected president in the world.[24] Without institutional constraints on his power, there is little to prevent superpresidentialism from degenerating into dictatorship.

The STF Renewal, April 1994

On 20 September, the IMF delayed disbursing the second tranche of the STF
($1.5 billion) because of Russia's failure to meet its inflation target. This was
a step with serious consequences, because it froze negotiations for up to
$10 billion of additional loans. Fund officials hinted that the money could be
disbursed by the end of the year if Russian policy improved. Yegor Gaidar,
who had recently returned to the government, abolished subsidized credits,
deregulated agricultural prices, and slashed expenditures by refusing to disburse funds. In November, interest rates finally became positive, and from
October through January, M2 grew by an average of less than 9 per cent per
month. Inflation fell to 13 per cent in December, the lowest figure since the
summer of 1992. In spite of the reformist consolidation in the Russian government, however, the budget deficit swelled alarmingly in the last quarter of
1993. Federal budget revenues fell from 33 per cent of GDP in the third
quarter to only 19.3 per cent in the last, opening up a budget deficit of 16 per
cent of GDP. Since this had to be financed by the central bank, the result was
a flagrant violation of IMF targets for CBR credit. This became seen as a test
of the IMF's resolve to enforce the budget agreement, and the IMF again
suspended the second tranche of the Systemic Transformation Facility,
which had been due to be disbursed in November.

Once again, however, Russia provided a crisis to test the Fund's resolve.
The electorate decisively rejected reform in the December 1993 parliamentary
elections. Gaidar's Russia's Choice party collected only 15.4 per cent of the
vote for its party list in the new State Duma.[25] The ultranationalist Liberal-
Democratic Party of Vladimir Zhirinovskii received the highest vote count
(22.8 per cent), followed by an alliance between the Communist Party
(12.4 per cent) and the Agrarian Party (7.9 per cent). The results of the election upon policy were indirect, because the new Constitution dramatically
reduced the role of the Duma, and Chernomyrdin remained at the head of
the government. However, the election represented a stark rejection of economic reform by the electorate; more troubling, it demonstrated disillusionment
with democracy as well, as voters deserted the center and embraced extreme
right- and left-wing alternatives. Gaidar, Fedorov, and most of the other
reformers left the government in January. The reaction of the market was
swift. In one week in January 1994, the ruble dropped 18.5 per cent against the
dollar. Inflation jumped from 13 per cent per month to 21 per cent.

Almost immediately, the Clinton administration signaled that it was time
for the IMF to relent. Vice President Gore, in St Petersburg, called the IMF
'insensitive' and argued that the West should help the Russian government to
subsidize Russian workers. In Germany, he suggested to Helmut Kohl that the
IMF should relax its inflation targets and accelerate aid to Russia. On
21 December, Warren Christopher and Strobe Talbott seemed to abandon the

stabilization agenda, criticizing the Russian reformers for callousness towards the pain of transition.[26] The next day, the IMF announced that it would consider relaxing its conditions. Ernesto Hernandez-Cata, the fund's chief negotiator with Russia, said that he would push for a monthly inflation target of 3–5 per cent for 1994, instead of the 2 per cent that he had been seeking.[27]

There was a gradual shift in the fund in 1993 and 1994 from a strategy of enforcing conditionality to a short-term bargaining posture, as the emphasis shifted away from past performance and towards bargaining over the minimum conditions that Russia must meet to receive the next loan installment. The Clinton administration intensified its criticism of the fund on 1 February, suggesting that the IMF had been slow to engage Russia in dialogue, and proposed that the G-7 take a more active role in monitoring negotiations between the IMF and Russia to resolve the continuing loan impasse. The pressure was intense enough that Camdessus felt compelled to respond. He spelled out a number of points that were under discussion, including industrial subsidies, price controls, privatization, and the budget deficit. His statement suggested, however, that the one irreducible IMF condition was that the Russian inflation rate fall back to the promised 10 per cent per month before the second tranche could be disbursed.[28] Meanwhile, the Russian government was continuing the efforts begun in the fall to reduce inflation. Although Chernomyrdin called for a more pragmatic approach to managing the economy and surrounded himself with industrialists, his policy in early 1994 was in fact designed to placate the market and the fund. Real interest rates rose steadily, to a peak of 10 per cent per month in March and April. In the first quarter of 1994, M2 grew at a modest rate of 7 per cent per month, and inflation finally dipped under 10 per cent per month in March. Camdessus took this as his cue, flying to Moscow and agreeing to renew the STF in return for promises of unspecified new taxes and spending cuts, a budget deficit for 1994 of no more than 10 per cent of GDP, and a target for inflation of 7 per cent per month by year's end. He announced that Russia was eligible to apply for a stand-by arrangement worth $4 billion of additional financing. In addition, the agreement made Russia eligible for up to $2 billion in loans from the World Bank that had been put on hold.

The fund had taken a firm stand for the second time, but had been forced to fight a rear-guard action that reduced its room for maneuver and strained its credibility. The fund imposed a cost on the Russian government by delaying the disbursement from September until April. This sent a signal that the fund would not sign a stand-by agreement or agree to release additional funds to stabilize the ruble until Russia had made clear progress on controlling inflation. It became increasingly apparent, however, that Russia was able to bring substantial diplomatic pressure to bear upon the fund, and that the fund had to modify its bargaining positions when Russia flexed its muscles. The fund gradually starting looking for an excuse to disburse the second tranche in spite of the violations of the 1993 agreement, and the bargaining came to revolve around the short-term measures that Russia could take to bring its policies back on track. The consequence was greater flexibility in the spring of 1994, which gave the fund greater leverage over short-term Russian policy, but also undermined Russia's long-term incentives to abide by the next agreement.

For a few months, the new government used the insulation from parliament afforded by the new constitution to continue the policy of stabilization. After the budget-tightening measures introduced in the fall, demand for dollars stabilized at a manageable level, and capital flight declined from the high of $4.5 billion per month in October to $1.5 billion in April. A new complacency crept into public statements about economic policy, as leading officials suggested that Russia's economic woes were largely a thing of the past (*Segodnia*, 1994a). The disbursement of the second tranche, however, seems to have removed the pressure for restraint. Almost as soon as the money was received, the period of active stabilization came to an end. The acting minister of finance, Sergei Dubinin, asserted 'without excessive optimism,' that hyperinflation had been avoided and that 'financial stabilization has taken place.'[29] Both fiscal and monetary restraint quickly fell victim to the new mood.

For the first half of 1994, most of the difficulty with the budget continued to be on the revenue side. Revenues declined to 8 per cent of GDP in the first quarter, and only recovered gradually (RET 1994, 3:1, p. 9, RET 1995, 4:1, p. 10). This had a variety of causes, including local fraud, the difficulty that the government experienced in collecting taxes from the new private sector, and the conflicts between the center and the regions over tax collection. The most important problem, however, was that the Russian government relied heavily upon tax favors as a way of building patronage. The revenue picture gradually improved during the year, but government spending also resurged, increasing by almost 50 per cent in each of the last two quarters. The federal budget deficit rose to 12 per cent of GDP in the third quarter of 1994 (RET 1995, 4(1), p. 10). Meanwhile, monetary policy returned to an expansionary course.[30]

The markets, once again, exacted a bitter revenge. Capital flight had slowed to a steady drain of $1 billion per month, but this was largely because Russian investors had found profitable ways to bet against the ruble or to shelter their funds in foreign currency. Demand for dollars surged 265 per cent during the summer, and the ruble steadily declined, indicating a deep lack of confidence in the government's policy. The CBR intervened furiously in September, spending four billion dollars in futile efforts to staunch the hemorrhage of rubles. Finally, when international reserves fell to only two weeks worth of imports, the CBR withdrew from the market. The ruble fell 40 per cent against the dollar on 11 October, which was dubbed 'Black Tuesday' in the Russian press. Inflation jumped to 15 per cent per month, and remained at 1993 levels until February. The flow of foreign investment into Russia, which had reached a peak of $500 million in August, fell to $100 million in November (Aslund, 1994, p. 206). The financial crisis provoked a full-scale secret police investigation directed at alleged profiteers and speculators, headed by Yeltsin's old friend Oleg Lobov (*Segodnia*, 1994c). Its overall impact, however, was positive for reform. Overruling Chernomyrdin, Yeltsin promoted the liberal Anatolii Chubais to first deputy premier and granted him control over the entire range of economic policy. Gerashchenko was replaced at the CBR by Tatyana Paramonova, who subsequently proved her dedication to a sound currency. Chubais announced a new policy course, which he dubbed the 'second stage of the Russian reforms' (*Segodnia*, 1994d). For the first time, the foreign exchange market had toppled a Russian government – something that even the Russian electorate was unable to do.

The IMF faced a bitter dilemma: to punish the newly-consolidated reformers for the sins of their predecessors, or to overlook the flagrant violation of the 1994 agreement? The fund's choice completed its transition from a reputation-building strategy to a strategy of short-term bargaining. The fund had slowed negotiations for a new stand-by arrangement when the budget deficit swelled. The Russian government had been clamoring for a new loan from the IMF since October to help cover a projected 1995 budget deficit of $26 billion.[31] In return, the IMF demanded a substantial policy down payment. Russia agreed to finally implement a 1994 decree to liberalize the oil sector, where prices remained 30 per cent below world levels.[32] In addition, Yeltsin signed decrees in March aimed at reducing corruption and increasing fiscal discipline.[33]

In April 1995, the Russian government signed its most far-reaching agreement with the IMF. Instead of downgrading Russia's credit as a result of its dismal performance in 1994, the fund offered a loan of $6.4 billion, the second largest in its history following the bailout of Mexico earlier in the year. The new agreement set an inflation goal of no more than 3 per cent per month by the end of the year and a budget deficit limit of 73 trillion rubles, or 5.1 per cent of estimated GDP. The Russian Duma furthermore agreed to prohibit the CBR from financing the Federal budget, compelling the Ministry of Finance to seek outside funding and to rely increasingly upon the domestic bond market. CBR net domestic credit, furthermore, was not to increase by more than 35 trillion rubles (RET, 1995, 4(1), p. 3). After the experience of 1994, the fund insisted on monthly disbursement in order to retain some leverage after the agreement was signed.

The Second Stand-by Arrangement, April 1995

Following a series of inauspicious beginnings, Russia finally succeeded in stabilizing its currency in 1995. Domestic political circumstances finally appeared favorable. By 1995, it had become clear that the State Duma was a rather tame legislature with limited power; the reformers had consolidated their control of the government after the currency collapse of October 1994; the CBR had finally joined the ranks of the reformers; and once again, inflation was high, underscoring the importance of restraint and limiting the gains from surprise. In addition, a number of technical and political obstacles to tax collection and deregulation had been overcome. IMF leverage appeared to be at an all-time high because IMF funding was explicitly written into the 1995 budget as a major source of noninflationary deficit finance.

In spite of the war in Chechnya, the Federal budget deficit remained below the agreed-upon ceilings.[34] Monetary policy was conservative, IMF targets for CBR credits and M2 were maintained, and the CBR substantially increased its foreign reserves.[35] As a result, the currency stabilized within an official exchange rate corridor, and inflation fell steadily, from a monthly rate of 17.9 per cent in January (an annual rate of 600 per cent) to 3.2 per cent in December (an annual rate of 40 per cent). The budget adopted for 1996, furthermore, called for even greater austerity, with a projected deficit of 3.9 per cent of GDP. Capital markets responded favorably: capital outflows fell to record lows of $500 million per month in the summer.

The campaign for the parliamentary elections in December led to a modest expansion of government spending in October and November.[36] The government resisted the temptation to override the IMF spending targets, however, even as the election campaign became increasingly desperate. In part, the government was complacent because the Russian constitution vests so little power in the parliament; it is apparent, however, that Chernomyrdin overestimated his popular appeal. The party-list voting was a disaster: the government party, Our Home is Russia, polled only 10.1 per cent of the party-list vote, putting it in third place behind its undemocratic opponents of the left and the right: Gennadyi Zyuganov's Communist Party (22 per cent) and Vladimir Zhirinovskii's Liberal-Democratic Party (11.2 per cent). Grigorii Yavlinskii's liberal Yabloko Party polled 6.9 per cent, and the rest of the vote went to small parties that failed to meet the 5 per cent threshold for representation in the Duma. Half of the seats were elected from single-member constituencies, however, which diluted the results. While the government was left controlling only 12 per cent of the total seats, no stable coalition emerged to oppose it. Since the Duma requires a two-thirds majority to pass legislation over a presidential veto or to block a presidential decree, even the disastrous defeat of the reformist parties in December barely impaired Yeltsin's ability to govern. However, it indicated the country's deep disillusionment with economic reform, and the willingness of substantial portions of the electorate to flirt with totalitarian alternatives. 84 per cent of Communist voters and 67 per cent of Liberal-Democratic voters endorsed some form of dictatorship; only 45 per cent of the electorate was unwilling to endorse either a return to Communism, dictatorship, or military rule (White *et al.*, 1997, p. 245). The long, painful transition had severely eroded the legitimacy of Russian democracy.

The Extended Fund Facility, February 1996

The current program was negotiated against the backdrop of a desperate presidential election campaign in which the Communist candidate, Gennadyi Zyuganov, seemed sure to prevail over an incumbent Yeltsin with an approval rating of 6 per cent. A Communist victory in Russia – unlike in Poland or Hungary – was very threatening to reform everywhere in Eastern Europe, and an ability to deliver Western assistance seemed to be one of Yeltsin's few electoral assets. Yeltsin was in a strong position, if in no other respect, at least in bargaining with the IMF.

As a signal about the upcoming Presidential election in June, the parliamentary elections in December were clear enough: the population was dissatisfied with Yeltsin's government. Yeltsin gave his economic policies a more populist cast in January, promising to pay wage arrears and reschedule $6.7 billion in taxes owed by enterprises. In order to end a nationwide miners' strike, the government allocated an additional $2.2 billion for the coal industry. Meanwhile, the Duma raised the ante, and pressed ahead with plans to raise the minimum wage by 20 per cent. Apparently signaling a change of course, Yeltsin fired Anatolii Chubais, his chief economic adviser, and replaced him with Vladimir Kadannikov, an industrialist and advocate of increased subsidies to industry.[37] Markets reacted swiftly. After more than six months of stability, the ruble fell almost 8 per cent in one week.

Meanwhile, the IMF came under oblique but public pressure from the Clinton administration to look the other way. After Chernomyrdin came to Washington to lobby for a new loan, Clinton stated that 'I believe the loan will go through, and I believe that it should.' US officials downplayed the importance of personnel changes in Moscow, and expressed understanding for Yeltsin's need to maneuver in advance of the elections. In a telling statement, Chernomyrdin observed that both countries were having presidential elections this year, lending 'a special tone' to their relationship.[38] The IMF was solicitous of the new Russian course, and Michel Camdessus again visited Moscow to smooth the way to agreement. In negotiations for a new three-year, $10.2 billion loan under the Extended Fund Facility, the IMF pushed for a number of institutional changes, including liberalization of foreign trade, resumption of privatization, and revisions in the tax code that would abolish preferences for some of Russia's most influential lobbies. However, in a clear concession to election-year pressures, the fund agreed to accommodate high levels of spending in the first half of the year.[39]

The Yeltsin campaign surged back from the brink of defeat by convincing voters that a Communist victory would be even worse than another term for Yeltsin. It was aided by Zyuganov's own mistakes, which allowed Yeltsin to portray him as an extreme Communist who would restore all of the horror of the Soviet Union. Faced with such a grim choice, a slim plurality of the electorate (35 per cent) chose Yeltsin in the first round of voting, and a short-lived alliance with the right-wing military officer Aleksandr Lebed gave Yeltsin a strong majority (54 per cent) in the run-off election. Skillfully managed by the Yeltsin campaign, the election became a referendum on Communism rather than on Yeltsin's policies: respondents' attitudes towards the former Soviet regime, rather than their economic fortunes during the transition, were the best predictor of votes for Yeltsin or Zyuganov (Colton, 1996). Anatolii Chubais quietly reemerged as Yeltsin's campaign manager, proved to be an invaluable asset, and rebuilt his political base. After the election, he became the president's chief of staff, and began his climb back to his former position of first deputy premier.

The election fell far short of Western norms of fairness. Yeltsin replaced the head of the All-Russian State TV and Radio Company with a loyalist, and appointed the head of Russia's only independent television station to his campaign. A study of the three national television stations' coverage of the campaign from May to July by the European Institute for the Media found that positive references to Yeltsin outnumbered negative ones by 492, while negative references to Zyuganov outnumbered positive ones by 313 (White *et al.*, 1997, pp. 251–2). Furthermore, the liberal press, which is usually quite critical of Yeltsin, rallied to his side once it became clear that it faced a choice between Yeltsin and Zyuganov. This probably would have happened in any case, but common interests were reinforced by the purchase of all of the major newspapers by financiers who supported the Yeltsin campaign. Throughout the campaign, media coverage remained extraordinarily one-sided, and Yeltsin's share of the vote gradually increased. Finally, it is a measure of the weakness of democratic norms in Russia that canceling the election was seriously discussed in the President's administration, and that the belief was widespread that Yeltsin would not step down if he were defeated.

The agreement with the IMF was severely tested by the presidential election of 1996, and familiar patterns of program slippage and benign neglect by the fund reasserted themselves. It was not until after Yeltsin had won the run-off election on 3 July and secured a second term that the IMF began to seriously scrutinize the Russian fiscal position, which had deteriorated considerably in the interim. Previous rounds of reform had restricted the use of direct subsidies and loans as instruments of patronage, so the government had turned to selective collection of taxes in order to cobble together a coalition and prevent lay-offs just before the election. The government had granted so many favors to influential firms that tax collections were 12 per cent below projected levels by July. The fund responded by delaying the monthly installment of $330 million of its loan that month, but signalled leniency by declaring that the disbursement could be made within weeks if Russia took action to increase tax collections.[40] The fund again accepted the reality of Russian pork-barrel politics and agreed to forgive the indiscretions of the election season, provided that policy improved afterwards.

A reformist coalition consolidated its position in Yeltsin's cabinet in the aftermath of the election, and by fall, Russian policy was gradually improving under Chubais' renewed leadership. Disappointing tax collections remained a serious hurdle, and prevented the disbursement of two more loan tranches, but the government's policy remained generally on track. Inflation fell, and foreign investment surged – driven in large part by low interest rates in the US and extraordinarily low interest rates in Japan, but also by a growing conviction among investors that Russia was recovering, and that its depressed assets represented the most attractive gamble on the market. Capital outflows, which had amounted to $16 billion during the campaign from January through June, returned to the low level reached in 1995 as soon as the election results were announced. In the next year, the Russian government floated Eurobonds successfully, as did major cities and even large enterprises. For the time being, Russia's isolation from international capital markets had ended.

CONCLUSION

Russia eventually succeeded in stabilizing its economy, but in the interim it demonstrated the limits of the fund's ability to enforce conditionality. Russia and the IMF have converged on an understanding that Russia is an unusual case, because it is very costly for the fund to enforce the conditions attached to its loans. As a result, these agreements are not constraining, and global capital markets have discounted them. Bargaining with the IMF has constrained Russian policy in the short term. In the long run, however, agreement with the IMF guarantees little, which accounts for the slow pace of foreign investment in Russia during the first four years of the transition. Russia has met the fiscal and monetary targets set forth in only two of its six completed programs. In two of the six cases, inflation rose and the ruble fell in the months following announcement of a stabilization program. In five of six, macroeconomic policy deteriorated immediately after a program was announced. The IMF seeks to enforce conditionality, but it labors under severe political constraints imposed by its major shareholders. The IMF repeatedly attempted to enforce conditionality by suspending loan tranches. However, in the face of insistent criticism from donor countries – in particular, from the United States – the fund was compelled to compromise. In each case, the fund adopted a bargaining strategy, trading additional credits for short-term improvements in policy, rather than investing in a reputation for enforcing conditionality. Russia is simply too important to the international system to be constrained by the IMF.

The cyclical expansion and contraction of Russian macroeconomic policy is explained by the political incentives generated by inflation rates, with their three- to four-month lags behind policy, and the capital flows that respond to them. When inflation is in a tolerable range, the argument for restraint is drowned by a chorus of demands for industrial subsidies and price controls. Injecting money into the economy at such times is tempting, because it generates a short-lived demand boom that raises the fortunes of sinking enterprises and allows the government to distribute favors to loyal banks and firms. The consequences can be put off for at least several months, which often gets the government out of a crisis or through an election. When inflation rates are much higher, however, the threats of uncontrollable hyperinflation, capital flight, and the collapse of the ruble become more hazardous than resisting political pressures. At such times, high inflation and a weak ruble become the strongest allies of reform. The burst of inflation that followed price liberalization in 1992 strengthened the hand of the reformers, but as soon as inflation came under control in late spring, the temptation to use monetary and fiscal policy to ease the pain of adjustment became overpowering. The ruble crashed and inflation soared. The new Minister of Finance, Boris Fedorov, was isolated in 1993 in a government of industrialists, but inflation was the wild card that allowed him to bid on a weak hand. Once inflation declined again, fiscal discipline was quickly abandoned. High inflation and growing budget deficits by the end of 1993 called for austerity again in early 1994, but again caution was thrown to the winds once lower inflation rates in the summer ushered in a new round of complacency. It took extraordinary inflation and the dramatic collapse of the ruble in 1994 to convince Yeltsin to delegate economic policy to a group of committed reformers, who carried out the successful stabilization of 1995.

In spite of Russia's low levels of foreign investment and tenuous integration into the world economy, capital markets displayed a striking capacity to discipline Russian policy through capital flight and by exerting pressure on the exchange rate. Markets were very sensitive to changes in government policies, and even to changes in the composition of the Russian government. The departure of prominent reformers from the government invariably shook the ruble and unleashed further capital flight. In return, the three crashes of the ruble in the autumn of 1992, winter of 1993, and autumn of 1994 exerted strong influences upon Russian policy, and in the last case led to the reorganization of the government. The government did not oppose devaluation per se, but the nominal exchange rate was a very visible symbol of its commitment to reform; when that commitment came into question, capital flowed into foreign investments, and the ruble fell. In each case, dramatic exchange rate movements ushered in tighter fiscal and monetary policies. The two most effective stabilization programs, in 1993 and 1995, each followed a collapse of the ruble.

Unfortunately, capital markets can only enforce discipline by proving that policies are disastrous, and democracy does not always survive the evidence. In the Russian case, three years were lost in which the foundations of a competitive economy and a consolidated democracy could have been built. There are at least three serious economic consequeces of failing to stabilize the economy in 1992. First, Russia is left with corrupt and unrestructured industrial, agricultural and service sectors. Interenterprise arrears and the reemergence of widespread barter are symptoms of the failure to restructure Russian industry, which occurred because of the ready availability of government favors. Second, Russia, one of the poorest industrialized nations, has exported $110 billion of capital since it launched its reform in 1992, and has attracted less foreign capital per capita than its more advanced neighbors. This represents a tremendous drain on the Russian economy which, if reversed, would have led to much faster growth. Third, the combination of high inflation, corruption and privatization has lent credibility to Communist propaganda: after five years of reform, Russia is now as unequal as its former archnemesis, the United States.

Sustained economic decline, deindustrialization, the widening gap between rich and poor, and the emergence of a corrupt elite have eroded the consensus in favor of democracy in Russia. In the referendum in the spring of 1993, after enduring more than a year of reform, a majority of Russians voters still supported Yeltsin and his package of economic reforms. In the parliamentary elections of 1995, in contrast, a solid majority supported authoritarian alternatives, and only a small minority supported the parties associated with economic reform. It is a hopeful sign that Yeltsin was able to come back from almost certain defeat in the presidential election the following year by capitalizing on the latent anticommunism of the Russian electorate – but it was a much closer thing than in 1991. Extremist politics does not have the same appeal in the countries that reformed their economies and tamed inflation quickly.

Finally, the legacy of a slow reform was a series of political confrontations that weakened the fabric of democracy and recast Russian institutions in a more authoritarian mold. Yeltsin launched reform in 1992 with strong popular support and the solid backing of the Supreme Soviet, and as time went on, both steadily eroded. As a result, it became ever more difficult to administer the painful medicine of economic austerity. However, as the transition progressed, the collapse of the state's ability to collect taxes, the declining credibility of the reform team, and the rapid exodus of capital raised the dosage necessary to cure inflation. By the time Yeltsin finally confronted the Supreme Soviet, he could no longer do so by constitutional means. As a result, the confrontation over economic policy caused far more damage to the tradition of constitutional democracy than would otherwise have been the case. The damage was normative, but tangible: Russians do not have confidence that scheduled elections will be held, that the competition will be fair, or that defeated incumbents will step down. Furthermore, the victory of one party in the constitutional struggle transfered tremendous powers to the President, undermining the careful balance of institutions that a compromise settlement sustains. The result is that Russian democracy remains unusually vulnerable to unscrupulous presidents.

In view of the damage done to democracy by high inflation in post-Communist countries, the IMF's advice to defuse inflation rapidly is sound. The fund cannot be blamed for the severity of Russian austerity programs because, first, they were not severe; and second, the fund had limited influence over Russian policy. If it can be blamed, it is only for failing to do more to constrain Russian policy – something that probably could only have been done if the United States were prepared to allow the fund to function as an independent actor. Instead, Russian policy was constrained only by the decentralized decisions of capital markets, and the result was a dangerous and damaging delay in the stabilization of the Russian economy.

Figure 8.2   Gross capital drain from Russia

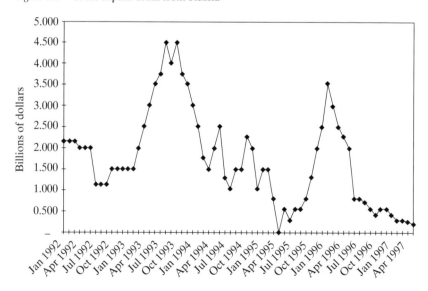

Source: ASIDA-Moskva.

Figure 8.3   Demand for foreign currency in Russia

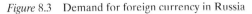

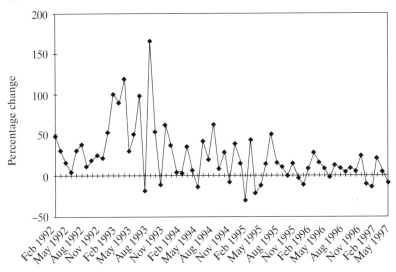

Source: Russian Economic Trends.

Figure 8.4   Monthly budget deficit in Russia as per cent of GDP

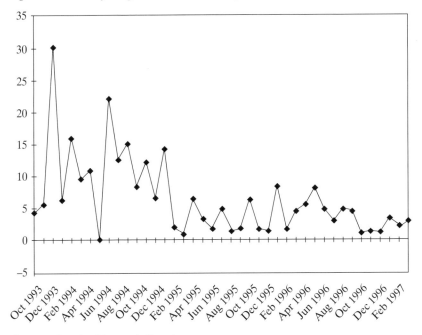

Source: Russian Economic Trends.

Figure 8.5   Change in the ruble/dollar exchange rate

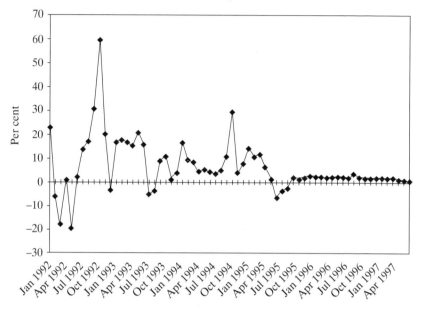

Source: Russian Economic Trends.

Notes

1. Note that there are some good reasons for questioning whether Chinese-style gradualism would be successful in the more highly-developed countries of Eastern Europe and the former Soviet Union (Woo, 1994).
2. Regressing annual growth rates from 1993 through 1996 in the countries of the former Soviet Union on the previous year's inflation rate produces a negative correlation, which is significant at the .06 level.
3. Similarly, the European Monetary System (EMS) has been modelled as a means for low-credibility countries to borrow credibility for their macroeconomic policies from high-credibility countries (Giavazzi and Pagano, 1988).
4. For a review of recent research on the political consequences of global capital flows, see Cohen (1996).
5. For a critique, see Goldstein and Montiel (1986).
6. For a discussion of the complexity of official creditor seniority, see Bulow, Rogoff, and Bevilaqua (1992).
7. For a formal model based upon this argument, and econometric tests using data from Russia, Poland, the Czech Republic, and Romania, see Stone (1997).
8. Russia was negotiating to join the IMF when it launched its reform program in January 1992, so it was unable to receive funding or sign a formal stand-by agreement. As a condition of the negotiations over membership, however, the government cleared its reform program with the Fund.

9. 'All the people that he regarded as authorities on economic matters – heads of enterprises, ministers, and so on, his old colleagues – were all telling him that we were carrying out a terrible policy that would lead to the ruin of the country. He kept supporting us, but his internal certainty declined.' Interview with Gaidar, 20 June 1997.

10. Most of the package consisted of debt relief on obligations that could not have been met in any case, and of export credits from budgets for agricultural programs.

11. *New York Times* (5 July 1992): A1, A6; (6 July 1992): A1, A7.

12. *New York Times* (6 July 1992): A1, A7.

13. Gaidar explains that Gerashchenko appeared at the time to be the best candidate who could be confirmed by the Supreme Soviet, but in retrospect he recognizes that this was a misjudgment. Interview with Yegor Gaidar, 20 June 1997.

14. ASIDA-Moskva (American-Soviet Investment and Development Associates, Moscow), courtesy of Kent Moors.

15. *New York Times* (27 March 1993): I, 1.

16. *New York Times* (1 April 1993): A1.

17. *New York Times* (3 April 1993): I, 4; (5 April 1993): A1

18. *New York Times* (14 April 1993): A1; (15 April 1993): A1.

19. *New York Times* (16 April 1993): A1.

20. *New York Times* (10 April 1993): I, 5.

21. *New York Times* (21 April 1993): A1.

22. Spending jumped to 40.5 per cent of GDP in the third quarter, with a deficit of 7.5 per cent of GDP (RET, 1994, 3(1), p. 9).

23. Interview with Yegor Gaidar, 20 June 1997.

24. The Russian president has more formal power, according to the Shugart and Carey scale, than any currently elected president in their study. Shugart and Carey (1992, pp. 150–5). Most of the countries that approach this concentration of power in the president have been authoritarian.

25. The 1993 Constitution provides for a combination of election to the Duma by single-member districts and by proportional representation.

26. *New York Times* (18 December 1993): I, 1; (19 December 1993): I, 19; (21 December 1993): A1.

27. *New York Times* (22 December 1993): A1.

28. *New York Times* (1 February 1994): A6; (2 February 1994): A1.

29. Dubinin predicted that inflation would run at 7–8 per cent per month by the end of 1994 and fall to 3–5 per cent by the end of 1995 (*Segodnia*, 1994b).

30. In April, M2 jumped by 17 per cent, and it continued to grow by an average monthly rate of 13 per cent through August. Monthly inflation had been brought down to single digits by the policies in place in the fall and spring, so this amounted to a real expansion of the money supply of almost 50 per cent over five months. In addition, the CBR gradually lowered interest rates, which became negative again in real terms in October.

31. *New York Times* (24 October 1994): A5.

32. *New York Times* (6 January 1995): A3.

33. *New York Times* (2 March 1995): A10.

34. RET/MU, 14 November 1995, pp. 3, 8.

35. Brigitte Granville, *Monetary Report*, 75 (7 September 1995): 12; *Russian Economic Trends Monthy Update* (14 November 1995): 7.

36. The government requested budget increases in several sensitive categories: 4.7 trillion rubles ($1.1 billion) to settle accounts with pensioners, 6.2 trillion

($1.4 billion) to rebuild Chechnya's economy, 10 trillion ($2.3 billion) to increase army wages and 2.3 trillion ($500 million) to provide the army with food. *Izvestiia* 29 September 1995, p. 2. In addition, it financed grain imports to prevent an increase in the price of bread due to the poor 1995 harvest. OMRI Daily Digest I, no. 205, (20 October 1995), p. 4. However, the budget deficit fell below 1.5 per cent of GDP in October and November.

37. In his first public interview, Kadannikov stated, 'We had to live under this strict regime for some time, but this time is over ... It is all leading to the death of all national industry.' *New York Times* (January 26, 1996): 1.
38 *New York Times* (31 January 1996): A8.
39. *Financial Times* (5 February 1996): 1.
40. *New York Times* (23 July 1996): A1, A4

Bibliography

Alesina, Alberto and Roberto Perotti (1995) 'The political economy of budget deficits,' *IMF Staff Papers,* 42(1), pp. 1–31.
——— and Howard Rosenthal (1995) *Partisan Politics, Divided Government, and the Economy* (Cambridge: Cambridge University Press).
Aslund, Anders (1994) *How Russia became a market economy* (Washington, D.C.: Brookings).
Barro, Robert J. and David B. Gordon (1983) 'Rules, discretion, and reputation in a model of monetary policy,' *Journal of Monetary Economics*, 12, pp. 101–20.
Bennett, Adam, Maria Carkovic, and Louis Dicks-Mireaux (1995) 'Record of fiscal adjustment,' in Susan Schadler (ed.), *IMF conditionality: Experience under Standby and Extended arrangements, Part II: Background papers* (Washington, D.C.: IMF).
Berg, Andrew (1994) 'Does Macroeconomic Reform Cause Structural Adjustment?: Lessons from Poland,' *Journal of Comparative Economics*, 18, pp. 376–409.
Bulow, Jeremy, Kenneth Rogoff, and Afonso S. Bevilaqua (1992) 'Official creditor seniority and burden-sharing in the former Soviet bloc,' *Brookings Papers on Economic Activity*, 1, pp. 195–233.
Cohen, Benjamin J. (1996) 'Phoenix risen: The resurrection of global finance,' *World Politics*, 48(2), pp. 168–96.
Colton, T. J. (1996) 'Voters' Behaviour in the Two Arenas,' Paper presented at the 28th National Countries Achievement of Slovic Studies, Bata, November 14–17.
Dhonte, Pierre (1997) 'Conditionality as an instrument of borrower credibility. International Monetary Fund,' *Paper on Policy Analysis and Assessment, PPAA* 97/2, February.
Fedorov, Boris (1994) 'Monetary policy and central banking in Russia,' *East European Constitutional Review*, 3(3–4) pp. 60–66.
Financial Times, various dates.
Fudenberg, Drew and David K. Levine (1989) 'Reputation and equilibrium selection in games with a patient player,' *Econometrica*, 57(4) pp. 759–778.
——— and Jean Tirole (1991) *Game Theory* (Cambridge, Mass.: MIT Press).
Giavazzi, Francesco and Marco Pagano (1988) 'The advantage of tying one's hands: EMS discipline and central bank credibility,' *European Economic Review*, 32, pp. 1055–82.
Goldstein, Morris and Peter Montiel (1989) 'Evaluating Fund stabilization programs with multicountry data: Some methodological pitfalls,' *IMF Staff Papers*, 33, pp. 304–44.

Russian Economic Trends (RET), various years (Moscow: Government of the Russian Federation).

Russian Economic Trends Monthly Update (RETMU), various years (Moscow: Government of the Russian Federation).

Granville, Brigitte (1995) *Monetary Report*, 75, 7 September, p. 12.

Haggard, Stephan (1986) 'The Politics of Adjustment: Lessons from the IMF's Extended Fund Facility,' in Miles Kahler (ed.), *The politics of international debt* (Ithaca, N.Y.: Cornell University Press).

Haggard, Stephan and Robert R. Kaufman (1992) *The Politics of Economic Adjustment* (Princeton: Princeton University Press).

Halligan, Liam and Pavel Teplukhin (1996) 'Investment Disincentives in Russia,' *Communist Economies and Economic Transformation*, 8(1), pp. 29–51.

Hellman, Joel (1998) 'Winners Take All: The Politics of Partial Reform in Post-Communist Transitions,' *World Politics*, 50(2), January.

Izvestiia, various dates.

Jones, Michael (1987) 'IMF surveillance, policy coordination, and time consistency,' *International Economic Review*, 28(1) pp. 135–58.

Kahler, Miles (1992) 'External influence, conditionality, and the politics of adjustment,' in Stephan Haggard and Robert R. Kaufman (eds), *The politics of economic adjustment: International constraints, distributive conflicts, and the state* (Princeton, N.J.: Princeton University Press).

Kapur, Ishan, and Emmanuel van der Mensbrugghen (1997) 'External borrowing by the Baltics, Russia and other countries of the former Soviet Union: Developments and policy issues,' International Monetary Fund *Working Paper*, WP/97/72.

Killick, Tony (1984) *The quest for economic stabilization: The IMF and the Third World* (New York: St Martin's Press).

Kirkpatrick, Colin, and Ziya Onis (1985) 'Industrialization as a structural determinant of inflation performance in IMF stabilisation programmes in less developed countries,' *Journal of Development Studies*, 21, pp. 347–61.

Kydland, Finn E., and Edward C. Prescott (1977) 'Rules rather than discretion: The inconsistency of optimal plans,' *Journal of Political Economy*. 85(3) pp. 437–91.

Linz, Juan (1993) 'Focus: Crisis in Russia,' *East European Constitutional Review* (Winter).

Lipson, Charles (1986) 'Bankers' dilemmas: Private cooperation in rescheduling sovereign debts,' in Kenneth A. Oye (ed.), *Cooperation under anarchy* (Princeton, N.J.: Princeton University Press).

Maxfield, Sylvia M. (1997) 'The Domestic Politics of Capital Flows and Securities Markets,' paper delivered at the 93rd Annual Meeting of the American Political Science Association, Washington, D.C., 28–31 August.

Mosley, Paul (1987) 'Conditionality as bargaining process: Structural-adjustment lending, 1980–86,' *Princeton Essays in International Finance*, no. 168. Department of Economics, Princeton, N.J.: Princeton University.

Nelson, Joan, (ed.) (1990) *Economic crisis and policy choice: The politics of adjustment in developing countries* (Princeton, N.J.: Princeton University Press).

New York Times, various dates.

OMRI Daily Digest, various dates.

Persson, Torsten and Guido Tabellini (eds) (1994) *Monetary and fiscal policy.* 2 vols (Cambridge, Mass.: MIT Press).

Przeworski, Adam (1991) *Democracy and the market: Political and economic reforms in Eastern Europe and Latin America* (Cambridge: Cambridge University Press).

Putnam, Robert D. (1988) 'Diplomacy and domestic politics: The logic of two-level games,' *International Organization* 42(3), pp. 427–60.

Remmer, Karen L. (1986) 'The politics of economic stabilization: IMF Standby programs in Latin America, 1954–1984,' *Comparative Politics*, 19(1), pp. 1–24.

Segodnia (1993a) 'New target for the Deputies: Minfin. Strengthening the ruble is considered criminal,' vol. 37, 27 July.

Segodnia (1993b) 'Supreme Soviet has planned a budget with a record deficit: popular "dirt scratchers" tear a hole for the government,' vol. 37, 27 July, p. 3.

Segodnia (1994a) 'The government prepares for an investment boom, investors seek guarantees,' 29 June, p. 2.

Segodnia (1994b) 'Minfin announces that financial stabilization is near,' 5 July, p. 1.

Segodnia (1994c) 'Read off the list, please, and seek out methods of punishment,' 4 November, p. 1.

Segodnia (1994d) 'Anatolii Chubais has introduced 'the team for the second stage of reforms,'' 12 November, p. 1.

Shugart, Matthew Soberg and John M. Carey (1992) *Presidents and assemblies: Constitutional design and electoral dynamics* (Cambridge: Cambridge University Press).

Sobel, Andrew (1997) 'Unequal Access: Borrowing in Global and National Political Institutions,' paper delivered at the 93rd Annual Meeting of the American Political Science Association, Washington, D.C., 28–31 August.

Spraos, John (1986) 'IMF conditionality: Ineffectual, inefficient, mistargeted.' *Princeton Essays in International Finance*, no. 166.

Stone, Randall W. (1997) 'The IMF and the Post-Communist Transition: Reputation, Bargaining, and Institutions,' paper delivered at the 93rd Annual Meeting of the American Political Science Association, Washington, D.C., 28–31 August .

Swoboda, A. (1982) 'Exchange rate regimes and European-U.S. policy interdependence,' *IMF Staff Papers*, 30.

Treisman, Daniel S. (1998) 'Fighting Inflation in a Transitional Regime: Russia's Anomalous Stabilization.' *World Politics*, 50 (2) (January), pp. 235–65.

Wallander, Celeste A., and Jane E. Prokop (1993) 'Soviet security strategies toward Europe: After the wall, with their backs up against it,' in Robert O. Keohane, Joseph S. Nye, and Stanley Hoffmann (eds), *After the cold war: International institutions and state strategies in Europe, 1989–1991* (Cambridge, Mass.: Harvard University Press).

Watson, James (1996) 'Foreign Investment in Russia: The Case of the Oil Industry,' *Europe-Asia Studies*, 48(3), pp. 429–55.

Wells, Robin (1993) 'Tolerance of arrearages: How IMF loan policy can effect debt reduction,' *The American Economic Review*, 83, pp. 621–33.

White, Stephen, Richard Rose, and Ian McAllister (1997) *How Russia Votes* (Chatham, N.J.: Chatham House Publishers).

Woo, Wing Thye (1994) 'The Art of Reforming Centrally Planned Economies: Comparing China, Poland, and Russia,' *Journal of Comparative Economics*, 18, pp. 276–308.

9 India: Financial Globalization, Liberal Norms, and the Ambiguities of Democracy[1]

John Echeverri-Gent

Financial globalization is commonly seen to be detrimental to democracy in developing countries. Writing for an international committee of 21 social scientists, Adam Przeworski asserts that 'modernization by internationalization' involves 'at least a partial surrender of national sovereignty in the political, economic and cultural realms' which weakens nascent democratic institutions (Przeworski *et al.*, 1995, pp. 4,10). In this volume, Tony Porter argues that financial globalization enables unaccountable international authorities to usurp control over key decisions about financial regimes from domestic authorities. Leslie Elliott Armijo expresses the concern that the shift from public to private capital flows that has accompanied globalization in the last 15 years may oblige states in developing countries to implement neoliberal policies regardless of their efficacy. Armijo contends that financial globalization will skew resources to disproportionately strengthen the political power of big business. She adds that the more liquid forms of international investment can destabilize democratic governments.

This chapter raises questions about the premises upon which the pessimistic view of the impact of financial globalization on democracy are based. I contend that the argument that financial globalization curtails democracy usually extrapolates from an obscure baseline founded on unexamined assumptions about the nature of financial regimes prior to globalization. I point out that it is misleading to draw conclusions about the impact of financial globalization on democracy without first considering the relationship between the financial sector and democracy prior to globalization. The case of India's stock exchanges demonstrates that prior to globalization India's capital markets had detrimental consequences for its democracy.

I also wish to scrutinize the assumption that state sovereignty and democracy are positively related. There are cases, such as international efforts to advance human rights, where the reduction of state sovereignty can lead to an increase in democracy. The relationship between financial globalization and democracy is more complex than pessimists contend because at the same

207

time that financial globalization limits state sovereignty, it promotes the spread of liberal norms which bolster democratic institutions. The experience of India demonstrates that even in countries with liberal democratic political institutions, the weakness of liberal economic norms – at least in terms of equitable procedures that regulate market activity – may facilitate the efforts of a privileged few to manipulate the stock exchanges to their personal advantage and allow the markets to serve as a channel for corruption that ultimately has a corrosive impact on a country's democracy. By promoting the spread of liberal norms, globalization has provided greater protection for domestic and foreign investors and reduced the opportunities for corruption. This contention does not dispute that control over financial policies is to some extent usurped by international investors and foreign authorities who promote financial reform largely for their self-interest. Instead, it observes that international investors' pursuit of predictability and calculability has promoted the spread of liberal norms which through their restriction on the arbitrary exercise of state power and their promotion of individual rights and equity of procedure have had a positive, albeit limited, impact on Indian democracy. To fully appreciate the impact of financial globalization on democracy we must account for the balance between the democratic deficit resulting from diminished control over fiscal and monetary policy, and the enhancement of democracy deriving from the spread of liberal norms.

Finally, I will investigate the argument that financial globalization produces inequalities that will inevitably curtail democracy. In multinational states such as India, the regional disparities generated by financial globalization are more likely to threaten democratic institutions than growing disparities between large and small business or wealthy and poor individuals. Financial globalization produces winners and losers. These are not only the wealthy and poor, corporations large and small. Perhaps more important, they are localities that reap the benefits of globalization by tapping into international capital flows and production networks and those that do not. When growing regional disparities coincide with ethnic and cultural differences, the losers may call the legitimacy of democratic institutions into question. At the minimum, coping with regional disparities is likely to be an issue that confronts the world's larger democracies. The exacerbation of disparities between individuals and corporations, however normatively undesirable, is less likely to undermine democratic institutions. This contention is founded on Huber, Rueschemeyer, and Stephen's (1997) distinction between formal, participatory, and social democracy. While vertical inequalities are detrimental to participatory and social democracy, they are quite compatible with formal democracy. The case of India suggests that the disparities resulting from financial globalization may not threaten the country's democratic institutions even while they erode democracy's participatory and social dimensions. Indeed, the era of financial globalization has been an age when democratic institutions have spread across the globe at the same time that economic inequalities have grown.

The chapter is organized in the following manner. I begin by examining the economic dimensions of financial globalization in India. Next, I describe the operation of India's stock exchanges prior to reforms. This discussion will provide a baseline necessary for understanding the impact of financial globalization on India's democracy. Then I investigate the impact of financial globalization on the operation of India's stock exchanges. In particular, I will examine its role in promoting the reform of India's stock exchanges. Finally, I demonstrate how financial globalization has created a new economic geography which more than any other development may cause tension in India's democracy.

THE ECONOMIC DIMENSIONS OF FINANCIAL GLOBALIZATION IN INDIA

Although during the 1980s India had taken advantage of financial globalization by securing commercial loans and accessing the savings of Indians abroad, the country made serious efforts to attract foreign direct and portfolio investment only after it initiated economic reforms in the wake of the 1991 balance-of-payments crisis. Total foreign investment, which averaged less than $100 million a year in the 1980s, increased to $6.4 billion in 1996–97 (USAID, 1990). Foreign direct investment (FDI) grew from $158 million in 1991–92 to $2.6 billion in 1996–97 (see Table 9.1). Despite this increase, FDI in India remains considerably below that of many developing countries. In 1996, India, a country with 19 per cent of the population of all developing countries, received only 2.9 per cent of all FDI to developing countries.[2]

The increase in FDI in India occurred in response to reforms designed to make the investment environment more attractive.[3] Prior to 1991, FDI was limited to 40 per cent of joint ventures, except in a few high-tech areas, and approval was time-consuming and arbitrary. In 1991, the Government of India permitted automatic approval for joint ventures with up to 51 per cent equity in 35 industries. It also established the Foreign Investment Promotion Board to provide single-window approval for other projects. When the United Front government came to power in May 1996, it announced the goal of increasing India's FDI to $10 billion a year by the year 2000. In December 1996, new guidelines were issued extending automatic approval for ventures with up to 51 per cent foreign equity in 13 industries and adding automatic approval for foreign equity up to 74 per cent in nine industries, predominantly in infrastructure, and of not more than 50 per cent in three mining industries. In limited circumstances, the new regulations permit 100 per cent foreign equity. The criteria for FIPB were codified and published for areas

Table 9.1   India's foreign investment flows (US$ millions)

	1990–91	1991–92	1992–93	1993–94	1994–95	1995–96	1996–97
I Direct investment	165	150	341	620	1 314	1 981	2 590
II Portfolio investment	0	8	92	3 493	3 581	2 096	3 850
(a) Foreign institutional investor	0	0	1	1 665	1 503	1 892	2 390
(b) Euro-issues/ GDRs	0	0	86	1 463	1 839	204	1 460
(c) Others*	0	8	5	365	239	–	–
III Total (I + II)	200	158	433	4 113	4 895	4 077	6 440

Note: *Includes NRI portfolio investments, offshore funds, and others.
Sources: Data for 1990–91 to 1995–96 from World Bank, *India: Country Economic Memorandum* (Washington, DC. World Bank, 1996), p. 7. Data for 1996–97 from Ministry of Finance press release, May 1997 as cited in Indira Rajaraman, 'A Profile of Economic Reform in India' (National Institute of Public Finance and Policy, New Delhi, June 1997).

without automatic approval, and a Foreign Investment Promotion Council was created to encourage FDI.

Portfolio investment in Indian firms was allowed only in September 1992. It has since grown to an annual net total of $3.8 billion with $2.39 billion coming from the purchases of Foreign Institutional Investors (FIIs) on India's capital markets and $1.46 billion acquired through Global Depository Receipts (GDRs). The 1992 reforms limited foreign portfolio investment to FII purchases of not more than 24 per cent equity in any firm with no single FII owning more than 5 per cent. In 1996, these limits were increased to a total ceiling of 30 per cent with a 10 per cent maximum on any single FII. Regulation of GDRs was liberalized in June 1996 expanding the eligibility for firms to enter foreign markets and relaxing the restrictions on the number of issues that a company can float and the end uses for such funds. In November 1996, allowed FIIs to form 'wholly debt-based' funds, replacing the 30 per cent limit that FII funds could hold in private debt. In January 1997, India opened its $36 billion government securities market to FIIs, taking the first step towards enabling the government to sell its debt in overseas markets. By the end of March 1997, there were 427 FIIs operating in India (GOI, 1997, chapter 4, p. 5).

The opportunity to attract foreign investment that was enhanced by financial globalization along with the proliferation of foreign actors on India's capital markets proved to be an agent of change which together with actions of the state transformed the institutions of the Indian capital market. To comprehend the dynamics of this transformation, we must first understand the nature of India's capital market institutions and key actors prior to the reforms. Only then can we understand the interplay between actors and institutions that shaped the trajectory of change in India's capital market and ultimately in the Indian state.

LEGITIMACY, DEPENDENCE, AND THE POLITICS OF REFORMING INDIA'S STOCK EXCHANGES

It is sometimes assumed that having long-established capital markets would facilitate efforts to attract foreign investment and reform the economy to promote greater efficiency. The case of India suggests that the institutional legacy of capital markets can impede as well as facilitate reforms. During the long history of India's stock exchanges social institutions and norms were constructed that impeded market efficiency. These institutions and norms also were barriers to attracting foreign investment.

Founded in 1875, the Bombay Stock Exchange (BSE) is the oldest exchange in Asia. Until 1995, it was by far the largest of India's 22 exchanges. The BSE lists almost 4500 of India's 7000 listed companies. Firms listed on the BSE account for more than 80 per cent of the $139 billion capitalization of India's stock exchanges. Some 650 of India's 2200 brokers work at the BSE. Many of them have traditionally come from a common ethnic (Gujarati) community, and in many cases, their family members have worked as brokers on the BSE for generations (Nicholson, 1995; *Financial Post*, 1995; *Institutional Investor*, 1995).

In the past, these brokers formed an exclusive club which exploited the Bombay and India's other stock exchanges for their personal advantage. Indeed, their ethic was similar to that depicted in Max Weber's concept of 'ancient capitalism.' Rather than increasing their profits by maximizing the volume of transactions that they conducted, the traders attempted to maximize their returns on individual transactions even if it meant manipulating institutions to the disadvantage of their transaction partners (Weber, 1981 [1927]). As a group, these brokers brazenly manipulated the investments of the public to enhance their private wealth, and they resisted modernizing the archaic technology because they feared that changes would transform their traditional business practices and curtail their opportunities to exploit the system. Furthermore, modernizing India's stock exchanges received low priority in the institution-building plans of India's Nehruvian state where it was envisioned that it was preferable to channel investment through public sector banks or the state itself. India's stock exchanges epitomized a classic rent-seeking equilibrium in which concentrated and powerful vested interests subjected diffuse public interests to their exploitation. If ever economic development confronted a collection action problem it was in the reform of India's stock markets.

The problems of India's stock exchanges have long been well known. They were outlined in great detail in a comprehensive review conducted by the High Powered Committee on Stock Exchange Reforms chaired by G. S. Patel, former Chairman of the Unit Trust of India and whose membership reads like a list of superstars of the Indian financial world.[4] In view of its membership, the committee issued a remarkable indictment,

> ... The security business in the country has tended to be in the hands of a few families of stockbrokers whose actions are primarily governed by the need to protect their own interests and bereft of the interests of the investing public and even obstruct the attempts of the Government aimed at making the Stock Exchanges efficient instruments for mobilising savings of the community for national development. ... (GOI, 1985, p. 10)

The stock brokers were criticized for being 'unprofessional and poorly skilled. Hardly five per cent are properly trained and equipped.' They were also charged with creating inordinate delays and an array of malpractices including insider trading, concealing speculative trading on their own accounts from stock exchange authorities, colluding with promoters to manipulate premia on new issues by buying up shares to attract investors and then selling the shares for a profit leaving unsuspecting investors with losses, and rigging stock market quotations to illegally enhance profits from options trading (GOI, 1985, pp. 9, 14, 16, 18).

India's archaic settlement system is at the root of many of the problems of its stock exchanges.[5] Some 80 per cent of all transactions for individual investors on India's stock exchanges are initiated through the more than 100 000 sub-brokers in India.[6] Brokers employ networks of sub-brokers as an economic means of reaching India's millions of small investors, a system which is especially convenient since the sub-brokers are not subject to legal regulation, and brokers are not legally liable for their sub-brokers' actions. Sub-brokers act as a blinder on transparency since they usually do not disclose the broker's costs for executing the transaction. Given the long delays involved in completing transactions (see below), the failure of disclosure provides a window of opportunity for manipulation.

The great paper chase necessary to complete transactions on India's stock exchanges begins with the requirement that each share certificate along with a transfer deed must be signed by the seller before a transaction can be completed. The most frequently traded shares legally should be delivered within a 14 day accounting period. However, many exchanges allow settlement of accounts within two periods or 28 days, claiming that this allows time to received shares and payments from clients in remote locations and process the necessary paperwork.

Large investors such as Foreign Institutional Investors (FIIs) face an additional problem. The size of share certificate denominations is small, usually in lots of 10 or 50 shares with 100 shares being the traditional maximum. This means that FIIs frequently end up acquiring thousands of share certificates, and the FIIs appoint banks as custodians responsible for completing settlements and registering their purchases. During an early peak period of activity from November 1993 to January 1994, FII purchases overwhelmed their custodians with a sea of paper creating a major bottleneck.

Changes in ownership must be registered by sending all share certificates and transfer deeds to registrars appointed by the company whose shares are being traded. Indian law stipulates that companies should register transfers of shares within 60 days. The present average for FIIs is nearly four and one-half months, and it can take much longer. If registrars discover problems with a seller's signatures on any of the transfer deeds, as they do with regularity, they return the shares and deeds to the owners or share custodians who in turn must contact the seller's broker to resolve the problem. But these brokers have little incentive to redress the situation, and they often produce exasperating delays. According to one estimate, 15–20 per cent of all FII transactions are in trouble at any single time (Nicholson and Nicoll, 1995, p. iv).

Brokers, issuing companies, and sellers each maintain a vested interest in India's byzantine system. Brokers use the periods between sales and settlement to speculate with their clients' money. Issuing companies, who legally can refuse to recognize the transfer of share ownership and indefinitely delay transfers through their registrars, use their control over the registration process to keep shares out of circulation and minimize sales that might depress the price of their stock. Companies also use their control over the registration process to prevent hostile takeovers. Sellers sometimes intentionally mis-sign their names as a hedge in case they later want to try to void transactions (*Global Money Management*, 1996, p. 2).

India's stock exchanges have been ineffectual in regulating the markets. According to the Patel commission, the governing bodies of the exchanges 'allow[ed] crisis situations to develop in the Stock Exchanges by neglecting to take timely action to curb excessive speculation.' The majority of India's stock exchanges remained closed 40 to 50 per cent of the year, and even when they were open they operated for only three hours a day. The board of directors of the stock exchanges were dominated by stockbrokers whose vested interest in maintaining the status quo has discouraged them from modernizing the operations of the markets, and they have frequently failed to take disciplinary actions against the unethical actions of their fellow brokers. Under their management, the stock exchanges were 'generally regarded to be relatively unsafe for the average class of investors' (*Global Money Management*, 1996, pp. 11, 18, 19).

How did public interests triumph over this rent-seeking equilibrium? It took more than two years after the release of the Patel Committee's report for the government to take action, and even then its action was largely symbolic. In April 1988, it established the Securities and Exchange Board of India (SEBI) to regulate the country's exchanges. However, SEBI could do little until it was given a statutory powers and legal sanctions.

The creation of SEBI appears to have been little more than a ritual enactment of a globally legitimated policy prescription (Thomas *et al.*, 1987). The best way to make sense of the establishment of the Stock Exchange Bureau of India (SEBI) in 1988 is as an attempt to enhance the legitimacy of India's capital market institutions in the eyes of the domestic and global public. It is otherwise difficult to explain why SEBI was established without the authority of legal sanctions and therefore was ineffectual in resolving the well recognized problems of India's capital markets. In 1989, shortly after it was founded, SEBI joined the Montreal-based International Organization of Securities Commissions (IOSCO), the institution which served as the center of the emerging regime for international securities markets during the 1980s and 1990s. It is likely that the activities of IOSCO's Development Committee, especially reports like its paper on 'Market Automation and its Implications for Regulatory Activities' were of considerable interest to Indian regulators. India's active interest in IOSCO's activities is evidenced by its election to IOSCO's executive committee in 1991. More recently, India has committed to raising its requirements for the capital of security market intermediaries in order to meet the capital adequacy norms prescribed by IOSCO.[7] India's interest in learning from foreign market institutions is also manifest by its agreement with USAID to sponsor the Financial Institutions Reform and Expansion Project to modernize its stock exchanges.

SEBI was a policy solution chasing after a policy problem. The balance-of-payments crisis of 1991, by creating a sense of urgency and thrusting new actors into positions of policy-making authority, created a window of opportunity for empowering SEBI and taking other measures to resolve the problems of India's capital markets.[8] Only after the balance-of-payments crisis of 1991 was SEBI given statutory authority through the SEBI Act (1992). The balance-of-payments crisis and pressures from international financial institutions stressed the need for fiscal austerity. As the limits of state resources became more evident, reform of the country's stock exchanges to make them a more viable source of finance for economic development became more desirable, at least in the eyes of economic policy-makers. India's economic crisis thrust Manmohan Singh into power as India's Finance Minister in order to avail the government of this Oxford-trained economist's technical expertise. It was Manmohan Singh who was primarily responsible for giving SEBI legal sanction and providing the support within the government that was necessary for initiating stock exchange reforms.[9]

In giving SEBI legal authority to regulate India's stock markets, the Government of India repealed the Capital Issues (Control) Act of 1947 and abolished the Controller of Capital Issues (CCI). This reform was a major step moving from direct government control to procedural regulation of the capital market since all firms wishing to enter India's primary market had to gain CCI approval for their issue and all the agency to set the price and premium for their issue. Under SEBI's regulation, companies were now free to enter the capital market and set their own prices after meeting SEBI's norms for their offer documents.

The SEBI Act of 1992 and the Security Laws (Amendment) passed on 25 March 1995 authorized SEBI to register and regulate all security market intermediaries including custodians, depositories, venture capital funds, FIIs and credit-rating agencies. In an effort to better protect investors, SEBI strengthened the standards of disclosure on primary markets, introduced prudential norms for issues and intermediaries, and streamlined issue procedures. The 1995 amendment to the SEBI Act for the first time enabled SEBI to file suits against violators of its regulations without prior approval of the central government. It provided SEBI subpoena powers for records, documents, accounts, and personal testimony, and it authorized it to levy fines in for certain violations of its regulations. The Securities and Exchange Board of India (Prohibition of Fraudulent and Unfair Trade Practices relating to securities markets) Regulations issued in 1995, defined fraudulent and unfair trade practices and authorized SEBI to take action against these practices.[10]

SEBI's exercise of its regulatory powers embroiled it in a protracted feud with India's stock brokers. The conflict between SEBI and members of the BSE was especially vehement. The BSE brokers went on strike for four weeks in the spring of 1992 in an effort to resist rules requiring them to register with SEBI. They also vehemently protested SEBI's 13 December 1993 ban on *badla* or carry-forward trading, securing the transfer of SEBI's chairman, and ultimately obliging SEBI to reintroduce a modified form in December 1995.[11]

SEBI has succeeded in asserting its authority over the BSE and India's other exchanges. It reconstituted the governing boards of the BSE and the other exchanges. It issued rules requiring that board members must be equally balanced between elected representatives of stockbrokers and its own nominees. SEBI has issued rules for making the client-broker relationship more transparent, in the process, regulating sub-brokers, segregating client and broker accounts, and introducing capital adequacy norms for brokers. SEBI directed all stock exchanges to set up clearing houses or clearing corporations and to provide trade guarantees. Under SEBI's guidance, all the exchanges set up surveillance departments, and have begun to coordinate their investigations with SEBI.

Stock markets are supposed to promote economic efficiency by enabling the takeover of inefficiently managed firms. In 1994, SEBI issued regulations intended to make the takeover process more transparent and protect minority shareholder interests. In January 1997, SEBI published a revised code that facilitates takeovers by, among other things, eliminating the requirement that a bidder's price be approved by regulators. The new code also offers better protection of the rights of minority shareholders. Any investor who takes a stake of 10 per cent in a company must then make an offer for a further 20 per cent; after that any substantial increase has to be by an open offer to all shareholders. Finally, the new code is intended to encourage changes in the management of 'sick' companies; saving jobs and protecting the interests of shareholders and creditors. Previously, companies whose entire net worth had been eroded were referred to the Bureau of Industrial and Financial Reconstruction which after completing lengthy hearings would determine whether to close down, restructure, or sell a company. Under the new takeover code, financial institutions can invite takeover bids after companies have lost only 50 per cent of their net worth.

The government's measures to create competition within India's established stock markets has in many cases been even more effective in securing reforms than has the efforts of its regulators. Just as the founding of NASDAQ in the United States created pressure for reforms of the New York Stock Exchange, India's National Stock Exchange (NSE) has pressured the BSE to reform. The NSE provides scripless (that is, paperless), on-line trading via a satellite-based network which by June 1997 linked brokers in 145 Indian cities. It opened for trading in equities in October 1994, and volume outstripped the BSE before the end of 1995 (Tassel, 1997).

The NSE is designed to be more investor-friendly than the BSE. NSE members must rectify bad deliveries within 48 hours. Bad and short deliveries that are not rectified are sold at an auction in which the erring broker is prohibited from participation. Deliveries are then completed with only a few days delay. Brokers on the NSE receive penalty points for defaults on deliveries and payments. They are fined when they accumulate more than 51 penalty points, and they are suspended from trading for five days when their penalty points reach 100. The NSE has created an Investor Compensation Fund (IFC) financed by a .001 per cent levy against the monthly turnover of member brokers and 2 per cent of the annual fees collected from all listed companies. The ICF is designed to reimburse any loss suffered by investors because of a member's default (*Institutional Investor* 1995).

Competition between the NSE and BSE has provided a strong impetus for reform of the BSE. The NSE was incorporated on November 1992 only after the BSE refused SEBI recommendations to admit new brokers, BSE brokers resisted registering with SEBI, and fought against SEBI's capital adequacy norms. In contrast to the BSE which is owned and managed by its broker members, the NSE is owned by state financial institutions and run by professional managers. Brokers pay a fee for using the NSE's services rather than buying seats on the exchange as they must for the BSE. While the NSE was set up with an electronic order-matching mechanism that matches buy and sell orders automatically, the BSE introduced the Bombay On Line Trading (BOLT) system only late in 1995 at roughly the same time that the NSE surpassed its daily turnover. The BOLT system still requires brokers and jobbers to quote prices. Competition with the NSE also encouraged the BSE's decision to reduce its maximum settlement period from two weeks to one week. Competitive pressures for reform are more intense than ever. By June 1996 average daily turnover on the NSE increased to $426 million while average turnover on the BSE totaled just $168 million.[12]

Many of the problems of India's stock exchanges could be alleviated through the creation of share depositories or clearing house systems that centralize share collection and use a computerized system of book entries to replace physical share transactions. Foreign financial institutions, in particular, have clamoured for the establishment of a depository (S. Sharma 1996). In October 1996, the NSE joined with the Industrial Development Bank of India and the Unit Trust of India to inaugurate the country's first depository, National Securities Depository Ltd. Development of the NSDL has been slow. In April 1997, received an expected boost when the NSDL received a favorable ruling from the US Securities and Exchange Commission permitting US institutions to participate in the NSDL even though it did not meet its criterion for $200 million net worth (*Asian Wall Street Journal*, 1997). By June 1997, the value of dematerialized shares was less than $750 000 or about 0.5 per cent of total market capitalization although the market capitalization of companies that have entered to agreements with NSDL equaled 25 per cent of total market capitalization (*Business Line*, 1997).

THE REFORMS, CORPORATE CULTURE, AND CORRUPTION

In a provocative essay, Phillippe Platteau (1994a,b) has argued that imposing markets in societies whose cultures are not supportive of market operations may create more problems than it solves. In Platteau's view, India remains a society where family and caste relationships take primacy over the liberal norms. As a consequence, many will exploit market opportunities to favor personalistic ties and take advantage of outsiders even when their actions are detrimental to the long-term health of the market. The operations of the BSE prior to the reforms seems to support Platteau's observation. However, analysis of recent changes in India's capital market demonstrates that Platteau underestimates the impact of globalization and reform of domestic institutions on the culture of corporate India.

Most Indian firms are family-owned and managed. Family businesses account for 70 per cent of the total sales and net profits of the biggest 250 private sector companies (*The Economist*, 1996b). The controlling interests of these families is only a small share of a company's total equity, typically less than 25 per cent (Ninan, 1997). Public sector financial institutions control roughly 40 per cent of large companies (*The Economist*, 1996b), with the rest owned by small investors. Many business families take advantage of pliant financial institutions and powerless small shareholders to conduct business off the books, have their companies pick up the tab for personal expenses, and so on (Kohli, 1997). According to one estimate, Indian business families have deposited $100 billion in Swiss banks (Kripalani, 1997). Some Indian firms exploit the stock exchange by manipulating their share prices and engaging in insider trading. Scandals involving Reliance Industries, India's largest private sector company, and CRB, a financial company, are indicative of much broader problems.[13]

India's regulatory agencies are understaffed and possess inadequate resources to prevent manipulation of the stock exchanges. SEBI for instance, has a total staff of only 300 – only 12 of whom are lawyers – compared to the Securities and Exchange Commission in the United States which has a staff of 3000, of whom 1800 are lawyers (Jain, 1996). The pre-reform culture of India's brokers, financial companies and corporations and the patently inadequate resources of SEBI highlight the problems of liberalizing the operations of India's capital markets, yet exclusive preoccupation with these problems neglects profound changes that already have occurred.

Despite these conditions, the culture and practice of India's capital markets and corporations are being altered by the institutional transformation that in large measure has been driven by diffusion of global norms. India's stock brokers are undergoing a wrenching shakeout. During the fall of 1996, the President of the Bombay stock exchange, M. G. Damani, predicted that one-quarter of the 641 members of the exchange would disappear in the following 12 months. Others predict that only 100 brokerages will survive (S. Sharma, 1996). From its founding in 1875 until 1992 when the government allowed domestic mutual fund concerns to set up brokerages, only individuals or sole proprietorships could be brokers on India's stock exchanges. The arrival of FII's, who are the most active traders of India's blue chips, and the establishment of the NSE, have shifted business to the larger, more professional brokerages with the capital to fund research departments and keep up with changing technology. A more subtle but more extensive change is occurring in the culture of corporate India. The greater activism and demands of FII's and Indian financial institutions who themselves are under new competitive pressures, along with changes in India's corporate legislative framework such as SEBI's new takeover code, are obliging Indian corporations to make their operations more transparent, meet higher standards of performance, and be more responsive to the interests of shareholders, foreign and domestic alike.[14]

By curtailing the exploitation of privilege and implementing institutional reforms that subject brokers to proper legal procedures, the reform of India's capital market has made a limited contribution to the more equitable operation of India's economy, and it has strengthened Indian democracy. Corruption in India's capital markets inevitably spills over to India's state institutions. Perhaps the best example of this is the $2 billion scam uncovered in April 1992.[15] The scam implicated not only the flamboyant broker Harshad 'the Big Bull' Mehta, but also 22 public sector enterprises – which illegally diverted funds worth billions of dollars to Mehta, the four largest foreign banks in India, a member of the Planning Commisson, and top officials in the Reserve Bank of India (India's central bank), including the Governor – who met with Mehta and listened to his request for special treatment. The Joint Parliamentary Committee convened to investigate the scandal concluded that the scam's irregularities were:

> manifestations of ... chronic disorder since they involve not only the Banks but also the stock market, financial institutions, PSU [public sector units], the central bank of the country, and even the Ministry of Finance, other economic ministries in varying degrees. The most unfortunate aspect has been the emergence of a culture of non-accountability which permeated all sections of the Government and Banking system over the years. (Lok Sabha Secretariat, 1993, p. 7)

That isn't all. In July 1993, Harshad Mehta claimed that he made an illegal political contribution to Prime Minister P.V. Narasimha Rao worth $360 000. The charge received widespread press coverage and remarkable public credulity despite the absence of corroborating evidence. Mehta's charge incited opposition parties to call for a parliamentary vote of confidence on 26 July 1993. Rao's controversial efforts to muster a parliamentary majority for his minority government ultimately led to his indictment along with 19 other politicians and bureaucrats for charges that they bribed ten opposition members in order to win the vote. The experience of the Harshad Mehta scam demonstrates that preventing such scams by subjecting capital market operators to the rule of law would make a substantial contribution to curbing the corruption of state institutions and enhancing their legitimacy.

INDIA'S GROWING ACCESS TO INTERNATIONAL CAPITAL MARKETS

Leslie Elliott Armijo argues in Chapter 1 that opening up international capital markets to the corporations of developing countries will favor large corporations with good reputations. Indeed, the most successful of India's GDR issues read like a Who's Who of Indian business. Reliance Industries, the flagship of Indian corporations, has raised the largest amount, $450 million. Other corporate stars raising large sums of money include Grasim with $190 million, Larson and Torboro with $150, and Ashok Leyland with $138 million. The benefits of foreign capital issues have not been confined to the private sector as a number of large public sector corporations also have taken advantage of the opportunities. Through 1995, about half of the GDR and FCCB issues have come from firms ranked among the India's top 20 according to sales with much of the balance coming from smaller but fast-growing companies in high-technology areas such as pharmaceuticals (Chopra *et al.*, 1995; R. Sharma, 1994).

It may be true that the advantages reaped from accessing international capital markets by big business in India enhances their political strength and makes them less politically accountable, but most democracies coexist with powerful corporations, even if the disparities in political power that they exploit diminish the equity of the political process. In India, the real danger from foreign capital flows and greater linkage with the global market comes from the geographical disparities that are likely to result.

GLOBALIZATION AND THE NEW ECONOMIC GEOGRAPHY

Democracies can coexist with much higher levels of foreign investment than India has seen in the recent past, or that it is likely to see in the foreseeable future. After all, advanced industrial countries in Western Europe have the highest levels of foreign capital flows and they are among the world's most stable democracies. However, India differs from western European countries in its size and social heterogeneity. India has 13 languages with more than 20 million speakers, and many other languages serving as the mother-tongues for a smaller number of people. Indian states are organized on linguistic lines. Each has its own distinctive culture and history. Indeed, many Indian states are larger in population and territory than European nation-states. Seven Indian states have more than 55 million inhabitants while from Portugal to Russia only six European states have more than 55 million people. Three Indian states have more territory than Italy, and a total of 13 have more area than Austria. India is much more heterogeneous than the most diverse state of Western Europe. In fact, in terms of social diversity it is more comparable to Europe as a whole. In Europe, uneven development and international capital flows have been an impediment to economic integration. In India, international capital flows may exacerbate uneven development and put pressures on the country's political integration. Below, I focus on two changes that are likely to increase regional economic disparities and exacerbate tensions between Indian states.

Competition among States and Inter-regional Rivalry

What do Jyoti Basu, a member of the Communist party of India (Marxist), Manohar Joshi, a leader of the Hindu chauvinist *Shiv Sena* party, and Laloo Prasad Yadav, a leader of the caste-based *Janata Dal* party, all have in common? Each visited the United States during 1995 as heads of Indian state governments attempting to promote foreign investment in their states. As fiscal pressures increasingly limit the financial largesse of the central government, state governments have initiated measures to curb wasteful expenditures and enhance their revenue base by attracting investment. As state and local governments become more involved in attracting investment, creating local infrastructure, and articulating industrial policy, economic liberalization has relaxed central government regulation of foreign investment and eliminated its licensing of industrial investment and production. The relative importance of state and local government policy in promoting industrial development has increased.[16] A clear manifestation of this change was the Enron controversy in which the state government of Maharashtra negotiated, renounced, and then renegotiated the largest foreign investment project in the history of the country while India's central government was relegated to the sidelines.

In contrast to the conventional wisdom that the states lag behind the central government, there are already indications that state governments are being transformed into engines of economic reform. For instance, while the central government is struggling to find ways to close down inefficient public sector enterprises (PSEs), the government of Uttar Pradesh has closed down 13 of its 50 PSEs, and it leased several of its 24 spinning mills to the private sector. Gujarat, Maharashtra, and Punjab have been leaders in contracting with the private sector for the provision of an array of municipal services. Maharashtra, Rajasthan and Punjab have privatized collection of octroi,[17] and Rajasthan has announced that it will privatize power distribution in selected districts.[18]

Attracting investment also has become a vital part of building local revenue bases and creating jobs. Virtually, all states have formed industrial development corporations to encourage domestic and foreign investment. Private investors now take advantage of the eagerness of state governments to attract investment to pressure them to arrange more favorable terms. For example, Ford was able to create a bidding war between the governments of Maharashtra and Tamil Nadu each of which were attempting to attract the automaker's investment to construct a plant for building the Fiesta (Subramaniam, 1996). The upside of these competitive pressures is that it may drive India's states to implement creative programs to promote local-level development. The down-side of the growing competition among states is two-fold. First, it creates a 'competitive concessionalism' whose tax concessions and subsidies are detrimental to fiscal and developmental efforts. Second, the competition will produce winners and losers. Those states with more dynamic governments, good infrastructure, strategic location, and well established industrial bases have been much more successful in attracting investment than have less dynamic states. The disparities are manifest in the contrast between the success in attracting FDI by Delhi, Maharashtra, and Gujarat and the failure of Bihar, Uttar Pradesh and Rajasthan. The former attracted 39 per cent of all India's FDI to just 15 per cent of the country's population. The latter states attracted only 3.5 per cent of India's FDI to more than 32 per cent of its population (see Table 9.2).

'Commodity Chains' and Growing Regional Disparities

Changing patterns of global production also may exacerbate regional tensions. Since the 1970s, a new form of international business organization has evolved: Economic enterprise is increasingly organized into international networks of firms designed to minimize costs and maximize flexibility and innovation. These 'commodity chains,' as Gary Gereffi has called them, reorganize economic space creating new regional disparities in the process. Bangalore – India's Silicon Valley – epitomizes how changing patterns of production and trade links have spurred regional development.[19] The metropolis that Jawaharlal Nehru called 'India's city of the future' with its three universities, 14 engineering colleges, and 47 polytechnic schools has been targeted as a center of Indian science since the days of the British raj. While it is home to modern industrial giants like Hindustan Aeronautics and Bharat Electronics, its most dynamic sector is software. Bangalore's 'Sultans of Software' include firms with technological expertise matching the world's most sophisticated software firms. Their satellite links with software developers around the world led American economist John Stremlau to observe, 'In cyberspace, Bangalore and Boston are practically in the same space'. Many of Bangalore's software firms are located in one of the city's dozen 'technology parks'. These self-contained communities usually have their own satellite communication system, power, sewage, and often their own stores, schools, and health care facilities. Life in these communities is increasingly detached from the rest of Bangalore, not to mention India's rural hinterland.

Table 9.2   Investment approvals in Indian states (August 1991 to September 1996)

State	Value of approvals (in Rs. billions)	Per cent of the value of all approvals	Share of population 1991
Delhi	165.6	19.2	1.1
Maharashtra	114.4	13.5	9.3
Gujarat	57.7	6.7	4.9
Tamil Nadu	50.1	5.8	6.6
West Bengal	49.0	5.7	8.0
Karnataka	47.5	5.5	5.3
Orissa	27.2	3.2	3.7
Uttar Pradesh	24.1	2.8	16.4
Andhra Pradesh	22.1	2.6	7.9
Madhya Pradesh	20.2	2.3	8.0
Punjab	8.0	0.9	2.4
Harayana	6.9	0.8	2.0
Rajasthan	5.1	0.6	5.2
Kerala	5.1	0.6	3.4
Himachal Pradesh	3.2	0.4	0.6
Bihar	1.1	0.1	10.2
Jammu & Kashmir	0.8	0.1	0.9
Others	255.2	29.2	4.1
All India Total	863.3	100.0	100.0

Sources: 'Foreign Investment Approvals and Actuals: A Profile', *Economic and Political Weekly* (10 May, 1997) pp. 987; and *Statistical Outline of India 1994–95* (Bombay: Tata Services Ltd., 1994) pp. 40–41.

Commodity chains can involve 'low-tech' as well as high-tech industries. Usage of computerized embroidery machines along with incorporation into multinational marketing networks has enabled the dusty provincial city of Tiruppur in the south Indian state of Tamil Nadu to increase exports from $25 million in 1986 to an estimated $1 billion in 1995 (Cawthorne, 1995; McDonald, 1994; Bhimal, 1994). Tiruppur's 100 big exporters and 1500 suppliers employ a total of some 150 000 workers, making the city one of the few places in India where there is a labor shortage. Tiruppur's garment makers are already increasing their value added by moving from T-shirts to sportswear, nightwear, and industrial garments. The city's producers sell to a broad array of companies including the trendy Italian firm Benetton. Although many production facilities in Tiruppur remain sweatshops and wages for many workers are barely above subsistence levels, many workers have acquired new skills, and some have started their own small firms. There is little doubt that export-led growth has benefited localities like Tiruppur. The key issue is how widely the benefits of exports can be spread. Will localities like Bangalore and Tiruppur become islands of prosperity amidst an ocean of poverty? Is it possible to create linkages that spread the benefits of development? Comprehensive analysis of this is beyond the scope of this paper. What is important for the purposes of this paper is that linkage with global production networks is likely to reorganize the economic geography of India in dramatic ways increasing regional disparities in the process.

Many regions of India during its pre-colonial and colonial eras were more closely linked to the global economy than during the first four decades of the post-colonial era. However, the new linkages that are being established are not simply taking India 'back to the future'.[20] Prior to independence India was not integrated into a single polity, even under the British. The mosaic of polities that was India made it difficult for, say, Kashmiris to complain about growing economic disparities between themselves and say, the Malabar coast. The economic regime of the first forty years of the post-colonial era made vigorous efforts to promote national unity by minimizing regional economic disparities at considerable expense to the country's economic dynamism. Central planning was used to build infrastructure in undeveloped areas and investment licensing was utilized to promote industrialization in backward states. Despite these efforts, and in part because fiscal resources and policy-making authority were increasingly concentrated in the central government, regional economic disparities produced violent political conflict in the Punjab, Kashmir, Darjeeling, Chotanagpur and so on.

The economic liberalization that has accompanied globalization may have produced one development that may mitigate the political tensions resulting from regional disparities. India's extensive state economic intervention and its centralization of authority during the post-colonial era politicized decisions affecting the distribution of benefits among regions. By extricating the state from the economy, economic liberalization may de-politicize issues of regional equity. Nevertheless, given the tremendous social heterogeneity that differentiates India's states and the history of contention over regional disparities in economic development, regional disputes are likely to gain prominence on India's political agenda even if they do not undermine the stability of Indian democracy.

CONCLUDING REMARKS

This chapter has focused primarily on foreign portfolio investment in the private sector and to a lesser extent on foreign direct investment. It does not really provide an adequate test for the impact of other modalities of financial globalization such as bank loans and foreign aid. Furthermore, since India, unlike other developing countries, has yet to experience volatile inflows and outflows of portfolio investment, it does not examine the implications of volatility for India's democracy. Yet my findings raise important questions about the pessimistic view of the impact of foreign portfolio investment on India's democracy. By discovering ways that foreign portfolio investment has strengthened India's democratic institutions, the chapter highlights several ambiguities in the relationship between financial globalization and democracy.

To understand the impact of financial globalization on Indian democracy we must first analyze the relationship between India's financial sector on Indian democracy prior to globalization. This analysis provides a baseline that is necessary to comprehend the consequences of financial globalization. This chapter has focused primarily on India's stock exchanges. Admittedly, the scope of the discussion has not addressed the constraints that integration with global markets might place on macroeconomic policy. I have contended that prior to globalization, India's stock exchanges were highly inequitable. These market institutions allocated the power to appropriate an unfair share of economic benefits to a small number of stock-brokers, privileged members of corporate India, bureaucrats, and corrupt politicians. When domestic institutions and actors are inequitable and unaccountable, the transfer of control from local market institutions to more remote international institutions does not undermine democracy. True, transferring authority to international organizations dominated by international investors may restrict the ability of a country's democratic authorities to control domestic stock exchanges in the future. But before domestic institutions and actors can be made democratically accountable, they must be subject to the rule of law.

Financial globalization reduced the scope for the arbitrary exercise of authority and strengthened Indian democracy by promoting liberal norms that expanded the 'rule of law' on India's stock exchanges. The point here is not that international investors are less susceptible to the blandishments of corruption than India's domestic investors and brokers – on the contrary, the participation of foreign banks in the Harshad Mehta scam is evidence of their willingness to exploit opportunities for corruption. Rather, the argument is that international investors, as a class, have a collective interest in rationalizing capital market institutions to enhance predictability and calculability. International investors also have access to institutions like IOSCO, USAID, the World Bank and so on which promote their collective interests. Financial globalization, by providing the opportunity to attract additional capital, has enhanced the Indian state's interest in rationalizing its capital markets. It was in part to attract foreign capital – but also to improve its capacity for raising and allocating domestic capital more efficiently – that India created the Securities and Exchange Board of India, the National Stock Exchange, and other institutional and legal reforms.

The impact of financial globalization on India's political system is mediated by India's political institutions and power structures even while it changes them. It is by no means inevitable that financial globalization will eliminate corruption and inefficiency. In some cases, it may create new opportunities for malfeasance. My argument is that over time it likely to reduce the arbitrary exercise of authority with stock exchanges and ultimately in corporate management. This trend enhances protection of investors' interests. In India, it is the twenty to thirty million small investors that suffer the most. It improves India's economic performance by increasing the efficiency of resource allocation and corporate management. By curtailing corruption in capital markets, it strengthens Indian democracy because the corruption inevitably spills over into the political system. This is true not only for India, but for countries around the world as diverse as Russia, Japan, and Brazil.[21]

Contending that financial globalization has enhanced democracy in India says little about its impact on inequality. While it may be analytically useful to adopt a definition of democracy limited to formal democracy or polyarchy,[22] it remains important to realize that changes in inequality will inevitably affect the capacity of different citizens to make democratic institutions accountable. In these initial years of India's economic reform, it is too early to grasp the impact of financial globalization on inequalities between economic strata. While there has been a remarkable increase in the incomes of corporate executives and a patent growth of middle-class consumerism, unlike other developing countries where economic liberalization has been accompanied by devastating cuts in social welfare expenditures, social welfare expenditures have increased as a per centage of central government expenditures during the reform period.[23] Poverty rates have also declined although the data are not strong enough to support an argument that the reforms have reduced poverty.[24] One thing is clear, financial globalization is creating a new economic geography which seems destined to exacerbate regional inequalities, especially as the regulations to minimize regional disparities under the pre-reform regime are dismantled. These disparities may create new problems, but at this point, India's democracy seems too resilient to be undermined by them. Less-consolidated political systems may not fare as well.

The experience of India's stock markets suggests that financial globalization strengthens the rule of law. However, financial globalization may promote the uneven development of legal systems by advancing laws that protect business and investor interests while leaving civil law protecting the social rights of citizens undeveloped (see O'Donnell, 1997). Yet the development of a more rigorous legal framework for investment and business is not necessarily antithetical to the promotion of citizen rights. Historically, liberalism's protection of property rights generated a legal framework that facilitated the advance of citizens' rights. Whether the equity of procedure implicit in the legal regimes promoted by neoliberalism can provide opportunities for enhancing citizens' rights in the world of global capital is an important subject for future research.

This study of financial globalization and democracy also points out important ambiguities in the process of democratization. The conventional wisdom is that political liberalization precedes the transition to democracy. Our case demonstrates that financial globalization can promote political liberalization in countries like India that have already made the transition to democracy. We need to be sensitive to changes in political institutions even after countries have completed a democratic transition. By promoting liberal norms, financial globalization may strengthen the economic and political institutions of Indian democracy by making them more liberal – even while it also generates new disparities that make them less responsive to broad segments of Indian society.

Notes

1. I would like to thank Gerard Alexander, Leslie Elliott Armijo, John Duffield, Elisavinda Echeverri-Gent, Charles Kromkowski, Herman Schwartz, Robert Wade, and David Waldner. I am especially grateful Aida Hozic for her important contributions to this essay first as a research assistant and then as a colleague. Any shortcomings are due to my stubborn refusal to heed the better judgment of my colleagues.
2. India's share of the total population of developing countries was computed from World Bank, 1996, pp. 188–9. India's share of net private capital flows to developing countries was computed from International Monetary Fund, 1997, p. 43.
3. For an excellent overview of India's economic reforms see Rajaraman (1997).
4. The committee's membership included: M. R. Mayya Executive Director of the Bombay Stock Exchange, E. R. Krishnamurti, Executive Director of the Madras Stock Exchange, D. H. Pai Panandiker, Secretary-General of the Federation of Indian Chambers of Commerce and Industry, D. R. Mehta, former Controller of Capital Issues, S. M. Dugar, Joint Secretary of the Department of Company Affairs, S. S. Nadkarni, Chairman of the Industrial Development Bank of India, K. V. Shanbhogue, ex-president of the Institute of Company Secretaries of India, L. C. Gupta, Dean for Research, Management Development Institute, and Paul Joseph, Joint Director (SE) Department of Economic Affairs, Ministry of Finance.
5. Descriptions of India's settlement system can be found in *International Money Marketing*, 1995; Nicholson and Nicoll, 1995, p. iv; Karmali, 1994, p. viii; and Crawford, 1994.
6. These figures come from GOI/MOF/SED 1991, p. 8 as cited in Gupta, 1996, pp. 751–7.
7. Personal correspondence from Tony Porter 13 March 1996. For overviews of IOSCO and the emerging regime for international security markets see Porter (1993), especially pp. 103–47 and Porter's chapter in this volume. India's commitment to meet IOSCO's capital adequacy standards is noted in GOI/MOF, 1996, p. 65.

8. The situation was similar to that depicted by the 'garbage can' model of policy making. See Kingdon, 1994; and Cohen, March and Olsen, 1972.
9. Interview with G. V. Ramakrishna, the first chairman of SEBI, 1989–93, New Delhi, 13 January 1995. The abolition of the Controller of Capital Issues and the subsequent empowerment of SEBI was also recommended by what became known as the Narasimham Commission on India's financial system. See GOI/MOF, 1991. The Narasimham Commission was convened after the World Bank made recommendations to the Government of India concerning financial sector reforms. Its recommendations closely reflected those of the World Bank. See Armijo, 1993, pp. 24–5.
10. Good summaries of SEBI reforms include GOI/MOF, 1996, pp. 60–3; and Gokarn, 1996
11. GOI/MOF, 1993, pp. 66–7, 69; Descriptions of the conflict between SEBI and the brokers of the Bombay Stock Exchange were provided to me in interviews with C. P. Thakur, Congress (I) spokesperson for economic policy, New Delhi, 23 June 1992, and Jay Dubashi, Bharatiya Janata Party, economic spokesperson, New Delhi, 25 June 1992. For more information on the broker's strike in April 1992 see D. P. Sharma 1992, p. 859. For discussion on SEBI's recent report on the BSE and other tensions with the brokers see Misra 1993, and *Economic Times*, 1993a, b and c. For the view of the first chairman of SEBI on the issues at stake in modernizing India's stock markets see *India Today*, 1991. The brokers ultimately succeeded in ousting SEBI's first chairman (Clift, 1993).
12. For a concise comparison of the NSE and the BSE see *The Economist* (1996a).
13. For the CRB scandal see Aiyar, 1997 and *The Economist*, 1997. For the Reliance controversy see Abreu and Raval, 1995; Jain and Rekhi, 1996; and Vekatesh, 1996. For an overview of other incidents of corporate corruption see Jain (1996).
14. Their clout within corporate India as well as the opportunities to raise even more capital from abroad is demonstrated by Reliance Corporation's decision to install an accounting system based on American standards.
15. For a lucid overview of the scam see Armijo (1993), especially pp. 22–30. For other accounts see *Business Today*, 1992; Mcdonald and Dalal, 1992; Dalal, 1992; *Economic Times*, 1992; Bidwai, 1992.
16. This point became clear to me in discussions with Ron Herring on 1 March 1996 in Charlottesville. For a provocative article that suggests that this is a general trend not only throughout the developing world but across the developed world as well see Chaudhury (1993).
17. Octroi are duties on trade entering into a state.
18. For an overview of state-level reforms see: World Bank, 1995, pp. 48–58. For a comparative discussion of the politics of privatization between different governmental levels in India and Brazil see Armijo and Jha forthcoming.
19. The discussion in this paragraph draws heavily from Stremlau (1996).
20. For an argument that the new globalization is returning the internal economy to economic integration roughly like that at the end of the nineteenth century see Schwartz (1994).
21. The impact of corruption dealings in capital markets is most patent in post-communist countries where 'nomenclatura privatization' and the subsequent operation of capital markets has benefitted a select few who have used their new wealth to enhance their influence within the new political system. For Russia see Aslund (1996) or Wedel (1997). Corruption in capital markets influences politics in developed as well as developing and post-communist countries. For the case of Japan see Sanger (1988) and *Economist* (1998).

22. For a discussion of polyarchy see Robert Dahl, *Polyarchy: Participation and Opposition* (New Haven: Yale University Press, 1971). For the distinction between the formal, participatory and social dimensions of democracy see Huber, Rueschemeyer and Stephens (1997).
23. While total expenditure of India's central government from 1990–91 to 1996–97 (revised estimate) increased by 92 per cent, expenditures on social services, employment, and poverty alleviation programs expanded by 138 per cent, increasing their share of the total budget from 9.48 per cent to 11.88 per cent. Computed from *Economic and Political Weekly* (1997).
24. The estimated proportion of India's population below the poverty line has declined by 2.9 per cent, from roughly 39 per cent to 36 per cent from 1987–88 to 1993–94. The Government of India's *Economic Survey 1996–97* asserts that an increase in employment generation from three million jobs in 1991–92 to more than seven million in 1994–95 has been responsible for the reduction in poverty. See GOI/MOF, 1998; Rajaram, 1997, p.14.

Bibliography

Abreu, Robin and Sheela Raval (1995) 'Reliance Industries: Duplicate Problems,' *India Today*, 31 December pp. 76–7.

Aiyar, V. Shankar (1997) 'C. R. Bhansali Scandal: Savings Swindle,' *India Today*, 9 June.

Armijo, Leslie Elliott (1993) 'Capital Unbound: National Resonses to Financial Market Scandals in Brazil (1989) and India (1992),' unpublished manuscript, Northeastern University.

—— and Prem Shankar Jha, forthcoming, 'Centre–State. Relations in India and Brazil: Privatization of Electricity and Banking,' in Satu Kahkonen and Anthony Lanyi (eds), *Institutions, Incentives, and Economic Reforms* (New Delhi: Sage).

The Asian Wall Street Journal (1997) 'Paperless Trading In India May See Boost from U.S. Investors,' 28 April p. 20.

Aslund, Anders (1996) 'Reform Vs. "Rent-Seeking" in Russia's Economic Transformation,' *Transition*, 26 January pp. 12–16..

Bartik, Tim (1991) *Who Benefits from State and Local Economic Development Policies?* (Kalamazoo, Mich.: W. E. Upjohn Institute for Employment Research).

Beck, Ernest (1997) 'Albania's Unrest Over Pyramid Schemes Puts Spotlight on Its Fragile Economy,' *The Wall Street Journal*, 30 January.

Bhimal, Shefali (1994) 'Against All Odds,' *India Today*, 31 March.

Bidwai, Prafulla (1992) 'Implications of the Mega-Scam,' *Mainstream*, 20 June.

Brace, Paul (1993) *State Government and Economic Performance* (Baltimore, Md.: Johns Hopkins University Press).

Business Line (1997) 'Depository brooks no delay,' *Business Line* (Internet edition), 13 June.

Business Today (1992) 'Big bull in big trouble,' 11 May, pp. 54–60.

Cawthorne, Pamela M. (1995) 'Of Networks and markets: The Rise and Rise of a South Indian Town, the Example of Tiruppur's Cotton Knitwear Industry,' *World Development* 31 (1), January, pp. 43–56.

Chaudhury, Kirin Aziz (1993) 'The Myths of the Market and the Common History of Late Developers,' *Politics and Society* 21 (3), September, pp. 245–74.

Chopra, Ajai, Charles Collyns, Richard Hemming, and Karen Parker (1995) *India: Economic Reform and Growth* (Washington, DC.: International Monetary Fund).

Clift, Jeremy (1993) 'India: Bourse Scourge To Be Replaced Amid Row,' *Reuters World Service*, 31 December.

Cohen, Michael, James March, and Johan Olsen (1972) 'A Garbage Can Model of Organizational Choice,' *Administrative Science Quarterly*, 17, March, pp. 1–25.

Comptroller of Publications (1991) *Report of the Committee on the Financial System* (New Delhi: Comptroller of Publications).

Crawford, Philip (1994) 'India: The Jewel Could Use Polishing,' *International Herald Tribune*, 30 April.

Dahl, Robert (1971) *Polyarchy: Participation and Opposition* (New Haven, Conn.: Yale University Press).

Dalal, Sucheta (1992) 'Bombay bombshell,' *Far Eastern Economic* Review, 4 June.

Economic and Political Weekly (1997) 'Special Statistics: Finances of Government of India' 32 (20–1), 17 May, pp. 1205–20.

Economic Times (1992) 'Text of the Janakiraman panel recommendations,' *Economic Times,* 3 June.

———— (1993a) 'SEBI Indicts BSE for Glaring Lapses,' *Economic Times*, 11 March.

———— (1993b) 'Purbhoodas & Co refuses SEBI accusations,' *Economic Times*, 12 March.

———— (1993c) 'Taxmen Stalk "Losing" Brokers,' *Economic Times* (12 March).

The Economist (1996a) 'India's Stock Exchanges: Duelling,' *The Economist*, 6 July, pp. 64–5.

———— (1996b) 'Riding a Cart and Bullocks through Indian Capitalism,' *The Economist*, 5 October, pp. 60–61.

———— (1997) 'Indian Finance: Imploding Star,' *The Economist*, 6 June, pp. 80–1.

———— (1998) 'Japan's Useful Scandal,' *The Economist,* 24 January, p. 37.

Eisinger, Peter (1988) *The Rise of the Entrepreneurial State* (Madison, WI.: University of Wisconsin Press).

Feller, Irwin (1992) 'American State Governments as Models for National Science Policy,' *Journal of Policy Analysis and Management*, 11, Spring.

Financial Post (1995) 'Intrigue on Bombay Exchange,' *Financial Post*, 23 March.

Foster, Scott (ed.) (1988) *The New Economic Role of American States* (New York: Oxford University Press).

Frydman, Roman, Kenneth Murphy, and Andrzej Rapacynski (1997) 'Capitalism With a Comrade's Face,' *Transition*, 26 January.

Gill, Stephen (1996) 'Globalization, Democratization, and the Politics of Indifference,' in James H. Mittleman (ed.), *Globalization: Critical Reflections* (Boulder, Col.: Lynne Reinner).

Global Money Management (1996) 'India's Custodians Look Forward to Depository System,' special supplement on Global Custody, 24 June.

Gokarn, Subir (1996) 'Indian Capital Market Reforms, 1992–96: An Assessment,' *Economic and Political Weekly*, 31 (15), 13 April.

Government of India, Ministry of Finance (GOI/MOF) (1991) *Report of the Committee on the Financial System* (New Delhi: Comptroller of Publications).

———— (1993) *Economic Survey 1992–93*. (New Delhi: Government of India Press).

———— (1995) *Report of the High Powered Committee on Stock Exchange Reforms* (New Delhi: Controller of Publications).

———— (1996) *Economic Survey 1995–96* (New Delhi: Government of India Press).

———— (1998) *Economic Survey 1997–98* (New Delhi: Government of India Press).

Government of India, Ministry of Finance, Stock Exchange Division (GOI/MOF/ SED) (1991) 'Report of the Study Group to Examine the Issues and Problems Relating to Unregulated Share Trading and Other Dealers in Securities' (New Delhi: Government of India Press).

Gupta, L. C, (1996) 'Challenges before Securities and Exchange Board of India,' *Economic and Political Weekly* 31 (12), 23 March.

Huber, Evelyne, Dietrich Rueschemeyer, and John Stephens (1997. 'The Paradoxes of Contemporary Democracy: Formal, Participatory, and Social Dimensions,' *Comparative Politics*, 29 (3), April, pp. 323–42.

India Today (1991) 'G. V. Ramakrishna: "The buck can stop here,"' *India Today*, 30 September.

Institutional Investor (1995) 'India: Moving With the Times: The National Stock Exchange,' international edition, December, p. S8.

International Monetary Fund (1997) *World Economic Outlook: May 1997* (Washington, D.C.: International Monetary Fund).

International Money Marketing (1995) 'Stock Exchanges Battle Archaic Laws,' 22 September.

Jain, Sunil (1996) 'Corporate Fraud: Shame and Scandal,' *India Today*, 30 November, pp. 54–61.

―――― and Shefali Rekhi (1996) 'Reliance Industries Limited: Fighting for its Reputation,' *India Today*, 15 January, pp. 68–70;

Karmali, Naazneen (1996) 'Survey of Global Custody,' *Financial Times*, 29 November.

Kenyon, Daphne A., and John Kincaid (eds) (1991). *Competition among States and Local Governments: Efficiency and Equity in American Federalism* (Washington, D.C.: Urban Institute Press).

Kingdon, John W. (1994) *Agendas, Alternatives, and Public Policies*, 2nd edn (New York: HarperCollins).

Kohli, Rajiv (1997. 'Giving India's Investors a Fair Shake,' *The Asian Wall Street Journal*, 4 March, p. 10.

Kripalani, Manjeet (1997) 'The Business Rajas,' *Business Week*, 14 April, p. 26.

Lok Sabha Secretariat (1993) *Report: Joint Committee to Enquire into Irregularities in Securities and Banking Transactions*, Vol. I, Report (New Delhi: Lok Sabha Secretariat).

McDonald, Hamish (1994) 'Made to Order,' *Far Eastern Economic Review*, 17 March, pp. 50–2

―――― and Sucheta Dalal (1992) 'Double Dealings: Indian Stock Crash,' *Far Eastern Economic Review*, 21 May.

Misra, Paromita (1993) 'Still no Enforcement Body for Investors,' *The Economic Times*, 7 March.

Nicholson, Mark (1995) 'Survey of Investing in India,' *Financial Times*, 13 March.

―――― and Alexander Nicoll (1994) 'Survey of Investing in India,' *Financial Times*, 13 March.

Ninan, T. N. (1997) 'Business Dynasties: Family Groups Face Struggle to Survive,' *The Financial Times* (special supplement on India), 24 June, p. 20.

O'Donnell, Guillermo (1997) 'Polyarchies and the (Un)Rule of Law in Latin America,' paper presented at the Annual Meeting of the American Political Science Association, Washington, D.C. 28–31 August.

Osborne, David (1988) *Laboratories for Democracy* (Boston, Mass.: Harvard Business School Press).

Peterson, Paul E. (1981) *City Limits* (Chicago, Ill.: University of Chicago Press).

Platteau, Jean-Philippe (1994a) 'Behind the Market Stage Where Real Societies Exist – Part I: The Role of Public and Private Institutions,' *Journal of Development Studies*, 30 (3), April, pp. 533–77.

―――― (1994b) 'Behind the Market Stage Where Real Societies Exist – Part II: The Role of Moral Norms,' *Journal of Development Studies*, 30 (3), April, pp. 753–817.

Porter, Tony (1993) *States, Markets, and Regimes in Global Finance* (Basingstoke,.: Macmillan).

Przeworski, Adam, Pranab Bardhan, Luiz Carlos Bresser Pereira, *et al.* (1995) *Sustainable Democracy* (Cambridge,.: Cambridge University Press).

Rajaraman, Indira (1997) *A Profile of Economic Reform in India* (New Delhi: National Institute of Public Finance and Policy).

Rosenbluth, Frances (1989) *Financial Politics in Contemporary Japan* (Ithaca, N.Y.: Cornell University Press).

Sanger, David (1988) 'Insider Trading the Japanese Way,' *New York Times*, 10 August, p. D1.

Schwartz, Herman (1994) *States versus Markets* (New York: St Martin's Press).

Sharma, D. P. (1992) 'SEBI: Misadventure,' *Economic and Political Weekly*, 25 April.

Sharma, Rahul (1994) 'India Changes Euroissue Laws to Curb Inflation,' C-reuters@ Clarinet.com, Clari.world.asia.india, clari.biz.economy.world, 28 October.

Sharma, Sumit (1996) 'India to Streamline Share Sales, Aiding Foreign Investors,' *The Wall Street Journal*, 25 July, p. A8.

Stremlau, John (1996) 'Dateline Bangalore: Third World Technopolis,' *Foreign Policy*, 102, Spring, pp. 152–66.

Tassel, Tony (1997) 'Culture Change on Dalal Street,' *Financial Times* special section, Survey India, 24 June, p. 21.

Thomas, George M., John W. Meyer, Francisco O. Ramirez, and John Boli (1987) *Institutional Structure: Constituting State, Society and the Individual* (Newbury Park, Cal.: Sage).

United States Agency for International Development (USAID) (1990) *India: Country Development Strategy Statement FY 1990* (Washington, D.C.: United States Agency for International Development).

Venkatesh, Latha (1996) 'India Moves To Discipline Reliance Firm,' *The Asian Wall Street Journal*, 17 October, p. 4.

Weber, Max (1981) [1927] *General Economic History* (New Brunswick: Transaction).

Wedel, Janine R. (1997) 'Cliques and Clans and Aid to Russia,' *Transitions* 4 (2), July, pp. 66–71.

World Bank (1995) *India: Country Economic Memorandum* (Washington, D.C.: World Bank)

——— (1996) *World Development Report 1996: From Plan to Market* (Washington, D.C.: World Bank).

10 Indonesia: On the Mostly Negative Role of Transnational Capital in Democratization
Jeffrey A. Winters

'Sad to say, it took a couple of dictatorships to get this ancient land moving.'

Andrew Tanzer (1995)

In 1995, Indonesians celebrated their 50th year of independence from the Dutch. But at the current rate of change, Indonesia's 200 million citizens may have to wait another 50 years before they can begin to celebrate their freedom. The fourth most populous country in the world, Indonesia has had just two presidents. General Suharto, now in his late-70s and in declining health, pushed aside President Sukarno in the bloody aftermath of an abortive putsch in 1965. With American complicity, General Suharto and his armed forces orchestrated a pogrom against the Indonesian Communist Party (PKI) that claimed between 500 000 and a million lives by the middle of 1966. Thus was the authoritarian tone set for Suharto's 'New Order' regime. With the passing of North Korea's Kim Il Sung, Suharto assumed the mantle of Asia's most enduring dictator. He is also by far the region's richest.[1]

In 1955, Indonesians participated in their first and last fair election. By 1959 parliament had been shut down – in part because the PKI was threatening to come to power through constitutional elections. When the country's representative institutions were reopened under General Suharto, the PKI had been decimated and the military was firmly in control of all branches of the government. To ensure that the party system would be dysfunctional, Suharto forced the 10 existing parties to squeeze together into three in 1973. The People's Consultative Assembly (MPR), the country's highest constitutional authority, meets only once every five years following the national elections to choose the president and set the broad guidelines for government policy. It has met six times since Suharto took over the country and has chosen the same president each time. In January 1998, Suharto confirmed that he would stand for a seventh term at the March MPR meeting. If he is chosen and if he survives until the end of his term in 2003, he will be 81 years old.

It is hardly surprising that Suharto keeps winning, since he has never allowed an opposing candidate to emerge. And, even if one did, Suharto need not be concerned because the president appoints the entire upper house of the MPR's 1000 members, as well as a portion of the lower house, the People's Representative Council (DPR). The 500 members of the DPR are meant to represent the voice of the people. The armed forces are guaranteed 75 DPR seats appointed by the president. The remaining seats are allocated through a tightly controlled voting process that cannot truthfully be called a general election, since during the 'campaigns' it is illegal to oppose the government, criticize the president, or discuss substantive policy directions. Parties must submit lists of potential candidates to Suharto for approval, and campaigning is limited to a period of just over three weeks, during which the three parties take turns every third day. Only GOLKAR (Suharto's political machine) is allowed to campaign down to the village level. The campaign is followed by a week of 'cool down' before the polls are opened and GOLKAR gets its traditional 65–75 per cent of the vote, giving Suharto a wide majority in the DPR and a super majority in the MPR. The DPR has never proposed a single draft law to the executive branch.

Projecting an image of familial harmony, Suharto has made much of the official state ideology, the *Pancasila*, or 'five principles'. Contrary to apologists both at home and abroad who suggest that the *Pancasila* reflect a distinctly Indonesian political and cultural form, Ariel Heryanto, a leading political scholar from Indonesia, notes that 'the image of familial harmony is deployed to justify the systematic suppression of any expression of grievances and political conflicts'. In his 1995 Independence Day address to the nation, Suharto justified his expulsion of two outspoken members of the DPR, the rounding up of activists and journalists, and the continued atrocities against unarmed civilians in occupied East Timor (invaded by Indonesia in 1975 with a wink and nod from President Ford and Secretary of State Henry Kissinger) by reminding his fellow Indonesians that only 'responsible openness' would be tolerated. Censorship and surveillance are the norm in Indonesia.

In June 1994, the government banned three major weeklies, two of which were the most prominent in the country (parallels in the US would be *Time* and *Newsweek*). All mass media, educational institutions, religious rituals, and artistic productions are monitored and policed for evidence of dissent. Elites brave enough to oppose Suharto's New Order have been harassed, ruined economically, black-listed, and jailed. Opponents from the lower economic strata in the cities and countryside receive similar treatment, though being beaten, raped, shot or crushed under armoured personnel carriers must be added to the price non-elites have paid for their dissent.

Even the United States government, which has backed Suharto unflinchingly since he deposed Sukarno, admits that Indonesia's economic development has been marred by political repression, corruption, wide disparities in wealth, and pandemic human rights violations. The State Department's 1994 human rights appraisal describes Indonesia as strongly authoritarian, despite a surface adherence to democratic forms. Apart from rhetoric and finger wagging, the substantive American response to political exclusion in Indonesia has been to focus on economic opening. It is an article of faith in American diplomatic and business circles that economic liberalization leads in some necessary, inevitable way to political opening.

The argument in this chapter is that foreign investments and those who control them have not contributed to a process of wider political participation in Indonesia. There has been significant economic opening, dramatic changes in the volume of capital flows and who controls them, as well as beneficial effects on job creation and living standards for many Indonesians.[2] But as an aid to political opening, economic liberalization and increases in all forms of capital are at best unreliable and at worst a convenient fig leaf for actors more interested in maintaining stable political conditions for profit-making than in advancing popular participation in the affairs of state.

Nor can it be said that massive capital outflows following a loss of confidence in a ruler like Suharto are necessarily beneficial to the project of democracy. Although the sort of currency and capital market crisis that hit Indonesia and other emerging markets in Southeast Asia starting in July 1997 certainly increased pressures on Suharto by antagonizing fracture lines in the regime, there are no guarantees that a more progressive government would replace the current dictator were his government to collapse. A major financial crisis can shake the political tree, but a broad range of political factors specific to each country determines into whose hands the fruit will fall. In Indonesia, where the domestic and foreign beneficiaries of Suharto's regime are grateful for the profitable opportunities and protections he has provided, the political situation does not favor greater popular participation in the short and medium term. This will come only when progress has been made in reversing the deliberate and total political demobilization of the society. So far no leaders have come forth to undertake this difficult task of channeling the aspirations of the scores of millions of excluded Indonesians into a constructive and progressive force. The result is a dangerous vacuum that instead could erupt into extreme violence and destruction.

With political opening on hold in Indonesia, it is timely to consider how the patterns of transnational investment have changed over the course of Suharto's New Order, and the mostly negative role these flows of resources and the actors controlling them have played as they helped postpone the struggle for political opening in Indonesia. Since 1965, Indonesia has passed

Table 10.1   Periodization of Suharto's new order Indonesia

		Economic factors	Political factors
1966–73	Pre-oil boom	Increasing flows of bilateral and multilateral credits and grants. Commercial borrowing by Pertamina beginning in late 1960s.	Foreign resources stabilize New Order economy. Suharto resists material constraints on regime consolidation. New Order honeymoon is brief.
1974–82	Oil boom	Tens of billions of dollars in windfalls from oil–gas sector. Foreign assistance remains significant. Some commercial borrowing by state firms.	Patron–client system flourishes. Political demobilization begins as Suharto crushes student movement, closes major newspapers, begins campaign of 'mysterious killings'.
1983–87	Post-oil boom	Precipitous fall in prices of fossil fuels. Cushioned immediately by billions in direct cash injections to Indonesian treasury from Japanese 'special assistance' and other bilateral and multilateral sources.	Suharto severely constrained to adopt policies more favorable to mobile capital. Deregulation begins, though Suharto's family and cronies remain protected. No significant signs of political opening.
1988 to present	Economic opening	Indonesia enters ranks of top 3 debtor countries; private borrowing becomes substantial. Capitalization of Jakarta stock exchange briefly surpasses total banking assets. Transnational investment pours in at record levels, especially from Asia. Huge financial crisis starting in summer of 1997.	As dependence on oil–gas exports declines, deregulation slows in tandem. Not yet encroaching on core Suharto economic interests. Still no political opening. Crackdown on dissidents. Suharto joins chorus of Asian dictators criticizing West for raising human rights issues. Continued massacres in occupied East Timor.

through four distinct phases based on changing forms and sources of capital and money resources. Table 10.1 briefly summarizes the phases.

Except for a brief honeymoon at the beginning of the New Order – before Suharto had consolidated his position within the Indonesian military and before political factions left over from the Sukarno years were crushed and demobilized – Indonesian society has remained highly controlled and highly depoliticized for over 30 years. For all its diversity, great geographic expanse, and history of political activity at home and abroad, Indonesia has been a quiet country politically for decades.[3] Indonesians have been so thoroughly intimidated that one rarely finds political graffiti of the sort so common in the 1950s and 1960s – not even scratched on the walls of public toilets.

There have been interludes of political opening when Suharto has eased his restrictions on the media and allowed more debate and dissent. But the periods have been short-lived, and seem to end as abruptly as they start – usually after criticism touches on Suharto and his family, or after opponents have revealed themselves enough to assist Suharto in making preemptive strikes. There is no plausible basis for linking these fleeting periods of political opening to the size, form or sources of transnational capital flows, nor to trends in economic opening. If anything, Indonesia has shown a fairly steady pattern of diminishing political participation even as capital resources from abroad have risen and fallen in importance. The 1997 national elections were less free and representative than the 1992 elections, which were less fair than the 1982 elections. Even the 1971 elections, the first after the massacres, were more open and participatory than the spectacles staged in the 1980s and 1990s. While it is true that changes in capital flows and those who control them have played a crucial role in the shifting strength and autonomy of the state and of Suharto himself,[4] the pressures from these actors, directly or indirectly, have never been for a *politically* liberalized regime. Through three decades of tightening political controls, transnational controllers of capital (finance or otherwise) have broken their measured silence on the matter of Indonesia's political exclusion only to shout down those who raise it.

CAPITAL AND INDONESIA[5]

The profile of capital flows for Indonesia presented in this section refers to conditions just prior to the deep crisis that gripped the country starting in July 1997. A brief postscript deals with some of the implications of the crisis itself. Indonesia, Malaysia, and Thailand are the main recipients of foreign direct investment in Southeast Asia. Direct investment to these three countries has risen sharply since the middle 1980s, surpassing total direct investment to the NICs by the early 1990s. In much the same way that transnational investment in China increased dramatically in the early 1990s following the massacre in Tiananmen Square, transnational investments in Indonesia surged in the middle 1990s despite a severe crackdown on press freedom in 1994 and the brutal destruction of the Indonesian Democratic Party (PDI) during the summer of 1996.

Approved foreign and domestic direct investment in Indonesia increased sharply since the middle 1990s, though realized investment continued to lag for both sets of investors – hovering around 40 per cent of approval levels because of bureaucratic obstacles and numerous inefficiencies in the Indonesian economy. Even so, the rates of direct investment since the early 1990s showed that private capital was responding favorably to liberalization efforts. The state played the dominant role in controlling investment resources during the oil boom years in the 1970s and early 1980s, but was thoroughly displaced by the late 1980s as the primary investor in the Indonesian economy.

Data on approved FDI by region or country of origin show that intra-Asian investment rose as the NICs and ASEAN states played a greater role in Indonesia's economy. Despite declining annual shares since the late 1980s, Japan is still the largest single foreign investor with 55 per cent of all approved FDI since 1967, totaling roughly $125 billion. The annual US share of FDI in Indonesia has been relatively low and is still concentrated heavily in mining and extractive sectors (with a market capitalization of $5 billion, the largest single transnational investment in Indonesia is Freeport-McMoran's copper and gold operation in West Irian).[6] Sharp upturns in US investment usually reflect large single projects, as with the massive Natuna Sea gas field at the opening of 1995 (for which President Clinton lobbied hard on behalf of Mobil Oil in the months leading up to the November 1994 APEC summit in Indonesia).

After first leading the country on a course of extreme dependence on oil and gas exports during the boom of the 1970s and early 1980s, Suharto reversed course and weaned Indonesia from its reliance on fossil fuels. From a high of 80 per cent of total exports in the early 1980s, oil and gas exports accounted for 46 per cent in 1994. That same year manufacturing accounted for 23 per cent of Indonesia's GDP of $158 billion. If services and tourism are included, the share jumps to 60 per cent of GDP. Despite these improvements, the country remains extremely vulnerable to balance-of-payments crises and continues to depend on massive annual injections of foreign assistance to close the gaping deficit on the current account. Indonesia's external deficit exposure has long been of great concern.[7] But the trends even before the severe financial crisis of 1997 were already alarming. The deficit on the current account began to rise toward $4 billion in 1994, exceeded $6 billion in 1995, and passed $7 billion in 1996 as rising imports needed to feed huge investments in domestic infrastructure continued to outpace growth rates in exports (which have slowed in textiles, garments, and plywood in the face of competition from China, Vietnam, and Malaysia).

A crucial part of the picture for Indonesia is the burden of repayments on the country's foreign debt. At the end of 1995, Indonesia's total foreign debt (public and private) was $100 billion. By the third quarter of 1997, the debt had grown by an additional $20 billion, making it the third largest in the world after Mexico's and Brazil's. Subsequent developments revealed that these official figures were gross underestimates, in large part because private commercial borrowing ballooned in Indonesia and the central bank was not able to keep track of these flows accurately. In 1993 combined principal and interest payments broke the $8 billion mark and increased steadily there-after. If the consortium of creditor countries and agencies (formerly chaired by the Netherlands, but in recent years renamed and now led by the World Bank due to Jakarta's anger over human rights criticisms coming from Amsterdam) did not provide huge new injections of aid each year, Indonesia would be unable to service its debt.

Whether measured using interest payments as a percentage of exports or total debt service as a percentage of exports, Indonesia's debt burden is more onerous than that of Mexico and Brazil. (Argentina, of course, faces the heaviest burden along these two measures). In the 1990s, Indonesia has spent more on debt repayment than on all compensation for the country's bloated civil service. Changes in the money supply and credits have been dra-matic since the 1970s. What is interesting, however, is that huge fluctuations caused mainly by external shocks before 1983 have been replaced by fluctua-tions caused by a dizzying series of policy moves that caused considerable instability in domestic finance – in particular the banking deregulations in the late 1980s when the ministry of finance and the central bank nearly lost control of the monetary system.

Partly to attract foreign capital to close the current account deficit, and partly reflecting the risks of bank lending in Indonesia, interest rates were kept extremely high. High interest rates on deposits have actually hampered the growth of Indonesia's capital market (about which more below). And even SBIs, Indonesian central bank certificates intended as an indirect instrument for regulating the money supply and interest rates, have been available at rates over 10 per cent per annum for most of the time since their introduction.

The turn toward indirect monetary instruments and the effort to shift financial intermediation increasingly to the private sector were at the heart of banking deregulation in the 1980s. The role of domestic private banks surged in a volatile environment where the government threw open the door for private banking without first developing even a rudimentary capacity for oversight (resulting in several spectacular defaults and widespread patholo-gies in bank portfolios, and contributing to the severe crisis toward the end of 1997). Significantly, foreign banks have seen their shares in total deposits actually fall since deregulation.

At least two preliminary observations emerge from these snapshots of changes in Indonesia's economy and external transactions. First, beginning in the 1980s private actors and private capital began to displace the dominant position of the state – both as micro-regulator of the economy and as the main controller and source of investment resources. This has reduced the autonomy of the Indonesian state mainly by tightening the constraints on (though by no means eliminating) Suharto's game of patronage and monopoly. But this rise of capital, to use Richard Robison's felicitous phrase (see Robison, 1986), has had limited beneficial effects for the vast majority of Indonesians when it comes to reducing bureaucratic red tape, illegal fees, and payments to corrupt petty officials. Indeed, if anything the effects have been mostly negative as powerful actors from Suharto on down have been forced to find new ways of feeding and lubricating the patron–client structures that pervade the New Order regime. With more control over capital directly in the hands of private investors, and with increasing pressures through GATT/WTO and APEC to reduce obstacles to free trade and investment, it is harder for Suharto to play the political game by the old rules.[8]

Second, neither the retreat of the state nor the reduced dependence on oil/gas exports helped diminish the volatility of the Indonesian economy or its exposure to potential balance-of-payments crises. The country's debt burden remained heavy, and even relatively minor shocks or surges in capital flight could set in motion a devastating downward spiral. This was evident during the summer and fall of 1997 when Indonesia's currency and capital market were shaken by a crisis of confidence in the region. The next section argues that the single greatest source of destabilization Indonesia now faces is precisely from such massive and rapid shifts in capital flows. The implications of these developments for political opening will be addressed in the concluding section.

THE JAKARTA STOCK EXCHANGE (JSE)

In addition to the sharp upturn in FDI, Indonesia saw the rapid development of its capital market starting in the early 1990s. Total market capitalization increased from Rp 12.4 trillion in 1990 to Rp 123.9 trillion in November of 1995, a ten-fold increase in five years. In 1995 the JSE finally surpassed the banking sector in total capitalization, though this trend was reversed when the market lost a third of its value in July and August of 1997 alone. Three-quarters of this capitalization was concentrated in just 40 Indonesian companies. The foreign share of Indonesia's capital market stood at 30 per cent at the end of 1995, amounting to roughly $16 billion. Of this, almost half was concentrated in shares held in just seven major companies.[9] Despite rapid growth in recent years, the JSE suffered from liquidity problems. Although foreign investors owned less than a third of the market, they tended to account for more than half of all transactions.

Prior to the emergence of a capital market in Indonesia, the only *daily* barometers of investor confidence were the exchange rate and outstanding SBI-SBPUs (central bank certificates). Private actors controlling financial resources have been highly attentive to the dangers of huge and sudden losses in Indonesia. This is evident from data on outstanding notes from the central bank. On rumors of a devaluation early in 1993, SBI-SBPUs in circulation dropped from Rp 23 trillion to Rp 12.5 trillion in 3 months – an outflow of about $4.7 billion. Another plunge of over $2 billion occurred in the aftermath of the Mexican meltdown at the end of 1994.

The stock market adds an additional daily barometer of investor confidence, but with the difference that not only is capital of higher velocity and higher impact involved, but the government has *no instruments* with which to control outflows of capital should a crisis (or even the mere perception of one) arise. The ministry of finance and the central bank could at least try to defend against runs on the rupiah by direct intervention and by playing with the volume and interest rates on SBI-SBPUs. Twice in the late 1980s, when indirect instruments failed to halt a run on the national currency, the minister of finance ordered all state companies (Indonesia has around 200) to withdraw all of their deposits from the banking system and purchase central bank certificates. This greatly reduced excess liquidity in the banking system and effectively stopped flows into foreign currencies.

Capital markets are different. The government has neither direct nor indirect instruments for stemming a severe decline on the Jakarta exchange. Also, the sheer speed with which value can be lost on the capital market surpasses anything the country or government officials have experienced before. This inexperience was painfully evident during the market crash of 1997, which was caused in part when Indonesian ministers tried to use old treatments for new ailments. As the sharp drop in the value of the Thai baht caused a domino effect for other currencies in the region, the Indonesian central bank tried to defend the rupiah by sharply raising interest rates. Interbank loan rates quickly reached 300 per cent. The impact of this move was two-fold. It made the Indonesian government appear desperate, which further worried investors (many of whom had only a superficial understanding of the country's political economy). But even more devastating, the high interest rates accelerated the flow of capital out of the capital market and into banks, causing the market to lose a third of its value in a matter of weeks. This caused still more alarm, setting in motion a second phase of financial crisis and instability for Southeast Asia. Almost all the countries in the region saw their projected growth rates cut substantially for 1998, and several, including Indonesia, were expected to actually contract. This change represents hundreds of billions of dollars in lost output.[10]

POLITICAL IMPLICATIONS

Despite countless studies over the past four decades trying to establish a basic causal connection between capitalism and democracy, it remains more an article of faith than demonstrable fact that economic opening, the spread of market forces, and capitalist industrialization pave the way for political opening, freedom, and popular participation. Capitalism has shown itself to function quite nicely with a remarkably wide range of polities over extended periods of time. That there is no linearity in the relationship is demonstrated clearly enough in Latin America, where capitalist development coexisted with representative democracies for decades, then continued on with (some say caused) military-dominated regimes, and most recently has continued on (some say caused) a swing back to greater political openness. That capitalist industrialization and the related emergence of a broad and prosperous middle class can occur with virtually no progress in political opening and democratization is evident in several places, but nowhere so plainly as in Singapore. With a GDP per capita second only to Japan in Asia, Singapore is as politically controlled and exclusionary today as it was in 1965, when the island was dominated by small farmers and large marshes. Indeed, political development in Singapore can only refer to a refining of the techniques of hegemony and domination by a state that is more deserving of the label 'totalitarian' than any communist regime ever was. Another troubling case is India, a country with a great deal of free expression and a pattern of regular elections spanning several decades. India is poor and was economically closed for much of the post-WWII period.

The evidence from Indonesia provides a useful reminder that the economic transformations heralded by market capitalism do not necessarily generate the expected or hoped-for systemic changes in the political realm. They often do not even produce truly systemic changes in the economic realm. Laudatory reports from the World Bank notwithstanding,[11] the picture that emerges in Indonesia is one of partial changes, contained benefits, limited transformations, selective and encapsulated bargains – with Suharto responding to demands for deregulation only when and as far as truly necessary. Indonesia's clientelist institutions and structures have been better at adapting to and resisting challenges than market capitalism has been at transforming or sweeping them away.[12] The country's most powerful actors, when pressed, have given with one hand while taking back with the other. In many instances they have not given at all. Sometimes they have yielded to demands for liberalization with great fanfare, only later to chip away at reforms much more quietly. The decidedly partial character of Indonesia's era of deregulation is evident in the fact that liberalization narrowly benefited the powerful, capital-controlling actors that are able to demand it while also stopping short of encroaching on the economic interests of Suharto, the many tentacles of his extended family, and his inner circle of friends, business associates, and top military figures. The deregulation packages announced in May 1995 and January 1996 followed a consistent pattern established since Indonesia adjusted successfully to the precipitous drop in oil prices in the early and mid-1980s. A number of cosmetic gestures toward liberalization were overshadowed by what the packages did not contain: any mention of the monopoly positions of Suharto's friends and family. Thus although the minister of industry and trade said publicly that the January 1996 reforms, which had been delayed three times in three months, would include fresh measures aimed at textiles, pulp, plywood and electronics, none was touched because Suharto's cronies were key players in each. The same is true in cement and auto parts, as well as in basic food commodities like flour, rice, soybeans, and sugar. The vast majority of Indonesian citizens pay huge monopoly rents to Suharto's billionaire associates because of these protections.

Economic liberalization is widely believed to usher in reforms in bureaucracy, the legal order, and in transparency and the public availability of information. Were these changes to be deep and wide, they certainly would favor political opening. In Indonesia, however, strategies for containing the wider *potential* effects of economic opening have been raised to a high art. Rather than reform the various government ministries, Indonesia offers investors 'one-stop' services designed to minimize the trouble and illegal fees incurred when permits and signatures are issued. The phenomenal rise of industrial estates and special economic zones – what I term 'zonal capitalism' – in places like Indonesia is due in part to the need to create hyper-attractive investment sites within decidedly less-attractive investment climates. The management companies that build and operate the zones shield their investor-tenants so that there is minimal contact with the state. Insofar as bribes and fees are paid, they get bundled together into a single service charge paid to the estate management company run by Indonesians, which then transfers the money to key officials.[13] This allows American companies operating inside the estates and zones to enjoy the competitive benefits of paying off corrupt officials, a practice forbidden by the US Foreign Corrupt Practices Act.

With investor pressures handled in this zonal or partial fashion, inefficiency and corruption get reduced only marginally at the central government level and not at all at intermediate and local levels for everyone else. For the great majority of Indonesians, liberalization has been a mean trick and a source of deep frustration and cynicism. Since the mid-1980s, Indonesia's leaders and the press have been talking incessantly about *deregulasi* (partly because the word 'liberalization' contains the word 'liberal' and is therefore politically taboo). Powerless to demand change, and with minimal or nonexistent benefits trickling down from state reforms given to mobile capital controllers, the average Indonesian finds in her interaction with the system that *deregulasi* is a sham. And worse, insofar as opportunities for lucrative skimming at the top have been curtailed, extraction from the middle and bottom has been increased to compensate. Thus the average bribe one must pay a traffic cop for a minor violation has increased five-fold during the last decade. Similar stories are told regarding illegal fees charged for the routine processing of identification cards, birth certificates, and permits to have a wedding party in one's home.

It is true that investors like rule of law because contracts are strengthened and risks are reduced once there is fairly predictable recourse in the courts. Indonesia's legal structure is outdated and the courts are thoroughly corrupt, relying more on money and the sway of patron-client relations than precedents in law. The pressures brought to bear by capital have not resulted in an overhaul of the legal system and an upgrading of the strength and independence of judges. Instead, the encapsulated response has been to finesse the problem by creating a separate commercial court that handles business matters from contracts up to intellectual property rights. The rest of the legal system – handling everything from family to criminal to political cases – remains largely intact, once again calling into question the purported political benefits of economic opening for the rest of society.

As for transparency and information flows, it is quite easy to open up the flow of information to business while controlling access for the rest of society. By putting a high price on information and by releasing it through exclusive channels, the government can ensure that investors get the timely information they demand while the public, except for a handful of elites who support the regime because it takes good care of them, is excluded. This explains how Indonesia can be lauded for its great strides in transparency even as it intimidates the country's media by closing down three major weeklies.

There are few indications that transnational investors support policy initiatives that would lead more directly to political reforms and democratization, and indeed there are strong reasons to suggest that it is in their objective interest not to push for such reforms. Instead, what investors really want is a climate of political and economic stability, even if it takes authoritarian governments to deliver it.[14] The rougher edges of the arrangement are smoothed over by an almost religious belief on the part of investors that their own pursuits of profits under authoritarian market capitalism will eventually help end the exclusionary system that serves them so well.

The American Chamber of Commerce in Indonesia (AMCHAM), in chorus with business interests around the globe, has consistently attacked even the most feeble gestures made by US representatives on behalf of human rights and political opening. From a competitive *business* perspective, raising issues of human rights hurts Americans in the same way that the Foreign Corrupt Practices Act forces US investors to bid for projects with one hand tied behind their backs. Echoing a sentiment expressed consistently by US investors, a CEO of a major US multinational preparing to open up a new headquarters in Southeast Asia observed:

> The French and the Germans and the Japanese don't have this problem of having to keep their governments focused on economic issues. It does no good in our business relations with Asian governments to have [US] officials making embarrassing and irritating comments on human rights. And it doesn't stop the violations by bringing these things up anyway.[15]

Asian governments protested strongly against including social and political issues within the Asia Pacific Economic Cooperation (APEC) framework, insisting instead that economic issues are discrete from political ones, and that the latter are strictly internal in character.

American business representatives agreed wholeheartedly and lobbied hard that human rights be addressed in a separate and unspecified forum. The United States government acquiesced to this pressure both at the 1994 meeting in Bogor, Indonesia and at the 1995 meeting in Osaka, Japan. Prior to the Osaka meeting, 28 US senators wrote to President Clinton urging him to make human rights abuses and the brutal occupation of East Timor top priorities in his discussions at the White House with President Suharto. Through his spokesman, Clinton refused to do this, keeping the up-coming APEC meeting in Osaka as the central focus. William Bodde, a former director of APEC, explained that Clinton's reason for down-playing human rights turned on the pivotal role Indonesia had played in Bogor to advance the cause of liberalization in investment and trade (Hader, 1995).[16] The US was especially eager to have Suharto pressure Japan and other countries to refrain from proposing various 'exception' clauses to the APEC pronouncements on trade. Toward this objective, Clinton was willing to ignore the urgings of the US senators and the constituencies they represented. As it happens, Suharto himself displayed a rather unreliable commitment to liberalization in Osaka whenever the discussion moved from talk and pledges to calls for concrete actions and schedules for policy reforms. Suharto not only escaped a lecture from Clinton on human rights abuses, but also proved to have a disconcerting penchant for exception clauses and other delays.[17]

Transnational investors have at least two objective reasons for not pushing for more political opening. The first has been alluded to, but deserves further elaboration. Aware that countries face a market in foreign investors and trading partners, transnational investors are reluctant to have their home governments agitating for political reforms because this undermines investors' relations with host governments and, as the US CEO said, gives advantages to other investors whose governments stay silent, as most do.[18] Thus for investors there are market-driven reasons that militate against even mentioning the issue of political opening, much less using leverage to push for concrete policy changes, as is routinely done in the economic realm.

A second reason transnational investors want to keep political opening off the agenda is that they benefit both at home and abroad from the *freedom gap* that separates the former colonizers from the former colonies. Greater political freedoms enhance labor's opportunities to gain a greater share of the economic surplus from owners and controllers of capital.[19] American workers, for example, have a clear interest in competing globally for jobs against workers that enjoy universal political guarantees and freedoms against beating, imprisonment, torture, and disappearance. The right to organize and protest against exploitative and dangerous working conditions is inseparable from other dimensions of being competitive, such as productivity. The authoritarian conditions that prevent workers from organizing and making demands are an integral part of the calculus that makes relocating capital and production facilities to Indonesia appealing in the first place. Closing the freedom gap would deprive transnational investors not only of the opportunity to produce cheaply in post-colonial states, but also of the leverage they have with labor back home when they can make credible threats to relocate to places where workers are cheaper, more pliable, and more intimidated.

Although there are certainly beneficial economic effects from inflows of capital, it is doubtful that the prospects for political development in Indonesia are being enhanced significantly by the presence of transnational capital. Indeed, the evidence suggests that capital controllers are hurting more than helping. This is no less true of finance capital than of direct investment. The new prominence of finance capital has created well-grounded fears in Indonesia that spooking high velocity capital could trigger a balance-of-payments crisis of mind-boggling proportions. This places a premium on rapid and decisive responses to signs of political challenge or instability in the Indonesian state. It is unlikely such responses will be toward more freedom and wider participation.

The first-order requirement of democracy under capitalism is that it serve the interests of those controlling the society's investment resources, or at a minimum that it not severely threaten them. In his work on Argentina, Edward Gibson has noted that

> for most of this century, party-based elite control over the political process in Latin America has served as a buttress against the substantive demands

of underprivileged strata on national political life. Democracy survived as long as elites controlled it, and as long as popular challenges could be neutralized through elite-controlled democratic institutions. (Gibson, 1996, pp. 23–4).

The same can be said of Indonesia. Many observers note with some admiration that Suharto has managed to maintain stability in Indonesia for three decades, despite a huge population, multiple ethnic groups, and a citizenry spread across an archipelago that is wider than the continental United States. The irony of this stability is that few people have any confidence that it can be maintained if the lid on the Indonesian pressure cooker is lifted.

POSTSCRIPT

As this book goes to press, there has been no resolution to the economic and political crisis in Indonesia, already in its seventh month. In the middle of 1997 the rupiah was trading at 2 400 to the dollar. In January 1998, despite major interventions by the US and the IMF, it had plunged to 17 000 to the dollar, sparking riots and panic in Jakarta and other cities on Java. Nearly all private Indonesian companies were rendered insolvent, and the market capitalization of the Jakarta Stock Exchange fell from $118 billion before the crisis began to just $17 billion at the beginning of 1998. Over the same period, the number of listed firms with a market capitalization over $500 million declined from 49 to 4.

These developments rocked the Suharto regime to its foundations. It is interesting to compare Indonesia with Thailand and South Korea, which have also endured tremendous economic difficulties since mid-1997. Considerably more participatory than Indonesia, Thailand and South Korea managed to change governments in the middle of the economic crisis without disruption or bloodshed. This has helped leaders in both countries separate themselves from many of the factors and power centers that contributed to the crisis in the first place. Thus while it cannot be said that financial market pressures necessarily helped promote participation in Thailand and South Korea, wider participation in both countries has helped them deal more effectively and legitimately with the financial crisis.

In Indonesia the opposite is true. The extreme absence of participation has meant that the country is at an impasse over how to get beyond Suharto's New Order, which is responsible for making Indonesia vulnerable to the crisis and which is the prime obstacle to moving forward with legitimacy to restore stability to the economy. The punishments of finance capital may not enhance the prospects for democracy and participation, but democracy and participation appear to enhance the prospects for restabilizing a punished economy.

Notes

1. The July 1997 issue of *Forbes* magazine listed Suharto among the three most wealthy dictators in the world, worth more than $16 billion. The GNP per capita in Indonesia was about $1000 at the beginning of 1997, and dropped to around $300 by the end of the year due to the collapse in the value of the Indonesian rupiah.

2. These benefits have been much more modest than World Bank reports or other writings on Indonesia claim. For a critique of Indonesia's development record, see Winters (1995).

3. With more than 13 000 islands and some 300 ethno-linguistic groups, Indonesia once had the largest Communist party outside a Communist country and was a founding member of the Nonaligned Movement.

4. For a more thorough discussion of this point, see Winters (1996).

5. All figures in this section are from Indonesia's Ministry of Finance, the Central Bureau of Statistics (*Badan Pusat Statistik*), and data supplied by ECONIT, an independent think-tank based in Jakarta.

6. The United States' Overseas Private Investment Corporation (OPIC) terminated Freeport-McMoran's $100 million insurance policy against political risk as of November 1995 because the company was spewing toxic pollutants into two rivers. And this was only part of the problem. Freeport ran into trouble in 1994 and 1995 on human rights grounds for its close cooperation with local members of the Indonesian armed forces, which the company hired privately for security services. Even the watered-down report from Indonesia's official human rights commission said that there have been 'indiscriminate killings, torture, unlawful arrests and arbitrary detention, disappearances, excessive surveillance and obvious destruction of local residents' property' in and around the Freeport mining concession. According to a Catholic bishop who interviewed more than 40 witnesses, people were kicked in the belly, chest, and head by people wearing army boots, beaten with rifle butts, forced to kneel with iron bars behind their knees, and shackled by the thumbs, wrists, and legs. 'Reports by the Catholic Church of Jayapura and the Indonesian Human Rights Commission confirmed numerous instances of torture and murder of local people by the Indonesian military, including one murder that occurred aboard a Freeport bus and torture that occurred at a Freeport security post.' Another respected Catholic organization alleged that 'Freeport security personnel were involved in some of the murders – a charge the company denies' (Bryce, 1996).

   Freeport hired Henry Kissinger (who is on the board of Freeport) and reportedly paid his company a $200 000 retainer and Kissinger himself a fee of $400 000 to lobby OPIC not to cancel the policy. During his 1995 meeting with President Clinton after celebrations at the UN, President Suharto asked that OPIC not to act against Freeport. Clinton declined to get involved. To lead the lobbying effort to reverse the OPIC decision, Freeport hired James Woolsey, a former director of the Central Intelligence Agency. Within Indonesia, Freeport also launched a campaign to cut off USAID and Ford Foundation funding to Indonesian non-governmental organizations (NGOs) that focus on the environment. This campaign, together with OPIC's actions, have helped harden Suharto's stance toward Indonesia's NGOs – one of the few democratic voices brave enough to speak up.

7. The Mexican crisis dealt a severe blow to Indonesia in January of 1995, prompting the central bank to intervene to support the rupiah by buying up hundreds of millions of dollars of the currency. In its 1995 annual report on

the Indonesian economy, the World Bank warned that 'the capital flight of early 1995 was small relative to the total amount of money that could flee the country should a serious crisis of confidence develop' (quoted in Mallet, 1995).

8. The lines of fracture and stress now apparent in the New Order state are linked to these changes, although they also reflect the age of the Suharto regime and its inability to adapt its ideological instruments of control to changing conditions. Casting every critic or opposition movement as Communist-inspired or an underground resurgence of the PKI is only the most obvious example of this. Even in authoritarian Indonesia, newspapers have ridiculed the New Order's tendency to trot out old ghosts and fears in its efforts to maintain exclusive control.

9. These are H.M. Sampoerna (a cigarette manufacturer), Indofood Sukses Makmur (food processing), Indosat (the government telecommunications satellite), Astra (car manufacturer and Toyota partner), Semen Gresik (a cement factory), Bank International Indonesia, and Indocement Tunggal Perkasa (cement).

10. It is worth noting that there need not be a real crisis for the stock market to start its downward spiral. Rumors about and perceptions of crisis are enough. And the sudden crash of the market, even if based on incorrect perceptions of imminent danger, can itself generate a very real crisis.

11. For a discussion of the World Bank's complicity in Jakarta's fraudulent claims regarding poverty reduction, see Winters (1995).

12. Both Edward Gibson and Blanca Heredia make similar points in their recent work on Latin American cases. See Gibson (1997) and Heredia (1996).

13. Investors in Indonesia like to joke that the only thing worse than paying a bribe is paying a bribe to the wrong official.

14. According to an individual who works in a close and official capacity to facilitate American investment in Indonesia, 'Western finance, trade and investment look primarily for stability, not type of government or flavor of capitalism. And Indonesia has been stable,' private correspondence, 25 January, 1998.

15. Confidential interview in Chicago, 9 February 1996. Similar sentiments were expressed by AMCHAM in Thailand when confronted with the prospect of US sanctions against the State Law and Order Restoration Council (SLORC) in Burma. In April 1996, and following immediately on the heels of a unanimous vote on a UN High Commission on Human Rights resolution condemning a consistent pattern of brutal human rights violations in Burma, AMCHAM of Thailand produced a position paper to express the views and interests of capital controllers to officials in Washington. AMCHAM called on the US government to promote business in Burma and to refrain from what it saw as negative policies. 'Restrictive policies or "sanctions" should not be adopted because they will limit contacts and positive influences of US business, government, and individuals in the development of Myanmar and the welfare of its general population,' the paper argued. It went on to blame the western press for exaggerating claims that 'slave labor' was being used to build UNOCAL's overland pipeline to Thailand, and added that 'there is a significant amount of misinformation about conditions in Myanmar.' Significantly, the paper concluded by noting that 'No other nation has adopted or will support such measures. Such policies would directly benefit foreign investors from Singapore, Japan, China, and other countries.' In short, the marketplace of possible investors militates against raising or enforcing a minimum standard of human rights practices.

16. Given the huge obstacle that Suharto himself represents to liberalization in Indonesia, Clinton was foolish to believe Suharto was a true believer in deregulation.
17. This posture was in evidence at Osaka, but it was even more evident in the Asian Free Trade Agreement (AFTA) talks going on within Asia. Indonesia sought to add fifteen items to the list of 'strategic' goods that could remain protected behind high tariffs, to the consternation of Thailand, one of the regions biggest exporters of agricultural products.
18. Dutch investors reacted sharply to their government's insistence on tying economic relations to improvements in human rights in Indonesia. The Suharto government responded by eliminating the Inter-Governmental Group on Indonesia (IGGI) that had been chaired by Amsterdam for two decades, and forming the Consultative Group on Indonesia (CGI) with the World Bank at the helm. It took a visit to Jakarta by Queen Beatrix, the first such visit since Indonesia became an independent country, to calm the ire both of Dutch investors and the Indonesian government. The Indonesians are masters of the surgical strike that sends a powerful message to others, whether at home or abroad, that might want to get out of line.
19. It is important to note that a significant proportion of transnational investment is not in labor-intensive sectors or activities. This does not mean that they tend to adopt a different stance on the question of raising issues of political opening or human rights. Rather, they tend to be either neutral on the question of how democratic or authoritarian a potential investment site is, or silent backers of those investors who have a direct stake in maintaining exploitative conditions.

Bibliography

Bryce, Robert (1996) 'Environment: Struck by a Golden Spear,' *The Guardian*, 17 January, p. 14.

Gibson, Edward (1997) 'The Populist Road to Market Reform: Policy and Electoral Coalitions in Mexico and Argentina,' *World Politics*, 49 (3), April, pp. 339–70.

— (1996) *Class and Conservative Parties: Argentina in Comparative Perspective* (Baltimore, Md.: Johns Hopkins University Press).

Hadar, Leon (1995) 'Clinton Sees Suharto's Support as Vital to Free Trade Plan,' *Business Times*, 30 October, p. 14.

Heredia, Blanca (1996) 'Recasting Political Order: Clientelism and Democratization in Mexico,' unpublished manuscript, CIDE and Northwestern University's Center for International and Comparative Studies, 8 February.

Mallet, Pascal (1995) 'Indonesia Not Immune from Confidence Crisis: World Bank,' *Agence France Presse*, 16 June.

Robison, Richard (1986) *Indonesia: The Rise of Capital* (Sydney: George Allen & Unwin).

Tanzer, Andrew (1995) 'The World's Best Kept Secret,' *Forbes*, 17 July, p. 112.

Winters, Jeffrey A. (1995) 'Suharto's Indonesia: Prosperity and Freedom for the Few,' *Current History*, 94 (596), December, pp. 420–4.

— (1996) *Power in Motion: Capital Mobility and the Indonesian State* (Ithaca: Cornell University Press).

11 Vietnam and Foreign Direct Investment: Speeding Economic Transition or Prolonging the Twilight Zone?

Jonathan Haughton

Since it committed itself to reform in late 1986, Vietnam has made a rapid transition from a planned to a market-driven economy. One of the first concrete steps towards reform was to promulgate a foreign investment law in 1988. The effect has been remarkable; in 1996, foreign investors committed themselves to projects worth $8.8 billion, in an economy with a GDP of $23.1 billion.

These flows give rise to a number of questions. First is the issue of the demand for foreign investment: why did the government of Vietnam decide to seek foreign investment, and how did it go about attracting it? Then there is the supply: why have foreign investors expressed such a keen interest in investing in the country?

The next set of questions are economic in focus. Has the foreign investment added to, or does it substitute for, domestic investment? Does the foreign investment contribute to economic growth? Does it enhance efficiency, or will it drain rents out of the country? Does reliance on such investment raise, or lower, the risk of financial crises? Is foreign investment playing a large role? Is it coming in too fast? Is it hurting exports?

The final group of questions are the broadest in scope. Is foreign direct investment in Vietnam a force for change? What effect does it have on national politics and policymaking? Does it reduce the scope for policy autonomy? Is there any discernible link to democratization? Consonant with the overall themes of the book, this chapter pays particular attention to these questions.

ECONOMIC REFORMS

Vietnam is one of the world's poorest countries, with a per capita GDP approaching about $310. When corrected for differences in purchasing power, Vietnam is probably at a similar level of affluence to Bangladesh, and at about half the level of China and a third of the level of Indonesia (Haughton, forthcoming). Despite its low level of income, Vietnam's social indicators are relatively good, with a life expectancy of 66 years and an adult literacy rate of 88 per cent. Nine out of ten one-year-olds have been immunized against measles. Vietnam today is poorer than Japan, Thailand or Taiwan when those countries began their rapid economic growth, but is at a level comparable to that of Indonesia in 1965 or Guangdong Province of China in 1978.

After independence in 1954, the economy of the North was based on the Soviet/Chinese model of a planned economy, and this model was applied to the South after reunification in 1975. Agriculture had been collectivized in the North in the late 1950s, and this was attempted, albeit with less success, in the South in 1976–77. A campaign against traders and industrialists in 1978 precipitated the exodus of the first wave of boat people. When Chinese aid dried up after the occupation of Cambodia in 1978, the country strengthened its links with the Soviet Union and joined the Council of Mutual Economic Assistance (CMEA).

Economic performance during the first five years after reunification was dismal, with a drop in GDP per capita of almost 2 per cent per year. This led to some efforts at reform in the early 1980s. A contract system was introduced in agriculture, similar in some ways to the Chinese reform of 1978, and this boosted agricultural growth. In industry the 'three-plan system' was instituted, which had the effect of permitting state industrial enterprises to pursue sideline activities. However by 1982 a backlash against the reforms occurred, driven in part by the rise in inflation to 95 per cent in that year, unaccompanied by an adequate adjustment to the salaries of civil servants.

By 1986, inflation had risen to 487 per cent, and incomes hardly rose. After a debate about significant reform, in the press and in the Politburo, the Sixth Party Congress introduced the policy of *Doi Moi* ('renovation'). While earlier change had sought to patch up flaws in the command economy, with *Doi Moi* there was greater willingness to replace, or at least augment, the old system with a new, more market-oriented economic structure.

After the call for *Doi Moi*, reform gathered momentum only slowly. The more relaxed atmosphere, along with the removal of internal trade barriers, led to a blossoming of the informal sector in 1987. The official exchange rate of 18 dong/$, which diverged dramatically from the parallel rate of 425 dong/dollar, was devalued sharply. The most important early reform was Politburo Decree 10 of 5 April 1988, which formally declared that henceforth the household would be the basic economic unit in the rural economy. The monopoly of the cooperatives was ended, and an estimated 200 000 managers lost their jobs. Land-use rights were granted for periods of 15 years.

A liberal law on foreign investment was passed in 1987 and promulgated on 1 January 1988, aiming to entice foreign investment into Vietnam. In September 1988, the State Committee for Cooperation and Investment (SCCI) was formed, to appraise and approve foreign investment projects, and by the end of the year over $370 million worth of such projects had been approved.

The culmination of reform came in March 1989, with a series of radical changes which formally swept away most of the remains of the command economy. Almost all administered prices were abolished, thereby ending the dual price structure; the remaining prices were generally raised to close to the free market level. Budgetary subsidies to state-owned enterprises were eliminated, as were the rice subsidies provided to civil servants and their families. The exchange rate was further devalued, and moved closer to the parallel rate; the two were essentially aligned from mid-1990 onwards. The growth of the money supply was sharply cut. Most import quotas and export subsidies were removed. Later in 1989 Vietnam withdrew fully from Cambodia and demobilized about half a million soldiers.

The results were spectacular, as Table 11.1 shows. Agricultural output rose 6.4 per cent in 1989, and the country went from being a rice importer to the world's third-largest exporter. Inflation collapsed from 308 per cent in 1988 to 35 per cent in 1989. The service sector rebounded, and coupled with the growth in agriculture these overpowered the shrinkage which occurred in most industrial sectors.

After 1989, the pace of economic reform was inevitably slower. Foreign and joint-venture banks were permitted from June 1991, as were limited liability companies. The government budget deficits were small from 1990 onwards, and a more modern (if still complex) tax structure was put in place. state-owned enterprises were rationalized, with as many as a million workers losing their jobs in the year to August 1991. A new constitution came into effect in April 1992 and paved the way for elections to an increasingly vigorous and vocal National Assembly in July 1992, with the most recent elections in July 1997. The foreign investment law has been revised periodically in the light of experience, with the most recent changes approved by the National Assembly in March 1997. The incentives for foreign direct investment in Vietnam compare favorably with those of its neighbors (Thien 1995, table 1).

The transition period was turbulent in other ways. A run on the credit cooperatives in 1990 led to the collapse of most of them, and of an estimated 2000 small enterprises which relied on them for working capital. By 1991, the country, with almost 70 million people, boasted a grand total of just 770 private industrial enterprises. Another shock occurred as a result of the ending of Soviet aid, which had peaked in 1989 at 5 per cent of Vietnam's GDP, and ceased completely in 1991. Vietnam's traditional export markets

Table 11.1 Vietnam: selected indicators of recent economic performance

	1976–80	1980–85	1986	1987	1988	1989	1990	1991	1992	1993	1994	1995	1996
Annual Growth Rates % p.a.													
Real GDP	0.4	3.5	3.3	3.9	5.1	8.0	5.1	6.0	8.6	8.1	8.8	9.5	9.3
Real GDP/capita	-1.8	1.6	0.9	1.4	2.6	5.5	2.8	3.6	6.1	5.6	6.6	7.3	7.3
Industrial output [GDP after 1989]	0.6	9.5	6.2	10.0	14.3	2.3	10.7	9.9	14.6	12.1	12.9	13.3	14.1
Agricultural output [GDP after 1989]	2.0	5.2	4.8	0.3	4.3	6.4	1.7	2.2	7.1	3.8	3.9	3.8	4.8
Inflation (Dec–Dec)	22	74	487	301	308	35	67	67	18	5	14	13	5
Levels of Output													
GDP, 1989 dong (bn)			20,579	21,395	22,497	24,308	27,014	31,286	33,991	36,735	39,982	43,797	47,888
GDP, current dong (bn)			595	2,863	15,374	28,226	41,829	76,707	110,535	136,571	170,258	222,840	254,500
GDP, $bn			1.40	2.25	3.07	5.84	7.71	8.70	9.79	12.96	15.47	20.20	23.10
Population (mid-year, '000)			60,249	61,750	63,263	64,774	66,233	67,774	69,405	71,026	72,510	73,962	75,355

255

Table 11.1 Continued

	1976–80	1980–85	1986	1987	1988	1989	1990	1991	1992	1993	1994	1995	1996
Exchange rate (dong/$) Official (mid-year)			18	225	900	3900	5150	11000	11290	10536	11007	11034	11018
Market (mid-year)			425	1270	5000	4832	5425	8820	11290	10536	11007	11034	11018
Electricity (m kwh)	3576	4481	5683	6213	6955	7948	8790	9307	9818	10851	12476	14665	16996
Cement ('000 t)	749	1018	1526	1665	1954	2088	2534	3127	3926	4849	5371	5828	6251
Grain output/cap (kg/yr rice equivalent)	169	203	198	185	201	216	211	211	227	233	235	243	247
Official hard currency exports ($m)	94	221	350	366	448	1138	1352‖	2087	2581	2985	4251	5220	7100
of which: oil				30	79	200	390	581	820	825	976	1130	1300
Official imports ($m)	512	449	509	523	804	879	1373	2338	2541	3924	5834	7520	11000
Number of visitors ('000)			7	40	60	187‖	136	188	308	528	941	1357	1600

8

256

Table 11.1 Continued

	1976–80	1980–85	1986	1987	1988	1989	1990	1991	1992	1993	1994	1995	1996
Foreign direct investment pledges ($m)	0	0	0	0	372	583	839	13 23	2168	3170	3765	7 620	8820
FDI disbursements ($m p.a.)	0	0	0	0	0	100	120	220	260	832	1048	1 782	

Notes: GDP series revised from 1991 onwards, so levels not comparable (but growth rates are accurate). Double vertical bars denote break in series or change in source of data.
Sources: Vietnam: General Statistical Office, *Statistical Yearbook 1996* (Statistical Publishing House, Hanoi) and earlier issues; *Vietnam Investment Review*, various issues. *Vietnam Economic Times*, various issues. IMF, *Vietnam – Recent Economic Developments* (Washington DC, 1996 and previous issues). Economist Intelligence Unit, *Vietnam Country Report*, various issues since 4th quarter 1995.). Economist Intelligence Unit, *Vietnam Country Report*, various issues since 4th quarter 1995.

in the Soviet Union and Eastern Europe also collapsed, and the country had to scramble for new markets.

By 1992 the economy was able to settle down to the business of growth. This it has done with great success, with GDP growing by an average of 8.9 per cent annually over the past five years. Since population growth is only about 2.1 per cent annually, this represents a remarkable two-fifths increase in per capita GDP since 1992. Inflation has been kept below 20 per cent annually. Exports have boomed, more than quintupling since 1990, albeit with some help from oil, which constitutes about a fifth of the total.[1]

One of the more surprising features of the recent growth is that the fastest-growing major part of the economy has been the centrally-owned state-owned enterprises, especially in heavy industries such as cement, steel and electricity, where output almost tripled between 1986 and 1995 (see Table 11.1). This is surprising in the sense that these sectors were favored under the command economy, and so one might have expected them to wane with the shift to a market-driven economy. There are a number of possible explanations for the phenomenon, which parallels what occurred during the initial years of economic reform in China. Some major projects, in which investment took place prior to reform, came on stream after *Doi Moi*; the investment boom of the early 1990s led to a high demand for the products of heavy industry, including cement and steel; state-owned enterprises may have received favorable treatment, particularly in the form of easier access to credit; and many enterprises teamed up with foreign firms, which combined local idle capacity and labor skills with modest amounts of technology and managerial expertise to yield large increases in output (and quality). Something similar occurred in Guangdong province during the first decade after the 1978 reforms (Vogel, 1989). The most interesting feature of this is that foreign investment in such businesses has had an immediate impact. Clearly the scale and scope of such investment calls for further attention, and to this we now turn.

FOREIGN INVESTMENT: THE FACTS

Information on the amount of money *committed* to new foreign investment projects is readily available. For a variety of reasons, however, the sums committed greatly overstate the actual inflows into foreign investment projects.[2] These realized inflows typically amount to about a quarter of the commitments in any given year; estimates of both are shown at the bottom of Table 11.1.

The most striking feature of the amounts pledged to foreign investment projects is that the sums have increased without interruption since 1988, reaching $8.82 billion in 1996. Given that total GDP in 1996 was $23.1 billion, this is a remarkably large amount (38 per cent of GDP) which, if implemented, will represent a degree of international penetration of the Vietnamese economy which is large by any contemporary or historical standard. Even the realized foreign exchange inflows are large, representing 9.4 per cent of GDP in 1995, or about 35 per cent of total investment. When combined with the domestic contributions to joint ventures, almost half of all the investment in Vietnam is currently taking place in foreign-invested projects.

Comparison with China

The importance of foreign investment in Vietnam may be compared with that of China, and this forms the basis for the recent analysis by Freeman (1994, see also Pearson, 1991 and La Croix *et al.* 1995). China began its economic reforms about a decade before Vietnam, and has not moved as far or as fast as Vietnam, but both countries have achieved similar success in the form of rapid economic growth and a massive reduction in poverty. China also opened up parts of its economy early on in the reform process, and extended a welcome to foreign direct investment. Both countries are now grappling with the challenge of building the institutions – property rights, prudential bank regulation, contract law, and the like – that will sustain rapid economic growth.

Figure 11.1 is key to the comparison, and shows annual foreign investment commitments (as a per centage of GDP) for the two countries. Several points emerge clearly. First, far more foreign investment has been pledged to ventures in Vietnam than in China, when the amounts are measured relative to GDP. Total pledged investment in China did not exceed 2 per cent of GDP between 1979 and 1990, while in Vietnam it has never been less than 7 per cent since foreign investment was permitted in 1988. The profiles are shown in Figure 11.1, where the rise in (committed) foreign investment in China is seen to be of recent origin. The high levels of investment pledges, relative to GDP, for Vietnam also carry a risk; if macroeconomic or other policies were to deteriorate, the stream of pledges could dry up, and economic growth could quickly stall. In effect Vietnamese economic policy has become hostage to the strong desire to attract foreign investment; this is not necessarily bad, but I return to the point below.

A second difference between the cases of Vietnam and China is that the typical project is far larger in Vietnam than in China, running to about $16 million (1988–May 1997) in the former and barely over $1 million in the latter. Even if one allows that many overseas Vietnamese may be quietly investing in unreported ventures, the difference remains and is striking. One explanation is that much of the investment in China consists of small ventures by Hong Kong entrepreneurs, who know China and can (and do) operate there even on a small scale. Most of the foreign investment flowing

Figure 11.1 Annual pledged foreign investment as per cent of GDP: China and Vietnam

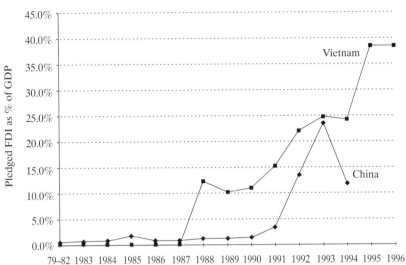

into Vietnam is going into joint ventures with state-owned enterprises; as a legacy of the period of planned economy, many of these enterprises are relatively large and are able to bring substantial assets (especially land) to the table. Moreover until investing in Vietnam becomes more convenient, only large projects may be able to bear the substantial upfront fixed costs which appear to be needed.

The third difference between the two countries is that about 60 per cent of the foreign investment in China is routed through Hong Kong. This contrasts sharply with the Vietnamese case, where no single country accounts for more than a fifth of the total. As of May 1997, the main sources of investment commitments were Singapore (19 per cent), Taiwan (14 per cent), Hong Kong (13 per cent), Japan (11 per cent), European Union countries (10 per cent), other ASEAN countries (9 per cent), South Korea (9 per cent) and the United States (4 per cent). The most important consequence of this diversity is that foreign investment commitments to Vietnam appear to be steadier than in China, and leave Vietnam less vulnerable to the passing whims or fashions in one or the other investor country.

The Pattern of Foreign Investment

The great bulk of the foreign investment originates from East and Southeast Asia, with just over half coming from the four Asian dragons (Taiwan,

Hong Kong, Singapore, and South Korea). The rapid increase in wages in these countries has prompted them to move the labor-intensive and less technologically advanced parts of their production overseas; while China is a tempting location, there is interest in diversifying, and Vietnam provides a convenient platform for such activity. A corollary is that foreign investment in Vietnam has moved remarkably quickly into production for export, 'funding the emergence of a rapid export-oriented growth pattern very early in the Vietnamese development process' (Fforde, 1994, p. 51).

Japan, whose economy generates 12 per cent of world GDP, accounts for just 11 per cent of foreign investment commitments. It surprises some observers that the Japanese presence is not larger. A similar pattern is observed in the case of foreign investment in China, with a Japanese share of about 10 per cent (Kamath, 1990; Xiaofang, 1990). We speculate that many Japanese companies find it difficult to compete, especially with firms from the nearby Dragons, in the low-technology activities which still characterize much of the foreign investment in China and Vietnam. Historical animosities between Japan and its East Asian neighbors may also play a role.

As in China, much of the initial investment in Vietnam went into natural resources, which in the Vietnamese case consist mainly of oil and gas. As opportunities dwindled in this field, investors moved on to investments in industry (46 per cent of all commitments as of May 1987), the now-saturated hotel and luxury housing sector (27 per cent) and, most recently, industrial zones (14 per cent). Less than 2 per cent of foreign investment has flowed into agriculture and forestry projects, and just 4 per cent into transport and communications, despite government urging.

An important feature is that the bulk of the investment has flowed into sectors which produce tradeable goods and services, or sectors where there is substantial competition (such as tourism). In such cases investors have to be mindful of the need to be efficient, and to be able to turn a profit at world prices. This contrasts with foreign investment which is lured to a country by import barriers, and aims to supply the protected, and high-price, domestic market; in such a situation foreign investment, by siphoning resources out of a country, may even be immizerizing (Fry, 1993). So far, Vietnam appears to have avoided this trap, but the recent easing of access to foreign exchange for foreign investors producing for the domestic market, coupled with some high and uncertain tariff barriers, runs the risk of attracting capital into inefficient activities in the future, moderated only by the likely continued vigour of smuggling.

Foreign investment commitments are distributed very unevenly across the major regions of Vietnam. Over 53 per cent of all pledged investment is destined for the Southeast region, which consists essentially of Ho Chi Minh City and its hinterland, but also includes the off-shore oil and gas fields of Vung Tau-Ba Ria. Since 1993 the predominance of Ho Chi Minh City in attracting foreign investment has waned, as foreign firms have been attracted to (or steered toward) Hanoi and Haiphong in the Red River Delta region of northern Vietnam. This is important, because a growing north-south gap would risk widening the major political, social and economic fault-line in Vietnam. The rest of the country, accounting for over half of GDP and almost 70 per cent of the population, is scheduled to receive just 12 per cent of foreign investment.

The concentration of foreign investment in the three major cities is not surprising, but it serves to exacerbate the existing income inequalities, particularly to the extent that it accretes in the comparatively affluent Ho Chi Minh City. On the other hand Chinese experience shows that over time investors spread their activities geographically, in order to avoid the congested and expensive cities. Indeed this is already happening in Vietnam, where investors in manufacturing are steering clear of the high rents and elevated labor costs of Ho Chi Minh City. Provinces such as Dong Nai and Song Be are also competing successfully for investors, offering reduced red tape and readier access to land.

UNDERSTANDING FOREIGN INVESTMENT IN VIETNAM

Why the Demand for Foreign Investment?

Not every country pursues foreign investment as vigorously as does the Socialist Republic of Vietnam. For instance Phongpaichit (1990) notes that Malaysia, Indonesia and Thailand were reluctant to welcome foreign investment prior to the mid-1980s. So what impelled, and continues to impel, this strong demand for foreign investment?

The answer lies, at least initially, in the change of heart which accompanied *Doi Moi*. It was recognized that Vietnam was falling behind its neighbors, and would need to boost domestic investment, acquire more up-to-date technology and know-how, develop its natural resources more efficiently, promote exports in order to earn foreign exchange, and create more jobs. Foreign investment was seen as a major contributor to all these goals.

Having set out to attract foreign investment, how did Vietnam do it? The first stage was to promulgate the Foreign Investment Law in 1988 and to set up the SCCI. The law was refined substantially and a new version came into effect in 1993 (*Saigon Times*, 4–10 March 1993). The law sets out the rights of investors, guarantees against nationalization, stipulates the tax regime and the main incentives, sets out the rules governing access to foreign exchange, and defines the role and functions of the supervisory SCCI.

However it is important to note that a Foreign Investment Law, while no doubt necessary, is unlikely to be sufficient unless many other pieces of the puzzle are in place, as experience in Laos and Mongolia shows. The government of Vietnam established its credibility in the macroeconomic arena by liberalizing prices and the exchange rate, and by taming hyperinflation. It has also shown a willingness to continue economic reform, with a land law which allows longer-lived usufruct rights, a new civil code, and more generous tax rules on imported inputs. Vietnam has moved faster and further than China in most of these areas.

This is not to underestimate the serious obstacles which remain. Investors complain of excessive red tape, of the need to get permission from too many levels of government, of an overvalued exchange rate, of corruption, of the need to hire personnel through labor bureaux, of changing rules and regulations, of 'unfair' competition from favored state-owned enterprises, and of unclear or varying taxes. As recently as 1994 it was generally accepted that two years were required between the identification of an industrial project and initial production for foreign investment firms, compared to one year for domestic firms. The reform-minded Prime Minister has since introduced changes aimed at simplifying the process, and Vietnam may soon reach the stage where most of the problems are those which face *all* investors, and not foreign investors alone.

Has Foreign Investment Lived up to Expectations?

Perhaps the first question which an economist might ask is whether foreign investment really adds to total investment. Starting with the national accounting identity

$$I = S + (T-G) + (IM-X)$$

one notes that investment (I) is financed by domestic private savings (S), government savings ($=$ net tax revenue minus spending on goods and services $= T - G$), and foreign savings ($=$ the *deficit* on the current account of the balance of payments). If S and ($T - G$) remain the same, then additional foreign investment will be reflected in a higher current account deficit, and will add to total investment. This outcome is not a foregone conclusion; if foreign investment merely takes the place of domestically-financed investment, then total investment will not change.

In a recent econometric study, Maxwell Fry (1993) found that foreign direct investment in five East and Southeast Asian countries added to overall investment, dollar for dollar, over the period 1966–88. On the other hand, in the 11 other countries in his sample, additional foreign direct investment did not raise overall investment; in part this arose because extensive privatization of state-owned enterprises, in Latin America and elsewhere, led to an inflow of foreign direct investment but little additional overall investment.

The data are too weak to permit a formal application of Fry's approach to Vietnam, but the underlying conditions in Vietnam are very similar to those in the other East and Southeast Asian countries in his sample. Moreover the evidence shows a substantial rise in the investment rate, from about 14 per cent of GDP in 1991 to about 28 per cent in 1996 (Vietnam: GSO, 1997). It is even conceivable that foreign investment may raise domestic investment more than proportionally, as it prompts the government to provide complementary investments such as roads, and provides an incentive for local firms to provided inputs or supply goods and services to the new employees. Vietnam is now seen as an attractive place for anyone – domestic or foreign – to invest; Fry argues that where the rules of the game and the pace of development make investment attractive in general, then foreign investment will want a piece of this action too, and this may now be an appropriate characterization of the situation in Vietnam.

Some are disappointed by the amount of realized foreign investment, arguing that its effect has been marginal, and barely worth the fuss. By the end of 1996 enterprises with foreign investment directly employed about 0.6 per cent of the labor force, or roughly 200 000 workers and probably generated no more than 10 per cent of GDP. While true, these understate the contribution of foreign investment, to the training of managers, to the transfer of technology, and to the effect which it is having on energizing domestic firms. These external benefits from foreign investment are also evident in China, and constitute the strongest argument in favor of welcoming such investment.

Why the Supply of Foreign Investment?

Why have investors shown such an interest in Vietnam? As documented above, Vietnam has proved to be relatively much more successful than China in attracting pledges, and even actual disbursements, of foreign direct investment.

The traditional answer is to point to the economic virtues of Vietnam, at least from the perspective of a potential investor (for example *Saigon Times*, 15–21 April 1993, p. 13). The workforce is young, hardworking, has a solid basic education, and is cheap. The country is located in the center of the fastest-growing region of the planet. The cost of production in the nearby Dragons has risen to the point where many industries have become uncompetitive, so they must move or die; and while China, even saber rattling, is an attractive destination, it is seen as unwise to put all one's eggs in that basket. In this context it is worth noting that much of Taiwan's investment in Vietnam has come from firms controlled by the Kuomintang, and a significant proportion of investment from Singapore has originated from state-owned enterprises such as the Keppel Group. Much of this investment has actually gone into developing Industrial Zones, which in turn are expected to entice more companies from the country of origin.

At least as important is the perception that the government is committed to staying on the track of reform, and of maintaining a relatively open economy. The root of this commitment to economic growth may be the need to maintain the legitimacy of the Communist Party, whose nationalist credentials no longer suffice and whose economic leadership during the period of the planned economy has been discredited. The party is not monolithic, however, and the powers of leadership are shared with the government and, increasingly, the National Assembly. Since the death of Ho Chi Minh in 1969, there has been no dominant leader, and major decisions are arrived at by seeking consensus at the top. This may not make for rapid decision making, but has the advantage that the resulting decisions are more likely to have staying power.

Similar considerations have led foreign investors into China. First Guangdong province was allowed to experiment with market mechanisms and to open its doors to outsiders. Hong Kong capital was attracted to the neighboring province because of the cheap, skilled labor. In due course other provinces began to compete for foreign investment, by streamlining the procedures and providing assurances that foreign capital would be welcome.

Is Foreign Investment a Force for Economic Change?

The desire to ignite economic growth led the government of Vietnam to undertake a series of important economic reforms. Since it would have been difficult to envisage rapid growth without at least some foreign investment to bring capital, managerial expertise, technology, and access to foreign markets, it was necessary to design a structure which foreign investors would find attractive. So initially at least, it was the desire to attract foreign investment, rather than the investment *per se*, which helped shape the reform agenda.

Once the foreign investment genie was let out of the bottle, the dynamic changed. The special case of oil and gas aside, most of the initial investment was in joint ventures *with state-owned enterprises*. Indeed joint ventures with private firms were not allowed until 1994, wholly foreign enterprises were initially discouraged, and foreign investors preferred to work with firms which they believed could cut through the red tape and get things done more quickly. The result has been to greatly strengthen the competitiveness and efficiency of the state-owned sector; over the past five years the labor productivity of state-owned industrial firms has doubled.

One might have expected success to breed success, as reformers pointed to the achievements of foreign investment and made the case for further liberalization. Quite the opposite seems to have occurred, with a reaction which is blocking some important further changes. These newly-strengthened firms typically have close links with the ministries, the Communist Party, and local officials. At best this helps them to operate effectively. At worst it encourages them to seek special favors in the form of privileged trading arrangements (as has occurred in the markets for rice and fertilizer) or impediments which make it difficult for private competitors to emerge.

The most dramatic example of reaction is seen in the current status of privatization, which the Communist Party opposes on ideological grounds, and some oppose because of concerns about a possible increase in unemployment. This aversion is shared by the managers of most state-owned enterprises, whose influence has been strengthened by their alliance with foreign capital. By pointing to big improvements in the quantity and quality of the output of state firms, they are in a position to cast doubt on the need to privatize. By and large the bureaucracy also resists privatization, fearing that this would reduce its ability to extract side-payments. The growth of corruption has prompted the government to introduce a program of 'administrative reform,' which despite occasional successes is generally pursued with more rhetoric than vigor, although the recent death sentences in 1997 meted out in the $40 million Legamex scandal may represent a substantial toughening of policy in this area.

For a while the reformers were able to make the case for equitization – a Vietnamese version of privatization which would first form joint stock companies with most of the shares held by the government and workers – but by early 1996 only three firms had actually been privatized. In late 1995, Do Quoc Sam, the then Minister of Planning and Investment and an active reformer, announced that 30 more companies were ready for equitization, out of about 6000 state enterprises; later in the year another minister announced a plan to privatize about 2 per cent (that is, 120) of state enterprises in 1996 (Economist Intelligence Unit, 1996, 1st quarter). In fact, no additional firms were equitized in 1996, despite continued prodding by the reform-minded Prime Minister Vo Van Kiet and some pressure from the IMF.

A corollary of the glacial pace of privatization has been the slow movement towards the establishment of a stock market, because of a shortage of potential stock offerings. Originally scheduled to be introduced in 1995, it is now unlikely to be in place before the year 2000. China has also moved very slowly towards privatization. Only at the September 1997 Party Congress in Beijing did it show some enthusiasm for divesting many of the inefficient state-owned firms, and it remains to be seen how quickly this will actually be achieved.

Delays such as these risk pushing Vietnam into what Dwight Perkins has called the twilight zone, where the economy would be caught between plan and market, half-reformed. Having made enough changes to ignite economic growth, the danger is one of complacency, and of believing that further changes are not so urgent. The consequence would be slower economic growth and a period of economic underachievement.

It would be wrong to leave the impression that Vietnam will inevitably find itself in the twilight zone, because the reformers have been active too. In an effort to break the close links between enterprises and their sponsoring ministries or provinces, the prime minister's office has encouraged the formation of larger conglomerates. The idea may be to encourage a form of competitive state capitalism, although it runs the very real danger that small, largely private, newcomers will be squeezed out. And Do Quoc Sam has argued that the need to attract foreign investment requires tackling the 'primitive infrastructure, the imperfect legal environment, officialdom, smuggling and corruption' (BBC Monitoring Summary of World Broadcasts, 2 February 1996).

The private business sector is remarkably small and has a strong ethnic Chinese presence. The ban, until recently, on joint ventures between foreign and private firms, was rationalized on the grounds that the local firms were too weak. But one effect has been to inhibit the reemergence of a Chinese business class. Phongpaichit argues that the rules applicable to foreign investment in Malaysia and Indonesia (but not Thailand) prior to about 1985 had a similar effect (Phongpaichit, 1990).

So far the argument has been that the desire to attract foreign investment prompted considerable liberalization, but that limits to change have emerged, originating in part from the very people most helped by this investment. But there is one final countervailing effect. A government which wants to *continue* to attract foreign direct investment has very little room for policy maneuver in the long run, despite the fact that foreign direct investment may not be as mobile as most other forms of international capital flows. The reason is not hard to see. Suppose that the government were to make a policy mistake, such as printing too much money. Its credibility as an economic manager would be undermined, and foreign investors would hesitate to propose new projects, in addition to delaying the implementation of those in the pipeline. Quite rapidly the inflow of foreign exchange would shrink, forcing a greater devaluation than would otherwise have been required. It could require some years of economic prudence before the credibility of policy makers would be restored.

Is Foreign Investment a Force for Political Change?

The conventional wisdom now holds that economic growth ultimately leads to political liberalization and democratization. Foreign direct investment, by helping promote growth, might thus be expected to hasten this process. Yet Vietnam remains a one-party state where the Communist Party is actively involved in the day-to-day running of government and the conduct of foreign policy. Dissidents are frequently jailed. The press is entirely state-owned, and an effort is being made to separate 'the fresh air from the dust' which blows in on the Internet. Given the small size of the private sector, most non-farming households depend on the state for their livelihood, and so are vulnerable to pressure to remain quiet. Family planning measures are barely short of coercive. It would seem that Vietnam has been insulated from pressures to democratize.

The superficial view is deceptive. Under the surface, political change is occurring rapidly. In recent elections, non-party candidates were permitted to stand, and a few were elected. The party is trying to encourage younger people to join the party, with some success. The National Assembly is increasingly vocal. The prime minister has said he wants the party to distance itself from the daily business of government, and to some extent this has occurred. The prison terms given to dissidents are frequently light (less than two years), and amnesties are common on auspicious occasions such as anniversaries or the Tet holiday. There has also been a large expansion of civil society, with the growth of associations such as those dedicated to environmental and architectural protection, and the reemergence of the churches (especially Buddhist and Christian) as important institutions.

The flexibility of the party has its limits however, and in the months prior to the Eighth Party Congress in June 1996 it moved to reassert its leading political role with two campaigns (see Economist Intelligence Unit, 1996, 1st quarter). One campaign, launched in January 1996, targeted 'social evils,' including prostitution, gambling, drug abuse, violent crime, and pornographic videos, all of which are seen as by-products of the more liberal economic environment. Hundreds of bars were closed, thousands of videos steamrolled in public, and the press told to emphasize good news. The other campaign, which began in December 1995, was aimed at 'foreign influences.' In a number of articles in *Nhan Dan* (the Party newspaper) and *Quan Do Nhan Dan* (the official army newspaper), the United States was accused of leading a 'soft and invisible attack wave,' and of seeking to effect democratic change by promoting 'peaceful evolution' and economic liberalization. The most visible effect of the campaign was the sudden enforcement of an old rule which requires Vietnamese words to be at least as large as foreign words on billboards and signs. In January and February of 1996 hundreds of signs were taken down, repainted, or covered in plastic sheeting in order to comply with the law.

The real target of the campaign was not foreign investors, but rather Prime Minister Vo Van Kiet and the reformers, who favor the development of the private sector and wish to see the party take a more minor role in public affairs. The accusers are the conservatives, who may be genuinely appalled by social evils and foreign influences, but who also see their influence waning. If the timing of the campaign was designed to influence the choice of a successor to Vo Van Kiet, then it failed, because his successor Phan Van Khai has even more robust credentials as an economic reformer.

While the reformers welcome foreign investment, the fact that the conservatives have not attacked it calls for some explanation. Now that Vietnam is no longer an international pariah, and is at peace, the party has been forced to turn to other sources of legitimacy. The most convincing of these is its claim to have brought rapid economic growth, and associated improvements in the standard of living for the bulk of the population. But this growth has only occurred since the country turned away from central planning and toward a market-oriented model of development, in which foreign investment plays a central role. The Communist Party in Vietnam, like its counterpart in China, needs capitalist foreign direct investment. But it remains suspicious, and General Secretary Do Muoi said in January 1996 that 'as Lenin taught, we are not afraid of capitalist enterprises, but of not being able to supervise and control them.'

Even though Vietnam remains very poor, and even though it is likely to remain a single-party state for at least a decade or two more, political change is occurring relatively quickly. A similar process was observed in China, with the democracy movement of 1989 coming little more than a decade after market reforms began in 1978. Without opening to foreign capital and markets, and without the growth rates that these have helped to bring, it is hard to believe that changes of this magnitude in Vietnam, or China, would have occurred so fast.

Does Foreign Direct Investment Foster Democracy in Vietnam?

In Chapters 1 and 14 of this volume, Leslie Elliott Armijo theorizes about the effect of the type of capital inflows on the development of procedural political ('liberal') democracy. Stripped to its basics, her thesis is that the shift of capital flows from aid towards portfolio investments is 'not entirely favorable for the oft heralded turn to democracy by developing countries in the late twentieth century'. The main reason is that portfolio investment carries a high balance-of-payments risk, strengthens the hand of big business (which tends to favor only limited political liberalization), and fosters 'neoliberal reforms' which are seen as weakening some of the pro-democracy actors.

She argues that foreign direct investment, which stereotypically comes from private companies and goes into private enterprises, has the virtues of giving a significant boost to economic growth, and of having low volatility and hence a low risk of leading to a balance of payments crisis. It tends to increase the influence of foreign business in the host country, and may indirectly boost support for the host country government; it also carries with it some pressure for the government to undertake economic liberalization.

Does this favor the transition to democracy? Armijo's answer is 'maybe'. On the one hand foreign-invested enterprises tend to favor some political liberalization, such as the free flow of information and the unrestrained movement of labor. On the other hand the presence of such enterprises strengthens the legitimacy of the incumbent government which, if it is authoritarian, may serve to delay the transition to a more complete form of liberal democracy.

With some modifications, these conclusions apply to the case of Vietnam. While most foreign direct investment comes from private firms, a significant proportion originates from state-owned companies abroad. Singapore's state-owned Keppel Group, and firms owned by Taiwan's Kuomintang, have invested heavily in industrial estates in Vietnam, in effect creating platforms for private firms from their countries. This gives foreign governments an economic stake in Vietnam, and is likely to color the official relations between the countries involved.

Until recently, most of the foreign investment flowing into Vietnam has gone into joint ventures with state-owned companies. The reason is straightforward: domestically-owned private firms are few and small, and the government has discouraged the development of 100 per cent foreign-owned firms. As a practical matter is it far easier to set up and develop a business in Vietnam if one has a local partner that can deal with obtaining land-use rights, permits and licenses. Joint ventures with state-owned businesses create a constituency within government for maintaining an atmosphere conducive to its businesses.

The difficulty here is that the government has two conflicting roles. As a participant in business it has an interest in making life difficult for potential competitors. But as an arbiter in the economic game its role is to encourage competition, set rules, and maintain a level playing field for the various economic actors. The danger is that this tension can result in incomplete economic reform: for instance, tariff barriers may remain high to protect established firms, only state-owned companies may receive allocations of quota for exporting garments to Europe, trading permits may be granted mainly to state-owned firms, and bank credit may favor state-owned firms because of their implicit government guarantee. Rules such as these tend to entrench the state-owned sector, ultimately inhibiting growth. While growth *per se* may not be related to democratization, affluence clearly is. Slower growth postpones the arrival of affluence and the liberal democracy with which it is almost always associated.

BEYOND FOREIGN DIRECT INVESTMENT

Foreign direct investment is easily the single largest source of foreign capital for Vietnam, financing about three quarters of the trade deficit in 1995 and about three-fifths of the official $3.9 billion trade deficit in 1996. This still leaves a substantial, and rapidly growing, gap which is covered by other sources of finance. Vietnam has no stock exchange, and the quantity of bonds that have been issued by government and enterprises is minuscule. Thus portfolio investment by foreigners is almost nonexistent. However three other sources of finance – remittances, aid, and short-term bank loans, are of some consequence.

Remittances

In 1995, Vietnam officially received $443 million in private transfers, mainly remittances from overseas Vietnamese (Viet Kieu). The actual flow is believed to be closer to $1 billion annually. According to information from the Vietnam Living Standards Survey of 1992–93, households who receive remittances from abroad spend most of the receipts on consumption (including school fees); these flows also have the effect of making the distribution of income less equal (Tam and Vinh, forthcoming). Perhaps in an effort to reduce this inequality, the government began to collect a 5 per cent tax on remittances in early 1997, but withdrew the tax a few months later when the official inflow halved. There is growing evidence that many overseas Vietnamese have invested in small projects, generally avoiding the standard licensing process required of all foreign investors.

The government is ambivalent about the inflow of remittances. On the one hand the money is welcome, and even more so if emigrés return with skills and technology too. On the other hand many overseas Vietnamese are stridently opposed to the current regime, and thus all overseas Vietnamese are considered somewhat politically suspect. There are about a million Viet Kieu in the United States, and many of them have been very politically active, and particularly successful in drawing attention to human rights problems in Vietnam. This in turn is likely to delay the granting of most-favored-nation status by the United States to Vietnam in the foreseeable future. The desire to maintain the inflow colors Vietnam's foreign policy as it seeks to soothe any ruffled feathers in the Viet Kieu community.

Aid

According to the Public Investment Plan published by the government in 1996, Vietnam expects to need $41 billion in investment between 1996 and 2000. Of this, $20 billion is to be financed from overseas, through foreign direct investment ($13 billion) and foreign aid ($7 billion). Over the last few years Vietnam has been one of the darlings of the donor community, attracting pledges of $1.9 billion of aid in 1994, $2.3 billion in 1995 and $2.4 billion in 1996. A little more than a quarter of the pledged amount has actually been disbursed, but the pace of disbursements has been quickening and rose to about $800 million in 1996 – well below the roughly $2 billion in disbursed foreign investment, but still a respectable 3.5 per cent of GDP and four times the level of 1991.

According to the figures published by the OECD's Development Assistance Committee, which may exaggerate the actual net flow, aid flows in 1994 came to $897 million; of this $645 million (72 per cent) was in the form of grants, and $586 million (65 per cent) came from bilateral donors. For the last few years the main donor has been Japan, which pledged a third of the total aid promised in 1996, and provides most of its aid in the form of low-interest loans which have a relatively modest grant element. Japan is far from being the largest investor in Vietnam, but its aid to Vietnam appears to be part of an effort to win other friends in the region, particularly countries that might stand as allies against China. Other important bilateral donors include Sweden (which has been a donor to Vietnam for many years), France, Italy and Germany.

The international financial institutions have been important in influencing economic policy, particularly the World Bank (which has pledged subsidized loans) and the IMF (which is not a *donor* in any meaningful sense, but agreed to a three-year Enhanced Structural Adjustment Facility (ESAF) in 1994). After several years of praising Vietnam's economic performance, both the World Bank and IMF began to take a markedly harder line by the summer of 1997. The World Bank is balking at extending a Structural Adjustment credit unless Vietnam commits itself to important further reforms, particularly the privatization of most of the state-owned enterprises. The IMF has postponed disbursing the next tranche of the ESAF pending more fundamental reforms. All of the IMF loan, and much of the money advanced by the World Bank, is fungible, and contributes importantly to the government budget. The loss of these funds would be more keenly felt by the government than much of the bilateral aid, a fact that gives the Bretton Woods institutions more leverage. Apart from a highly visible training project, the United States does not yet provide significant aid to Vietnam; if and when it does, the aid is likely to be conditional on visible progress in the human rights arena.

Short-term Capital

Net inflows of short-term capital were estimated at $124 million in 1994 and $311 million in 1995, and may have risen to as much as $1 billion in 1996 if one includes letters of credit used for trade finance. Sometime in 1996 importers found that they could get ready access to letters of credit and other forms of finance for imports, and rapidly tapped this new source of funds. One consequence was an import binge which raised the trade deficit to a remarkable $3.9 billion (17 per cent of GDP); this borrowing also delayed downward pressure on the dong, which became increasingly over-valued by late 1996.

The borrowing binge came to a rapid halt in early 1997 when a number of domestic firms were unable to repay their letters of credit and the leading state-owned bank expressed reluctance to stand by the letters of credit it had guaranteed. This was a serious blow to the confidence of the banking system. The dong was allowed to depreciate by about 5 per cent, the government imposed a temporary ban on a range of significant imports in May 1997, and access to further letters of credit was tightened. Although the immediate sense of crisis has passed, the financial system remains edgy and very fragile. The most important result of the incident may be that there is now a clear recognition of the fragility of the banking system and this is leading to efforts to improve the system of banking regulation and oversight.

CONCLUSIONS

In 1986 Vietnam received just 7000 visitors from the outside world. This year (1997) the figure is expected to be 1.8 million. In tourism as in commerce and finance, Vietnam is opening up rapidly to the outside world. Nowhere is this more evident than in the case of foreign investment, which is now associ-ated with almost half the investment in the country. In embracing foreign capital, Vietnam has been obliged to accept the rules of the game, allowing information to flow, markets to function, and workers to move to find jobs. While quibbling over the side-effects, both conservatives and reformers agree that foreign direct investment has helped transform the economy in a very short time, and that there is no realistic alternative to it. China has reached the same conclusion, as have all the fast-developing countries of Southeast Asia, and all the developed world. Compared with other capital flows, foreign direct investment is seen as relatively benign; it flows into pro-ductive activities, it cannot be withdrawn very quickly, and it is part of a package that includes access to foreign markets and the transfer of know-how. Because most of this investment has, until recently, flowed into joint ventures with state-owned enterprises, it has served to strengthen the status quo, wherein most industrial activity remains in the hands of state-owned enterprises or the firms in which they have an important stake.

Until very recently, foreign aid was also pursued with vigor by the govern-ment because it was seen as entirely advantageous to the country. But donors, and particularly the World Bank and IMF, are beginning to set con-ditions to their further generosity, calling for continued substantial economic reforms. Although it would be impolitic to admit so openly, the economic reformers probably welcome this pressure, provided it is applied discretely and does not engender a nationalist backlash. This pressure may help weaken the resistance to further reform. Certainly it is geared to promoting change on the most contentious issue of all: what to do with the state-owned enterprises. The World Bank, the IMF, and most reformers want the state-owned enterprises to be equitized rapidly, while the economic conservatives are content to see privatization proceed at its current snail's pace.

Vietnam is not expected to have a stock market before 1999 at the earliest, and so the country has not yet had to contend with the volatile flows of portfolio investment. This has not prevented domestic firms from tapping short- and medium-term, hard-currency loans overseas. The danger to economic policy-making is that this creates a strong domestic constituency which resists any depreciation of the dong, because this makes repayment more expensive (in dong terms). The combination of state-owned companies contracting loans overseas (with an implicit government guarantee) and a fragile banking system is dangerous; if and when some of the borrowing companies are unable to service their loans, this could cause great stress on the banks and precipitate a banking crisis. With a trade deficit of 17 per cent of GDP in 1996, which had to be financed through a combination of direct investment inflows, loans, aid and remittances, Vietnam is taking advantage of the benefits of world financial flows, but at the cost of becoming much more vulnerable to unforeseen shocks.

Has foreign direct investment led to more political change? Superficially it would seem not. The Communist Party has no intention of permitting rival political parties; the press is state-owned, dissidents are sometimes jailed, and the party still intervenes actively in the running of the government. But under the surface there is substantial movement, as was the case in the decade following economic reform in China. Some non-party and independent candidates have won election to political office; the press has more freedom to speak out; the Party has stepped back from some of the daily chores of government; the institutions of civil society are strengthening; and the party is often an agent for change, being in a position to act as a counterweight to narrow-minded or venal local officials. With economic growth, and particularly growth with a strong foreign investment component, people and information have to flow more freely. With these freedoms will eventually come calls for greater political pluralism.

This does not mean that major political changes are just around the corner. All the successful economies of Southeast and East Asia were ruled by a single political party for at least the first two decades of their economic transformations, and Vietnam sees no reason why it should not experience something similar – economic reform and growth coupled with political loosening but not political pluralism, perestroika without much glasnost. Capital flows, whether direct or otherwise, are unlikely to change this at all for another generation.

Notes

1.   More details about the transition are to be found in Haughton (1997), Riedel (1993), *The Economist* (1995), the IMF (1994) and the Vietnam Country Reports of the Economist Intelligence Unit (1996–97).
2.   A good deal of hyperbole surrounds the discussion of foreign investment in Vietnam, so some care is needed in separating the rice from the chaff. Starting in 1988, when foreign direct investment was first permitted, through the end of 1993, 802 projects with foreign investors were approved by the State Committee for Cooperation and Investment (SCCI). The total capital approved for these projects was $8.455 billion, which is an indication of the intentions of the parties to the investment, both foreign and local. Of the total pledged capital, $4.647 billion constituted legal capital, which the parties to the investment are required by law to contribute to the venture and which may not be taken out of the enterprise unless it is wound down.

There is always a gap between intentions and reality. Of the 802 projects approved, 481 had been activated by the end of 1993, and these represented a commitment of $5.581 billion in capital overall. This too overstates actual investment, because only part of the capital committed to these projects had actually been paid up. The first firm number is therefore the total value of activated capital, which was $2.653 billion, or 31 per cent of the total pledged amount. Of this total, 58 per cent ($1.542 billion) had been received from abroad in the form of loans and equity, and the remaining 42 per cent constituted the contribution of domestic partners. The foreign component is a true measure of foreign direct investment, and amounted to 18 per cent of the amount pledged. More recent information which breaks down foreign investment in this way is not available, but informal estimates indicate that in recent years, actual inflows of direct investment have been running at about a quarter of the level of total reported foreign investment project commitments.

Most of the foreign direct investment is contributed in the form of money, but about in the period through 1993 about $200 million was contributed in kind, mainly in the form of equipment. This is a contentious issue, because foreign partners have been keen to contribute used equipment to their ventures in Vietnam, and frequently over-value it. On the other hand over 80 per cent of the Vietnamese contribution to joint ventures has been in the form of natural resources (mainly oil and gas) and land, and the value of these tends to be inflated too. Legally, the capital contributions of the parties to a joint venture must be valued in 'international market prices,' but in the words of one legal advisor, 'there is really no substitute for hard negotiation between the parties' in this area (Clifford Chance, 1994). By the end of 1993 the turnover of projects with foreign investment was estimated at $1.226 billion, which would imply a plausible capital–output ratio of about 2.2.

Bibliography

British Broadcasting Corporation (BBC), various dates for 1996–97, *Monitoring Summary of World Broadcasts* (London).

Clifford Chance Law Firm, around 1994, *Vietnam: A Guide to the Legal Framework* (New York: Clifford Chance).

The Economist (1995) 'The Road to Capitalism: A Survey of Vietnam,' 8 July.

Economist Intelligence Unit (1996–97) *Country Report: Vietnam*, quarterly (London: Economist Intelligence Unit).

Fforde, Adam (1994) *Economic Commentary and Analysis* (Canberra, Australia: ADUKI Pty Ltd).

Freeman, Nick J. (1994) 'Vietnam and China: Foreign Direct Investment Parallels,' *Communist Economies and Economic Transformation*, 6 (1).

Fry, Maxwell (1993) *Foreign Direct Investment in Southeast Asia: Differential Impacts* (Singapore: Institute of Southeast Asian Studies).

Haughton, Jonathan, forthcoming, 'Overview of Economic Reform,' in David Dapice, Jonathan Haughton, and Dwight Perkins (eds), *In Search of the Dragons' Trail: Economic Reform in Vietnam* (HIID/Harvard University Press).

International Monetary Fund (1994) *Viet Nam – Recent Economic Developments* (Washington, D.C.: IMF).

—— (1996) *Vietnam – Recent Economic Developments* (Washington D.C.: IMF).

Kamath, Shyam J. (1990) 'Foreign Direct Investment in a Centrally Planned Developing Economy: The Chinese Case,' *Economic Development and Cultural Change*, 39 (1), pp. 107–30.

La Croix, Sumner J., Michael Plummer, and Keun Lee (eds) (1995) *Emerging Patterns of East Asian Investment in China: From Korea, Taiwan and Hong Kong* (Armonk N.Y.: M. E. Sharpe).

Pearson, Margaret M. (1991) *Joint Ventures in the People's Republic of China* (Princeton, N.J.: Princeton University Press).

Phongpaichit, Pasuk (1990) *The New Wave of Japanese Investment in ASEAN* (Singapore: Institute of Southeast Asian Studies).

Riedel, James (1993) 'Vietnam: On the Trail of the Tigers,' *The World Economy*, 16 (4), July, pp. 401–22.

The Saigon Times, various issues (Saigon).

Tam, Le Minh and Nguyen Duc Vinh, forthcoming, *Remittances and the Distribution of Income*,' in Dominique and Jonathan Haughton *et al.* (eds), *The Vietnamese Household: Explorations Using the Living Standards Measurement Survey 1992–1993* (Singapore: ISEAS Press).

Thien, Tran Dinh (1995) 'Foreign Direct Investment in Vietnam,' *Vietnam's Socio-Economic Development*, 4, Winter.

United Nations (1996–97) *Statistical Yearbook*, various issues (New York: United Nations).

Vietnam Investment Review (1996–97) various issues (Hanoi).

Vietnam: General Statistical Office (1997) *Statistical Yearbook: 1996* (Hanoi: Statistical Publishing House).

Vietnam: Office of the Prime Minister (1996) *Public Investment Program 1996–2000* (Hanoi).

Vogel, Ezra F. (1989) *One Step Ahead in China: Guangdong Under Reform* (Cambridge, Mass.: Harvard University Press).

World Bank (1995) *Viet Nam: Economic Report on Industrialization and Industrial Policy* (Washington, D.C.: World Bank).

World Bank (1996) *Vietnam: Fiscal Decentralization and the Delivery of Rural Services* (Washington, D.C.: World Bank).

Xiaofang, Shen (1990) 'A Decade of Direct Foreign Investment in China,' *Problems of Communism*, March/April, pp. 61–74.

12 Thailand: What Goes Up...

Danny Unger

We can help trace links between the institutional form of capital entering developing countries and the emergence of political democracy by making explicit our assumptions about the critical economic, political, and social variables that intervene between capital flows and political effects. If inflows of portfolio capital either strengthen or weaken organized labor or rural producers, for example, what effects do we anticipate to follow for democratic development? Do business interests enjoying enhanced control over political resources advance political democracy? Are political leaders more apt to be able to forge stable ruling coalitions in a context of political democracy when they endorse broadly orthodox economic policies or, on the contrary, do departures from that orthodoxy boost their abilities to deliver economic stability, reward supporters, and thereby create enduring coalitions?

Suppose we had some confidence about the impact of international capital flows, as they increasingly assumed the form of portfolio investments, on the distribution of political resources in developing countries. We might, for example, be able to assert (as Leslie Elliott Armijo suggests in Chapter 1) that the result of capital flows increasingly assuming portfolio forms was to foster economic instability, enhance the influence of state technocrats advocating orthodox economic policies, and raise the influence of business at the expense of state officials and politicians. What effects flow, in turn, from these developments? Do they bolster political democracy? Extending our causal argument to reach conclusions about the development of democracy requires that we articulate comparably clear hypotheses linking those immediate effects on the distribution of political resources to ultimate outcomes in terms of political change. If we knew that rising portfolio capital flows tended to induce adoption of orthodox economic policies, would we also know what impact those policies would have on political change? Or about the effects of variations in the political resources of private capitalists and state officials on political developments?

I belabor these questions because of a suspicion that the assumptions informing Armijo's hypotheses emerge in large part from analyses of political conflict and change in Latin America. These assumptions may be less reliable when applied to the Thai case. To state the case crudely, for many scholars of Latin American politics, to say nothing of Latin democratic

276

activists, a central issue concerns political conflict pitting the privileges of capital against the interests of the rest of society.[1] With this expectation as backdrop, enhancing the resources under the control of business and curbing the capacity of state officials to channel resources appears to work against the entrenchment of democracy.

Even when stated in such caricatured form, these assumptions have a firm logic. Suppose we make the following assumptions: democracy requires the support of the mass of the population; voters' choices reflect their short-term material interests; at least in the short term, orthodox economic policies tend to aggravate income inequality; the existing distribution of material resources and market skills within national economies is highly skewed, further aggravating the impact of market policies on income distribution; and orthodox economic policies require the curtailment of welfare policies that might otherwise cushion the blows suffered by those short on those resources and skills. These not unreasonable assumptions foster expectations that, by restraining the hand of the state and its capacity to protect disadvantaged actors in competitive markets, portfolio inflows of capital would to some extent inhibit the emergence of stable political democracy.

The argument sketched above suggests that variation in the distribution of resources across economic groups disposes or impedes the appearance of particular political regimes, including political democracy. A central obstacle to strengthened political democracy is the great sway exercised by the concentrated interests of capital.

At first blush, the Thai case might seem to conform to the broad contours of such an argument. In the 1980s, political party leaders became increasingly powerful at the expense of government officials, particularly the military. Parliament constituted the institutional base of party leaders' growing power. The ascendance of party politicians appeared all the more pronounced when the military followed a successful coup in 1991 by botching its effort to consolidate its political roles in 1992. The military was in retreat: votes and the representatives they elected assumed greater importance.

Beginning in 1995, however, ruling party leaders received increasingly pointed criticism for their mishandling of economic policymaking, as well as rampant corruption. This criticism assumed far more force the following year as the export sector began to stall, the financial sector weakened, and external economic imbalances grew. The financial and currency crisis in 1997 pushed concern about economic mismanagement still further and aroused speculation that the military might reassume more active political roles. Party leaders were in retreat: the prospect of more direct military roles in governance appeared less remote. Votes might again decline in significance. In fact, in 1997 parliament approved a new constitution with the potential to strengthen democracy and a new party-based government came to power in November. Given the prominent roles that unstable short-term capital inflows played in fuelling the Thai economy, and ultimately precipitating the financial meltdown and the baht crisis, it would not require a great stretch to argue that those inflows were inimical to the development of political democracy in Thailand. In this chapter, however, I tell a different story.

For most champions of democracy in Thailand the first and greatest obstacle to their ambitions were officials of the state and, in particular, the military. In this respect, political development in Thailand was similar to that elsewhere in East Asia and, in the broadest terms, presented a contrast to the arenas of political contestation in Latin American countries. The latter, older states established themselves in the era of private sector dominance associated with Britain's nineteenth century hegemony. Private actors dominated markets and exercised great sway over politics as well. Many of the East Asian states, by contrast, emerged in contexts marked by the relative absence of societally-based political power (this was particularly true in Thailand). Large capital inflows in the 1950s and 1960s came into the hands of East Asian officials trying, at least in some cases, to nurture strong domestic firms. Hence (to overstate the distinction), if many advocates of democracy in Latin America in the 1990s believed that the great obstacle to democracy was the entrenched dominance of ruling socioeconomic classes, in East Asia that impediment was the state. Where many observers believe political contest in Latin America revolved around socioeconomic class competition for control over the state, in East Asia most would point to shifting relations among the state, business and civil society. The result is that while we may view the rise or consolidation of business dominance in Latin America as threatening to meaningful political democracy and requiring countervailing political forces (see Armijo's discussion in Chapter 1), in East Asia we see the same development as an assault on the state's monopoly of political power and a possible step toward greater political pluralism.

The key obstacles to stronger political democracy in Thailand, I suggest, lie in the power of the state and the dominant institutional form of political expression exercised by capital (clientelism). Stable political democracy in Thailand is not likely to emerge until powerful political organizations with roots outside the state (and either representing private capital or reflecting an unprecedented degree of organization among Thai popular groups) perceive that their interests are served by supporting democratic political institutions. Developments that redistribute political resources away from state officials and into the hands of private actors may eventually encourage the emergence of more democratic politics in Thailand even if they tend, particularly in the short-term, further to aggravate income inequality.

In the absence of powerful, enduring organization among social groups, political competition in Thailand is likely to revolve around those able to organize violence and those with money. Weaknesses in the state's administrative capacities make it relatively difficult to envision the emergence soon of a regime dominated by state officials outside the military. To the extent that state officials are able to wield dominant political influence, ongoing social and economic diversification is apt to express itself in pluralist clientelism. This would mean that critical decisions often would be made not through parliamentary or party deliberations, but through a struggle to influence policymaking within the state itself. This form of politics, in which politicians' key roles center on their brokering capacities, characterizes most East Asian polities.

In order for representative institutions to emerge as effective political instruments of governance, and to use parliament as a base for policy debate and decision, those institutions will have to reflect the concerns of dominant interests outside the state. In Thailand, that can only mean business interests. With high levels of integration with the international economy, private firms have incentives to demand minimally competent regulatory performance on the part of state officials. The financial crisis of 1997 underscored this point. Hence, we can hope that, over the long run, by strengthening private business and diversifying its interests, capital will become champions of the representative institutions they will be able to dominate. Diversity among business interests may foster the development of regularized political competition among parties representing those interests. And, eventually, that competition could encourage parties to reach out to other groups as the latter enhance their own capacities for effective political organization. In short, it may be that the best prospect for the emergence of effective and stable political democracy in Thailand lies in something like the stylized tale of its prior emergence in European contexts (Moore, 1966; Hirschman, 1977).

CAPITAL INFLOWS AND POLITICAL EFFECTS

Historically, capital inflows into Thailand were of modest size compared to those received by other developing countries, including those within East Asia. In large part the small scale of these inflows resulted from the absence of significant plantation or mining sectors and from Thailand's political independence sustained through the colonial era. In the nineteenth and first half of the twentieth century, capital flows to Thailand were lower than those to neighbors. Thailand's independence may have exposed foreign businesses to higher levels of market competition than they faced in colonies entirely controlled by their governments. In addition, the institutions necessary to reassure investors, including reliable property guarantees, were less developed in Thailand. The result was lower levels of investment. Trade, rather than investment, drove Thailand's integration into the world economy.

If capital inflows were at low levels, the roots of democratic politics or of any broad forms of political participation also were only rudimentary. Thailand was an absolute monarchy until 1932. The economy's rapid integration into global markets had remarkably little effect on traditional rural economic and social organization. This social stability resulted primarily from the availability of surplus land that enabled farmers to expand production without significantly changing traditional forms of economic and social organization; the rising rice harvests that paid for the country's imports; an enduring rural economy that served as a buffer as economic resources, including labor, moved into new activities (Phongpaichit and Baker, 1996); and the limited developmental ambitions of the Thai elite that obviated the need for significant mobilization of the population.

By the mid-1990s these conditions had changed radically. As a state on the front lines of the Cold War in the late 1950s, Thailand had become a significant recipient of US, multilateral, and then, in the 1980s, Japanese public capital flows and private bank loans to state firms. Then, in the late 1980s, Thailand sucked in huge net private capital inflows. Initially, these took the form primarily of direct investments, but, increasingly after 1992, portfolio inflows assumed importance. The offsetting enormous current account deficits suggested to many observers by the mid-1990s that the baht would have to be devalued. As a result, the baht was one of the principal targets of speculative attacks early in 1995 following the Mexican peso crisis, and again in 1997. Thai officials' staunch defense of the baht finally crumbled with a sharp devaluation in July 1997 and continued weakening into 1998.

Thailand's politics also changed sharply beginning in the 1970s, ending the military's political dominion that began soon after the overthrow of the absolute monarchy in 1932. In the early 1970s, rising business interests teamed with a growing middle class in Bangkok, spearheaded by university students, toppled a military government and brought forth a brief period of parliamentary democracy. Subsequently, despite frequent reversals, the power of parliament, political parties, and their patrons expanded inexorably. Electorally based political competition became more deeply entrenched by the mid-1990s, even as the creation of effective representative democracy remained a distant goal.

My task in this chapter is to try to discern what if any connections there may be between these two stories, one concerning changes in the institutional form of capital inflows, the other involving shifts in political actors, institutions and regimes. In short, the analytical focus of this chapter involves an effort to make of these two sets of developments a single, causally linked, story. The bulk of this chapter covers the development of Thailand's politics and economic policies since the ending of the absolute monarchy. The latter part of this section emphasizes shifts in Thai financial sector and capital account policies, and in the size and composition of capital inflows. The latter part also analyzes the causes and possible political effects of the repeated speculative attacks on the baht in the mid-1990s. In the final part of the chapter I amplify the argument outlined above and reflect further on some of the hypothesized relationships developed by Armijo in Chapter 1.

THAILAND'S POLITICAL ECONOMY AFTER 1932

After the overthrow of the absolute monarchy in 1932, bureaucrats (particularly the army) dominated Thai politics.[2] A combination of weak organization and active state repression prevented the emergence of politically significant societally-based political actors. State officials engaged in factional struggles for power but their rough and tumble had little impact, particularly after the late 1950s, on the relatively consistent framework of economic policies. Fred Riggs described the Thai political system of the day as a bureaucratic polity in which officialdom formed the prime minister and cabinet's principal constituency and bureaucrats exercised power by and for themselves (Riggs, 1966). While this system did not undermine policy or social stability, neither did it provide political continuity. Between 1932 and 1998, Thailand had 16 constitutions and well over 50 cabinets.

These unstable political conditions were not supportive of the development of democratic political institutions. Neither did they help to attract significant capital inflows. In fact, until communists came to power in China in 1949, Thailand often was a net capital exporter as Chinese resident in Thailand sent money to relatives back home. In any case, the insular nature of political competition during this period generally divorced political competition from concerns with broad macroeconomic issues.

Marshal Sarit Thanarat staged a coup in 1957, ousting his two main rivals and the following year began to recast the framework of Thailand's political economy. Sarit overthrew the 1932 political system in favor of a polity dedicated to nation, religion, and monarchy, as well as economic development. The newly established Revolutionary Council threw out the constitution and the national assembly, and banned political parties, trade unions and strikes.

Under Sarit, officials established new state economic institutions and adopted a market oriented import-substituting industrialization strategy. Thereafter, the state enterprise sector that had grown rapidly after 1932 retreated. Development strategy emphasized greater reliance on the private sector and provided investors with guarantees against competition from new state enterprises. Thailand's economy grew steadily and rapidly.

Private Thai financial institutions expanded impressively during the country's rapid economic growth. The Bangkok Bank, founded in 1944, grew to be the largest financial institution in Southeast Asia. Thai banks played key roles in financing and coordinating the Thai private sector. The organization of Chinese family-based business banking groups acted in some respects similar to universal banks and provided elements of private sector governance. They also were key conduits between local producers and foreign producers and markets. In the 1970s, with the retrenchment of foreign direct investment, the banks helped to supplant the roles of foreign firms, for example in the textile industry.

The United States government approved of Sarit's anticommunism and support for private investment. American assistance increased, particularly economic aid. American private investment also flowed into Thailand, primarily in mining and services. Japanese investors responded to the new investment promotion measures and higher tariffs hindering their access to the local market by establishing many of Thailand's modern manufacturing industries. Nonetheless, capital inflows were not large. As late as the early 1970s, one study noted that among Southeast Asian countries, 'Thailand was the principal exception to the strong dependence on foreign financing for capital formation' (Wu and Wu 1980, p. 15).

As a result of state rationalization measures implemented under Sarit, by the mid-1960s Thailand had in place much of the state institutional and physical infrastructure necessary for economic development. When US spending in the region increased sharply with the commitment of US combat troops in Vietnam, Thailand was poised to exploit the ensuing economic opportunities. Subsequently, US spending in Thailand increased sharply. This included US aid, spending by troops on rest and recreation, spending on US military bases in Thailand, and increased exports to South Vietnam (Stubbs, 1989, pp. 526–8). Between 1950 and 1970, US aid averaged 0.7 per cent of Thailand's GNP (Muscat, 1990, p. 8).

With its open trade regime, agricultural abundance, and low levels of foreign investment, Thailand was slow to develop a modern manufacturing sector. In 1960, food processing and tobacco accounted for over half of all manufacturing value in Thailand. As late as the end of the 1960s, manufactured exports accounted for only 3–4 per cent of total exports. Indeed, even in 1982, primary commodities accounted for 70 per cent of Thai foreign exchange earnings (ESCAP/UNCTC, 1988, p. 468).

Until the late 1960s, and even into the early 1970s, Thais enjoyed impressive macroeconomic stability. Ammar Siamwalla (1975, pp. 27–30) suggested that Thailand's open economy during a period of low global inflation, balance of payments surpluses sustained by US military spending in the region, and fiscal drag that reduced the possible inflationary consequences of those surpluses, all helped sustain economic stability up to 1973.

From 1960 to 1985, manufacturing in Thailand grew at over 10 per cent a year. It failed, however, to generate either adequate employment or foreign exchange to offset the cost of rising imports. The exhaustion of easy import-substituting opportunities in the 1970s and the need to continue importing capital goods, parts, and components resulted in regular trade deficits and increased foreign debt. Officials tried to boost exports by various means beginning in the early 1970s. The strength of the baht hindered these efforts as did officials' failure to coordinate policies to shift incentives decisively away from import substituting production and toward foreign markets. The external stability that underpinned Thailand's macroeconomic performance collapsed in the 1970s, and Thailand's economy and politics followed suit.

During the 1960s, the number of university students in Thailand swelled. By the end of the decade, they had become a new force in Thai politics. Students led a campaign resisting bus fare increases in 1969 before moving on to stage demonstrations that toppled the military government in 1973. The years of open politics (1974–76) that followed ruptured Thailand's political stasis, ushering in a period of sharp social and political polarization and instability.

Following the 1970s economic and political shocks, observers in Thailand and abroad grew more concerned about weakening economic fundamentals in Thailand. Disaster eventually hit the financial sector with the collapse of a major finance company, spilled over into the local stock exchange in 1979 and a subsequent series of financial institution collapses, and exacerbated economic doldrums in the mid-1980s. Foreshadowing the crisis of the mid-1990s, many financial institutions' losses came from heavy exposure to affiliated firms, particularly in property speculation.

With the political opening in the 1970s, business participation in government increased rapidly. Early business inroads came from relatively established Bangkok figures, often with strong links to other power centers, including military personnel. In rural areas, however, a new breed of Thai political actors emerged. They grew wealthy and built local support bases serving as brokers between Bangkok and the regions. Their importance stemmed in part from both the state's relatively weak administrative reach into local areas and the comparative absence of strong local institutions through which central state officials could operate. These 'new men' exploited emerging business opportunities, often illegal or requiring political connections. With their wealth and local ties they established the first effective electoral vehicles in rural Thailand. Whether backing candidates or running themselves, buying candidates or buying votes, by the late 1980s they had become powerful political actors (Phongpaichit and Piriyarangsan, 1994, pp. 11–18, 55–73, 80–86).

Other groups played political roles for the first time in the 1970s as well. Students helped to mobilize workers in Bangkok and, initially dispatched by the government, farmers in the provinces. Farmers' groups spread rapidly before subsiding in the face of renewed state suppression after 1975. Communist insurgencies gained in strength in the countryside and even the Buddhist clergy became sharply polarized (Suksamran, 1982). In response to instability, radicalization, and fears stemming from communist gains in Indochina in 1975, the military staged a coup the following year. Two generals later, in 1980, Prem Tinsulanonda assumed office. He remained there until 1988, presiding over a period of economic turmoil and then recovery as well as the gradual growth in the power of politicians, parliament, and political parties.

Prem placed macroeconomic policymaking in the hands of a circle of technocrats. Based in a handful of state institutions, these officials grappled with an accumulation of economic ills, including high energy prices, a financial sector meltdown, low commodity prices for Thai exports in the mid-1980s, and global recession and rising protectionism that limited demand for Thai manufactured exports. The government ran deficits and the country's foreign debt (most of it incurred by state enterprises) grew rapidly, the debt service ratio reaching over 27 per cent in the mid-1980s (Overholt, 1988, p. 179).

To offset these trends, Thai firms needed to deepen the country's industrial structure and to expand their own exporting capacities. Thai officials, scholars, and multilateral development agency officals agreed on the need to restructure tariffs, to improve access to export finance for smaller exporters, to raise the efficiency of revenue collection, expand infrastructure, and boost spending on education and rural development.

Meanwhile, over the late 1970s and into the early 1980s, the importance of US aid declined while that of the IMF and World Bank continued. By the early 1980s, Thai officials were trying to curb offshore borrowing, particularly by state-linked firms. Japan increasingly became a dominant source of foreign capital. At the same time, Japan became more attractive to some Thai officials as an economic model. A lack of resources, however, ultimately limited the scope for expanded public sector investments, frustrating the ambitions of officials favoring more activist state roles in promoting industrial development.

With only modest policy changes, most critically the currency devaluations of 1981 and 1984, Thailand's economy began to grow rapidly in the latter 1980s. Manufacturing grew very quickly, boosted by rising exports. For the first time, private capital inflows played crucial roles in the Thai economy. Earlier direct investment had helped to improve local technological capabilities as well as management, creating new industries in the process. This continued to be the case. In addition, however, the sheer size of the capital inflows was of a different magnitude. Direct investment inflows grew some seven-fold between 1987 and 1990, to about $2 billion. Inflows fluctuated around that level into the mid-1990s. Macroeconomic stability returned and for the first time since the 1960s, the government regularly ran fiscal surpluses. Domestic savings increased, investment grew still faster, and Thailand's torrid economic growth in the late 1980s and early 1990s produced large current account deficits.

Stable politics helped Thai policymakers take some of the steps necessary to adjust to the economic shocks of the 1970s. Prem's coalitions in the 1980s forged compromises between bureaucratic dominance and wider political participation, particularly during the years after 1983 marked by coalition governments (Samudavanija 1989, p. 13). Political parties and parliament enjoyed greater influence over policy, but technocrats with cabinet portfolios or serving as economic advisers continued to dominate macroeconomic policymaking. The military maintained a check on political parties through its influence in the unelected upper house of parliament.

Many military leaders saw their political role as insuring social stability, the maintenance of the ideology of Nation, Religion, and Monarch, and protecting poor Thai farmers from an emergent plutocracy. Most soldiers had rural roots and perceived themselves as having close links to farmers. Officers insisted they were responsible for protecting the people from unscrupulous 'capitalists' and 'dark influences' (by which they meant the new class of rural power brokers.) This perception encouraged continuing military intrusions in politics, and occasionally into economic policy-making as well.

The military's claims of paternalistic concern for Thai farmers reflected, in part, the growing economic dominance of Bangkok and the Central Region of Thailand. Through the 1980s the gap between the center and the regions was growing. At the same time, however, political power moved away from Bangkok. With political parties' powers increasing, parliament also grew more powerful. Among these parties, the most influential were rural-based ones using extensive vote buying and often dominated by godfather-like figures. By comparison, the Bangkok-based parties were relatively weak. The vast majority of the rural population, however, gained little share either of the economy's growing wealth or of the provinces' rising political influence. At least until the early 1990s, income distribution worsened.

When Chatichai Choonhavan assumed the premiership in 1988, he was the first elected MP and nonsoldier to hold the post since the mid-1970s. It soon appeared that the parties were entrenching their power and severely curtailing the military's political roles. With budget coffers flush, the Chatichai government was able to dispense largesse freely while still running huge fiscal surpluses (about 4.5 per cent in 1990 and 1991). The dominant economic orthodoxy began to relax its grip on policy-making.

Chatichai's aides, however, baited military leaders, perhaps with the intent of establishing civilian supremacy. Politicians' growing confidence apparently went too far, particularly given the level of unity within the military in the early 1990s. When Chatichai intervened in the military's promotion process, the military struck back, staging a coup in 1991. The new ruling Revolutionary Council justified its action by pointing to the pervasive corruption of the Chatichai government. The military regime placed Anand

Panyarachun, a former civil servant and major business figure, at the helm of the government and over the next year the Anand government pushed through an impressive list of long-planned economic reforms.

Seizing the opportunities afforded by strong growth, beginning in the late 1980s, officials in the Ministry of Finance and Bank of Thailand began to push a comprehensive set of financial reforms. By and large, the powerful banks supported the reform agenda. They faced increased competition from finance companies and the Stock Exchange of Thailand, while large local firms had increasing access to foreign bank loans. Nonetheless, the banks were prospering and promoting firms' export initiatives. Bank assets grew six-fold between 1985 and 1994 to over $180 billion. Finance companies' assets expanded almost ten times to nearly $50 billion (Phongpaichit and Baker, 1996 p. 38).

Pressure from the GATT and, more directly, the United States, reinforced moves to deregulate and liberalize entry into the financial sector. By the end of the decade, both bankers and state officials were hoping to expand Thailand's economic roles in neighboring countries and to develop an off-shore banking market. Officials no longer pursued only the goal of system stability, or even efficient or equitable financing of economic activity. Increasingly, financial policy became industrial policy as officials promoted the industry for its own sake. Thai bankers and state regulatory authorities increasingly came to view financial sector development as a means of enhancing efficiency, extending Thai economic activity abroad, and an independent locus of entrepreneurship.

A series of policy changes in the late 1980s and 1990s aimed to boost local savings; enhance the financial sector's ability to compete in international markets and exploit new opportunities abroad; meet demands emerging under negotiations on the General Agreement on Trade in Services; facilitate the creation of a secondary capital market; encourage local financial institutions to raise long-term funds; make it easier for state firms to issue debt; help the central bank manage domestic liquidity; and create new financial institutions, such as an Export-Import Bank and a credit-rating agency, that would relieve the Bank of Thailand of some of its policy responsibilities.

Officials deregulated capital flows in the early 1990s. In May 1990, the Chatichai government announced Thailand's adoption of the International Monetary Fund's Article VIII status, signifying that it had removed most capital controls. Further deregulation continued into 1993, by which time foreign exchange liberalization largely was complete.[3] The impact of these changes was evident, and of considerable concern, in the mid-1990s with speculative attacks on the baht and increased difficulties controlling the money supply.

After early 1992 elections, the military tried to keep its grip on power. The public, which had acquiesced to the military coup in 1991 with scarcely any dissent, grew restive with this evidence of the military's interest in entrenching its political power. The popular governor of Bangkok led protests against the new government. When these led to bloody clashes, the king used his tremendous prestige to intervene and ordered a settlement of the crisis. Anand again assumed the leadership, his government prepared new elections, and by the fall of 1992 a career politician became the new prime minister. The military had overplayed its hand and sped up the secular decline in its influence. Military representation continued in the unelected upper house but the military was unable in the mid-1990s to prevent interference in its promotion decisions by a former Army chief of staff turned civilian minister of interior and later prime minister.

Officials in the early 1990s launched initiatives that helped to bring on Thailand's currency and financial crises in 1995 and, especially, 1997. The key reform that played the most direct role in inducing the baht crisis in the mid-1990s involved the creation of offshore banking facilities.

In the early 1990s, financial officials promoted Bangkok as an offshore capital market. The Bank of Thailand wanted to make Bangkok a financial center, particularly for services business with Burma, Cambodia, Laos, and Vietnam. Authorities used foreign pressure to liberalize the local financial market as an opportunity to launch Bangkok International Banking Facilities through which foreign financial institutions could increase their business in Thailand while Thai firms enlarged their business abroad. Authorities hoped the new facilities also would enable the Thai economy to cope with its continuing shortage in local savings and boost skills in the financial industry.

In March 1993, authorities approved 47 Thai and foreign applications to establish international banking facilities. During the first year of operations, the new facilities handled over $6 billion in business and continued to expand rapidly (*The Economist*, 5 February 1994, pp. 81–2). By 1995, officials grew concerned that the bulk of new business was out-in lending, with Thais borrowing foreign exchange and increasing the local money supply. Capital inflows continued to grow. Net direct investment inflows continued to run around $2 billion a year. Portfolio inflows rose rapidly beginning in 1992 and expanded about 12 times by 1994, rising above $3 billion. Offshore lending to local banks and finance companies surged. By this time, late in a sustained investment boom, capital increasingly pursued more marginal projects, particularly speculation in assets. Even after the local stock exchange collapsed in 1994, money continued to flow into the property sector.

Finance authorities finalized an overall plan for the financial sector early in 1995. The plan called for new legislation to facilitate authorities' prudential supervision of financial institutions and aid Bank of Thailand monetary policy implementation. Broadly, it aimed to foster greater competition at home to prepare local institutions for increasing penetration of the Thai market by foreign financial institutions. Indeed, for the first time in 30 years, the Bank of Thailand would issue new commercial bank licenses.

Rising levels of foreign investment over the late 1980s made the Thai economy more vulnerable to financial shocks coming from abroad. By early 1994, some Thais expressed concern about rising dependence on short-term inflows of capital and suggested that a devaluation of the baht might be necessary. Foreigners were investing in the Thai equity market and Thais were borrowing abroad to take advantage of lower interest rates. The new offshore banking facilities proved an irresistable temptation given the combination of large interest rate differentials and the fixing of the bahts' exchange rate that removed the need to consider exchange rate risk when borrowing in dollars. The current account deficit had peaked in 1990 at 9 per cent of GDP, but began to soar again in 1994, climbing back over 8 per cent in 1995 and remained at about that level over the next two years. Higher interest rates abroad helped to spark an abrupt move out of the Thai stock market early in 1994, sending shares plummeting. Market capitalization dropped 6 per cent in 1995 (*FEER*, 11 January 1996, pp. 79–80). By mid-1997 it had reached depths not seen since the late 1980s.

The first assault on Thailand's rapidly changing financial and monetary policy framework in a context of growing dependence on foreign capital inflows followed the Mexican peso collapse. When the financial crisis induced by the peso's collapse hit in early 1995, the baht momentarily devalued, the Stock Exchange of Thailand slumped, and interbank loan rates jumped. The Bank of Thailand adeptly managed the ripple effects of the Mexican financial crisis.

In 1995, a new prime minister, Banharn Silpa-archa, marked a further high point for the ascendance of political parties and the provincially based power brokers. Banharn typified many of the qualities in politicians that long had led military leaders to resist 'parliamentary dictatorship' and the dominant role it gave to money in politics. Money was indeed the critical force in Thai electoral politics. Pollwatch, a Thai organization, estimated that the Chart Thai political party spent $60 a vote in some tight races during the 1995 election (*FEER*, 13 July 1995, pp. 17–8). Estimates also suggested that to buy a shoe-in candidate for a seat in parliament cost parties some $800 000 and that candidates and parties spent $680 million during the 1995 elections (*FEER*, 29 July 1995, pp. 14–9). Estimates ran considerably higher ($800 000–1 200 000) for the November 1996 election (*BPWR*, 29 November 1996, p. 5).

By the mid-1990s, political parties and their rurally-based backers had established their political dominance. The military and Bangkok-based business firms also remained powerful actors. And Bangkok's middle class grew into a potent political force, powerful enough to bring down governments, although without the votes to elect new ones (Christensen and Siamwalla,

1993, p. 30). Thailand no longer was a bureaucratic polity. Political parties gaining power through elections increasingly dominated politics.

Thailand's 1990s-style democracy had few admirers. Political leaders' policy choices eventually proved their ability to damage the country's economy. Electoral vehicles operated through the purchase of votes and of MPs. The large amounts spent gaining power had as their object the securing of ministerial portfolios that politicians then used to recoup their investments. Money politics ruled and the economy's rapid wealth creation slowed in 1996 and nearly halted the following year, disproportionately benefited the better off.

Political competition affected regulatory policies and seemed to undermine the probity and effectiveness of top level bureaucrats, even in the most powerful government agencies. In 1995, the prime minister faced difficulty filling the finance portfolio and turned to an inexperienced figure who soon became embroiled in a series of controversies. Top level technocrats bickered late in November 1995 when the Bank of Thailand governor set up a $400 million fund to refinance margin loans in an unsuccessful effort to prop up the Stock Exchange of Thailand (SET). The bank governor eventually forced the resignation of his deputy, also the head of the Securities and Exchange Commission, in late December 1995.

A new finance minister resigned in May 1996, soon after the Bank of Thailand took over the Bangkok Bank of Commerce with its $3 billion in bad loans. Some of those losses resulted from loans to figures with close government ties (*FEER*, 15 August 1996, p. 44). Critics maintained that for political reasons the central bank waited too long before moving in on the bank (*FEER*, 15 August 1996, p. 47). The ensuing controversy helped induce the resignation of the central bank governor in July 1996. The turnover of top financial officials was unprecedented.

These difficulties in the financial sector fuelled opposition to the Banharn government. The prime minister insisted that 'Bangkok is not Thailand' (*BPWR*, 6 September 1996, pp. 8–9), hoping to rely on his power base in the provinces and to ignore growing calls in Bangkok for his resignation. Rising pressures, however, including from within his ruling coalition, forced him from office. An election late in 1996 returned power to an increasingly familiar cast of politicians, led by Prime Minister Chavalit Yongchaiyudh.

Coming on the heels of this confusion, the tasks confronting the government elected in November 1996 appeared formidable. The prime minister's closest economic advisor secured only the finance ministry portfolio for himself and the commerce ministry for an ally. Other economic portfolios went to coalition partners. The new government cut public spending in its budgets for the 1997 and 1998 fiscal years, primarily by reducing military hardware expenditures. Ultimately, however, officials could not stem the gathering forces working against the Thai financial system and the baht's rigid peg. As a result, the government fell late in 1997 to be replaced by a new party-led coalition.

Meanwhile, Thailand adopted a new constitution. The push for a new charter came from a broad variety of civil society groups hoping to stem the influence of money on Thai politics. Late in 1996 Thais elected nominees from whom parliament selected 76 (one from each province), adding 23 academics, to comprise a Constitution Drafting Assembly. The assembly went to work in 1997, generating publicity and relatively broad popular participation, and drafted a document that it then submitted to parliament. After amendments, parliament passed the new charter in the fall of 1997.

The new constitution is a major departure in its guarantees of individual rights, decentralization of state power, and efforts to impose on officials and politicians accountability to citizens. Reflecting a pervasive distrust of politicians, the charter doles out authority to a host of independent ombudsmen, commissions and courts. The constitution and the process through which Thais adopted it confirm the rising political power of Bangkok's middle class. It is far from clear, however, that the country's institutions are strong enough to make a success of this very complex constitution with its mandated decentralization and delegation of authority.

The many scandals that embroiled Thai financial authorities assumed significance beyond their titillating appeal. Tales of malfeasance diminished confidence in Thai financial officials' competence and integrity, and helped to bolster skeptical assessments of the baht's strength. Battles among officials also may have contributed to their failure to effectively regulate financial institutions' lending activities that underpinned the burgeoning property boom. At the very time that the boom threatened the health of the financial system, the economy's real sector was undergoing severe pressures as well, as evident in the stagnation of exports from 1996. All these factors combined and aggravated the consequences of the 1997 baht crisis.

Thailand's screaming economic growth hit a wall in the mid-1990s. The equities market collapsed, exports stalled, the foreign debt and current account deficit ballooned, and the fiscal surpluses disappeared. The SET had stopped growing, and began to sink, early in 1994. As the financial sector in Thailand became increasingly shaky, foreigners grew concerned. Between 30 and 40 per cent of their holdings in Thai equities were in bank shares (*The Economist*, 12 October 1996, p. 80). Exports recorded almost no growth in 1996 after expanding by over 20 per cent in 1995. Thanks to the new offshore banking facilities, foreign debt jumped from $28 billion in 1990, reaching some $90 billion by 1997 (*The Economist*, 22 February 2997, pp. 80–5).

Thai authorities pegged the baht to a basket of currencies in which the dollar's weighting (some 80 per cent) was far greater than justified by Thai trade patterns (*FEER*, 6 March 1997, pp. 48–50). Officials resisted IMF advice to shift the weighting of the currencies in the basket (*The Economist,*

24 May 1997, pp. 69–71). The dollar peg severely limited officials' ability to increase interest rates as part of tight money policies. It also hurt exports by inducing modest currency appreciation as the dollar rose against the yen in 1996. The liberalization of capital controls and the rapid expansion of off-shore banking services enabled local firms to borrow abroad at low interest rates without incurring foreign exchange risks. Capital inflows stimulated monetary expansion and boosted investment in marginal projects, particularly in property (*The Economist*, 24 May 1997, p. 15; *FEER*, 12 June 1997, p. 71).[4] By 1997, some $70 billion of the total $90 billion foreign debt was in private hands (*The Economist*, 17 May 1997, p. 82). The fragility of the property sector and its financial backers made it still more difficult to use higher interest rates as a monetary policy tool.

Speculative attacks on the baht increased in the spring of 1997 and forced the central bank to intervene on a very large scale to shore up the currency. Thai authorities received assistance from regional financial authorities who honored agreements reached in 1995 and 1996 in the wake of the Mexican peso crisis and its reverberations. The Thai central bank also intervened in the forward market and by the end of April had committed billions of its reserves. In mid-May, officials instructed Thai banks to desist from lending baht to foreigners and buying baht-denominated offshore bills (*The Economist*, 24 May 1997, pp. 69–71).

The next month officials issued decrees (bypassing parliament) ordering sixteen finance companies to stop business and seek buyers. Then, in early July, authorities acknowledged defeat, floating the baht and turning to the IMF for advice. Officials continued, however, to resist IMF loans and their attendant conditions. By the end of the month, this resistance too collapsed as Thais turned to the IMF for a line of credit of some $17 billion. In return, authorities promised to cut government spending further and to craft a plan to restructure the financial sector. One of their first steps was to close 56 finance companies. Other steps, however, emerged only after a new government came to power in November 1997. By that time, international investors were increasingly confident that Thai authorities were taking steps necessary to return investor faith in the economy. The Thai crisis, however, had triggered a region-wide series of currency and financial disasters that, in turn, raised questions about Thailand's own economic recovery.

The baht crisis developed across several dimensions simultaneously. On the one hand, in many respects, Thailand's economy and finances looked sound. The country had large foreign exchange reserves, at least when the speculative attacks began. The sudden slowing of economic growth in 1996 was, at about six per cent, still impressive by most standards. Many analysts expected the investment boom, peaking in 1995, to significantly boost local exports and to help reduce soon the current account gap. The ratio of M2 to total reserves was low.[5] Exports appeared to be recovering slightly in 1997.

And most estimates suggested that the baht was not dramatically overvalued (when authorities allowed the currency to float in July 1997, however, it immediately depreciated 20 per cent and thereafter continued to fall, over 50 per cent by early 1998).

On the other hand, the sudden collapse in export expansion in 1996 seemed to reflect in large part the long anticipated difficulty that Thai firms would have, given weaknesses in human capital, infrastructure, and public sector performance, in moving from labor-intensive to more skill intensive exports. Competitive pressures grew when the Chinese yuan devalued in 1994. More significant in the medium term was the speculative bubble that had emerged in property. With many firms and their lending institutions perilously weak, authorities were reluctant to devalue the baht and bankrupt the majority of lenders that had not arranged to limit their risk to exchange rate shifts. Officials also were concerned about the impact of interest rates, 13 per cent and higher since early 1995, on smaller firms borrowing in the local market (Bowring, 1996, pp. 5–6). With the property market in doldrums and turnover virtually nil, valuing assets became increasingly difficult. Officials tried to force sickly firms to merge with government help (*The Economist*, 1 February 1997, p. 78; 24 May 1997, pp. 69–71; *FEER*, 6 March 1997, pp. 48–50). Worse, building of office space continued so that even after the July 1997 devaluation, the property linked-financial sector crisis remained very serious with significant additional office space in Bangkok due to become available between 1997 and 1999. As noted above, these factors grew more alarming given the inflexibility of the currency peg and the apparent chaos among financial and monetary policy-making officials.

Ultimately, perhaps the most important causes of the baht crisis were the liberalization of the financial system coupled with the loosening of capital controls over the early 1990s under a fixed exchange rate system. The latter factors allowed local investors easy access to investment funds and fuelled the property boom even when local interest rates were at high levels. Liberalization of the financial markets increased competition for lending and pushed investment toward increasingly marginal projects without accompanying increases in the effectiveness of prudential supervision (what the *Far Eastern Economic Review* termed 'half-hearted liberalization and imprudent supervision') (*FEER*, 12 June 1997, p. 70).[6] Financial sector regulations continued to limit finance companies' abilities to compete in various areas, encouraging their concentration on the property sector, with disastrous results. At the end of 1996, estimates suggested that at least one-fifth of their loans were bad (some estimates ran significantly higher), and put the share of bad loans held by the banks at near 10 per cent.

At a time when increasing fragility of the country's currency and general financial health put a premium on skilled management, the growing financial and macroeconomic policy influence of party politicians complicated the jobs of officials tasked with making financial and monetary policies. By the late 1980s and early 1990s, increasing politicization of relations between the Bank of Thailand and the Ministry of Finance also was evident. In 1990, the finance minister dumped the Bank of Thailand governor. This move simply added to worries about the central bank's independence that had been generated by an earlier sacking of the country's central banker in 1984.

Subsequent struggles between the central bank and the Ministry of Finance developed under later governments as well. Some observers felt the finance minister serving under Prime Minister Chuan in the early 1990s intruded into policy areas once reserved for the Bank of Thailand. During the fallout from the peso crisis in 1995, the central bank governor unsuccessfully advocated recourse to exchange controls. He was opposed by the finance minister and the central bank's deputy governor, also head of the SEC.

CONCLUSION

In Chapter 1, Armijo traced four different intermediate factors (economic growth, shifting the distribution of resources across domestic actors, changing vulnerability to balance-of-payments crises, and pressures to adopt orthodox economic policies) through which the institutional form of capital inflows may affect political democracy in developing countries. She concludes that, all else equal, and with the partial exception of the situation of incumbent democratic regimes, greater dependence on portfolio investment is apt to militate against the entrenchment of political democracy. In this section, I suggest possible grounds for arriving at more optimistic conclusions.

First, it may be worthwhile saying a word about the size of capital inflows. Armijo suggests that in order to gauge the impact of the form capital assumes as it enters developing countries, we control for the size of those flows. On first blush, that decision seems sensible. On further reflection, however, there are grounds for doubting our ability to reflect on real world conditions while continuing to control for the differing size of capital flows associated with the rising importance of portfolio flows of capital. Is what we are doing akin to trying to control for variation in energy supply so that we can assess the impact of its different forms (beasts of burden versus electricity, for example)? In both cases, size of supply may be central to the story, so that controlling for its variation makes little sense.

The institutional developments associated with rising portfolio flows of capital are very important, suggesting the potential of rising shares of rich world savings becoming available for investment in capital scarce developing countries. This increased investment might help to boost economic growth in those countries and that, in turn, might bear a relationship in the medium to long-term with the strengthening of democratic politics. Other possible effects may be less obvious, but are worth considering.

Increased capital inflows that reduce the scarcity of capital in developing countries could have significant effects on those countries' institutions and politics. Many of the classical works on the political economy of late development have emphasized the need for institutions capable of amassing capital in a context of its scarcity.[7] We often associate, for example, concentrated banks, combines, and business groups, backed by state officials, with late industrialization. If global capital flows continue to grow around the world through the institutional development of equity markets, and have the effect of diminishing scarcity, could that have an effect on the institutions, both private and public, that we expect to emerge in late developing countries? And could any such institutional effects, in turn, influence the development of political democracy? (Unfortunately, the most obvious and immediate impact has been the collapse of financial systems adapted to the task of rationing relatively scarce capital as the supply of capital suddenly increased sharply.)

Political implications could also flow from the decreasing relative scarcity of capital. As the cost of capital fell with its greater supply, we might expect the political influence of owners of capital to diminish as well, even if the influence of capital in the aggregate increased. This would depend, however, on the extent to which changes in the supply were correlated with shifts in the numbers of institutions and individuals able to control the allocation of capital.

The comments above concern not only the institutional form of international capital flows, but some of the possible effects of the increased size of those flows. What impact might portfolio investments have, independent of the size of flows? Armijo suggests in Chapter 1 that inflows of portfolio capital are apt to enhance the influence of those local agents that can attract those flows (big business), generally at the expense of incumbent officials and politicians. On the whole, this conclusion seems convincing in light of the Thai case. There does appear to be, however, at least one avenue by which public officials and politicians might also benefit from these inflows: increased tax revenue. Tax revenue might rise as a result of larger capital inflows that boost aggregate economic activity (again for a moment suspending the control on the size of capital inflows), because changes in local accounting practices necessary to attract foreign capital resulted in less concealment of profits by local firms, or because economic activity became more efficient (so that a given investment yielded a larger increase in economic activity) or concentrated in activities on which the state relied for a greater share of its revenue (though there are no *a priori* reasons for expecting either of the latter two results, unlike the argument about changing accounting practices). Certainly the increases in direct investment inflows in Thailand in the late 1980s helped to boost economic activity and state revenue, to the benefit of (incumbent) political leaders. The Thai case seems in several respects to support Armijo's hypotheses concerning the impact of shifting institutional forms of capital inflows on political democracy. She notes, for example, that as inflows shift from the public to the private sector, business groups in the latter are apt to gain greater political influence. Consistent with (the reverse of) this expectation, advocates of greater democracy in Thailand frequently argued in the 1960s, 1970s, and 1980s that extensive US aid to Thailand, much of it military assistance in various forms, helped to entrench military rule at the expense of democratic forces. As official inflows became relatively less important in the late 1970s and into the 1980s, and the US share of those inflows fell, other societal groups did indeed become more powerful at the expense of the Thai military. We could also note that increasing Japanese bilateral assistance, crucial in the early and mid-1980s, coincided with greater interest among some Thai officials in more activist state policies and that those officials' influence waned later in the decade as private sources of capital, first direct and then portfolio investments, came to assume enhanced importance. These relationships are certainly far more complex than hinted at here, but we find, perhaps, shreds of evidence in support of these hypotheses.

As portfolio capital inflows to Thailand assumed increased importance in the late 1980s and 1990s, what trends did we see in Thailand's politics? As discussed above, state actors, the military in particular, grew weaker. Was big business in Thailand the principal beneficiary? This does not seem to be the case. Big business prospered under military and other state-dominated governments. While its interests were hardly ignored under subsequent party-dominated coalitions, the real winners were local gangsters and godfathers, the brokers who crafted means of tying the mass of rural voters to the centralized decisionmaking apparatus in Bangkok. In addition, groups in Thailand's civil society showed impressive new capacities in 1997 in directing the writing and passage of a new constitution designed to significantly increase officials' and politicians' accountability to the public.

If big business was not the principal political beneficiary of growing portfolio investment inflows, what of its position following the 1997 financial and currency collapses? Did its ability to attract foreign capital enhance its powers? Certainly something similar happened to the influence of technocrats in earlier periods when their ability to pull in funds from international financial institutions, foreign aid donors, or direct investments by foreign firms assumed greater importance in contexts of economic hardtimes. The problem for big business in Thailand, however, is that it has yet to create an institutional apparatus through which to exercise its enhanced control over economic resources. Its economic power has not translated into effective political power. The Nam Thai political party in 1995 was a striking, but unsuccessful, effort to forge an institutional vehicle capable of drawing the approval and funds of big business and Bangkok's middle class, and the votes of Thai farmers. Among Thailand's major political parties, only the Democrats approximated this achievement. Until Bangkok's big business interests create such an institution (or a powerful, corporatist alternative), they are likely to continue to exercise primarily structural power or power channeled through accustomed clientage networks. Their power will be either too broadly diffused, or too narrowly focused to serve either their longer-term interests or those of democratic development. So long as those conditions persist, Thailand's democracy is likely to be weaker, not stronger, than it will be when its potentially most powerful socioeconomic group is able openly to exercise power in support of its preferences. Nonetheless, the coming to power in late 1997 of a new Democrat Party-led government in the midst of currency, economic, and financial crises, suggested that the instability induced by portfolio (out)flows were strengthening the hands of big business and Bangkok's middle class, those groups most apt to be able to strengthen democracy in Thailand.

Notes

1.   It is of course not difficult to cite exceptions to this generalization. See, for example, the contributions in Chalmers, Souza, and Boron (eds) (1992).
2.   This section draws on Unger (forthcoming).
3.   In the case of smaller transactions and all capital imports, officials removed all controls. Exports over approximately $20 000, not including remittance of investment funds and foreign loans, required nominal official approval. Authorities planned to continue to loosen remaining controls.
4.   A near two-fold rise in Thailand's incremental capital–output ratio between 1988 and 1991 supported the notion that investors were pursuing rapidly falling profits. *FEER* (6 March 1997), pp. 48–50.
5.   This ratio is emphasized in Sachs, Tornell, and Velasco (1997). Ratios after the peso crisis calculated using IMF (1997).
6.   Sachs *et al.* (1997, pp. 8, 54–56) emphasize the role of domestic financial deregulation in the currency crises in Mexico and Argentina late in 1994 and early in 1995.
7.   Gerschenkron (1962) provides the argument in its classic form. A more recent variant stressing the particular characteristics of different sectors, appears in Shafer (1994)

Bibliography

Bangkok Bank Monthly Review, 37 (10), October 1996.
Bangkok Post Weekly Review (BPWR), various issues.
Bangkok Post Year-end Review (1996).
Bowring, Philip (1996) 'In search of a soft landing,' *Nikko Capital Trends* 1 (7), July.
Chalmers, Douglas A., Maria do Carmo Campello de Souza, and Atilio A. Boron (1992) *The Right and Democracy in Latin America* (New York: Praeger).

Christensen, Scott and Ammar Siamwalla (1993) 'Beyond Patronage: Tasks for the Thai State,' Thailand Development Research Institute, 1993 Year-End Conference, Chonburi, Thailand, 10–11 December.

Economic and Social Commission for Asia and the Pacific, United Nations' Center on Transnational Corporations (ESCAP/UNCTC) (1988) *Transnational Corporations from Developing Asian Economies, Host Country Perspectives*, Publication Series B, No. 12 (Bangkok: United Nations).

The Economist, various issues.

Economist Intelligence Unit (EIU), various issues.

Far Eastern Economic Review (FEER), various issues.

Gerschenkron, Alexander (1962) *Economic Backwardness in Historical Perspective* (Cambridge, Mass.: Harvard University Press).

Hirschman, Albert O. (1977) *The Passions and the Interests, Political Arguments for Capitalism before Its Triumph* (Princeton, N.J.: Princeton University Press).

International Monetary Fund (1997) *International Financial Statistics* (Washington, D.C.: International Monetary Fund), June.

Moore, Jr., Barrington (1966) *Social Origins of Dictatorship and Democracy, Lord and Peasant in the Making of the Modern World* (Boston: Beacon Press).

Muscat, Robert J. (1990) *Thailand and the United States; Development, Security, and Foreign Aid* (New York: Columbia University Press).

Overholt, William H. (1988) 'Thailand: a moving equilibrium,' in Ansil Ramsay and Wiwat Mungkandi (eds), *Thailand–US Relations: Changing Political, Strategic and Economic Factors* (Berkeley, Calif: Institute of East Asian Studies, University of California, Berkeley).

Phongpaichit, Pasuk and Sungsidh Piriyarangsan (1994) *Corruption and Democracy in Thailand* (Bangkok: The Political Economy Centre, Faculty of Economics, Chulalongkorn University).

— and Chris Baker (1996) *Thailand's Boom!* (Chiang Mai, Thailand: Silkworm Books).

Riggs, Fred (1966) *Thailand: the Modernization of a Bureaucratic Polity* (Honolulu: East–West Center Press).

Sachs, Jeffrey, Aaron Tornell, and Andres Velasco (1997) 'Financial Crises in Emerging Markets: The Lessons from 1995,' Working Paper Series no. 97–1, Center for International Affairs, Harvard University, January.

Samudavanija, Chai-Anan (1989) 'Thailand: a stable semi-democracy,' in Larry Diamond, J. Linz, and Seymour Martin Lipset (eds), *Democracy in Developing Countries: Asia* (Boulder, Col.: Lynne Rienner).

Shafer, D. Michael (1994) *Winners and Losers, How Sectors Shape the Developmental Prospects of States* (Ithaca, N.Y.: Cornell University Press).

Siamwalla, Ammar (1975) 'Stability, Growth and Distribution in the Thai Economy,' *Finance, Trade and Economic Development in Thailand* (Bangkok: Sompong Press for the Bank of Thailand).

Stubbs, Richard (1989) 'Geopolitics and the Political Economy of Southeast Asia,' *International Journal* (Canada), no. 44.

Suksamran, Somboon (1982) *Buddhism and Politics in Thailand* (Singapore: Institute of Southeast Asian Studies).

Unger, Danny, forthcoming, *Building Social Capital in Thailand: Fibers, Finance, and Infrastructure* (Cambridge: Cambridge University Press).

Yuan-li Wu and Chun-hsi Wu (1980) *Economic Development in Southeast Asia, The Chinese Dimension* (Stanford, Calif.: Hoover Institution Press).

.

Part III
Conclusions

13 Tequila versus the Dragon: Comparing the Crises in Mexico and Thailand

Walter Molano

Since the 1982 debt crisis, Latin American economic policy makers have become quite accustomed to looking to East and Southeast Asia as models of export-led growth, low inflation, and market-oriented regulatory frameworks. Even those analysts who granted that the 'East Asian model' had a significant component of *dirigisme*, rather than being stellar examples of *laissez faire*, perceived Asian economies to be structured much more soundly than those of most developing countries in the western hemisphere (Amsden, 1989; Wade, 1990; Stallings, 1995). The Mexican devaluation of December 1994 and the subsequent 'tequila crisis' seemed to confirm this pessimistic assessment of Latin America.

Yet a mere three years after the Mexican devaluation, Thailand faced a similar crisis that spread throughout East Asia. It became known as the 'dragon crisis'. Many observers initially saw little to worry about in the Asian region despite the widespread contagion, given that the economic fundamentals appeared strong. This chapter takes a contrarian view by arguing that, while the two crises had similar origins and short-term results, the domestic economic restructuring needed in Southeast Asia may be more profound than that which followed the crisis in Latin America.

ORIGINS OF THE TWO CRISES

The roots of the Mexican crisis have been the subject of much analysis and debate (Calvo, Goldstein, and Hochreiter (eds), 1996; Edwards and Végh, 1997). Most analysts agreed that the Mexican crisis was driven by both domestic and external factors, with the first major factor being Mexico's low savings rate. The relatively large gap between the savings and investment rate forced the Mexican economy to be heavily dependent on external savings. The Mexican government allowed credit to expand sharply though the state-owned development banks on the eve of the 1994 presidential

301

elections. As a result, the current account deficit rose quickly, reaching 8 per cent of GDP by the end of 1994. This was soon followed by a series of internal shocks, such as the assassinations of presidential candidate Donaldo Colósio and Attorney General Ruíz Massieu. Another important factor, as detailed by William Gruben in his chapter in this volume, was the government's decision to cede monetary policy by pegging the exchange rate. Yet external factors were also very important. Early in 1994, Federal Reserve Chairman Alan Greenspan abruptly raised interest rates, pushing up the external cost of capital. Furthermore, economic woes in Japan led to a repatriation of capital and a decline in global liquidity.

The Mexican government could have adjusted to the changes by slowing the economy, but it was unwilling to so on the eve of the elections. Therefore, the Mexican central bank tried to circumvent the situation by dollarizing the debt through the issuance of *tesobonos* (see Gruben's and Elizondo's chapters for more detailed analyses). This was a high risk bet since the public sector assumed all devaluation risk. Yet, as Leslie Elliott Armijo points out in Chapter 1, portfolio capital flows are extremely volatile and unforgiving. Hence, there was no tolerance for the increase in risk. Furthermore, a series of subsequent policy mistakes led to a final depletion of international reserves. The Mexican central bank was finally forced to devalue the peso, pushing the economy into a deep recession.

The origins of the Thai baht crisis also lay in both domestic and external factors. In the 1980s the government carried through a major stabilization program, and the Thai government, like Mexico's, ceded monetary policy by fixing the exchange rate. The model was highly successful and the economy grew rapidly, averaging 8 per cent growth per year for over a decade. However, by the 1990s the economy was starting to face important bottlenecks and constraints. The appreciation of the Japanese currency and rising real wages reduced the competitiveness of Thai products. An attempt to improve income distribution and move up the development curve led to important shortages in skilled labor. Yet such a qualitative transformation is slow and the external accounts began to deteriorate. Therefore, it was evident that an economic adjustment would be required. The government was hesitant since a new administration was in the process of taking over. Danny Unger's chapter in this book details some of the political constraints on Thai Prime Ministers Banharn Silpa-archa (1995–96) and Chavalit Yongchaiyudh (1996–97).

Second, financial deregulation led to a sharp expansion of credit to the private sector through the banking system. In the late 1980s, the Bank of Thailand controlled and restricted the growth and allocation of credit by imposing 'voluntary' guidelines on the banking sector. In an effort to bypass these constraints, non-bank financial institutions – investment companies specializing in financing the rapidly growing property sector – came into existence. Many investment companies, however, were controlled by politically powerful individuals. An over-expansion of the financial system and subsequent problems forced the central bank to secretly intervene. However, it was not until August 1997 that the Bank of Thailand announced that it had lent more than $19 billion, or 10 per cent of GDP, to the private financial sector.

While Thailand benefited from high savings and investment rates, these did not prevent a crisis from occurring. The high rate of investment masked the fact that many projects were inefficient or unproductive. The easy access to domestic and international credit resulted in a surge of real estate investment, resulting in a large property asset bubble. In fact, most of the Southeast Asian economies witnessed a sharp expansion of credit to the private sector as shown in Table 13.1, and an explosive surge in foreign debt as in Table 13.2.

By the mid-1990s, there was little investment in Thai productive capacity; foreign direct investment in 1996 covered only 9 per cent of the current account deficit. The result was an ever-widening deficit, which by 1996 had surpassed 8 per cent of GDP. The Thai economy funded the current account deficit via accumulation of private sector debt to international lenders. By 1997, the stock of short-term private sector external debt rose to $37 billion, much of it dollar denominated. Short-term debt, indeed, accounted for 40 per cent of the country's debt. The government was very slow in addressing the burgeoning external imbalances, and hence the economy became highly vulnerable to external shocks.

The third major cause of the Thai crisis was external. The economic slowdown in Japan reduced the demand for Thai exports. Furthermore, it is

Table 13.1 Southeast Asia: credit to the private sector
(increase as per cent of GDP)

		1991	*1992*	*1993*	*1994*	*1995*	*1996*	*1991–96*	*1992–96*
Thailand	DMBs 1	67	72	80	92	100	101	34	29
	Total 1	88	92	104	120	133	135	47	43
Malaysia	DMBs	77	75	76	77	91	105	28	30
	Total	n/a	110	112	115	136	158	n/a	48
Philippines	DMBs	18	21	26	29	38	46	28	25
	Total	22	25	32	36	45	51	29	26
Indonesia	DMBs	50	48	45	49	52	55	5	7

Note: DMBs = deposit money banks.
Source: SBC Warburg Dillon Read, data files.

Table 13.2   Southeast Asia: net external debt

	Net external debt, $ billions							
	1991	*1992*	*1993*	*1994*	*1995*	*1996*	*Change in $bn*	*Change in USD debt 1991–96 (%)*
Thailand	18.4	22.2	28.2	37.4	50.5	62.2	43.8	238
Malaysia	13	9.1	6.5	7.1	12.7	15.5	2.5	19
Philippines	28.2	27.7	33.7	40	42.1	42.1	13.9	49
Indonesia	64.1	65.3	71.1	80.5	88	91	26.9	42
Total	123.7	124.3	139.5	165	193.3	210.8	87.1	70

Source: International Institute of Finance, data files.

important to note that globalization had a hand in the Thai crisis. Thailand's exports to the US fell in the aftermath of the Mexican devaluation. Mexican products were not only more competitive after the devaluation, but there was more integration of the two economies through the North American Free Trade Agreement (NAFTA). Moreover, expanding capacity in Asia produced a massive decline in export prices. Instead of growing at a pace of 10 per cent per year, as in the 1980s, export prices in the mid-1990s fell 4 per cent per annum due to over-capacity.

Speculative attacks started in May 1996, and the central bank depleted international reserves by $4 billion. The attacks accelerated in June 1997 when Moody's downgraded Thailand's short-term deposit rating. After defending the baht for more than a year, and expending another $12.8 billion in international reserves, the central bank was up against the wall. Although the central bank reported that international reserves were $33 billion, it omitted the fact that it had committed an estimated $25 billion in forward contracts. Therefore, net reserves were now estimated at below $8 billion. The final blow came on 2 July 1997 when the Czech central bank devalued its currency, signalling the start of a new wave of speculative attacks on weak currencies. The Bank of Thailand decided it could no longer sustain another attack and decided to float the baht.

POLICY RESPONSES

The events of late December 1994 in Mexico revealed a lack of cohesion and policy coordination. On 19 December 1994, the Mexican central bank decided to devalue the peso by 15 per cent. No formal announcement, however, was made and the decision to devalue the peso was leaked out to a radio show early in the morning. One reason for the confusion was that the economic team was newly installed. Nevertheless, the devaluation process undermined investor confidence and there was a further run on the currency. Unable to sustain the exchange rate, the central bank was forced to float the peso less than a week after the initial devaluation, and eventually, the peso depreciated 122 per cent. The government also knew it had to instill confidence in the markets if it wished to stabilize the currency. Therefore, Finance Minister Jaime Serra was dismissed and Guillermo Ortiz was installed. In March 1995 the government announced a comprehensive program, in conjunction with the IMF and US government, to stabilize the economy and address the financial sector crisis. Of the $50 billion rescue package, $28.2 billion came from the US. Still, the Mexican economy was devastated, and GDP fell 11 per cent, monthly inflation spiked to 8 per cent and the unemployment rate almost tripled.

The Bank of Thailand was forced to float the baht on 2 July 1997 and the currency immediately devalued by 17 per cent. The small devaluations injected a lack of confidence into the markets, and by the end of October 1997 the government had devalued by 45 per cent. Thailand's crisis was also fraught with mismanagement and policy mistakes. Banking supervision, for example, was poor and highly politicized. Although restructuring of the financial sector would have been the best option, the government was forced to opt for a bailout since that was being demanded by political interest groups. Another important factor was political fragility. Thailand has a history of weak political institutions, and military intervention in 1992, for example, had led to widespread unrest. The political team was also new. Prime Minister Chavalit Yongchaiyudh was elected in November 1996, and his fledging government was a loose coalition of diverse political parties. The main faction was the Chart Pattana party, led by former Prime Minister Chatichai. The incumbent, Chavalit, was weak in his ability to dictate policy. Soon after the start of the crisis the congress held a no-confidence vote and all the members of the cabinet resigned in order to create a new cabinet. Although Prime Minister Chavalit might have survived the no-confidence vote, the key coalition partner – the Chart Pattana party – called for a major cabinet reshuffle.

The government was also slow in approaching the IMF. On 28 July 1997, the Thai government approached the International Monetary Fund (IMF) for a standby line of credit. The IMF organized a $17 billion standby package in August 1997 – the largest bailout after the Mexican package. The World Bank provided $1.5 billion and the Japanese government contributed $4 billion. Japan, indeed, had a large interest in Thailand, some Japanese companies had large foreign direct investment projects in the country. For example, Japanese car makers had boosted their production in Thailand, and Toyota had 28 per cent of the Thai auto market. The Japanese banks also held about $17 billion in Thai corporate debt. Given the staggering $233 billion in delinquent loans already held by Japanese banks, the new Thai obligations would be another painful blow. While the Japanese provided the largest contribution of any country, it was still small in comparison to the US assistance program to Mexico. The reason was because other countries in the region required similar assistance and Japan was undergoing one of its worst recessions in the postwar period. Consequently, Japanese Finance Minister Hiroshi Mitsuzuka stated that the government was reaching its limits in assisting these countries. By the second quarter, the economy had contracted 11 per cent as compared to the previous year, and the government was trying to close the fiscal deficit.

However, Thailand was hesitant to adopt the terms needed to receive the $17 billion assistance program. Some of the demands of the IMF were higher oil taxes, a balanced budget, and the revision of the banking code. The Thai banking code dates back to 1940 and provides only an arduous and expensive route for creditors to recover their money. The coalition refused to accede to all of the demands of the IMF and Finance Minister Thanong Bidaya resigned, followed in early November 1997 by Prime Minister Chavalit.

REGIONAL CONTAGION

The Mexican and Thailand crises are interesting for many reasons. They show the hazards of rapid financial deregulation (see Manzocchi's chapter in this volume) and the perils of fixed exchange rates. However, they also show the contagion effects of currency crises. In 1995, the Mexican crisis spread to Argentina and Brazil. Argentine GDP growth plummeted from 3.13 per cent in the first quarter of 1995 to negative 7.7 per cent in the third quarter. Likewise, Brazilian GDP growth plunged from 10 per cent to 1 per cent during the same time period. Both countries had overvalued exchange rates, large external imbalances, and fiscal problems. The countries were attacked by financial speculators and many people took their money out of the countries. Hence, they had to make major alterations in their macroeconomic policies. A similar result occurred when Thailand devalued. Its neighbors in the Association of South-East Asian Nations (ASEAN) were confronted with intense speculative pressures. The crisis immediately spread to the Philippines, Indonesia, and Malaysia, and later to South Korea and Hong Kong. On 11 July the Philippines abandoned the defense of the peso and on 14 August the Indonesian government floated the rupiah. The decision by the ASEAN governments not to defend their currencies reflected a variety of pragmatic considerations, including a desire to eliminate easy targets for speculators. Ironically, the result has been tremendous uncertainty, which has fueled hedging and heightened speculative activity. Investors identified a regional pattern of slowing export growth, increasing global capacity, rising current account deficits and weak banking systems. Market participants realized that concerns about relative competitiveness would cause these currencies to move in tandem since the so-called Asean four – Thailand, Malaysia, Indonesia and the Philippines – compete in broadly the same export markets. Hence, a devaluation in one country would force the other countries to follow suit. Moreover, a long tradition of regional exchange-rate stability had encouraged domestic investors to assume significant currency risk. The abrupt withdrawal of Southeast Asian central banks from the foreign exchange market – with the encouragement of the International Monetary Fund – left companies with large foreign currency exposure. As they scrambled to hedge these liabilities, pressures on the region's currencies intensified.

CONCLUSION

The currency crises in Mexico and Thailand underscore the dangers facing developing countries. Both countries were once paradigms of development and economic reforms, yet both showed the fragility of their economic and political systems. The two crises had many similarities, but also key differences. The similarities lie in fragile political systems, high levels of corruption and lack of transparency. Other problems included the politicization of the financial system, the lack of independent institutions, the mismatch of assets and liabilities, and the inability of the government to respond properly to external and internal shocks. There were also important differences. First, the public sector was the root of the Mexican crisis, while it was the private sector that drove the Thai crisis. Yet the most important contrast was in the financial sector, where both governments ceded their monetary policies by pegging their exchange rates. Yet this decision, as argued by Gruben, was incompatible with an expansive domestic credit sector, and the result was an eventual crisis. Although the collapse of the Mexican financial sector was costly, the Thai damage was more extensive due to its larger financial sector, as shown in Table 13.3. Thai household wealth declined by 70 per cent and property values dropped by 50 per cent. The Mexican crisis produced a 35 per cent decline in household wealth and a 25 per cent decline in property prices. The concentration of the Thai crisis in the private sector also deepened the crisis. Mexican companies were much less indebted than in Thailand both in domestic and local currency terms; hence, the damage was less.

The two crises also mark an important transition point for developing countries. The goal of this book has been to assess the effects of foreign

Table 13.3   Mexico and Thailand: financial indicators in the aftermath of the crises

	Mexico	Thailand
Stock market index	–40%	–70%
Property values	–30%	–50%
Household wealth	–25%	–70%
Non-performing assets of the financial sector (percent of GDP)	–18%	–30%

Note: Data presented are 6–12 months after each crisis.
Source: SBC Warburg Dillon Read, data files.

capital inflows on macroeconomic policy-making and democracy. The Thai and Mexican cases showed that attempts by governments to shrug off monetary policy by pegging their exchange rates, while pursuing expansive credit sectors, was a form of moral hazard that would be brutally punished by the market. In my view, in other words, free forms of capital flow do not themselves directly hamper or bolster democracy in developing countries. However, open capital markets in this era of volatile cross-border portfolio investments cruelly punish macroeconomic mistakes. This lesson in macroeconomic reality forces governments to mature and endogenize monetary policy. The lesson may be expensive since it may shave several years of growth, but it is an important lesson that will lead to more prudent macroeconomic policy-making in the future.

Bibliography

Amsden, Alice (1989) *Asia's Next Giant: South Korea and Late Industrialization* (New York: Oxford University Press).
Calvo, Guillermo, Morris Goldstein, and Eduard Hochreiter, (eds) (1996) *Private Capital Flows to Emerging Markets after the Mexican Crisis* (Washington, DC : Institute for International Economics).
Edwards, Sebastian and Carlos Végh, forthcoming, 'Banks and Macroeconomic Disturbances under Predetermined Exchange Rates,' *Journal of Monetary Economics*.
Stallings, Barbara (ed.) (1995) *Global Change, Regional Response: The New International Context of Development* (Cambridge,.: Cambridge University Press).
Wade, Robert (1990) *Governing the Market: Economic Theory and the Role of Government in East Asian Industrialization* (Princeton, NJ: Princeton University Press).

14 Mixed Blessing: Preliminary Conclusions
Leslie Elliott Armijo

The premise of this book has been that the quality as well as the quantity of cross-border capital flows makes a difference to emerging market countries. The particular characteristics of greatest interest have been the institutional forms of foreign capital, ranging from foreign aid to portfolio flows. The outcomes this volume has focused on have been political, as well as economic. This conclusion attempts, in a very preliminary fashion, to draw generalizable lessons from the country cases. I look at country cases illustrating each type of capital flow to see whether the expected consequences manifest themselves. Since no country case is a pure example of a single type of capital flow, these remarks should be understood as impressionistic.[1] Furthermore, since all types of capital inflows tend to strengthen incumbents, while all financial crises tend to weaken them, the most important predictor of the political consequences of net foreign capital inflows is the characteristics of the incumbent political regime. The discussion, summarized in Table 14.1, thus distinguishes between authoritarian and democratic capital importers that have experienced each type of inflow.

Foreign Aid

Our expectations of *foreign aid* (see row 1 of Table 14.1) were that it would make a rather small contribution to economic growth in the recipient country, that the locally-relevant political influence of donor governments (or international organizations) would be strengthened, as would governing incumbents, and that this form of foreign capital transfer posed a comparatively low balance-of-payments risk. External actors would be relatively unlikely to pressure the sitting government for specific economic reforms, neoliberal or otherwise. The consequences of official grants and credits for democracy in emerging market countries thus mainly hinged upon the goals of the main donor government(s) and the pre-existing characteristics of the government in the recipient country.

United States' aid to the Philippines under Ferdinand Marcos through the late 1970s illustrates foreign aid to an authoritarian government. In return for secure leases for military bases that the US considered essential to its East Asian strategy, the US gave generous aid commitments and for many

Table 14.1 Types of capital flows and democracy: country cases

Prominent financial instrument	Authoritarian capital-importing country	Democratic capital-importing country
Foreign aid	• Philippines under Marcos • Zaire under Mobutu	• India under Nehru • Russia under Yeltsin
Foreign direct investment	• Indonesia under Suharto • Vietnam in 1990s	*'Pessimistic' outcome*: • Chile under Frei, then Allende (1964–73) • Brazil under Kubitschek, Quadros, Goulart (1956–64) *'Optimistic' outcome*: • Argentina, Brazil in late 1980s, 1990s • South Africa under Mandela
Bank loans to govt.	• Argentina, Brazil, Mexico in 1970s	• India in 1980s
Bank loans to private firms	• Chile, Argentina, Brazil in 1970s	• ??
Portfolio investments with govt.	• Mexico under Salinas (1988–94)	• Argentina under Menem (1990s)
Portfolio investments in private firms	• South Africa under apartheid • Singapore in 1990s (equity) • Indonesia in 1990s (short-term debt)	• India, Chile in 1990s (corporate bonds, portfolio equity) • Thailand, South Korea in 1990s (short-term debt)

years downplayed credible reports of human rights abuses. Moreover, the Marcos administration apparently used its overall control of resources and influence (although not necessarily foreign aid dollars in a traceable fashion) to perpetuate dense networks of patronage and to corrupt many government-business links. The US government avoided pressuring the Philippines for significant economic reform, although the multilateral development banks sporadically tried.[2] However, in the early 1980s the US altered its perception of 'US interests' in the area and gave important support to the 'people power' movement of democracy campaigner Corazon Aquino. The large sums of bilateral and multilateral aid to the Philippine government, along with the strong historic ties of the islands to the *de facto* ex-colonial power, gave the United States government substantial influence over the progress of the eventual democratic transition. In the Philippines, then, foreign aid began to contribute to the circumstances promoting democracy only when this became an outcome important to the country's major aid donor.

Zaire provides a second case of aid to an authoritarian regime. American, French, and other foreign aid from the 1970s through the early 1990s to Zaire under President-for-life Mobutu Sese Seko pursued goals of anti-Communism, strengthening post-colonial francophone ties, and assuring access to huge copper and mineral reserves for commercial uses and possible military contingencies. With such a full agenda of strategic goals, human rights and democratic concerns were consistently and thoroughly downplayed in the relations of the major donors with the authoritarian government.[3] Although Zaire admittedly was an extreme case, it provides a textbook example of the contribution of foreign aid to government economic mismanagement and the propping-up of an oppressive government and political regime.

An example of a democratic recipient of foreign aid is India in the 1950s through the 1960s, during these years one of the largest aid recipients among all developing countries, albeit one of the smallest in per capita terms. Aid from western democracies, both from multilateral sources such as the World Bank and through bilateral programs like the US Food for Peace donations, provided important budgetary support to the Indian government in its first decades, becoming at least one of the factors that enabled Indian democracy to survive. Large quantities of foreign aid to India not only strengthened the ability of elected rulers to deliver some of the material goods their constituents desired. Foreign assistance also reinforced the government's freedom to pursue its preferred economic policies, which it described as 'democratic socialism'. These policies included construction of a huge state productive sector, and extensive affirmative action and regional redistribution programs, all intended as a way of enhancing citizen support of the incumbent democracy (and the long ruling Congress Party) within a multi-ethnic state riven with deep caste and class inequalities. They were the antithesis of neoliberal policies. With hindsight, the majority of Indian economists agree that many of India's statist economic policies also were rather inefficient. However, because the population by and large perceived their redistributive element as just and moral, they played an important role in legitimating democratic government in a setting that many observers initially thought would be an unlikely home for it.[4]

The experiences of the Philippines, Zaire, and India generally confirm our expectations of foreign aid. Few observers believe that external assistance made great contributions to economic efficiency in any of these countries. Nor did foreign aid, even from democratic donors, necessarily make great contributions to hastening the transition to democracy. Instead, aid resources gave incumbent governments additional room to manuever, both economically and politically (so long as the foreign patron government could achieve its *de facto* core goals), without greatly increasing policy-makers' worries that a sudden foreign exchange crisis might develop. More recently, the newly and precariously democratic Russian federation has received large quantities of multilateral assistance, especially – and unusually – from the International Monetary Fund. Randall Stone's chapter in this volume puts a compelling, and rather darker, twist on the likely consequences of massive quantities of foreign aid coming to a young and weak democracy. The political incumbent, President Boris Yeltsin, indeed has been strengthened, Stone argues, but at the cost of both sound economic policy and institutionalizing democracy.

Foreign Direct Investment (FDI)

Foreign direct investment (row 2) should have a significant positive impact on economic growth, should heighten the political and policy influence of multinational corporations, and should not be prone to sudden capital flight. I assume that multinational corporations (MNCs) always become players in the domestic politics of the host country, however much they may publicly disavow having any such intent. Most often their political involvement is limited to discreet lobbying on behalf of a 'good' investment climate. Thus, MNCs may intrigue against what they view as 'politically-motivated regulatory red tape' or 'irrational' restrictions on their right to hire and fire at will, and so on. If the country's current rulers are authoritarian leaders, they should be strengthened by FDI inflows. However, authoritarian regimes also may experience subtle pressure from foreign corporations to liberalize politically, for example, by expanding freedom of the press. Policy-makers may also find multinational direct investors urging them to liberalize the economic policy regime.

Indonesia and, very recently, Vietnam are authoritarian countries that have captured large direct investment inflows (see Winters and Haughton in this volume). Loudly anticommunist and authoritarian, Indonesia under General Suharto received large amounts of FDI from the late 1960s through the 1990s. Communist and politically-authoritarian Vietnam has garnered truly astonishing pledges of foreign investment since its embarkation on the path of economic liberalization in the early 1990s. There are some interesting similarities between these otherwise diverse cases. The symbolic vote of confidence from outside, and the economic stimulus, have helped each economy. In both cases generous foreign investment apparently bolstered the political fortunes of the authoritarian incumbents, arguably encouraging them to continue suppressing political dissidents. Foreign direct investment thus did little or nothing to promote democracy. Multinationals have insisted upon some economic reforms, generally ones aiming to make the internal economic regulatory environment more predictable and more similar to business conditions prevailing in advanced industrial countries.

Nonetheless, the political incumbents were perhaps encouraged to perpetuate certain economic irrationalities, such as large-scale corruption in the management of public-sector investments, that did not negatively affect foreign investors' profits. That is, direct investors, like local big business actors, in both countries have been more concerned with ensuring their own freedom of action than with increasing the overall efficiency of the economy. In addition, Jonathan Haughton notes that Vietnam's Communist government has required joint ventures between state-owned enterprises and MNCs, thus strengthening government incumbents more than with ordinary FDI, while diluting the presumed 'efficiency effect' of having foreign capital inflows spent by private, rather than public, actors.[5] FDI has the advantage of not being highly volatile. The spread of the 1997 East Asian financial crisis to Indonesia, but not (as of mid-January 1998) to Vietnam, probably can be attributed to the much greater role of liquid portfolio investment in the former. FDI also gives the host government useful friends: western and Japanese direct investors in Indonesia have used whatever influence they have over their home governments to encourage them to participate in the rescue package.

If the incumbent government is instead democratic, and if it can limit the political and lobbying activities of foreign businesses to actions that are not regime threatening, then the additional private investment and growth provided by FDI should strengthen democracy. However, emerging market country governments are not always able to control the domestic political activities of foreign business. Chile in the early 1970s illustrates the case of foreign direct investors – who originally had entered the country under a succession of politically and economically conservative though mostly democratic previous administrations – confronted with a newly elected, politically weak, democratic government espousing radically redistributive, populist economic policies. Officers of American multinational companies actively intrigued with representatives of the US government and the Chilean military to overthrow President Salvador Allende, who lost his life in the coup that initiated 17 years of often brutal military rule (Treverton, 1990). The Chilean experience illustrates the pessimistic hypothesis about the increased influence of foreign business in host country politics. Similar events transpired with the João Goulart administration (1961–64) in Brazil and the second Peronist government (1973–76) in Argentina, each of which the country's military officer corps, with the tacit support of traditional politicians and business leaders, also displaced by force.

There is another possible twist on these stories, however. Most contemporary economists, including many on the left, probably would agree that the economic policies of Allende, Goulart, and Isabel Perón were, in fact, unsound and unsustainable. Each of the three presidents, for example, raised civil service and public sector union wages when the treasury had no funds to back this move. Arguably, had multinational investors successfully pressured these governments to adopt less radical economic policies, then economic conditions would have improved and the excuse for a military coup could have evaporated. This second line of argument, the optimistic hypothesis, also plausibly applies to the more recent experiences of new democracies in emerging markets that have decided to welcome foreign direct (and portfolio) investors. These include Argentina and Brazil from the mid-1980s, or South Africa in the 1990s. In each case, the policy-makers in the new government who historically had been associated with economic nationalism gradually adopted many of the programs of neoliberals (on Argentina, see Armijo, 1994 and Gibson, 1997; for post-apartheid South Africa, see Daniels and Daniels, 1995). Also in each case, this shift in the overall tenor of public policies was initiated by technocrats, politicians, and other policy elites from the 'top down,' had to be sold to sceptical voters whose first preference was for classically populist economic policies, and was at least partly a response to political incumbents' perceptions of the need to attract foreign capital, especially in the form of direct investment.

Commercial Bank Loans to the Public Sector

The third category of international investments is *commercial bank loans to the public sector* of the emerging market country (row 3 of Table 14.1). I argued that bank loans to government should have a lesser impact on economic growth, while expanding the resources available to the political authorities to use for either developmental or directly electoral purposes with, in practice, comparatively little creditor oversight or external pressure to follow 'sound' economic policies, however defined. The risk of a balance-of-payments crisis, however, is higher with loan finance than with official credits or FDI. During the 1970s the authoritarian governments of Argentina and Brazil, and the civilian, semi-authoritarian government of Mexico, each received large quantities of foreign bank loans. In all three cases, foreign loans to non-democratic incumbents shored up unrepresentative political regimes by allowing political leaders to extend favors to politically crucial groups.[6] Interestingly, another consequence of foreign borrowing was to increase the *de facto* economic policy autonomy of governments from both foreign and domestic pressure to reform.[7] Finally, capital account surpluses due to foreign borrowing in all three Latin American countries served to make large current account deficits surprisingly painless, at least for upper-income groups, and thus probably deprived the democratic opposition of many potential allies among salaried workers and the business community. Until the 1982 debt crisis, the incumbent regimes in each of these countries continued to claim, with some plausibility, that they should be maintained in office because of their singular success in national economic management. Foreign loan inflows not only insulated the military regimes in these countries from foreign pressures to alter their regulatory regimes; they also protected authoritarian incumbents from criticism from domestic political opponents.

However, bank loans, even long-term ones, are a more volatile form of capital flow than foreign aid or direct investment. In Argentina, Mexico, and Brazil the effect of the 1982 financial crisis was a loss of credibility for authoritarian incumbents leading to dramatic changes of regime in Argentina in 1983 and Brazil in 1985, as each country returned to procedural political democracy. However, had the international environment of the 1980s been less favorable to democracy, the successor regimes in Brazil and Argentina might well also have been authoritarian. Mexico's civilian 'soft' authoritarian regime experienced no sudden, dramatic crisis, but rather a gradual erosion of public confidence (important to authoritarian as well as democratic regimes, albeit in somewhat different ways) throughout the 1980s. One consequence was to give previously feeble opposition parties a opportunity to press for fairer, more genuinely democratic, rules of the national political game (see Elizondo in this volume).

Commercial bank loans to a democratic government can also augment its resources and bolster its credibility. In the 1980s India, a democratic country which had resisted the blandishments of international bankers throughout the 1970s, became a large commercial bank borrower. Tellingly, one of the hopes of Indian politicians and policymakers was that, by borrowing from the foreign private sector, they could escape the economic policy conditionality imposed by public sector lenders, such as the International Monetary Fund, to which Prime Minister Indira Gandhi very reluctantly had had to turn for a large loan in 1981. As had been the case with Latin American sovereign borrowers of the 1970s, the foreign resources gave additional room for fiscal maneuver (or irresponsibility) to the incumbent government – though this time the incumbents were democratic. India experienced another external payments crisis in 1991, which led the country to another reluctant turn to the IMF and provoked policy-makers into beginning long-needed economic liberalization.[8] Fortunately for the long dominant Congress (I) Party, it was a short-lived coalition government of the non-Congress left parties that made the politically unpopular decision to turn to the IMF in early 1991; the Congress itself, under newly-elected Prime Minister P.V.N. Rao, took the onus of devaluing the rupee by 22 per cent in July of that year. Overall, since the external crisis was contained, access to foreign loan capital served to support both the political incumbents during most of the 1980s, that is, the Congress (I) Party, and also India's democratic political regime.

The cases of three large Latin American borrowers in the 1970s, and of India in the 1980s, thus generally confirm our suspicions that cross-border private bank lending to the public sector in emerging market countries increases both the economic and the political bargaining power of incumbent governments – unless and until a serious external payments crisis causes the economic management skills of the political leaders suddenly to be called into question.

Commercial Bank Loans to the Private Sector

This volume has suggested that the effects of *commercial bank loans to the private sector* (row 4), are likely to include a greater stimulus to economic and industrial growth and an increase in the political weight of large borrowing firms in domestic policy councils. The inflows should increase the bargaining chips of big business *vis-à-vis* the incumbent government. If local big business firms bring in significant quantities of foreign commercial bank loans, then authoritarian regimes should experience pressure from their entrepreneurs to liberalize, at least in the areas of respect for property, legal and predictable regulatory enforcement, and sometimes human rights. Of course, many of the most closed regimes, from China to Burma, during the 1970s heyday of commercial lending to developing countries lacked a business class that could directly attract foreign bank loans. Other authoritarian countries with private firms that might have borrowed abroad, such as the East Asian tigers like South Korea, operated domestic regulatory and financial environments that strongly encouraged local firms to depend on state banks instead.[9]

As it happens, the main examples of developing countries whose private firms directly contracted large quantities of medium and long-term commercial bank loans abroad are precisely those Latin American countries whose governments also were large borrowers, thus confounding our attempts to distinguish the effects of government versus private sector long-term borrowing. One proposition I suggested in Chapter 1 seems not to hold true in these cases, however. There does not seem to be evidence that countries that had a particularly large share of direct private sector borrowing abroad, such as Chile or Argentina, spent their borrowed funds, on average, more wisely than those with relatively smaller shares of private in total foreign borrowing. In fact, most observers have considered that Chile, along with Brazil, apparently invested with a reasonable degree of efficiency, while Argentina wasted a large portion of the funds it borrowed (Frieden, 1991, p. 80). One plausible explanation that is consistent with the logic developed in chapter one, however, is that the private sector in many of these countries, but perhaps in

Argentina particularly (see Lewis, 1990), was characterized by what has come to be known as 'crony capitalism,' in which firms' profits depend less on competitive efficiency and more on political connections that give them access to economic rents. Under these political conditions, private borrowers may expect that any exchange rate or other losses they experience are likely to be 'socialized' by the central government.

The expectation that big business would increase its bargaining power with the authoritarian central government, and then would tend to push for political liberalization if not full democracy, seems to have described outcomes in Brazil (where business dissatisfaction with military rule was crucial in accelerating democratization, as Peter Kingstone notes in his chapter in this volume), but not in either Chile (where big business could not even protect itself from waves of bankruptcy when the debt crisis hit in 1982–83, much less impose a liberalizing political agenda on military incumbents) or Argentina (where crony capitalism prevailed, linking military officers and big business in non-productive rent-seeking). In these three countries taken together, there is not strong evidence that big businesses used their ability to attract foreign loans to enhance their politically-relevant domestic resources, or even that big business' political preferences tended toward political liberalization, though not always the transition to full mass democracy. If the expected effect is present, it has been swamped by other, more powerful, influences.[10]

I do not know of a good empirical example of a democratic developing country whose private firms directly tapped multinational commercial banks for large quantities of long-term loans. This cell in Table 14.1 is thus empty.

Portfolio Flows to the Public Sector

This fifth category of international financial flows is shown in row 5 of Table 14.1. Our expectations of their effects on the borrowing country's political economy were quite similar to those postulated for commercial bank lending. *Portfolio inflows to the public sector* should provide a lesser stimulus to economic growth than those going to the private sector, but a greater political resource for the sitting government. As noted, portfolio flows differ from bank loans in one important respect: balance-of-payments crises provoked or exacerbated by large-scale overnight capital outflows are much more likely to occur with securities explicitly marketed to their purchasers as being highly liquid.

Mexico during the early 1990s provided a reasonably clear example of several hypothesized consequences of portfolio flows coming into government coffers (see the chapters by William C. Gruben, Carlos Elizondo, and Walter Molano).[11] The substantial portfolio capital inflows to the government, beginning in the very late 1980s and accelerating in 1993, on the whole strengthened the semi-authoritarian regime, and its domination by the Mexico's longtime ruling political party, the Partido Revolutionário Institucional (PRI). Foreign purchases of portfolio capital inflows in the Mexican government peso-denominated *cetes* securities, and later the dollar-indexed *tesobonos*, enhanced the freedom of maneuver of the PRI political incumbents, just as the earlier commercial bank loans had done in the 1970s. As Mary Ann Haley and Jeffrey Winters emphasize in their contributions to this book, foreign portfolio investors seek political stability. However, as Carlos Elizondo notes in his essay, sometimes a preference for political stability, in practice, can be a preference for a process of gradual, orderly democratization to continue. Thus, in 1994, the enhanced visibility of Mexican politics in the US as a consequence of the North American Free Trade Agreement (NAFTA) had made US investors aware that a possible source of instability in Mexico was popular protests against the continuing legacies of soft authoritarianism in Mexico, such as election fraud. That is, the need to retain the confidence of notoriously fickle foreign investors put pressure on the out-going Salinas administration to run clean elections. Business confidence prior to the election, of course, was helped by the fact that it looked as though the leftist PRD, whose standard bearer, Cuauhtémoc Cárdenas, had come close to winning the 1988 election, had no chance in 1994. In August PRI candidate Ernesto Zedillo, as expected, won easily.

Unfortunately, the story did not end there. For a variety of reasons, both economically sound and politically opportunistic, outgoing President Carlos Salinas chose not to devalue despite a widening trade deficit.[12] His administration convinced world markets that it would not precipitously devalue by replacing peso-denominated treasury securities, as they came due, with dollar-indexed bonds offering an attractive interest rate. In December 1994, Zedillo's economic team finally devalued the peso by 15 per cent, an intrinsically reasonable amount in terms relative to price inflation prevailing in Mexico as compared to the US Nonetheless, the markets panicked. By early February 1995, the peso's value stabilized at 40 per cent below its earlier level, only stopping there due to the firm backing of a $50 billion rescue package engineered by the Clinton administration.[13] The Mexican population, which had endured a drop in the real urban minimum wage of more than 50 per cent following its 1982 international debt crisis,[14] and only had begun to see economic recovery in the early 1990s, was stunned to discover that further years of austerity were in store.

The consequences for Mexican democracy over the subsequent three years of the peso crisis were fairly consistent with our theoretical expectations. On the one hand, the PRI stopped looking like a miraclemaker, and the stock of opposition parties rose. Greater transparency of political activity, and incremental progress towards fairer formal rules of the game (election procedures and campaign financing, for example) resulted.[15] These trends were democratizing, and contributed to the opposition victories in the mid-1997 elections. On the other hand, the economic consequences of the peso crisis clean-up have, as also theorized, undercut the social and economic positions of several groups whose active participation in writing new 'rules of the game' might be expected to ensure full and fair mass participation in democratic processes. As has happened in country after country, middle class unionized civil servants and public sector industrial workers were laid off in large numbers, weakening these groups as political actors. Post-crisis structural adjustment also has made the poor, both urban and rural, more desperate than ever, encouraging the twin responses of apathy and resignation for the majority, along with a turn to violent protest for a minority.[16] The interim bottom line is thus something like this: Mexico's peso crisis has brought greater political freedom and competitiveness, but has heightened economic insecurity and inequality. The fact that government short-term debt was a large part of the problem has put the public sector on a particularly tight rein.

Turning to the case of portfolio capital inflows to the government of an already democratic emerging market country, we could expect many of the same outcomes: the direct positive impact on economic growth probably would be limited because public sector borrowers have a political as well as an economic investment agenda; while they lasted, portfolio purchases of government bonds could provide a welcome source of fungible resources to the political incumbents – but portfolio inflows would be prone to sudden reversals, possibly bringing political as well as economic crises for the country and/or its rulers. Argentina in the early 1990s, under President Carlos Menem of the Justicialist (Peronist) Party, was a newly-democratic country that allowed itself to sell large quantities of government debt to buyers bringing capital from abroad.[17] As it happened, the Menem team had occasion to regret its reliance upon portfolio inflows for government deficit financing. When Mexico's peso crisis exploded in late December 1994, first-world investors, as had happened in 1982, tended to generalize their pull-out across other emerging markets, especially in Latin America, without a great deal of regard for the possible differences among countries. In early 1995 Argentina, Ecuador, Brazil, and others experienced the 'tequila effect' of a backlash from Mexico's crisis.[18] While Menem, along with Argentina's decade old democracy, survived the dramatic ebb of capital, the government budget (which thereafter incorporated much higher interest rates on the public debt) and the Argentine economy (where an incipient recovery from the recession of the 1990s was dashed) paid the price.

The tequila effect was not sufficiently severe to have unbalanced Argentina's new democracy. However, it is not too difficult to imagine a scenario in which it might have. President Menem himself was quite lucky in the timing of Argentina's narrowly averted financial crash: the movement to alter the Constitution to allow him to run again, and his victory in that election, already had passed by early 1995 when the run on the Mexican peso began to batter the Argentine peso. Had the Argentine electoral calendar been otherwise, he might well have lost his bid for reelection.

Portfolio Investments to the Private Sector

The final type of cross-border capital flow is *portfolio investments in private sector securities* (row 6). With an authoritarian regime in the capital-importing country, our expectations would be that such flows would make a potentially large contribution to private investment by the country's largest firms (that is, those whose shares constitute the blue chip investments in the local stock exchange, or who are able to issue bonds or commercial paper in global markets), that the heads of these firms would tend to join foreign direct investors overtly or covertly in pushing for greater political liberalization (in the sense of a rule of law and civil liberties protections) without necessarily risking too much to call for full democratic elections, and that the desire to avoid the ever-present potential of a major capital outflow would lead to a fairly cautious and deferential attitude on the part of the authoritarian rulers towards their business supporters. Preemptive neoliberal economic policy reforms also should be likely.

South Africa in the 1970s and 1980s provides an interesting case. Rich in diamonds, gold, and minerals, it long had one of the most active stock and securities exchanges outside the major industrial democracies. It also had a special kind of authoritarian political system, one that provided liberal democracy for a minority, but used apartheid to exclude the black majority from economic, social, and political power. Generalizing very roughly, in recent decades black Africans were the workers and small farmers, Afrikaaners the civil servants and commercial family farmers, while English-speaking whites dominated the liberal professions and upper reaches of business. British capital was long the largest source of foreign investment, both direct and portfolio, in a tradition dating back to the late nineteenth century. Under these circumstances, foreign capital inflows to the local private sector on the one hand tended to strengthen the white minority, the elite who benefited from authoritarian rule over all non-white residents. At the same time, business links to the outside probably strengthened the English-speaking minority within the overall white minority that ruled the country. Under these particular demographic circumstances, the predicted politically liberalizing effect of capital inflows to the business class was muted by the solidarity of the white community as a whole. Nonetheless, the English-speaking white community was somewhat more open to a gradual transition to democracy than the Afrikaaner one, perhaps partly because of its greater familiarity with the larger world through international business links. As was the case in our examination above of commercial bank lending to the private sector in authoritarian Latin America, there does not seem to be compelling evidence that private portfolio inflows to the South African private sector during the 1970s and 1980s was a great source of pressure for economic efficiency, although my judgment on this point is quite impressionistic (see Daniels and Daniels, 1995).

Another obvious case is that of Singapore, in the 1980s and early 1990s both an Asian 'tiger' and a hot emerging stock market. As of the mid-1990s, Singapore's longtime strongman and patriarch, Lee Kwan Yew, was respected at home and throughout the region because of the country's great economic advances under his tutelage. At the same time, Lee and his proteges, including Prime Minister Goh Chok Tong, could not afford to alienate their business leaders, on whom the country's prosperity and ultimately their own political tenure depended. In the case of Singapore, many business families within the country also had extensive ties with the overseas Chinese community around the world, including those who had located in the advanced industrial democracies. The Singapore business community was quite far from sharing, for example, the political opinions of radical students who wished to move rapidly to full democracy. However, the internationally competitive business community also was sensitive to its image abroad, collectively wincing when, for example, a Japanese popular song mocked Singapore as the place where chewing gum was a banned substance.

Financial globalization in Singapore had resulted in a somewhat freer press, a dawning but vigorous debate over the pros and cons of paternalistic government, and signficant moves toward political liberalization – stopping well short of formal representative democracy – over the decade ending in the mid-1990s. Interestingly, Singapore to mid-January 1998 had escaped serious damage from the East Asian financial crisis, at least by comparison with its neighbors. This was probably because there are important distinctions among the various types of new cross-border portfolio investments in the emerging market country's private sector, beyond the obvious differences between portfolio flows and the other less-volatile flows discussed in this book. Singapore, although an important emerging stock market, did not suddenly in late 1997 reveal large amounts of short-term foreign borrowing by local banks – a major source of trouble in Thailand, Indonesia, and South Korea.

Indonesia is another authoritarian country that in the 1990s received increasing amounts of portfolio capital inflows into its private sector, particularly the banking system. Like Lee in Singapore, Indonesia's Suharto benefited from large portfolio capital inflows, in that they made his regime and government look like excellent economic managers. However, and unlike Singapore, Indonesia has had a serious financial crisis; as of this writing the currency had dropped 80 per cent against the US dollar, compared to its level in early 1997. What are the apparent implications for democracy? Jeffrey A. Winters, who was able to revise his chapter on Indonesia, is struck by the much more facile and effective social and political response to the financial crisis in democratic Thailand and South Korea, as compared to authoritarian Indonesia. President Suharto's initial response to the crisis seems to have been to promise the IMF whatever it wanted, and then, in his government's budget of early January, as well as his plans to be succeeded by his high-spending Vice President Habibie, to have attempted to continue with crony capitalism – with large areas of the economy reserved for his own family – as usual. The incumbent authoritarian government was proving extremely resistent to neoliberal economic reform, even after a violent balance-of-payments crisis and the forced retirement of Suharto in May 1998. Unfortunately, the first few months of the Habibie government did not result in significant structural reforms of Indonesia's underlying political economy. Perhaps because Indonesia's poor and middle sectors, but not yet its top elites, had thus far paid the bulk of the costs of the crisis.

I close the case studies with a look at portfolio flows to the local private sector in three democratic or democratizing emerging market countries: India, Thailand, and South Korea in the 1990s. Although all types of foreign capital inflows tend to assist political incumbents – so long as a balance-of-payments crisis is avoided – I argued in Chapter 1 that those flows whose local disposition is in the hands of the private sector could be more problematic for the often weak or fragile democratic governments in emerging market countries. Portfolio flows controlled by private entrepreneurs should stimulate productive investment while empowering local big business as a potential counterweight to the national political leaders.

India had been securely democratic for decades. Its portfolio flows to the private sector in the 1990s, in contrast to most of the East Asian countries that had trouble in late 1997, had been mainly in the form of equity and bond flows, particularly those associated with large Indian firms raising funds directly by securities floated in international markets, global depository receipts (GDRs). Although even limited entry by private investors directly into Indian capital markets has had an important influence on the shape of Indian financial regulations, as detailed by John Echeverri-Gent in his essay, the Reserve Bank of India, the country's central bank and main commercial bank regulator, placed strict limits on the amount of short-term foreign loans and deposits that commercial banks could contract, resulting in a regulatory regime with substantial capital controls still intact. This regulatory caution appears to have paid off; through mid January 1998, India had not yet caught the 'Asian flu'.

India also is a case where our predictions about the political and policy consequences of capital inflows to private big businesses provide a plausible description of reality. On the one hand, the private sector became increasingly important to the balance of payments in the 1980s and early 1990s, both as a source of exports and as an investment destination for foreign funds. Economic policies, meanwhile, became more market-oriented, particularly since 1991, and the profession of businessperson, by all accounts, has higher status and greater attraction for the 'best and the brightest' than it did in the first three decades after independence in 1947. There is a chicken-and-egg problem here, as it is hard to know whether businesspersons have become more politically and socially prominent as a consequence of economic policy changes initiated by government bureaucrats and senior politicians, or whether the generally pro-market preferences of an increasingly confident private sector wield more influence than previously. Both are probably true. The causes of India's recent economic liberalization are in any case over-determined (Varshney, 1996; Echeverri-Gent, 1997). In his carefully nuanced contribution to this volume, Echeverri-Gent suggests a new twist on the 'optimistic hypothesis' about the effects of private foreign capital flows: by forcing greater regulatory transparency and breaking up cosy oli-gopolies, democratic integrity is preserved and deepened, as small businesses and small investors get a more level playing field and, most importantly, a corrupting influence from the crony capitalists to the government is damp-ened. At the same time, he concedes that trade and financial globalization in India in general already have widened interregional income disparities – and probably will continue to do so, with potentially ominous implications for democratic and political stability.

The final examples are Thailand and South Korea, newly-democratic countries that received large amounts of portfolio capital inflows to their private sectors in the 1990s, with particularly large flows of short-term hard currency debt, often borrowed by local banks who then would relend in local currency, making their profits on the spread.

Danny Unger's chapter summarizes Thai political economy since the mid-1970s. While agreeing that local big business prefers political liberalization to full democratization, Unger sees the strengthening of local private capital in Thailand in the 1980s and 1990s as an important counterweight to a still very powerful military-bureaucratic-civil service complex, which the prolifer-ating clientelistic political parties had utterly failed to rein in. That is, given Unger's assessment of the stage of Thai democratization, he sees redistribu-tion of economic and political power in the direction of local big business prior to the financial crisis as, on balance, having increased political competi-tion and accountability. Moreover, although he is less explicit on this point, Unger tends toward the 'optimistic' interpretation of the post-crisis increased indirect influence of foreign institutional investors on Thailand's economic policy choices, suggesting that sounder macroeconomic and regu-latory policies may result. It is also possible to imagine that the balance-of-payments crisis could weaken Thai democracy, at least in the short-run, by reinforcing the impression that civilian politicians are both incompetent and corrupt, and implying that the Thai military is neither. However, as both Winters and Unger note, Thai adjustment to its financial crisis in late 1997 and through January 1998 was reasonably rapid, arguably *because of* its comparatively democratic political game.

A related dynamic seemed to be at work in Korea. That country's balance-of-payments crisis hit before the December 1997 presidential election, in contrast to events in Mexico in 1994, and served to discredit both the conservative government of incumbent President Kim Young Sam (a former dissident who owed his election to a rapprochement with the outgoing military rulers) and the *chaebol*, powerful and long-favored oligopoly business conglomerates (Kim, 1996; Amsden, 1989). Long-time dissident Kim Dae Jung won a plurality in a three-way race and used the opportunity given him by the crisis to win striking early negotiating victories even before formally assuming office.[19] As in Thailand, the financial crisis may prove to have a silver lining in that it gives reforming democratic governments some leverage to reduce some of the cosy ties between big business and the state. However, as in Mexico, those who suffer most in the short run will be those in the lower, and to a lesser extent the middle, income groups. Political democratization may be accelerated, but the economic pain will be considerable. Furthermore, if the Rueschemeyer, Stephens, and Stephens (1992) analysis is correct, then the apparent weakening of groups such as labor unions during the transition to democracy might hold worries for the future. The alternative hypothesis is that, by being flexible and 'reasonable' in this time of crisis, Korean union leaders may permanently earn themselves a place at the table. Moreover, to the extent that the foreign investor community sees cautious progress in democratization as a key indicator of that highly-desired quality, 'political stability' (see Elizondo in this volume), then the financial crises in Thailand and South Korea may work to secure those countries' democratic openings.

       *   *   *

I ended Chapter 1 with a series of expectations. Based on the evidence presented herein, how have they fared?

1. I suggested that, contrary to the too-facile expectations of many in the business and policy communities, economic growth does not necessarily promote political democracy, at least not for poor and middle-income countries. While this collaborative project has not directly addressed this link, it seems implicit in the stories told of Mexico and Brazil before the 1982 debt crisis, and Indonesia and Vietnam in the more recent period. What economic growth does do, for as long as it continues, is to

legitimize incumbents. Conversely, however, where authoritarian regimes have wrapped themselves in the flag of successful economic management, they can be denuded rapidly by financial blowups. This happened to authoritarian rulers in Argentina, Uruguay, and Brazil in the early 1980s (though Chile's General Augusto Pinochet held on), and was a factor in the overthrow of Philippine dictator Ferdinand Marcos and gradual liberalization of Mexico's civilian one-party state.

2. No contributors to this volume rigorously tried to test the hypothesis that inflows controlled by the private sector within the emerging market country, or by foreign direct investors, would be allocated more efficiently, resulting in greater increments to growth, although Stefano Manzocchi summarizes related literature, finding the links between private foreign capital and growth more tenuous than sometimes assumed. Walter Molano's contribution is implicitly provocative on this point, however, as he suggests that the long-run economic consequences of the Thai and East Asian crises of late 1997 could be more serious than the Mexican crisis of 1994–95, precisely because the borrowers in East Asia were in the private sector, whereas Mexico's peso crisis was first and foremost a crisis of the government's ability to meet its short-term debt obligations. This apparent anomaly – that capital flows coming to the local private sector might produce deeper economic crises than public-sector portfolio borrowing – is perhaps explained by the fact that many of the private borrowers in East Asia were banks and financial institutions operating in newly-liberated capital markets with inadequate regulatory oversight (see Amsden and Euh, 1997). In fact, several of the authors note that greater transparency and predictability in national financial regulation – often missing in emerging markets – would be a good thing, whether for better economic results in the capital-importing country (see Manzocchi), for foreign investors (Molano), for small investors and ordinary citizens within the emerging market country (Echeverri-Gent), or even for the institutionalization of democracy itself (Stone).

3. Different institutional forms of cross-border capital flows would, I thought, differentially promote the fortunes, and local political influence, of four different political actors: foreign governments and international organizations, incumbent governments in the capital importing country, foreign direct investors, and local big business. The evidence of increments of both political and economic influence accruing to foreign lender/donor governments and/or to borrower governments as a consequence of different institutional forms of cross-border capital flows is straightforward and consistent with these predictions. With the relative decline of foreign aid, for example, not only have borrower governments lost resources, but foreign governments (often to their surprise) also

have lost influence. It is worth pondering the consequences of the fact that the currency trader George Soros in the early 1990s gave more aid to promote democracy in Central and Eastern Europe than the US government.[20]

With respect to foreign business, my initial decision to call the influence of multinational direct investors 'political,' but to exclude the indirect influence of global private portfolio investors (before any financial crisis) from this framework seems to have underemphasized important facets of the story. Thus, for example, Haley, Porter, Stone, and Echeverri-Gent in this volume each detail some of the different ways in which the mostly neoliberal preferences of private global investors (in the case of Russia, Russian owners of wealth who had the connections to engage in capital flight) have constrained public policy choice in emerging market countries, even when the foreign investors did not actively lobby incumbents. Moreover, once a financial crisis looms, private portfolio investors may become directly involved, as in the cases of foreign institutional investors in Mexico in 1994–95, or private multinational banks who made short-term loans to domestic banks in East Asia in 1997. Tellingly, South Korean President-elect Kim Dae Jung granted George Soros an audience in the first two weeks after his December 1997 upset victory, making sure the financial endorsement of Korea implied by the meeting was well-photographed (Burton, 1998).

The findings on the political consequences of foreign inflows coming under the control of local private business firms were intriguing but difficult to generalize. In some authoritarian countries, from Chile and Argentina in the 1970s to Indonesia in the 1990s, the private business community was so dependent upon the political authorities that even an ability to attract foreign capital inflows seemed not to give it much of an independent voice. Nor was it clear that these borrowers favored even limited political liberalization. In fact, strengthening business families close to the regime has often propped up authoritarian rule indirectly – at least unless and until a financial crisis shook the system (see Winters, this volume).

In other developing countries, private business has been a vocal and somewhat independent political actor. Where private capitalists have been able to attract foreign capital without the assistance or intermediation of their government, they have often asserted themselves in domestic policy debates. In both authoritarian and democratic Brazil politicians needed business support at least as much as the reverse (see Kingstone, this volume). Private business borrowers in newly-democratizing countries such as Thailand and South Korea, or newly market-oriented democratic countries like India, were also flying high before the late 1997 crises, partly because of their importance to the balance of payments.

Danny Unger's chapter suggests that increased influence and independence for the domestic business community was a welcome source of pluralism, given Thailand's long tradition of a centralized, closed, state bureaucracy. With the late 1997 crisis, both government and business leaders lost credibility with the Thai public, although the medium-run consequences of this remain unclear. Similarly, Korea's large integrated financial–industrial conglomerates, the *chaebol*, in the mid-1990s had used their access to foreign funds as yet another advantage *vis-à-vis* small firms. The *chaebol* have been humbled by the late 1997 financial crisis, quite plausibly strengthening President-elect Kim Dae Jung's hand in enacting needed regulatory reforms.

India's business community in the 1990s both aided the country's balance of payments by being able to tap global capital markets and increased its public voice in the policy arena, although the precise connection between these two trends is unclear. John Echeverri-Gent argues that the greater transparency demanded by foreign institutional investors as a quid pro quo for bringing their monies into the country has had the salutory effect of curbing corruption in local business practices. This, he concludes, strengthens democracy, because it reduces the incentives for local business leaders to attempt to suborn politicians to cover up corruption. That is, while Indian big business has been strengthened in some ways, it also has been held to account and disciplined in other respects. We can probably conclude that direct loans to and/or investments with the local private sector do increase big business' control over politically-relevant resources. How much, and with what political consequences, cannot be answered outside of the context of individual countries.

4. There can be little doubt that balance-of-payments crises are bad for political incumbents, both in terms of the credibility of their economic policies (see Gruben) and the length of their political tenure, a point stressed by Elizondo and Kingstone in particular. On the other hand, and provocatively, democratizing polities that are relatively pluralist and open to policy debate may be more able to cope with financial crises flexibly and effectively than authoritarian regimes (see Winters).[21] Thus, in late 1997 both South Korea and Thailand changed both economic policies and chief executives while continuing their democratic opening. By January, 1998 Indonesia had not made either shift. Both China and Vietnam have been protected from the Asian financial crisis thus far by a combination of reliance on FDI rather than portfolio flows, plus continued capital controls (see Haughton). It is hard to imagine the non-democratic, secretive regimes in either country responding successfully to a financial crisis should one hit.

5, 6. Chapter 1 also expressed concerns over the medium-term political consequences of the worsening of income distribution that often – or always? –

accompanied post-balance-of-payments crisis structural adjustment programs. Even more ominously, the same effects on income distribution (and the subsequent distribution of political influence), I argued, might be expected from preemptive neoliberal economic reforms of the sort that emerging market country governments often have had to enact in order to head off a financial crisis that threatened. This hypothesis is hard to evaluate because it requires the construction of counter-factual scenarios, but a few concluding words may be relevant.

The post-1982 debt crisis period of structural adjustment in Latin America is the best source of data, since the waves of financial crisis associated with the portfolio flows of the 1990s occurred too recently to evaluate them. Three trends were apparent.

- First, poverty and inequality worsened dramatically throughout Latin America during the debt crisis decade. Moreover, neither poverty nor inequality was reduced in the early 1990s, even when most countries of the region began to grow again.[22]
- Second, procedural political democracy took hold and deepened throughout the region.[23] A contributing factor was the discrediting of military regimes throughout the region that had legitimized political repression in the 1970s by rapid economic growth.
- Third, the room for public policy maneuver by Latin American governments in the 1990s clearly had shrunk by comparison with previous decades, particularly the 1950s through the 1970s. The neoliberal policy preferences of the late twentieth century's global portfolio investors led them to shun countries that adopted leftist policy agendas that, for example, redistributed land or other assets, made the tax system more progressive, increased social spending, and so on (see Haley and Porter, this volume).

From the viewpoint of the distribution of political power within Latin American emerging market countries the news was thus both good and bad. On the one hand, political pluralism and the openness and competitiveness of politics increased as a consequence of the external debt crisis of the 1980s. On the other hand, those groups whose politically-relevant resources already were scarce had their *economic* power diminished even further just as the rules of the successor democratic games were being negotiated. Meanwhile, the debt crisis also had negative consequences for the international *distribution of political power* between the governments of developing countries and foreigners, both private investors and their home governments (see Porter).[24]

The optimistic comeback to these observations might make some of the following points. Latin America is not the world; there is thus no reason to believe that its experience of structural adjustment predicts anything about East Asia, Eastern Europe or anywhere else.[25] After all, income distribution was infinitely more unequal in Latin America in 1980 than in East Asia in 1995; perhaps initial inequality is the main determinant of structural adjustment that makes the already poor relatively poorer.

Moreover, international trade theory predicts that the locally abundant factors of production – typically including unskilled labor in emerging market countries – will see their relative economic returns rise as a consequence of greater integration with the global economy, because these factors will be relatively scarcer on the world stage (Stolper and Samuelson, 1941; Frieden and Rogowski, 1996).[26] The recessions and cuts in government spending associated with structural adjustment may be particularly burdensome for the poor, yet inflation stabilization, also demanded by global private portfolio investors, disproportionately benefits lower income groups since the poor and unsophisticated typically lack access to the diversified asset portfolios that upper income groups use to protect themselves from price volatility (see Stone in this volume, and Armijo, 1998). Finally, and most persuasively, neoliberal reforms, although they cause transitional pain, plausibly improve the functioning of the economy in the medium and long run. In particular, they eliminate most opportunities for politically-protected, but economically-wasteful, rent-seeking by petty government bureaucrats.[27]

7. The most important conclusion of Chapter 1, finally, was that little could be said about the likely consequences of the changing forms of foreign capital flows for democratic development in emerging market countries in the absence of knowledge about the current political system. In general, net inflows of all types boosted incumbents, while sudden net outflows destabilized them. Portfolio flows – including stocks, bonds, and short-term debt – have in the mid-1990s, unfortunately, more than lived up to their reputation for volatility.

There thus are some reasons to believe that current trends in global financial markets are not entirely favorable for the oft-heralded turn to democracy by developing countries in the late twentieth century. Still, given the conditions of global economic competition today, most developing countries would be worse off in the absence of foreign capital inflows, whatever their form. So long as they do not exit immediately, most capital inflows do promote economic growth in the recipient country, particularly when the funds are invested with an eye to market rather than political criteria. In the long-run (if not necessarily during the interim) capitalist economic growth does seem to be associated with liberal democracy. Liberal democracy ('procedural political democracy'), in turn, provides at least limited protections to the economically disenfranchised, and is a political system superior to any variety of authoritarianism (military–technocratic, fascist, Communist, theocratic, or whatever) for all but the dictator and his or her group. This conclusion's implicit policy recommendation, therefore, is not the naive advice that emerging market countries somehow ought to resist the blandishments of foreign portfolio investors. Rather, the lesson may be that developing countries (both governments and citizens) consider opening their markets up to global financial flows at least somewhat cautiously and with an educated awareness of the risks involved.[28]

Notes

1. The countries assigned to particular cells had larger than modal capital inflows of the type indicated; however, the type of capital flow indicated, as for example 'bank loans to private firms,' was not necessarily the single most important source of foreign capital inflows for that country in that period.

2. Some observers argue that the World Bank, for example, was a significant influence moving economic policy in the Philippines in a generally neoliberal direction. See Broad (1988). In my view, the portfolio investment received by the country in the 1990s has been infinitely more effective in producing macroeconomic policy changes in an orthodox direction.

3. On US policies toward sub-Saharan Africa, see Clough (1992).

4. A plurality of bilateral donors also came in handy for India and some other aid recipients. When western foreign aid donors attempted to impose economic and political conditions that Indian Prime Minister Indira Gandhi found onerous (for example, US pressure to devalue in 1966, US opposition to Indian involvement in the war over Bangladesh in 1971), then the Indian goverment sought alternative sources of foreign assistance from the Soviet Union.

5. In general, the notion that MNC investors help promote 'sound' economic policy should not be taken too far. MNCs also can tolerate large deviations from impersonal, market-oriented economic policies when their own profits are large. For example, many MNCs have been happy to engage in high-cost, tariff-protected production for local markets.

6. Foreign funds permitted, for example, economically questionable but politically useful policies such as the purchase of new weapons for the military in Argentina, expansion of export and farm subsidies in Brazil, and extension of generous benefits to members of public sector unions in Mexico, Argentina, and Brazil.

7. In Brazil, for example, accelerating levels of inflation and public-sector debt seemed an acceptable tradeoff to governing elites as long as rapid economic growth continued and foreign capital inflows kept domestic interest rates from rising significantly (see Fishlow, 1989).

8. The payments crisis' proximate causes were the rupee's overvaluation and the sudden strain caused by the several effects of the Persian Gulf War, from higher oil import prices to the loss of substantial workers' remittances from Indians employed in Kuwait. When the financial scare hit, the main capital outflows were private portfolio investments in so-called NRI (non-resident Indian) deposit accounts; nonetheless, the fact that India's total foreign debt had risen to close to $90 billion constituted an additional worry.

9. On the role of state control of financing in South Korea, see Kim (1996), and Woo (1991).
10. Jeffry Frieden (1991) suggests what the missing variable might be. He explains variations in local business' policy preferences between Brazil, the members of whose business community competed with one another for sector-specific subsidies from government, and Chile or Argentina where business accepted radically pared down government and neoliberal policies, by reference to Chile and Argentina's higher historical levels of class conflict which made private business more dependent upon the state's repressive apparatus. Thus the Brazilian business community, less dependent upon the state for internal security, felt free to demand both more economic benefits from government – and more rapid and substantial political liberalization.
11. By early 1994 foreign participants accounted for as much as 70 to 80 per cent of daily trading in Mexico's stock market (Fidler and Frasier, 1994). They also held around 40 per cent of outstanding federal government debt, according to Banco de México figures showing a breakdown of holders of all outstanding government debt supplied to the author by the International Institute of Finance in Washington, D.C. As of February 1994, 1.4 per cent of federal government debt was held by Mexican banks, 25.1 per cent by the Banco de México itself, 40.7 per cent by foreigners, and 32.8 per cent by the non-financial sector resident in Mexico. I note again that the form in which most international financial statistics are collected makes it difficult to distinguish between portfolio flows destined for the capital-importing country's public and private sectors. My choice to assume that most short-term debt flows were destined for the private sector, as reported in the summary statistics in this volume's introduction and first chapter, will have understated the Mexican government's borrowing abroad.
12. Many observers have argued that Mexico's December 1994 crisis was more of a liquidity than a solvency crisis. If private investors had not reacted so precipitously, neither the subsequent balance-of-payments nor fiscal crises need have reached anything like the magnitude that they did. On the economic issues, see Gruben and Molano in this volume; Sachs, Tornell, and Velasco (1995); Roett (1996); Passell (1995). On the politics of Mexican international financial policies in 1994, see Elizondo in this volume; Starr (1997).
13. The package included $20 billion in loans and guarantees from the US, a then unprecedented $17.8 billion from the International Monetary Fund (IMF), and a similarly noteworthy $10 billion from the Bank for International Settlements (BIS), the bankers' central bank.
14. In 1990, the real urban minimum wage in Mexico City was 45.5, where 1980 was 100. Real average wages in manufacturing were 77.9, with the same base year. ECLAC (1993), pp. 34–5.
15. My reading of Mexican politics is that Zedillo himself is sincere about democratizing reform, although progress undeniably has been two steps forward, and one and a half back. See Dillon (1996); Crawford (1997).
16. Even the Zapatista movement in Chiapas state, which predates the 1994 financial crisis, is largely a reaction against neoliberal economic reforms, in this case mainly the land-tenure changes that accompanied Mexico's accession to NAFTA.
17. In the case of Argentina, much of the 'foreign' capital was undoubtedly returning flight capital, that is, money that Argentine citizens, often illegally, had spirited out of the country from the late 1970s through the 1980s to place in safe havens abroad. From the viewpoint of the present analysis, however, this

interesting fact is irrelevant, since the behavior of the owners of the portfolio investments is equivalent.

18. On Brazil's experience, see Kingstone in this volume. On the tequila effect, see Roett (1996), and Molano (1997).

19. The President-elect prevailed upon the outgoing incumbent to pardon two former presidents, Chun Do Hwan and Roh Te Woo, facing life sentences for corruption and abuse of power. By this act, Kim Dae Jung looked magnanimous (President Chun had planned to execute the dissident, only desisting because of vocal and high-level international pressure) and won friends among the military and traditional economic elites. In early January 1998, Kim Dae Jung got at least initial agreement from normally militant trade union leaders for their acquiesance to some layoffs, in exchange for an extension of Korea's thin social safety net.

20. The Soros Foundation spent more than $123 million in Central Europe between 1989 and 1994, about five times the US government's National Endowment for Democracy (Miller, 1997).

21. *New York Times* columnist Thomas L. Friedman (1998) distinguished among countries with modern 'transparent' domestic financial regulation, that have been hurt least (Taiwan, Hong Kong, Singapore), countries with 'democratic, but corrupt, systems,' that 'were hurt second worst' but already have begun to adjust (Thailand, South Korea), and the 'corrupt, authoritarian regime that can't adapt' and 'is going to melt down' (Indonesia).

22. The Inter-American Development Bank (1997, pp. 17–18), which favors market-liberalization and generally tries to put a positive face on neoliberal structural adjustment, put it this way: 'After falling continually throughout the 1970s, poverty increased dramatically in Latin America during the 1980s ... [D]uring the 1990s, the distribution of Latin American income did not improve, though the persistent deterioration that characterized the late 1980s was arrested ... [P]oorer income groups typically benefit disproportionately from economic recovery, just as they are disproportionately hurt by bad times... But the relatively well-off groups of Latin American society appear to have benefited from the recovery of the 1990s more than the poorest classes'. For more critical views of structural adjustment , see Veltmeyer, Petras, and Vieux (1997), Oxhorn and Ducatenzeiler (1998), or Boron (1995). Baer and Maloney (1997), on the other hand, conclude that neoliberal reforms will not worsen Latin American income distribution in the long run.

23. The literature is vast. See Diamond, Linz, and Lipset (eds) (1989). On democratic consolidation in the 1990s, see Domínguez and Lowenthal (eds) (1996).

24. Interestingly, the perception among policy-makers and intellectuals in *advanced industrial countries* is also that financial globalization has limited public policy autonomy in their countries, shifting 'power' abroad (see Underhill (ed.), (1997); Schrecker (ed.), (1997); Strange (1986); Cerny (ed.) 1993). The relative gainers were not emerging market countries, of course, but rather private owners of capital. Dani Rodrik (1997) provides a resolutely moderate synthesis of the overall globalization debate, that nonetheless acknowledges the increased bargaining power of capital.

25. Sub-Saharan Africa's experience of structural adjustment in the 1980s was even more depressing than Latin America's, though the causes of this failure are wildly overdetermined (Poku and Pettiford (eds), 1998).

26. For a contrary argument that is empirically rather than theoretically based, see Cohen (1998). He noted that globalization in the 1990s in Mexico, Brazil, and Argentina, Latin America's three largest emerging markets, seems to have

worsened income differentials and decreased the returns to unskilled labor, as governments undermined collective bargaining traditions in order to attract foreign capital, while local capitalists shed workers and adopt the latest (capital-intensive) technology in order to compete globally.

27. On the theory of economic 'rents,' see Krueger (1974). For arguments in favor of market reforms to eliminate corruption and rent-seeking that were written about India, but apply more generally, see Jha (1980), and Bardhan (1984).

28. The crises in portfolio flows of the mid-1990s have led to renewed interest in those countries that have retained substantial capital controls, including Chile (see Fidler, 1998) and China.

Bibliography

Amsden, Alice (1989) *Asia's Next Giant: South Korea and Late Industrialization* (New York: Oxford University Press).

Amsden, Alice H. and Yoon-Dae Euh (1997) 'Behind Korea's Plunge,' *New York Times*, 27 November.

Armijo, Leslie Elliott (1998) 'Political Finance in Brazil and India: An Argument about Democracy and Inflation,' unpublished book manuscript.

Armijo, Leslie Elliott (1994) 'Menem's Mania?: The Timing of Privatization in Argentina,' *Southwestern Journal of Law and Trade in the Americas*, 1 (1), Fall, pp. 1–28.

Baer, Werner and William Maloney (1997) 'Neoliberalismo e distribui*cão de renda na América Latina,' *Revista de Economia Política*, vol. 17, no. 3 (67), July–September, pp. 39–62.

Bardhan, Pranab (1984) *The Political Economy of Development in India* (Oxford: Blackwell).

Boron, Atílio A. (1995) 'Argentina's Neoliberal Reforms: Timing, Sequences, and Choices,' in Leslie Elliott Armijo (ed.), *Conversations on Economic and Political Liberalization: Working Papers of the Southern California Workshop* (Los Angeles: Center for International Studies, University of Southern California).

Broad, Robin (1988) *Unequal Alliance: The World Bank, the International Monetary Fund, and the Philippines* (Berkeley: University of California Press).

Burton, John (1995) 'South Korea to borrow $35 billion in first quarter,' *The Financial Times*, 5 January.

Cerny, Philip (ed.) (1993). *Finance and World Politics: Markets, Regimes and States in the Post-Hegemonic Era* (Aldershot, England: Edward Elgar).

Clough, Michael (1992) *Free at Last?: US Policy Toward Africa and the End of the Cold War* (New York: Council on Foreign Relations Press).

Cohen, Roger (1998) 'Argentina Sees Other Face of Globalization,' *New York Times*, 6 February.

Crawford, Leslie (1997) 'Mexican opposition snubs Zedillo,' *The Financial Times*, 23 January.

Daniels, Nomsa D. and Francis Daniels (1995) 'Reform Politics in South Africa: The African National Congress and Foreign Investors,' paper presented at the Conference on Financial Globalization and Emerging Markets, Watson Institute, Brown University, 18–19 November.

Diamond, Larry, Juan J. Linz, and Seymour Martin Lipset (eds) (1989) *Democracy in Developing Countries: Volume 4, Latin America* (Boulder, CO: Lynne Rienner).

Diaz-Alejandro, Carlos F. (1986) 'Some Unintended Consequences of Financial Laissez-Faire,' in Alejandro Foxley, M. McPherson, and Guillermo O'Donnell (eds), *Development, Democracy, and the Art of Trespassing: Essays in Honor of Albert O. Hirschman* (Notre Dame, Ind.: University of Notre Dame Press).

Dillon, Sam (1996) 'Zedillo Lectures the Mexicans: Obey the Law,' *The New York Times*, 1 October.

Domínguez, Jorge I. and Abraham F. Lowenthal, (eds) (1996) *Constructing Democratic Governance: Latin America and the Caribbean in the 1990s – Themes and Issues* (Baltimore, Md: Johns Hopkins University Press).

Echeverri-Gent, John (1997) 'Explaining the Paradox of India's Economic Reforms: Globalization, Partisan Competition, and the Incentives to Reform,' unpublished paper, University of Virginia.

Economic Commission for Latin America and the Caribbean (ECLAC) (1993) *Preliminary Overview of the Economy of Latin America and the Caribbean 1993* (Santiago, Chile: United Nations, ECLAC).

Fidler, Stephen (1998) 'Chilean lessons for Asian crisis,' *Financial Times*, 14 January.

Fishlow, Albert (1989) 'A Tale of Two Presidents: The Political Economy of Crisis Management,' in Albert Stepan (ed.), *Democratizing Brasil: Problems of Transition and Consolidation* (New York: Oxford University Press).

Foxley, Alejandro (1983) *Latin American Experiments in Neo-Conservative Economics* (Berkeley: University of California Press).

Frieden, Jeffry A. (1991) *Debt, Development, and Democracy: Modern Political Economy and Latin America, 1965–1985* (Princeton, NJ: Princeton University Press).

Frieden, Jeffry A. and Ronald Rogowski (1996) 'The Impact of the International Economy on National Policies: An Analytical Overview,' in Robert O. Keohane and Helen V. Milner (eds) *Internationalization and Domestic Politics* (Cambridge: Cambridge University Press).

Friedman, Thomas L. (1998) 'Heal Thyself,' *New York Times*, 7 February.

Gibson, Ed (1997) 'Making Market Reform Politically Viable: Federalism and Electoral Coalition-Building in Menem's Argentina,' paper presented at Second Conference on 'The Economic and Political Challenges of Market Reforms in Latin America,' Tower Center, Southern Methodist University, 4 October 1997.

Inter-American Development Bank (1997) *Latin America after a Decade of Reforms: Economic and Social Progress, 1997 Report* (Washington, D.C.: Inter-American Development Bank), September.

Jha, Prem Shankar (1980) *India: A Political Economy of Stagnation* (Bombay: Oxford University Press).

Kim, Eun Mee (1996) *Big Business, Strong State: Collusion and Conflict in South Korean Development, 1960–1990* (Albany, NY: SUNY Press).

Lewis, Paul H. (1990) *The Crisis of Argentine Capitalism* (Chapel Hill: The University of North Carolina Press).

Miller, Judith (1997) 'A Promoter of Democracy Angers the Authoritarians,' *New York Times*, 12 July.

Molano, Walter (1997) 'Financial Reverberations: The Latin American Banking System During the Mid-1990s,' paper presented at the Annual Congress of the Latin American Studies Association, Guadalajara, Mexico, April.

Oxhorn, Philip and Graciela Ducatenzeiler, forthcoming 1998, 'The Problematic Relationship Between Economic and Political Liberalization: Some Theoretical Considerations,' in Philip Oxhorn and Pamela Starr (eds), *Markets and Democracy in Latin America: Conflict or Convergence?* (Boulder, Col: Lynne Rienner).

Passell, Peter (1995) 'Economic Scene: In Mexico-style crises, the IMF Could be a Bankruptcy Court,' *The New York Times*, 22 June.

Pastor, Manuel, Jr. (1992) *Inflation, Stabilization, and Debt: Macroeconomic Experiments in Peru and Bolivia* (Boulder, Col.: Westview).

Poku, Nan and Lloyd Pettiford (eds) (1998) *Redefining the Third World* (Basingstoke, Macmillan).

Rodrik, Dani (1997) 'Sense and Nonsense in the Globalization Debate,' *Foreign Policy*, no. 107, Summer, pp. 19–37.

Roett, Riordan (ed.) (1996) *The Mexican Peso Crisis: International Perspectives* (Boulder, Col.: Lynne Rienner).

Sachs, Jeffrey D., Aaron Tornell, and Andres Velasco (1995) 'Lessons from Mexico,' working paper of the Center for International Affairs at Harvard University, March.

Schrecker, Ted (eds) (1997) *Surviving Globalism: The Social and Environmental Challenges* (Basingstoke, Macmillan).

Starr, Pamela K. (1997) 'Monetary Mismanagement and Inadvertent Democratization in Technocratic Mexico: Are Market Reforms Doomed?,' paper presented at Second Conference on 'The Economic and Political Challenges of Market Reforms in Latin America,' Tower Center, Southern Methodist University, 4 October.

Strange, Susan (1986) *Casino Capitalism* (London: Basil Blackwell).

Stolper, Wolfgang Friedrich and Paul A. Samuelson (1941) 'Protection and Real Wages,' *Review of Economic Studies*, 9, pp. 58–73.

Treverton, Gregory F. (1990) 'Covert Action in Chile, 1970–1973,' *Pew Case Studies in International Affairs* (Washington, DC: Institute for the Study of Diplomacy, Georgetown University).

Underhill, Geoffrey R.D. (ed.) (1997) *The New World Order in International Finance* (Basingstoke, Macmillan).

Varshney, Ashutosh (1996) 'Mass Politics or Elite Politics?: India's Economic Reforms in Comparative Perspective,' paper presented at the Conference on India's Economic Reforms, sponsored by the Center for International Affairs and Harvard Institute of International Development, Harvard University, 13–14 December.

Veltmeyer, Henry, James Petras, and Steve Vieux (1998) *Neoliberalism and Class Conflict in Latin America: A Comparative Perspective on the Political Economy of Structural Adjustment* (Basingstoke, Macmillan).

Woo, Jung-en (1991) *Race to the Swift: State and Finance in Korean Industrialization* (New York: Columbia University Press).

Index